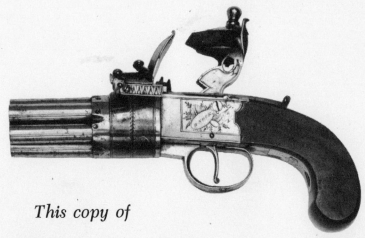

This copy of

the Collecting of Guns

is the property of

· ·

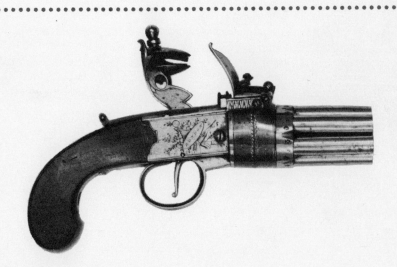

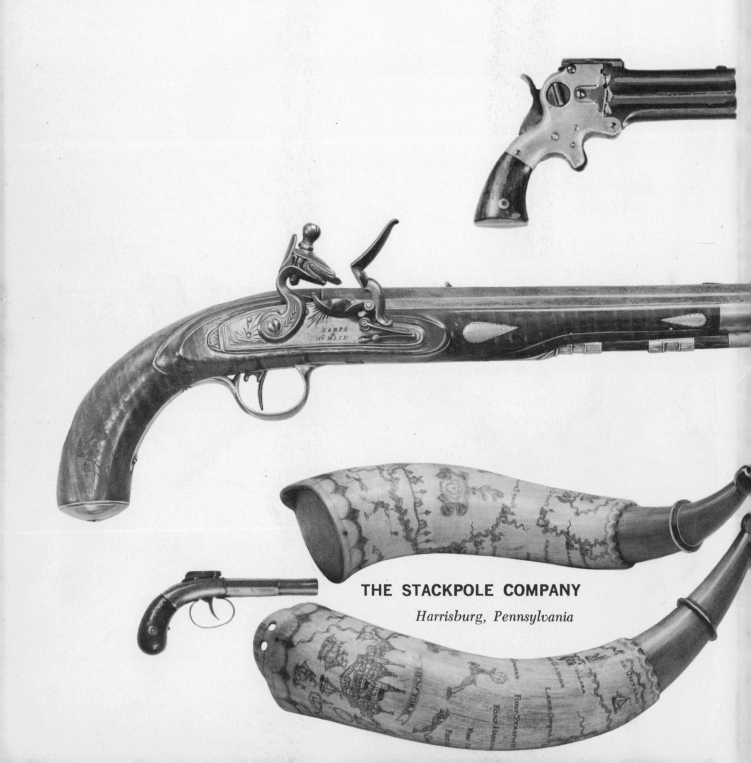

design and layout by SIMON FRANKEL

THE STACKPOLE COMPANY

Harrisburg, Pennsylvania

the Collecting of Guns

EDITED BY JAMES E. SERVEN

William A. Albaugh III
Graham Burnside
Dr. J. E. Byrne
James C. Drummond
John S. du Mont
William E. Florence
Col. Arcadi Gluckman
James J. Grant
Thomas E. Hall
Dr. Thomas T. Hoopes
Frank R. Horner
Leon C. Jackson
Harry C. Knode
Herschel C. Logan
Harry H. Mann
Karl F. Moldenhauer
Harold L. Peterson
William G. Renwick
P. L. Shumaker
Samuel E. Smith
Henry M. Stewart, Jr.

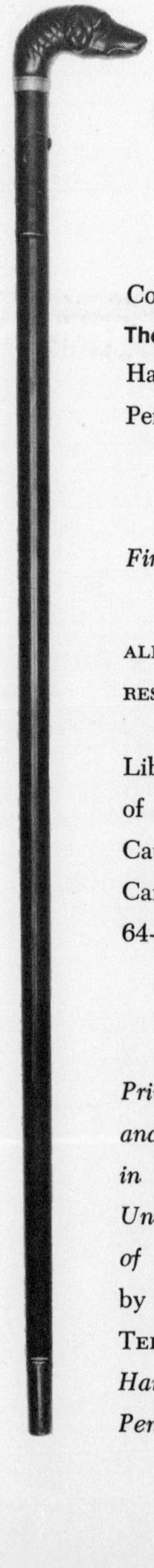

Copyright © 1964 by
The Stackpole Company
Harrisburg,
Pennsylvania

First Edition

ALL RIGHTS
RESERVED

Library
of Congress
Catalog
Card Number:
64-14890

*Printed
and bound
in The
United States
of America
by* THE
TELEGRAPH PRESS
*Harrisburg,
Pennsylvania*

Dedication

To the

**Collectors' and Shooters'
Associations of America and
the Old World**

who, by their exemplary
standards and organized
efforts, have done so
much to encourage the
collecting and preserva-
tion of historic weapons;
and who have contrib-
uted greatly in providing
a better public under-
standing of the true roles
played by firearms, vital
tools used in shaping
world history.

Contents

Contents

Guide to the Illustrations

The first numeral denotes the chapter; the second numeral denotes the illustration. If more than one weapon is described in an illustration, a third numeral indicates specific items of that group beginning at 1 and counting down from the top. If there is more than one row of weapons *in an illustration, a subhead indicates "Left row" or "Right row"; as before, numerals start with 1 at the top of each row. These numerals key to the captions which accompany the illustrations. The page number on which the illustration appears follows the caption.*

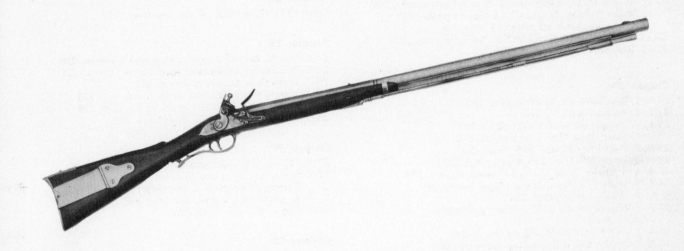

Index

13

JAMES E. SERVEN

...And those who served as Co-Authors:

**III
William A. Albaugh**

Graham Burnside

John E. Byrne, M.D.

James C. Drummond

Jim Serven's interest in guns was aroused many years ago when his father bought a small group of Civil War carbines from Francis Bannerman's store in New York City. While still a young man Jim became one of the most active collectors in his native state of New York. In 1932 he helped to organize, and then served as an officer in, the pioneer Eastern Arms Collectors Association, one of the first formally o r g a n i z e d gun collector groups and now known as the New York State Arms Collectors Association. After moving to the West, Jim's talents were honored by his election to the presidency of the two largest California gun collector associations. Among later honors he has been awarded honorary memberships in various collector associations throughout the country, made a Fellow of the Company of Military Historians, and has been repeatedly named to the Gun Collectors Committee of the National Rifle Association. Jim Serven's contributions to firearms research and literature are extensive. His rich experience as a collector and arms dealer, coupled with his professional ability as a writer and editor, have made him eminently qualified to edit this work and write some of its chapters.

It was only natural that Bill Albaugh, the great grandson of a Confederate officer, should take a keen interest in arms of the Confederacy. After attending Randolph Macon College, Bill served as an officer in Naval Intelligence during World War II. He saw action in both the Atlantic and the Pacific, surviving two torpedoings. His survival was indeed fortunate for gun collectors; since the 1930s his tireless research and capable writings have given us scholarly works on Confederate a r m s. He is presently an investigator for the U. S. Civil Service Commission but finds time for continuing r e s e a r c h activities. Bill Albaugh's contribution on these pages gives impressive evidence of his thorough knowledge in the Confederate arms field.

Graham Burnside was born just one hundred years after the birth of his famous relative, General Ambrose E. Burnside of Civil War and gunmaking fame. He is an ardent shooter and collector as well as a staff writer for gun magazines. Even while serving with the U. S. Marines in the Pacific during World War II, Graham devoted any available time to gathering cartridge specimens. After completing graduate work at Wyoming State University, he t a u g h t in h i g h schools for e i g h t years. In 1959 he turned to full-time writing and research in the firearms field. His articles have appeared in many publications. Graham lives at Dundee, Illinois, in a house built in 1840, where he is happily surrounded by a 5,000 specimen cartridge collection, guns, and books.

John E. Byrne, M.D. is not only greatly respected in his profession but he is also highly regarded and widely known as a researcher and historian. He has been collecting and studying Smith & Wesson revolvers for thirty years; his study of Smith & Wesson arms has included the broad field of infringements and evasions of the basic Rollin White patent. Dr. Byrne is a member of a number of arms collectors associations and currently vice-president of the Missouri State Skeet Shooting Association. His present interest continues in the Smith & Wesson field but as an additional project he is compiling a history of the St. Louis gunmakers, suppliers of the trappers and emigrants who opened up our American West.

James C. Drummond learned the gunmaking business at an early age from his father who was Chief Engineer at the Ross Rifle Co. in Canada and at the Savage Arms Co. in Utica. Young Drummond served in World War II in the R.C.A.F. as a technician and instructor in small arms. After the war, as a skilled gunmaker in S o u t h Shaftsbury, V e r mont, he converted military arms to sporting guns, then specialized in restoring valuable and historic weapons, perfecting new and better ways to clean and repair important antique weapons. Museums and collectors from all over the country found Drummond's shop in Cheshire, Connecticut, a place where a master craftsman always treated an old gun with respect and scientific skill.

meet the

John S. du Mont

John S. du Mont of Greenfield, Massachusetts, has been an active gun collector for thirty years. He was the founder and first president of the Massachusetts Arms Collectors Association; he is a member of the Armor and Arms Club of New York; a Fellow of the Company of Military Historians; member of the N.R.A. Gun Collectors Committee; and he is a member of many other important associations. John du Mont has been a frequent contributor to leading publications in the firearms field and was coauthor with John E. Parsons of the monograph *Firearms in the Custer Battle*. His counsel is often sought by prominent museums and other organizations. World War II military service saw him at Leyte, Philippine Islands, from which campaign he emerged with two combat medals.

William E. Florence

Few men can attain the prominence enjoyed by Bill Florence in only fifteen years of gun collecting. In this relatively short time he has become well-known from coast to coast as a collector of extremely rare and fine guns. While his interest covers the entire weapons field, Bill has devoted special attention to collecting Remington arms. He is a past president of the Massachusetts Arms Collectors and a member of five other gun collectors associations. Bill Florence's arms displays at the various gun association meetings are always outstanding. After many years as a resident and business man in Massachusetts, Bill recently retired and now makes his home in Florida.

Arcadi Gluckman, Colonel, USA, Ret.

Colonel Arcadi Gluckman, USA, Retired, developed an interest in military arms when he was first commissioned an officer in World War I. He applied for voluntary retirement in 1950. In 33 years of service, much of it spent abroad, Colonel Gluckman was awarded the Silver Star, Legion of Merit, Army Commendation Medal, Purple Heart with Oak Leaf Cluster, and many other commendations and honors. He is a versatile linguist, and an expert on military history. Among books written by Colonel Gluckman are: *United States Martial Pistols and Revolvers; United States Muskets, Rifles and Carbines; Catalogue of U. S. Military Short Arms; American Gun Makers* (with L. D. Satterlee), and a supplement to the same. He is considered one of America's foremost authorities in the martial arms field, and one of our most thorough researchers.

James J. Grant

Since the publication of his two books devoted to single shot rifles, Jim Grant has been recognized as the leading authority in this field. Jim is dear to the hearts of both shooters and collectors; he likes to collect the old black powder guns and he likes to shoot them. He was one of the charter members of the Ohio Gun Collectors Association and has been a National Rifle Association member for over thirty years. Not only his books, but his articles in magazines have always been interesting and informative. When James J. Grant writes about single shot rifles, their cartridges and accessories, it is always factual and well researched.

Thomas E. Hall

Thomas E. Hall, curator of the Winchester Gun Museum, has since the age of twelve devoted much time and study to the firearms and ammunition of the world. He is an authority on antique arms, of which the Winchester Museum has one of the finest collections in the world. The gift of an old flintlock pistol on his twelfth birthday was an acquisition which set Mr. Hall's life pattern, first as a hobby, and now as a career. Mr. Hall is a member of the Armor and Arms Club, the American Society of Arms Collectors, Arms and Armor Society of England, Antique Arms Collectors Association of Connecticut, Connecticut Gun Guild, and the Pennsylvania Arms Collectors. Many arms researchers turn to Tom Hall for information, and acknowledgements of his assistance will be found in many of the most useful firearms books.

Dr. Thomas T. Hoopes

Few men attain the honors and distinctions which have accrued in the career of "Tommy" Hoopes, as he is known by his many friends. This amazing scholar, with both Master's and Doctor of Philosophy degrees, has such a record of fellowships, publications (in English and foreign languages), lectures, radio and television participation, travels, aviation service, and other activities that the listing would take many pages. Suffice it to say here that Dr. Hoopes, who recently retired as Curator Emeritus of the City Art Museum of St. Louis, is one of the world's foremost authorities on early weapons. He is a member of the Armor and Arms Club of New York and other important societies.

Authors

Frank R. Horner

A native of Missouri, Frank R. Horner moved to Madison, Wisconsin, forty-five years ago to teach at the University of Wisconsin. Several years later he entered the insurance business in which field he has risen quickly to the top, now being an "Emeritus Agent" at Madison and a life member of "The Million-Dollar Roundtable" of the National Association of Life Underwriters. As Frank was forging ahead in his field of business, he also forged ahead in his hobby field. One of the founders of the Wisconsin Gun Collectors Association, he has built over the years not only an outstanding collection of Pepperbox arms, but in his gunroom can be found a fine collection of American martial arms and some very interesting firearms curiosa. He is representative of the many busy, successful men who have found gun collecting a great source of pleasure and relaxation.

Leon C. Jackson

The career of Leon C. Jackson has been varied—teacher and boxing instructor at college, public relations, and business machine dealer— which led finally to the business he enjoys most and in which he has been eminently successful, the antique weapons business. Coming out of World War II a Lieutenant Colonel, "Red" Jackson reentered the business machine field, moving from Louisiana to Texas. But soon the gun business became a full-time job and, assisted by his personable and very capable wife, Elsie, he has made Jackson Arms of Dallas one of the world's leading establishments of its kind. The Jackson Arms periodic illustrated catalogs are very informative and a real contribution to firearms literature. A member of many collectors associations, "Red" Jackson is also very active in National Rifle Association affairs, serving on the Executive Committee. He has been effective in combatting anti-firearms laws and in promoting firearms safety programs. His broad knowledge of the firearms field as a collector and dealer, coupled with intimate knowledge of legislative matters applying to firearms, made him an ideal choice for the subject assigned to him in this book.

Harry C. Knode

A collector for 35 years, Harry C. Knode is one of the most versatile men in the collecting fraternity. An excellent organizer, he put together and was first president of the American Society of Arms Collectors. A charter member and past president of the Texas Gun Collectors Association, he also served as co-editor of their publication *The Texas Gun Collector;* more recently he has edited the bulletin of the American Society of Arms Collectors. Not only have Harry's writings won him national acclaim, but his skill as a free lance photographer has placed his work on covers of the *American Rifleman* and other important magazines. The Knode home and business office address is Harry C. Knode & Co., P. O. Box 12274, Dallas 25, Texas. Harry is currently a member of the N. R. A. Gun Collectors Committee.

Herschel C. Logan

Many interests appear in the background of Herschel C. Logan of Salina, Kansas. His writing credits include the books: *Other Days, Hand Cannon to Automatic, Romance of the Old West, Cartridges, Buckskin and Satin, Underhammer Guns,* plus a great many magazine articles devoted to firearms. Honored in "Who's Who in America" and other important publications, Herschel Logan has devoted most of his life to the field of art. Few have ever been able to match him in firearms illustration. He is a Fellow of the Company of Military Historians, and enjoys many other honors and affiliations.

Harry H. Mann

Guns have long been Harry H. Mann's hobby and his business. An active collector for 35 years, he has assembled one of the West's outstanding firearms collections. As operator of a prominent shooting gallery and gun store for many years before his retirement, his place of business was a mecca for collectors and shooters. He is the winner of many pistol and rifle matches and often serves as an official N. R. A. referee. One of his hobbies has been hunting big game with flintlock and percussion muzzle-loading rifles. Still a relatively young man, Harry is an active member of collectors clubs from California to Texas, and is the director of highly-regarded semi-annual antique gun shows at Las Vegas, Nevada, where he lives.

Karl F. Moldenhauer

Karl F. Moldenhauer learned during his studies at Marquette University and in the manufacturing and construction companies bearing his name, that research is often the key to success. After buying his first old gun, obtained merely to hang over the fireplace, Karl became curious. The gun was a Remington, and there were things about it that did not conform to the printed information available. Thus began a search for more information— and then more Remington arms! Encouraged by his lovely and sympathetic wife, Karl has brought to his home in Cedarburg, Wisconsin, one of the finest Remington arms collections ever assembled. Guns have not been the only items which have accrued through Karl's interest in this hobby. His library and files are filled with a wealth of reference material which has made him one of the most knowledgeable men in this field. Active in gun collector's associations, which he has served in many capacities, Karl counts as one of his greatest accomplishments in collecting, the many fine friendships established through his interest in guns.

| Harold L. Peterson | William G. Renwick | Paul L. Shumaker | Samuel E. Smith | Henry M. Stewart, Jr. | Philip F. Van Cleave |

Since receiving his Master's Degree at the University of Wisconsin in 1947, Harold L. Peterson has been one of America's most active researchers and writers in the weapons field. He is Chief Curator of the National Park Service, and has served as honorary curator and consultant for a number of our important museums. The list of publications credited to Harold Peterson is long and outstanding, from his *The American Sword* in 1954 to *The Treasury of the Gun* in 1962. Many magazine writings are also the product of his capable pen. He has received many awards and honors as an historian, writer, and lecturer. A past president and Fellow of the Company of Military Historians, he is also a member of many arms and armor associations in America and abroad; he serves as a member of the N.R.A. Gun Collectors Committee.

The great private arms collections of the world are usually built by men who have the resources, the time, and extensive knowledge. Such a man is Major William G. Renwick. Following Harvard law school, Bill Renwick successfully practiced law in Boston. He served his country in vital areas involving both combat and intelligence in World War I. Formerly a resident of Weston, Massachusetts, the Major is now retired and resides in Arizona. In his collection are assembled some of the world's finest European arms, an excellent section of Kentucky rifles, countless beautifully cased arms, a group of typical Western frontier weapons, and an outstanding variety of revolving-cylinder shoulder arms, some of them illustrated on following pages. Great collections often grow from small beginnings. The seed for the Renwick collection was planted when Bill's Sunday School teacher gave him an old Franco-Prussian War musket.

Paul Shumaker began collecting at the age of seven; that was quite a long time ago, since he has been an engineer with the Ohio Bell Telephone Company for 37 years. After joining the Ohio Gun Collectors Association in 1938, Paul's collecting interest took on new momentum. His talents were soon recognized and he was made a director, moving through the offices to serve two terms as president of our largest gun collector's association. Through his guidance, the Columbus meeting of the association has grown to an affair requiring 600 display tables. Paul Shumaker's published works include an excellent study of Colt's Old Model Pocket Pistols. He is currently a member of the N.R.A. Gun Collectors Committee.

Sam Smith's great grandfather traveled out to Wisconsin by covered wagon in 1846, and this branch of the Smith family has been firmly rooted there since. Sam is a director and officer at the Markesan State Bank. He started collecting guns as a boy in grade school and never once, even as a conservative banker, changed his view that old guns were a good investment. Among his many gun collector activities Sam Smith founded the Wisconsin Gun Collectors Association, and served five times as president. He is a member of many other associations. His experience and counsel are important in meetings of the N.R.A. Gun Collectors Committee on which he now serves. A very thorough researcher, the writings of Sam Smith have appeared in many magazines devoted to guns.

Henry M. Stewart, Jr., started collecting guns in 1925. Since that time he has built up one of America's finest collections, numbering almost 1500 arms, ten percent of which are to be found in their original casings. A keen student of arms and meticulous in research, Henry Stewart has contributed greatly to broader knowledge in many different fields of gun collecting. He is a member of numerous collectors' associations, serving in high offices and adding much to their firearms displays by his outstanding exhibits of rare and unusual firearms. Few men have ever gained the broad knowledge of the entire firearms field possessed by Mr. Stewart.

Philip F. Van Cleave's interest in antique arms goes back to his junior high school days when he obtained his first firearm (flintlock pocket pistol) as a graduation gift from his father, the late Harley J. Van Cleave. Phil's enthusiasm was so infectious that within a year's time, both father and son were actively specializing in the arms produced by the firms dominated by Ethan Allen. A career employee of the National Park Service for the past twenty-two years, Phil is presently Chief Park Naturalist at Carlsbad Caverns National Park, New Mexico. He is interested in anything and everything relating to the Allen firms, and hopes eventually to publish the fruits of the extensive collecting and research activities of his father and himself.

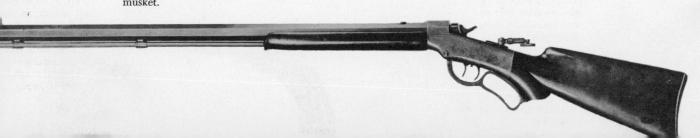

*F*ew things which inspire collector activity can equal firearms for the multiplicity of types, sizes, shapes, finishes, makers, and periods. Gunmaking dates back over four hundred years and, as the trade grew, it eventually came to be practiced in every country.

Central Europe, Italy, France, Spain, and the British Isles were leaders in arms development during the initial centuries, but following the migration of many old-world gunmakers to America in the 1700s, many of the forward strides since that time have been made here.

The American settlements were born in a period of zealous world colonization; the older nations were reaching out militantly for new territories. Not only did the early settlers need firearms to provide their meat and fowl, but guns were their major means of defense. It often took a good gun and a keen eye to keep one's scalp in unfriendly Indian territory.

Added to the Indian dangers, there was almost continual cold or hot warfare between England and France over American territory, with Spain and Russia also reaching covetously for parts of richly-endowed North America. Eventually the American colonists had to fight desperately for freedom from foreign domination of any kind. All their struggles, added to the burdens of sustaining one's self in a new, undeveloped land, made the gun especially important. American gunmakers, starting with the small one-man shops and on to the big manufactories, met this challenge. From their efforts came a continual progression of new and improved gun models until the world looked to America, not Europe, for the most advanced designs.

The collector will find graceful Pennsylvania-made long rifles of small bore, used in early days for self-protection and for hunting the light game found in the East. These are full stocked with beautiful grained woods. As the frontier moved westward, heavier guns of larger bore were needed for the buffalo and the grizzly bear. American gunmakers provided them. As America grew and the need developed, gunmakers produced suitable pocket pistols, house pistols, belt pistols, and big holster pistols, along with a variety of shoulder arms.

When multi-fire was needed, there came the multi-barrel, multi-cylinder, and many other systems to provide more than one shot without reloading. Some of these inventions were very successful; others were cumbersome and unreliable but the collector will find all interesting. Throughout the history of gunmaking, the transitional periods of change from one basic system to another provide many fascinating and some rather curious weapons.

The approach to gun collecting can be made from so many directions that the demands of every taste can be successfully fulfilled. Whatever period you select, or whatever types you choose, there

Introduction

will be an intriguing array of specimens for you to find. Collectors often remark that life took on greater zest for them when they turned to gun collecting and its challenging goals; every trip takes on greater purpose and added pleasure when there are old shops to visit and gun "leads" to explore. As one collector expressed it, he no longer merely "drags the scenery by" when he drives down new highways.

National pride and greater availability influence a majority of our collectors to concentrate on weapons produced in the United States. Within this book you will find outlines devoted to some of our American weapons. Obviously, we could select only a few of the most popular types; there are many others equally worthy of the collector's interest and investment, including the fine European arms which space permits us to give but brief treatment here.

The mission of this book is to provide the best available information on the subject of gun collecting. Because the research and knowledge of one author cannot encompass all fields of learning in such a vast sphere, there is brought to you here the counsel and experience of a team of twenty-two authors. These are all men who, by their accomplishments, have earned national recognition and acclaim in their respective fields.

I take this opportunity to thank each of our authors for sharing their valuable knowledge with us, and for the meticulous care they have devoted to the preparation of their contributions. Appreciative acknowledgement is also due those who have provided many of our illustrations; among these are: E. Irving Blomstrann, Barlow E. Williams, James A. Mills, Dick Friske, Harold Phelps, William Wollin, Abbie Rowe, Howard Bettersworth, Frank E. Bivens, Jr., Colonel Roy C. Kuhn, Milo B. Taylor, Charles H. Bradford, Philip R. Phillips, Archer Jackson, Clay P. Bedford, Ray Riling, Olin Mathieson Chemical Corporation (Winchester Museum, New Haven), The Smithsonian Institution, The Metropolitan Museum of Art, Springfield Armory, and others.

The *Collecting of Guns* represents a careful assembling of vital data condensed into a compendium of what is most important to anyone interested in firearms evolution. Its pages outline the history, development, manufacture, use, care, collection, and study of small arms. It provides information in related areas that are very important today—and will be perhaps even more important tomorrow. There are many carefully selected illustrations to provide precise interpretation of text details; special attention has been given to making the text concise, easily understood, and vitally interesting. We believe this is a book you will find truly *useful,* and that you will turn to it often for pleasure and profit. A history, guide, and technical reference volume in one, *The Collecting of Guns* is designed to help you to the better understanding and full enjoyment of a great hobby.

James E. Serven

1.

the
Romance and
Adventure
of
Gun Collecting

*I*t is not uncommon that a thousand-dollar profit is made from the sale of an antique firearm. This profit potential in itself is a great attraction to collectors, but there are many other rewarding, non-monetary inducements that draw men to gun collecting. This strong interest in guns is found all around the world.

The urge to collect is born in most of us. As children we collect baseball player cards, unusual rocks cr shells, and any number of other things. When we grow up, this inclination to collect takes different forms. For some it is pushed into the background by a demanding profession or other absorbing pursuit, some merely become haphazard accumulators; but an increasing number now become discriminating adult collectors. And it is through their intelligent efforts and industry that we have the rich historical treasures in our museums, in our libraries, and in our great private collections.

An ideal field of collecting embraces subjects which combine the qualities of beauty, fine craftsmanship, historical importance, fascinating interest, and established values. No field meets these requirements better than gun collecting.

Down the ages, the finest artisans—goldsmiths, silversmiths, engravers, woodcarvers—have executed on the surfaces of guns beautiful designs created by talented artists. The mechanical progression of weapons was engineered by the genius of the keenest minds of the day. And surely no product of man's hand has shaped his destiny more than the gun. In the gun there are enduring materials which, if properly cared for, make the gun an object of everlasting beauty and increasing worth.

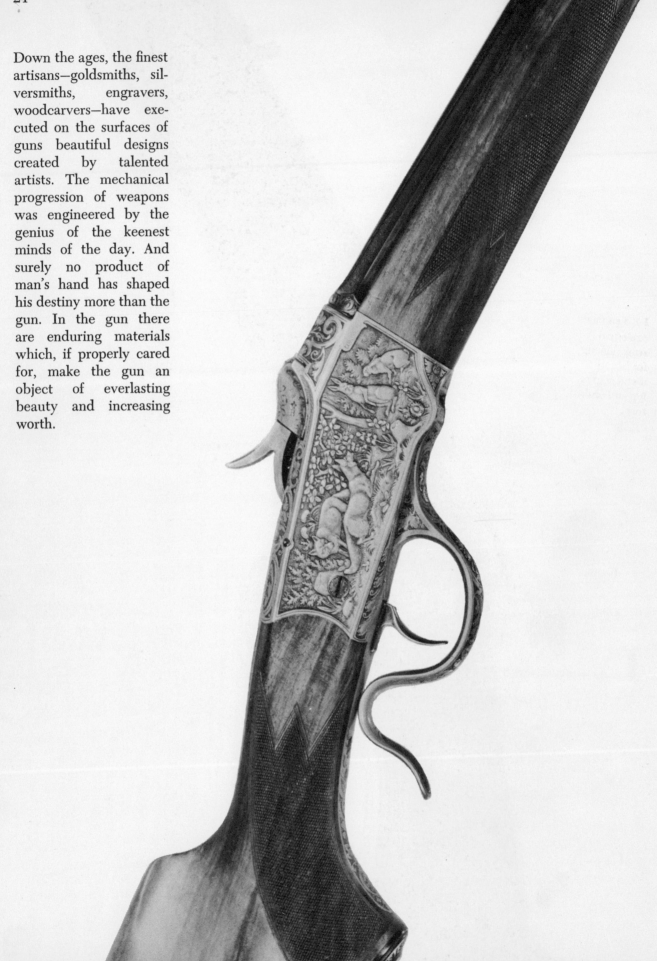

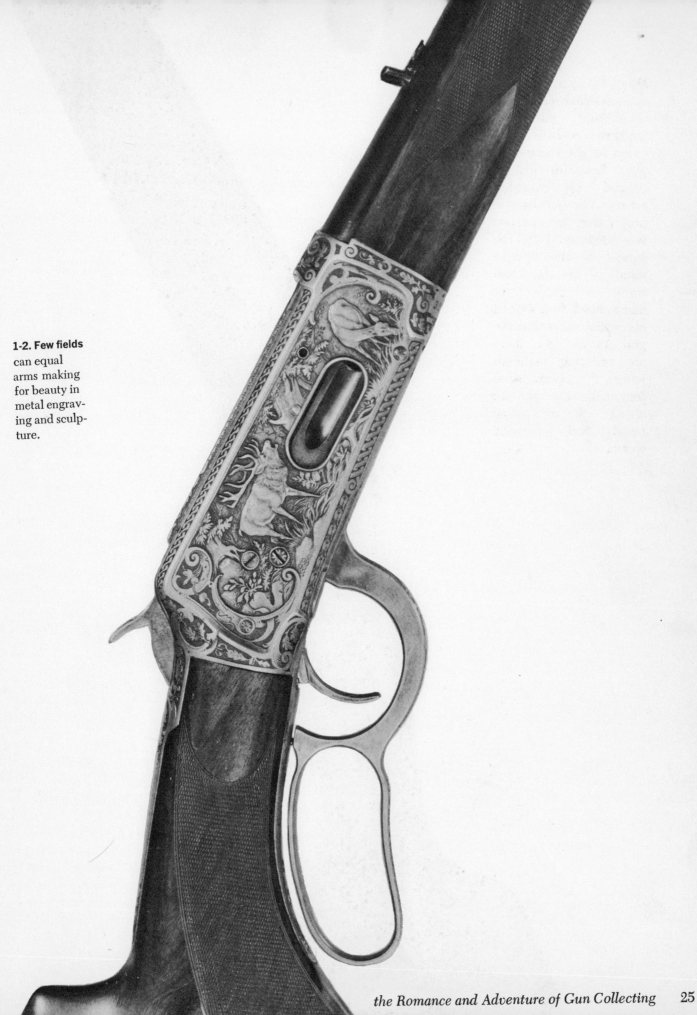

1-2. Few fields can equal arms making for beauty in metal engraving and sculpture.

1-3. Historic association often adds special luster to some of the guns in a collection. These Philadelphia-made flintlocks are said to have been used in guarding the famous Liberty Bell while it was being carried off from Philadelphia to Allentown and hidden under the floor of Zion Reformed Church during the American Revolution.

We speak of the gun here in its broad generic sense, including in the meaning of the word all the forms of firearms. There are diverse interests which contribute to the motivation of individual collectors. One may have had an ancestor who fought in the Revolution, and an old musket from those days was handed down in the family. Starting with this one family heirloom, a large collection of different muskets may be assembled. Another may have had relatives who crossed the plains in a covered wagon; for him a great number of the favorite frontier arms have special interest. Civil War weapons are now actively sought by collectors. Very few of our older families escaped some involvement in that unfortunate struggle, and the tools with which the war was fought arouse great curiosity and interest. Prominent in Civil War battles, in great variety, were rifles, carbines, pistols, revolvers, and heavier weapons.

Family association is only one of many motivations that can head a man toward serious gun collecting. Behind every old gun lies a record which is often filled with adventure, spiced with danger, and sometimes even heroic in its details. The record of individual guns may be well documented, but more often the record is obscure and presents a fascinating realm of mystery into which the collector can, by research, try to make his way. In the quiet of his gunroom, one may devote pleasant meditation to the probable role of that old gun. In such studies and reveries there is a break and separation from the tensions of everyday life. Doctors tell us that there is wonderful therapy in a hobby; they apparently take their own advice and that may be one reason why there are so many doctors in the gun collecting fraternity.

1-4. The gunroom becomes a sanctum where one separates himself from the tensions of everyday life and turns his mind to contemplation of the things that please him.

1-5. Many Col-
lectors enjoy
the fun and
pageantry
often associ-
ated with
shooting old-
time guns.
Here members
of the Califor-
nia Muzzle
Loaders and
Collectors As-
sociation,
shown against
the back-
ground of an
ox-drawn cov-

ered wagon,
prepare to give
an exhibition
of flintlock and
caplock rifle
shooting be-
fore an audi-
ence of several
thousand inter-
ested specta-
tors at a '49er
Commemora-
tive Encamp-
ment.

Webster defines a hobby as: "Something a person likes to do or study in his spare time—a favorite pastime or avocation." Perhaps the reason so many gun collectors are successful is because they truly enjoy what they do and what they study in connection with their hobby. The *study* is an important feature, for as a man's knowledge increases his pleasures and profits grow.

As an organized hobby, gun collecting is relatively new, but in the past quarter century it has broken from the confines of latent interest to assume the proportion of a collector's "gold rush." This is, of course, merely a figure of speech; in the heightened interest and enthusiasm for gun collecting, it has become an absorbing and very important pastime but not necessarily a hectic or demanding one.

Many American men are hunters and many of them are or have been soldiers. Their modern guns have caused them to become curious about the weapons their fathers and grandfathers used. Was that old muzzle-loader as accurate as claimed? Did it kick like a mule? This natural curiosity has led many to acquire muzzle-loading guns and to try them out at targets and on game. As a result, a new national shooting sport was developed, now numbering in its ranks thousands of muzzle-loading shooters and collectors. Another area of collector-shooters is in the field of single shot cartridge rifles. Here one will find some of the finest rifles ever to come off a workbench, many barreled by such perfectionists as Pope, Schoyen, Zichang, and Peterson. They are beautiful to adorn a collector's wall, and thrilling to shoot (mostly with black powder).

The man who has a flare for history finds an especially rich field in gun collecting. America has led the world in the development of guns since the days of the Long Rifle. The gun has remained ever present through the many vital periods of our history. One can visualize the embattled farmers and their big smoothbore muskets at Concord and Lexington—the long rifles of Kentucky and Tennessee backwoods-

men driving back the British invaders at New Orleans—the Mexican War, where the "Mississippi" rifles, and Colt's big Whitneyville-Walker Dragoon pistols, bravely employed, helped to bring victory—we think of the early western movement, and the rough-living Mountain Men armed with Hawken rifles—there was that intrepid early trader, Josiah Gregg, leading his caravan down the Santa Fe trail with a Colt cylinder rifle across his saddle and five extra loaded cylinders in his saddle bags—then the tremendous buffalo harvest with the Sharps rifles, and the heroic stand made by buffalo hunters at Adobe Walls—and how a few trail-weary cowboys led by Nelson Story used their new rolling block Remington rifles to drive off 3,000 Indians up on the Bozeman trail of

1-6. Great military engagements of the past such as this 1815 battle for New Orleans inspire history-minded men and those with soldier ancestors to collect examples of the weapons used.

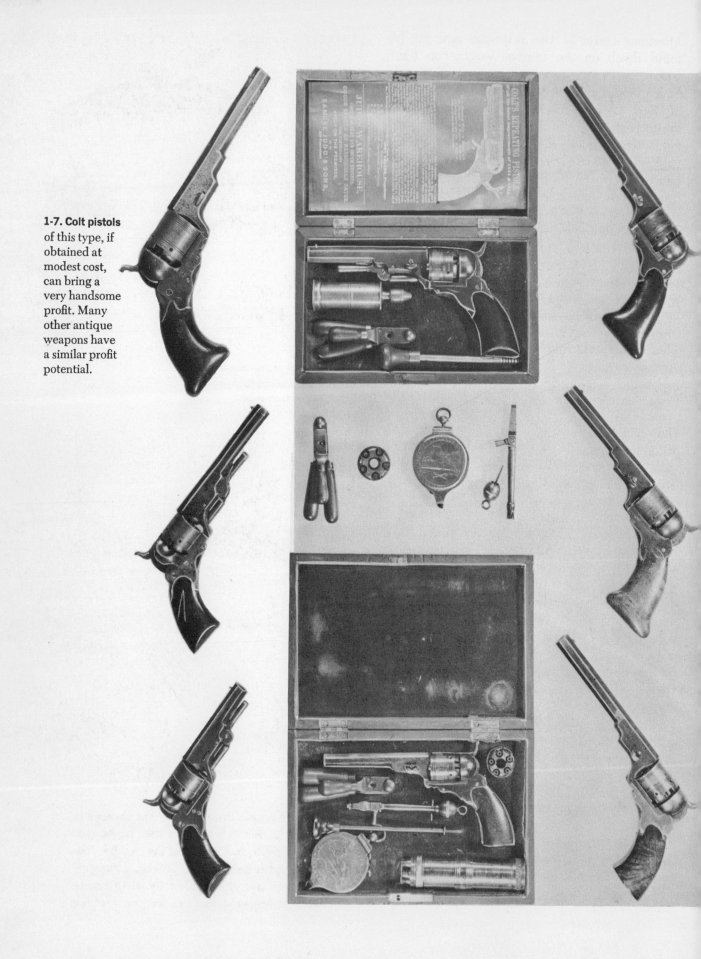

1-7. Colt pistols of this type, if obtained at modest cost, can bring a very handsome profit. Many other antique weapons have a similar profit potential.

Montana—certainly the historian will let his mind dwell on the famous wagon-box fight, where our soldiers, armed with newly-issued Springfield trapdoor rifles, gave a howling horde of Red Cloud's Sioux the surprise of their abruptly ended lives—then to the California gold fields where good men and bad kept a Colt caplock pistol or a "pepperbox" pistol close at hand—down to Texas where the famous Rangers brought law and order to the frontiers of that state with their Sharps and Winchester carbines, along with the ever-present bowie knife and Colt "six-shooter"—these are but a few of the historic subjects which, in the quiet of a collector's gun-room sanctuary, may pass before the mind's eye. A gun in that very room may have been present in one of these exciting fields of action!

There is a practical side to gun collecting which appeals to many who, either by necessity or by inclination, subject their spending of time and money to the cold rules of safe investment.

One does not buy stock, a piece of real estate, or an automobile without knowledge of the fair value. The same rules of prudence apply to gun collecting—a reasonable knowledge of the subject is the key.

Only one man among a large crowd did have this all-important knowledge a few years ago at a county auction in upstate New York. There was the usual array of furniture, crockery, old clocks, miscellaneous implements—a tremendous number of articles. The auction was well publicized and had drawn many buyers. Among the odds and ends was a box which when put up for sale was shown to contain a pair of old pistols. Only one buyer seemed to have more than cursory interest, and the box with its pistols was sold to him at a small figure. The hesitant competitive bids had served to allay any suspicions of the auctioneer that he might have something especially valuable.

The net result of his special knowledge was that this man obtained a great prize and sold his "buy" to a wealthy collector for a larger sum than was collected for *all* the articles sold at that auction.

Some years ago a dealer purchased a rare Ameri-

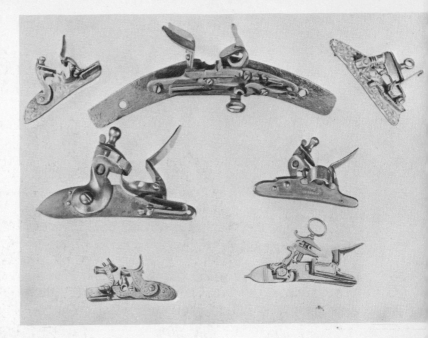

1-8. In gunlocks alone there are hundreds of varieties to fascinate the mechanically-minded collector.

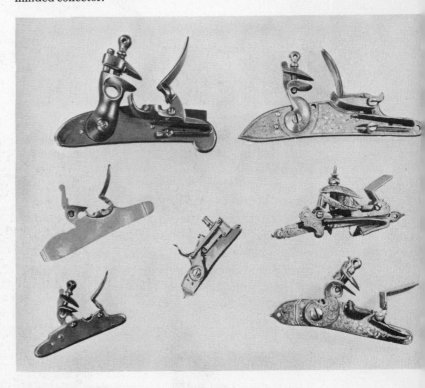

can pistol in Canada for $1,500. Soon thereafter he sold it for $2,000. A few years later he bought it back for $3,500 and resold it for $5,000. Today it is valued much higher. This and the preceding incident are cited primarily to illustrate the occasional big opportunities for profit which come to informed dealers and collectors alike. A carefully conducted study has revealed that antique firearms as a group are now valued at six times the prices they brought in 1938.

The profit potential explains to some degree the great zeal we find in gun collectors, but the profit motive is only one of many elements of the picture. We will find wealthy men more enthusiastic about obtaining a wanted old gun than if they had just closed a million-dollar business deal. Pride of discovery and accomplishment is very strong among gun collectors.

The rather ingenious mechanical systems employed in arms manufacture, dating from the 1500s, fascinate many whose work or general interests include mechanics, engineering, and science. Studies of some of these old systems have given birth to ideas applicable to modern manufacture. The principle of interchangeable parts, for instance, had its great initial success in early gunmaking.

Gun collecting often appeals to those who have some talent in the writing field. It presents a challenge to explore areas of specialization, gather more information than anywhere recorded, and publish the findings—bringing honor to one's self and rendering a real service to fellow collectors.

*A*ntique firearms, as a business, have attracted many in recent years. Some collectors who have felt the urge to get away from their lathes at machine shops have gone into the business of making parts for restoring old guns, or accessories and other items for muzzle-loader shooters. Some men have merely set up small shops where they may repair, buy, sell, or trade

old guns. You will find, however, whatever role a man may play in the antique firearms field, he usually has assumed that role by choice and through a fondness for old guns.

Few other fields are equal to gun collecting as a social leveler. At annual meetings in Washington, D. C., one can rub elbows with Congressmen and other government leaders, even perhaps the President or Vice-President of the United States, who satisfy their personal interests in old guns by attending the arms exhibitions presented by the National Rifle Association.

Leaders among our armed services are enthusiastic participants in these and many other gatherings where collectors meet and exhibit their guns. Leading industrialists, State Governors, stars of the entertainment world, bankers, doctors, lawyers, men in the highest and men in the humblest positions share a common interest and a sympathetic comraderie that knocks down all bars of social prejudice or reserve.

Gun collections involve little upkeep; depreciation is seldom a factor, appreciation being the general rule; and there is no deterioration in the materials of which guns are made if they are properly protected and cared for.

The gun is truly an American symbol—a symbol closely associated with the freedom and liberty so dear to men's hearts. These pages could suggest only a few of the reasons why men collect guns; there are many other reasons. We can produce material evidence of the good profit potential, but the far greater dividends in happiness, health, and education are more difficult to define.

"Why do men like and collect guns?"

We asked Dr. W. R. Funderburg, past president of the American Society of Arms Collectors, why men like and collect guns. He replied as follows . . .

"To one who has studied guns, loved guns, and avidly collected guns for twenty-five years, the question seems absurd. It is like asking why men like apple pie, risqué stories, Scotch whiskey, or curvaceous gals in Bikinis. How is it possible *not* to like and collect guns?

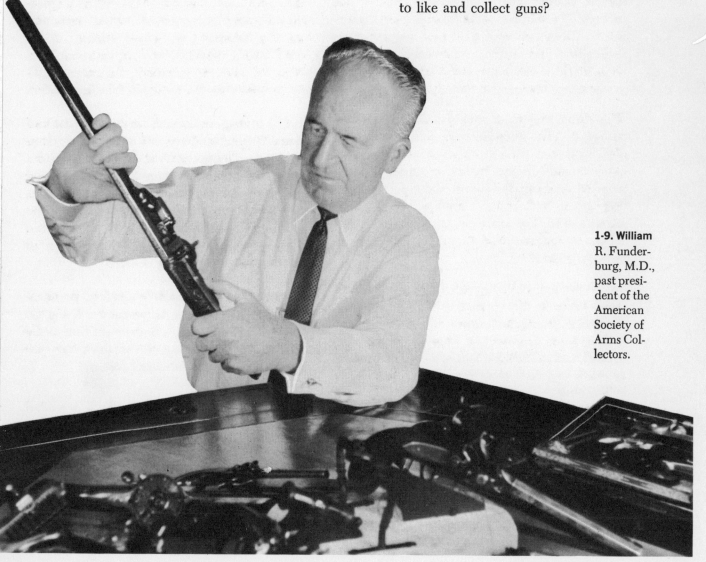

1-9. William R. Funderburg, M.D., past president of the American Society of Arms Collectors.

"The Author and Romanticist—What can have more romantic appeal than the vision of two stalwart gentlemen gravely carrying their Wogdons or Mantons to the Field of Honor at dawn; there, meticulously adhering to the "Code Duello," to have their trial by combat to defend the honor of a lovely lady, or cleanse a stain placed on their own honor?

"The Historian—The world's history has been molded by man's ability to develop weapons. The historical outline of man's past five hundred years lies clearly written in any comprehensive collection of guns. Since the invention of firearms, wars have been won or lost depending upon the ability to devise, manufacture, and strategically use these weapons.

1-10. Admiral Mumma, Congressman Flynt, and Colonel Jackson were among hundreds from all walks of life who enjoyed a Dallas, Texas, exhibition of antique firearms valued at over one million dollars.

"In seriously trying to analyze the appeal of guns and the hobby of collecting them, it becomes apparent that this hobby has a facet to attract almost every type of individual. Let me give only a few examples:

"The Mechanic—The problems of developing multiple fire and more efficient detonation have taxed the mechanical ingenuity of man for five hundred years. Where could one find a more fascinating series of mechanical devices than the different mechanisms of firearms?

"The Artist—Look at the beautiful patterns worked with inlaid ivory in a Saxon Dag. Examine the finely engraved designs of animals and birds chiseled into the cold steel barrels of Italian wheel locks. Notice the intricately carved ebony stocks of French dueling pistols—the gold overlay on the barrels and locks—the flowing lines—the perfect balance. Certainly this is the very essence of high art!

"But why continue? To me personally, gun collecting has been an all-absorbing hobby. It has served me as an excellent panacea to ease the tensions and disappointments which plague most of us today. When I reach home at night after an exhausting, frustrating day in the operating room, with tensions screwed to the snapping point, I can effect a magic cure by simply walking into my gunroom. There I can pick up several 'Old Friends.' I examine them and take them apart for the hundredth time. Miraculously the 'cares that infest the day' no longer seem so important. Suddenly I am relaxed, as I sit half dozing, dreaming of a bygone era. Things move back into their proper perspective, as I realize how insignificant are my petty troubles and tribulations. Modern medicine has yet to develop a tranquilizer comparable to this.

. . . And you ask me, 'WHY DO I COLLECT GUNS?'"

1-11. Collectors who are handy with tools very often enjoy working on their old guns and restoring them to good firing condition.

2.

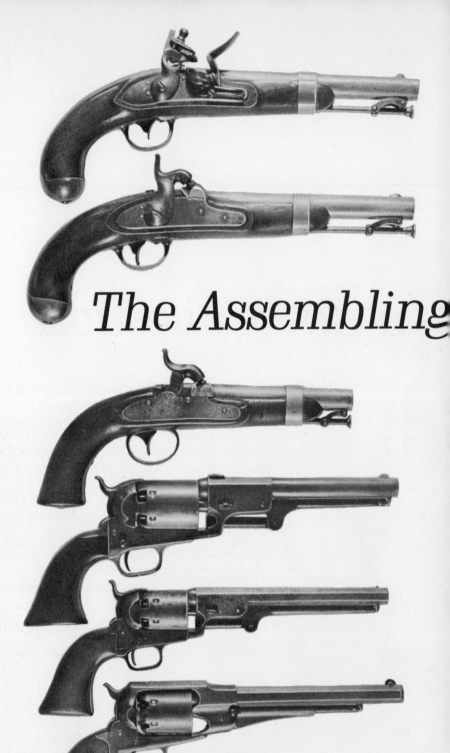

The Assembling

2-1. Novices do well to generalize at first, collecting various kinds of old guns which may come their way at modest prices. A good rule is to purchase only complete, clean specimens. Guns that have been extensively restored, refinished, or badly battered have very low value appreciation and poor salability.

# of a Gun Collection

The past twenty-five years have seen a great shifting of the available antique firearms supply. Where once many old guns might be found in the hands of private owners who cared little for them, or in antique shops and secondhand stores where they were not highly valued, the situation is very different today.

Private owners have become more conscious of the value of antiques; information regarding values is more easily accessible. Antique shops, and all other shops where old guns are sold, often have before them the latest price lists and seldom underprice their merchandise. Thus opportunities for picking up "sleepers," as collectors like to call underpriced items, are relatively few. But opportunities still do exist for the alert student of arms and for the astute negotiator.

Possibly the first and most important decision a man should make when he plans to build a gun collection is to become a student. One must be able to recognize opportunities before he can grasp them. The nuggets of information you gather can pave the way to golden rewards in gun collecting.

Fledgling gun collectors normally have only a rather hazy understanding of the almost endless variety of weapons produced during the past five centuries. One has to acquire not only the essential book learning but also the needed "feel" or experience of collecting by actually locating and buying his first guns.

It is generally recommended that the beginner make his way conservatively, first buying those guns which are in relatively good supply and hence moderately priced. The main concern should be in buying complete, clean specimens—guns that have not been refinished and have not been subjected to major restoration. These inexpensive

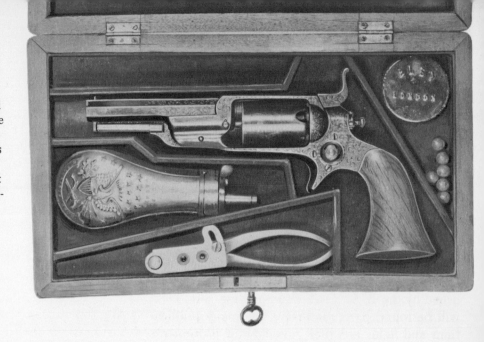

2-2. A very valu-able engraved pistol like this, presentation inscribed and fitted with a stock made from the famous Charter Oak, was located through an advertisement in a rural publication and purchased for a few dollars.

types of today may gain substantial value with time, but if you have a poor specimen with which to begin you will not profit much; it is invariably the all-original, good condition guns that enjoy the greatest rise in values.

Once a collector has gained the basic knowledge that makes him qualified to invest wisely and safely, he may wish to sell or trade some of his early acquisitions and specialize in collecting the arms of one type, one manufacturer, one country, one region, one caliber; he may be attracted to the varied ignition systems, the artistic qualities, the odd mechanisms, or some other special category.

How then are the best ways to find these guns? And if necessary to sell or trade, how is the best way to go about it?

These are not questions for which there are simple sure-fire answers. Various geographic areas and even different kinds of guns may call for different methods. A good knowledge of the subject, a certain amount of ingenuity, a lot of patience, and a generous amount of effort are the principal qualities on which you must rely.

As to ingenuity, collectors have traveled down many diverse trails to locate desirable antique guns. Advertising in the gun magazines for wanted items is a common practice and often produces good results. Every collector, whether he may be a collector of guns, books, coins, or other things, holds steadfast to the hope of finding a rare specimen at a very low price. This is a normal desire and part of the joy in collecting. When you advertise in a gun magazine (where readers are usually experienced), your chances of getting a specimen you need are very good, but it will take a keen knowledge of rarity and value to make a spectacular "buy."

The spectacular finds are usually made in the out-of-the-way places, where knowledge of gun values is limited. The classified sections of farm papers have been quite productive for some collectors. A valuable Paterson Colt pistol was obtained for $35 through an advertisement in a New York farm paper. A California collector purchased a beautiful engraved Dragoon Colt and several Confederate pistols at very low prices through ads in several Southern farm papers. Many other collectors have done as well.

Classified advertisements in outdoor magazines occasionally turn up good collector items, for readers of these publications usually are outdoorsmen who have some general knowledge of guns. The collector will do well to visit his local library and consult Ulrich's Periodicals Directory, published by the R. R. Bowker Co. of New York. Data will be found here concerning the many publications and fields in which classified advertisements may be employed.

When your classified advertisement brings in replies, you must then pursue an effective course in turning good prospects into successful purchases. One favorite method is to provide a printed folder which illustrates items wanted by the collector and points out features the seller should describe when sending information. This can save a lot of misunderstanding and wasted transportation costs. When possible to do so, it usually is a better negotiating technique to induce the seller to name a price. If it is low, you can make a quick, good purchase; if the price is a bit high, you can dicker.

There are two schools of thought about local newspaper advertising and local publicity concerning one's gun collection. One group shies away from advertising locally for fear that this publicity will focus attention on their collections not only by those who might have some old guns to sell, but will also make their gun collections a target for burglary. The opposite view is that professional burglars seldom are tempted by antique guns and the rewards of local publicity are far greater than the dangers of theft.

Although there has been some increase in recent years, the incidence of antique firearms theft is relatively small; antique guns are easily traced and their sale involves markets not ordinarily familiar to those who steal for profit.

Collectors enjoy telling stories of how this or that rare gun "walked in off the street," a term used to describe purchasing a gun from someone who had

2-3. Gun-minded owners of businesses have found that displays of their old weapons create great interest. Often people bring in old guns they wish to sell.

heard the collector bought old guns and brought one in to sell. These opportunities would not be present unless the collector's desire to buy old guns was generally known. To spread this word around, collectors have calling cards printed which on one side provide the name, address, and telephone number, and on the other side a message (sometimes illustrated) which plainly conveys that old guns are wanted. These cards, left at antique shops, gun stores, gunsmiths, fix-it shops, pawnshops, and other likely places, may be quite productive. Word of mouth publicity and post cards showing their guns have helped to build valuable exhibits for owners of saloons, hotels, and other public places where the guns are employed as an attraction.

A word of caution should perhaps be injected at this point about buying from strangers. In addition to local people who come in with a gun or two to sell, the collector may be visited by itinerant gun dealers who have the back of their car full of guns to sell or trade. These men should not be confused with fellow collectors on vacation who enjoy a visit with others in the firearms fraternity, and who trade a gun occasionally for the pleasure of it. Some of the professional, itinerant gun dealers to which reference is made here are honest and reliable men—others are not. Thus the collector must be on guard, for more unfortunate "deals" have turned up in this kind of selling than any other. In any case, it is wise to obtain convincing identification from strangers, make a note of auto licenses, and if a purchase is made have the seller sign an effective bill of sale—such as that prepared by the Gun Collectors Committee of the National Rifle Association, a copy of which is illustrated (see 2-4).

Thus far we have given our major attention to a few of the methods employed to locate old guns in the hands of non-collectors; we know that it is reasonable to expect that old guns may be obtained from these people occasionally at favorable prices. But it is no longer true that guns in the hands of non-collectors represent the bulk of the supply. The major supply now is possessed by collectors and by dealers.

A few years ago you could count the antique gun dealers on your fingers; now there seems to be one in every hamlet. There are a few dealers of established national reputation who dominate the busi-

BILL OF SALE FOR ANTIQUE FIREARMS

RECEIVED OF ...., residing at ....
...., the sum of .... dollars ($........................) and
.... in trade in full payment of the following described firearm:

Maker's Name ....
Maker's Address ....
Country and Date of Manufacture ....
Model .... Serial Number(s) ....
Condition (See other side for NRA Condition Standards) ....
Ignition System ....
Barrel(s) .... Barrel(s) Length ....
Caliber(s) or Gauge(s) ....
Over-all Length .... Weight ....
Accessories Included ....
Markings, Engravings and Inscriptions (Describe) ....

Stocks or Grips (Describe) ....

Alterations and Replacements (Describe) ....

Historical Claims (Authenticity and Origin of Arm and/or Inscriptions, etc.) ....

I certify that the above information is true and complete, and that I have the right to sell and give possession of the firearm described.

SIGNED AND SEALED this .... day of ...., 19......

Name of Seller

Federal Firearms License No. ....

Address of Seller

Received the firearm described in the foregoing Bill of Sale:

....

2-4. Bill of Sale.

ness, but many others enjoy a profitable trade either on a full-time or part-time basis.

Another factor affecting the buying and selling of old guns is the changed economic picture. Many collectors feel forced into a certain amount of gun trading to pay for guns they otherwise might not now be able to afford. This more active buying, selling, and trading on the part of collectors, coupled with the increased number of dealers, has contributed greatly to the rapid spread of antique

2-5. At gun collector's meetings and gun shows collectors display their guns, sometimes buy, sell, and trade. Here are made many pleasant social contacts; there is good camaraderie, and quite often a collector will go home with some good profits. Even the ladies, as evidenced here in the background, find much to interest them.

gun shows. Commercial gun shows have thus become an important market place for the collector; they are now held occasionally in almost every section of the United States. Added to these commercial shows, one finds an increased amount of buying, selling, and trading at the regular meetings of our many gun collector associations.

Occasional auctions which include antique guns are held and these offer opportunities for adding to one's collection. At the usual auction house all sales are final and guns are offered "as is," features which may bring costly disappointments. Years ago, at Walpole Galleries and other New York and Philadelphia auction houses, gun auctions were very popular and were a major source of supply, but in recent years this is a form of selling which has declined in favor and importance. Today, the biggest and best available supply of antique guns will be found in the showrooms of the full-time arms dealers.

Publications which currently carry the advertisements of gun dealers are listed under "Current Publications" in the Bibliography at the end of this book. Many of these dealers publish priced catalogs, some well illustrated. In fact, a large percentage of present-day antique gun sales can be credited to the reliable dealers who send out priced sales lists. Many older collectors can recall pleasant hours spent thumbing through the old Bannerman priced catalogs or through the old priced and well-illustrated lists of F. Theodore Dexter. These catalogs and lists retain good reference value to this day, but prices are now merely indicative rather than currently informative.

Although the collector must expect to pay dealers a full market price, he usually gets in return a wide selection from which to choose; there is the privilege of returning anything not satisfactory for full refund; and the buyer obtains experienced protection against spurious merchandise. Through buying large collections, the dealer can keep the "finding" cost per unit low, whereas a collector often must spend a lot of time, money, and effort in pursuit of one piece. Furthermore, cordial collector-dealer relationships are often very helpful if the collector wishes to sell rather than buy, for the dealer usually has special knowledge about

where your guns will sell best. A friendly dealer is helpful also when a collector wishes to upgrade his collection and trade in certain weapons toward the purchase of desired items in the dealer's stock.

Regardless of what markets the collector may explore to find his guns, a basic knowledge of values must be acquired. With thousands of different models, types, and variations it is impossible to keep the precise value of each in one's head, but it does pay to consult available books, magazines, priced auction catalogs, and dealers' price lists to become familiar with the price ranges in major areas.

Unlike many commodities, the value of collector firearms is not affected by fluctuating supply—the supply changes only in the sense of a slow diminution. Small supply by itself is not a reliable guide to value, strange as that may appear to some. As an example, twice as many pistols as rifles were made on Colt's first firearms system; yet the pistols bring more than twice the price of the rifles. There are many instances where arms made in small quantity command lower prices than others which

2-6. The major supply of old guns is no longer in the hands of non-collectors; it will be found in established gun collections and in the gunshops.

are far more numerous. To bring top prices, there must be that rather fickle quality, *demand*.

Demand is generated by a wide range of factors. Colt collecting is popular because Samuel Colt produced the first successful repeating pistols; Colt, himself, had an ebullient personality; the name Colt became a synonym for pistol around the world; there are many interesting models available to the collector. The Winchester rifle has many collector devotees because of its important role in opening the West; here, as with Colt, we find a manufacturer long in production, and whose arms are associated with the writing of our dramatic national history. Many weapons, some beautifully finished and made in small numbers, may bring only a modest price—possibly because the manufacturer was not long in business, his arms were designed more for a bureau drawer or hall closet than in the holster of a dashing Pony Express rider or western sheriff; they may have no memorable association with martial fields of honor.

The judgment of collectors has not always been infallible, however, in establishing popular trends. A survey devoted to the price patterns from 1900 indicates that long-existing inequities in the values of antique weapons now are fast adjusting themselves. As an illustration, pepperbox pistols were long given little attention and their prices remained low, while other values were climbing rapidly upward. Then suddenly collectors woke up, and now many collect only this one kind of pistol, in which it was found there are many interesting variations. Values have increased almost 800 percent since 1938.

Generally, because of limited space and easier handling, American collectors have preferred handguns over shoulder arms; they have also shown a very strong preference for the plainer American-made weapons over the more elaborately crafted early European arms. Although surveys have shown there are more shotguns than rifles and pistols in American homes, shotguns have never enjoyed much collecting activity. Truly fine or unusual specimens are valued, but collections devoted exclusively to shotguns are few. The collector must keep facts like this in mind. If he strays too far from the types of weapons which have appeal for others, he will perhaps suffer difficulty and loss when he may wish to sell.

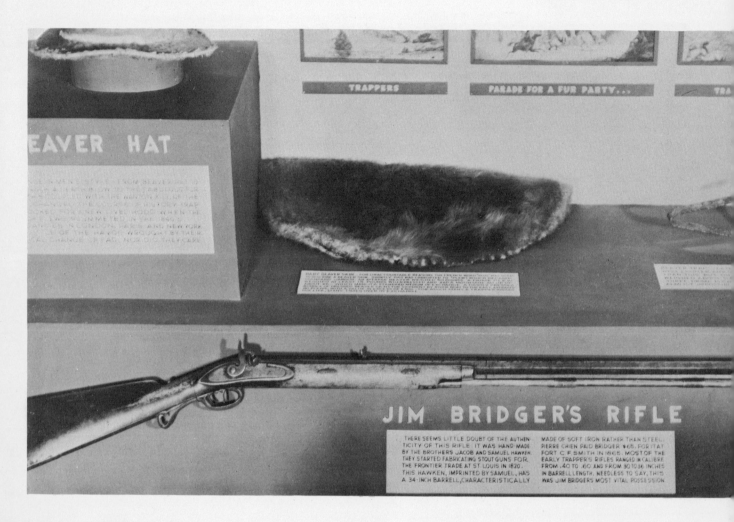

BEAVER HAT

TRAPPERS   PARADE FOR A FUR PARTY...   TRA

JIM BRIDGER'S RIFLE

*I*n the past few years, either through more widespread education or through necessity born of scarcity and economics, more collectors are turning to long arms and to European weapons. The movement into a neglected field is influenced somewhat by the hard facts of desirable buying opportunities. If a collector can foresee an impending trend of popular demand and acts on it wisely, his foresight can be very profitable.

In addition to demand, the greatest other single factor in establishing value is condition. Perfection must not be expected in an old gun where an honest patina of age gives it respectability and authenticity—but the manner in which a gun has weathered the years is important. If it has grown old without the scars of misuse, retaining a good percentage of its issue appearance, the value is

high; if it has suffered major operations, replacements, alterations, and refinishing through a rough career, much of the desirability and value is forever lost.

There was a day when collectors passed up very favorable "buys" merely because the weapon offered was one in which they had no personal interest. Seldom do experienced collectors do this today, for they have learned that there is a collector somewhere who will want that particular type or model; between true collectors it is sometimes easier to make a trade than to pry loose a cherished gun for money. Trading is part of the fun of collecting, too, for each party may get something he personally enjoys more, and thus each has profited regardless of the relative market values. Being human, the collector finds more flavor in the

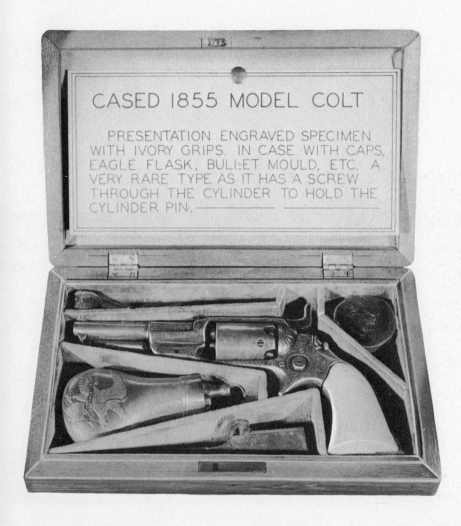

CASED 1855 MODEL COLT

PRESENTATION ENGRAVED SPECIMEN WITH IVORY GRIPS. IN CASE WITH CAPS, EAGLE FLASK, BULLET MOULD, ETC. A VERY RARE TYPE AS IT HAS A SCREW THROUGH THE CYLINDER TO HOLD THE CYLINDER PIN. ———————— ————————

2-8. When visiting museum displays, note all the minor details which point to the scarcer variations of a standard model. Sometimes small things, like the screw in the cylinder of this pistol, can add considerable value.

deal if he feels he has come out with a better value. And being human, not all are above glossing over faults in their trading stock—somewhat like the horsedealer who salved his conscience when selling a horse with one blind eye by telling the buyer, "He don't *look* so good right now, but he's a well-bred horse."

Behind this writing are many years of active research, study, buying, and selling in the antique firearms field. Some of the lessons learned, if reduced to a very simple set of rules, are these:

1. Study basic books and dealers' catalogs carefully, before and when you embark on any energetic collecting program. Visit other collectors and view museum exhibits, observing details closely.

2. Gain your experience first among the less ex-

pensive items, acquiring in the process such rarities which chance may bring your way at modest prices.

3. Avoid guns which have been badly used or extensively restored unless they may be great rarities. Bad pitting, mismatched serial numbers, and replaced grips or gunstocks are features which greatly lower desirability and value.

4. The firearms field is too vast to embrace in its entirety. Limit your ambitions to your pocketbook, the space you will have available, and the weapons that not only have personal appeal but which you have a reasonable chance to acquire.

5. Do not collect in a haphazard manner. Your guns may grow to represent a very substantial investment. Therefore, a well considered plan or

goal is important. There is a big difference in the appreciation rate of well chosen and poorly chosen antique weapons.

6. The program you follow to attain your goal is the element which will spell success or failure in building a creditable collection at proper cost. On the preceding pages some of the methods of finding guns have been briefly outlined. Each collector must, through experience, take those paths which serve him best. One of the first steps suggested is active membership in the National Rifle Association of America and membership in one or more of the gun collector's associations affiliated with it.

7. Keep well informed on firearms laws. Our hobby is affected by some of the provisions of the Federal Firearms Act and the National Firearms Act. Every collector should have a copy of these laws. State or local laws may also apply. Avoid those weapons or practices which are the particular target of these laws.

8. Accurate records are vitally important. Photographs and a carefully prepared card index file can be of inestimable value in many situations.

9. Do not let the persuasive voice of greed blind you when confronted by an apparent golden opportunity to buy a great rarity at half price. There are, for instance, more spurious or replica models of the rare Walker-Whitneyville Colt floating around the country—some planted with "history-minded" Grandpas—than there are originals. Have valuable rarities carefully checked by an expert before buying; then insist on a carefully drawn bill of sale. (See illustration page 40.)

10. Fine antique guns are a precious and irreplaceable part of our national treasure. Through carelessness and attrition, the supply grows smaller. It becomes the responsibility and the self-interest of every collector to acquaint himself with methods that give his guns the finest care and protection. Proper cleaning and legitimate repair, safe display provisions, careful handling of one's guns or those of others—these are all a part of this responsibility. Helpful information on these subjects will be provided in later chapters.

*T*here are no magic formulas to success in gun collecting, but success does come most often to those who listen, observe, study, and pursue a carefully planned program. If you follow these practices, you will soon find that few fields of recreation can equal the c l o s e comraderie, the educational enrichment, and the thrilling adventures which are the rewards of the firearms collecting fraternity.

2-9. Do not neglect oppor-tunities to acquire valuable items associated with firearms history—the accessories, the old catalogs, and old prints such as this one (on the left) titled "With the Wolfhounds." It was produced from a painting by Frederic Remington and offered by Smith & Wesson in 1902 to popularize their big top-break revolvers in the West.

the Assembling of a Gun Collection

3-1. If you ship a gun to a buyer or return it to a seller, you have a serious responsibility to box it carefully. Carelessness was responsible for the broken stock on this valuable "One of One Thousand" Model 1876 Winchester.

the Rules and Ethics of Gun Collecting

_3._

Among all true sportsmen, and especially in a gentleman's hobby like gun collecting, there are certain things one does or does not do if he wishes to retain the respect of his fellows. Down the years definite standards of conduct have come to be a requisite to first-class membership in the firearms collecting fraternity. Occasionally some of these rules are broken innocently through lack of knowledge, and that is a major reason for their discussion here. The actions of collectors with fellow collectors and the nature of relations between dealers and collectors are very vital to the full enjoyment of collecting.

First let us consider basic practices which affect collecting generally. It is widely accepted that all sales, either made directly or by correspondence, should be subject to prompt refund, adjustments, or other corrective action if the buyer is dissatisfied and makes prompt declaration of that fact, especially if there may have been any misleading claims or the omission of important details in the negotiations.

Where a buyer is merely disappointed in the quality of an arm he purchases by mail, having visualized something different, he is expected to pay the transportation both ways and return the arm at once, in the same condition as received; if the seller has grossly misrepresented the gun in question or has misstated the generally-used standards of condition, he would be morally bound to pay at least half the transportation costs and perhaps all.

Devious practices designed to trap the inexperienced or unwary, such as trumped-up appraisals to establish inflated values, efforts to screen bad faults, dishonestly claiming a gun had been the prize possession of a prominent and discriminating collector, or any other shady methods of entrapping a buyer, are a form of _caveat emptor_ (let the buyer beware) which honest gun collectors do not tolerate. Deliberate deceit, planned efforts to attach spurious historical or prestige association, and conscience-pricking silence concerning known grave faults are

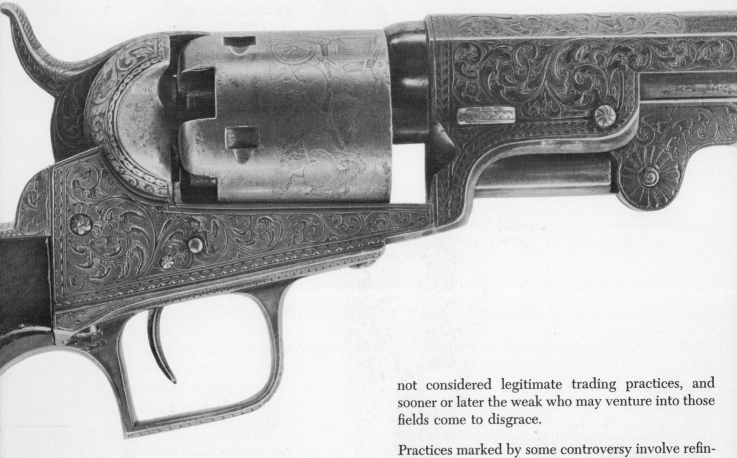

3-2. Collectors must learn
to recognize the character
of original factory en-
graving and a true straight-
back trigger guard, as on
this authentic Colt Navy
pistol. Modern engraving
to boost the value of an old
piece or altering parts to
give the appearance of a
more valuable variation are
practices not tolerated by
ethical collectors.

not considered legitimate trading practices, and
sooner or later the weak who may venture into those
fields come to disgrace.

Practices marked by some controversy involve refinishing and non-issue engraving on old guns. Most
collectors frown on non-factory finish and on any
form of decorative treatment applied by other than
the manufacturer or at least by craftsmen contemporary with the period of manufacture. If rebluing,
browning, or plating are done, and if the gun is
engraved, etched, or inlaid at a period not consistent
with the manufacturing date—then it is honest practice that the arm be so marked in an inconspicuous
place (usually in areas concealed by the grips or
stock), and that the seller state unequivocally that
such refinishing or recent non-factory decorating has
been done. One of the first things a collector must
learn is to distinguish between original factory finish and re-finish; he must be able to recognize the
difference between old engraving and modern work.
Factory-original work often brings hundreds of dollars more than modern field work on the identical
model. There are fine custom engravers today, as

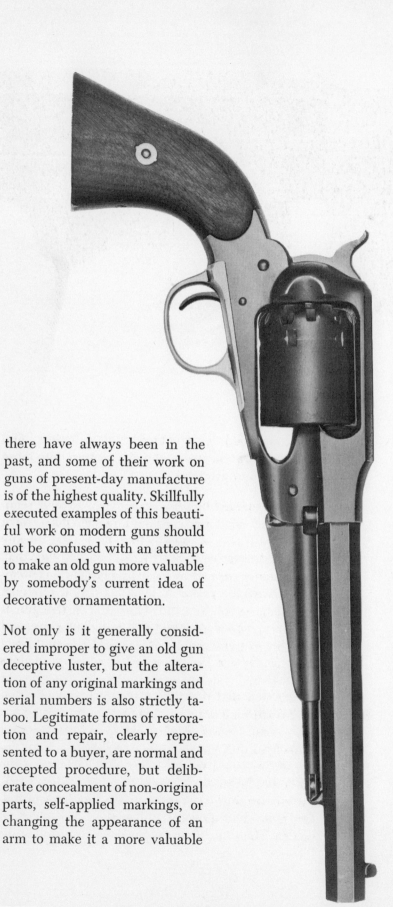

there have always been in the past, and some of their work on guns of present-day manufacture is of the highest quality. Skillfully executed examples of this beautiful work on modern guns should not be confused with an attempt to make an old gun more valuable by somebody's current idea of decorative ornamentation.

Not only is it generally considered improper to give an old gun deceptive luster, but the alteration of any original markings and serial numbers is also strictly taboo. Legitimate forms of restoration and repair, clearly represented to a buyer, are normal and accepted procedure, but deliberate concealment of non-original parts, self-applied markings, or changing the appearance of an arm to make it a more valuable

variation depart far from the realm of allowable practice and into the field of fraud.

Even more controversial than the field of refinishing has been the business of replica making, a relatively recent development. One can now buy full-scale replicas of a great many of the valuable Colt percussion arms, Remington pistols and rifles, United States martial arms, Confederate pistols, derringers, and other types. Many collectors maintain that full-scale models of valuable collector's arms, regardless of modern markings (easily effaced), are not in the best interests of gun collecting. It is inevitable that some of these replicas fall into dishonest hands and come on the market "convincingly scarred and aged" as rare original specimens.

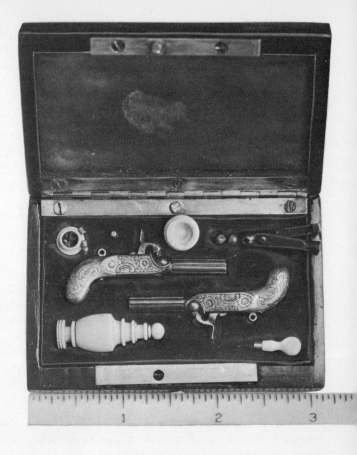

3-4. Replicas
which all consider a very worthy endeavor are miniatures. Full-scale guns which do not copy the patterns of old-time gunmakers or are made purely to demonstrate a man's personal skill and craftsmanship are also free of criticism.

On the other side of the coin, there are those who defend replica making as a useful undertaking, claiming that the makers provide weapons needed for those who like to shoot the old blackpowder style guns—and thus valuable antique specimens need not be endangered by firing them. Some take the view they never could afford to pay the market price of the original more valuable arms but will be content to own a replica costing a hundred dollars or less.

Whatever may be the merits or the demerits in opposing views of replica making, replicas are apparently with us to stay. In self-protection, the purist collector must acquaint himself with the warning signals which point to a replica. They can be detected no matter how clever a backroom mechanic may be in trying to eliminate honest manufacturers' markings and make a gun "old before its time."

On one point there can be no dispute—it is definitely dishonest and unethical to manufacture and offer for sale a spurious copy of a valuable firearm, representing it to be an authentic factory original or failing to make it crystal clear to the buyer that the arm is a replica of modern manufacture.

There are other points, too, in the modern manufacture of old-time style weapons where collectors and shooters are in general accord. No criticism is made of the manufacture or sale of firearms and accessories which cannot be easily mistaken for long-established models of specific manufacturers. These might take the form of miniatures, plastic or clay replicas, firearms of original design regardless of the antiquity of their firing system, or guns made up to demonstrate individual skill and craftsmanship (provided they are not the scaled design of any famous old-time gunmaker).

Ethics in gun collecting are much the same as in many other collecting fields; the keynote is integrity. And a good rule is to deal only with those known to possess that quality.

We come now to the approved standards of conduct; we know these also as proper manners or good etiquette, and they are here applied to gun shows, gun club meetings and exhibits, at gun shops, and to visits between collectors. No effort is made to make this part of the chapter an Emily Post sort of rule book, but there are some rules worthy of mention which benefit all gun collectors and safeguard a good public image of gun collecting.

In 1953 the National Rifle Association sponsored the formation of a nation-wide Gun Collectors Committee and it has functioned actively since that time. Members are selected from important collectors' associations throughout the country. Their mission is to represent the interests of all gun collectors, to study collectors' problems, and to initiate such actions as may be found desirable and proper. One of the first acts of the original Gun Collectors Committee was to pre-

pare a code of conduct for gun collector meetings and exhibits. The writer was present at that meeting and helped to draft the code. Copies of the suggested code were sent to all the leading collector's organizations in America for their comment; the code was unanimously approved —it was that important. Because the code does have such stature and general acceptance, and although it has had wide publicity, we print it here for those who may find it useful:

1. **All firearms and accessories in possession or on display** at collectors meetings must have proper legal status as defined by federal, state, and local laws.

2. **Displays shall be confined to collectors weapons and re**lated material, provided that exceptions may be granted by club officials to meet special situations. New, currently manufactured arms, unrelated accessories, and sporting goods shall not be offered for sale.

3. **Live explosives in the form of fuses, grenades, and like** items shall not be exhibited, and no firearms shall be loaded with a cartridge, cap, or powder.

4. **Collectors meetings are encouraged to offer construc**tive educational programs in the form of exhibits and informative talks. Educational displays should include informative labels.

5. **Replicas, or arms and accessories extensively repaired** or otherwise not authentic, shall not be displayed unless clearly labeled to indicate their true nature. This shall apply to engraving that is not contemporaneous with the manufacture of the arm.

6. **Members, guests, or spectators shall not handle any** exhibit without permission of the owner. Each member shall assume full responsibility for the proper instruction and conduct of his guests, especially minors.

It is true that much of our gun collecting activity is conducted at club meetings and at gun shows, but the home and the gunshop are equally important; each has its form of etiquette. The degree to which a visitor may observe good habits will have a big influence in determining his future welcome.

The gunshop, by its nature, has a somewhat more liberal view of gun handling than one may expect to find in the private gunroom. Here visitors come presumably to buy, and close inspection is a necessary part of buying. By observing a few general rules the customer will eliminate the major causes of dealer's complaints:

Learn to hold all pistols or guns properly, keeping hands on grips and stocks and off metal parts as much as possible. Fingerprints on metal often produce corrosion.

If you must test the action of a gun, do not jerk it or work it rapidly and repeatedly. On the older pieces, ask the dealer to demonstrate the action for you—any responsibility for damage will then be his.

Never snap hammers. One reason is a safety measure. Without careful examination you cannot tell if a muzzle-loading barrel contains a charge. Flints are easily chipped, nipples can be badly battered when unprotected by a copper cap, and other gun parts sometimes suffer when there is no cartridge to receive the blow of the hammer.

Don't spin cylinders. This favorite moving picture gesture is as ridiculous as it is harmful. And by all means, don't try to spin a pistol by the trigger guard. If you want to take a chance on wrecking your own pistol, that is up to you; but don't be a Hollywood cowboy with the dealer's guns. One dealer has a sign on the wall of his shop which he claims saves him a lot of trouble from broken gun parts. It pictures a mouse about to be caught by the neck in a trap. Above the mouse are these words: "It's the thoughtless guy who always gets it in the neck! Never fool with a machine you do not understand!"

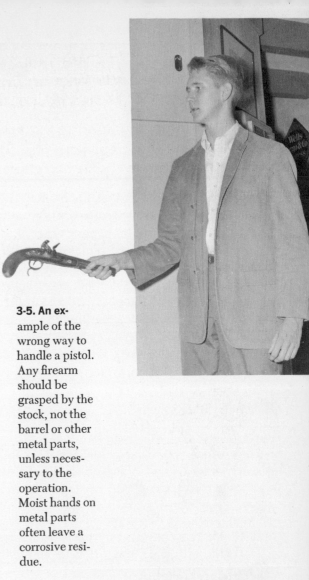

3-5. An example of the wrong way to handle a pistol. Any firearm should be grasped by the stock, not the barrel or other metal parts, unless necessary to the operation. Moist hands on metal parts often leave a corrosive residue.

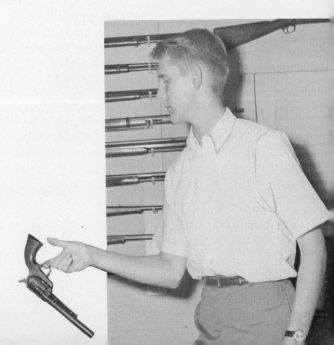

IT'S THE THOUGHTLESS GUY WHO ALWAYS GETS IT IN THE NECK!

.....NEVER FOOL WITH A MACHINE YOU DO NOT UNDERSTAND!

If a gun is examined, be sure to replace it securely in its rack, or return it to the dealer's care. A pistol knocked off a showcase, or a rifle that falls to the floor can be greatly damaged. One of the things one would first notice about the old-time custom gunmakers was their slow, deliberate manner of handling guns. Axel Peterson of Denver is especially remembered for the graceful movement of his hands—he never grabbed anything, always seemed to caress it. This is a trait for the gun collector to cultivate —a slow, careful manner of handling all guns, his own and the other fellow's.

Conduct expected in the private gunroom is more restrained than that in the public gunshop. Here you are a guest, not a customer. The guns you will be viewing are the fond possessions of the owner, not merchandise for sale. If you wish to handle any weapon here, it is good manners to request the owner's permission.

If your curiosity about the action of a gun prompts the owner to volunteer demonstrating it, that is fine. But unless working an action is very important to you, be reluctant to request it; old working parts may be brittle, and once an original part is broken a certain amount of the untouched originality of that gun is forever gone. And thus the pleasure of your visit may be clouded by the owner's misfortune.

A favorite practice of those who have valuable guns and enjoy showing them to other collectors is to keep a supply of cotton gloves on hand. Visiting collectors and the owner, thus equipped, may handle the guns without danger to the finish. Some hands contain an exudation

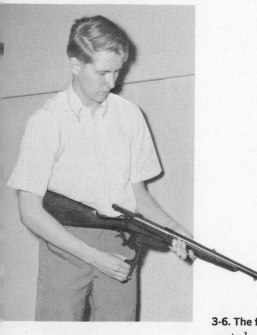

3-6. The fast and repeated working of a gun's mechanical action is a sure way to give the owner nervous prostration. If you must test the action of a gun, do it slowly and carefully.

-7. If you want to ractice spinning handgun like a 'V cowboy, don't lo it with some- ne else's pistol r in their gun- oom. It is a prac- ce that can be as armful as it is idiculous.

which, if not quickly removed, creates a very unfavorable corrosive action on metal.

Courteous self-discipline should be observed, too. Asking a gun collector how much his collection is worth is like asking a cattleman how many cows he owns—the same as "how much money have you in the bank?" Don't press a fellow collector to sell you a gun you particularly fancy if he clearly indicates he has no desire to sell. While perseverance is one of the building blocks to success, it should be evident only in those areas where it is welcome. Success comes to a collector sometimes after ten years of longing for a certain cherished gun; a major reason for this eventual success may be that over those years he tempered his desire for the gun with consideration for the owner's feelings and a respect for his expressed wishes. There is little welcome anywhere for the over-zealous and "pushy" collector.

The stature of gun collectors as a group is well above average. For the majority, the common

3-8. Never leave an- another man's gun (or your own) in this position. Any gun, and especially full-stock rifles and those with heavy barrels, can suffer broken stocks and other serious damage if left where they can topple to the floor.

points of ethical conduct and good manners need no telling here. If our principal concern may seem to have been with improper practices, it is not because they are predominant. But in every field of endeavor there are varying and comparative degrees of conduct—we can fall into good habits or bad habits. A reminder of the good and the bad once in a while can help us all toward a greater enjoyment of our hobby.

3-9. Handling swords and guns with attached bayonets in the gunroom must be attended with great caution. This is not the place for wildly demonstrative gestures with any weapons.

O

ver the years, literally hundreds of thousands of words have been devoted to the history and development of firearms, for this is an important subject. Often it has been necessary for the student of arms to wade through many pages to learn the vital facts.

What may be considered somewhat of an innovation is employed here. By means of a brief "chronology" and simple pen and ink sketches it is hoped that this presentation will provide the story of firearms evolution simply, clearly, and concisely.

Missing will be the lengthy details of inventions, patents, and wordy descriptions of various ignition systems. By this direct method it is believed the reader will be able to grasp and understand the story much more quickly—and will retain it longer.

All dates and events are taken from the most reliable sources. Where definitely known, the actual dates are given. In the early periods of firearms development a range of dates must suffice—as in the invention of gunpowder, the actual origin of which is lost in the mists of antiquity.

With this brief introduction, there now follows our outline of the fascinating story of firearms development—from the burning stick of the crude *hand cannon* to the modern, efficient metallic primer in the present-day *automatic*.

4.

the Chronology and Evolution

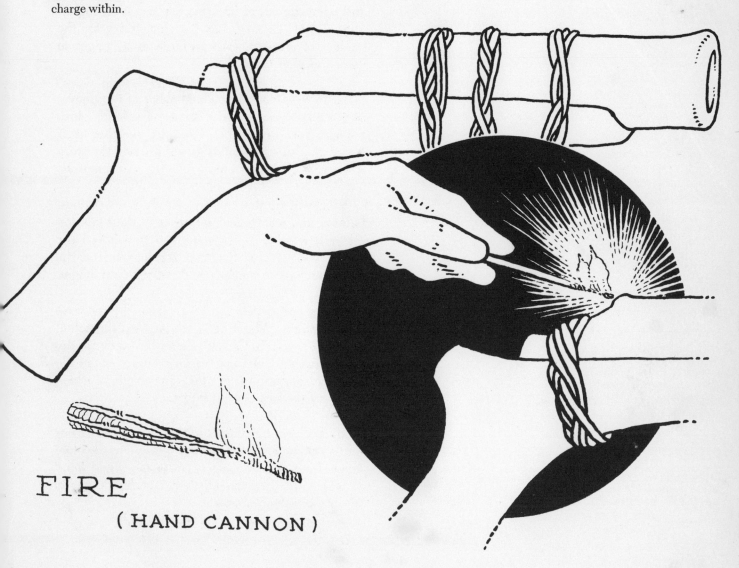

4-1. A burning stick applied to a speck of powder at the touchhole of the barrel set off the main charge within.

FIRE

(HAND CANNON)

of Firearms

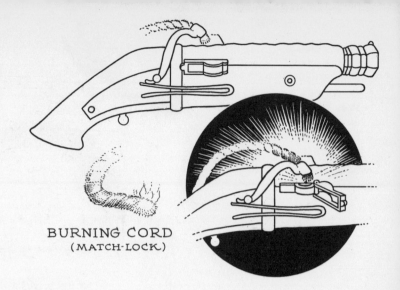

4-2. A specially prepared cord, or "match," was lowered to a pan containing a bit of powder. Resulting flash entered the touchhole leading into the bore of the barrel to detonate the charge.

BURNING CORD
(MATCH-LOCK)

1225-1250

..Discovery of gunpowder

..*Roger Bacon* wrote a formula in secret code

1300-1325

..Advent of large cannon-like firearms

1326

..Earliest picture of a gun (Manuscript by *Walter de Milemete*)

1339

..First mention of a multi-shot cannon

1350

..First dated cannon (Museum of Stockholm, Sweden)

1350-1400

..Portable small arms, such as hand cannons, first came into being.

1400-1450

..Transition period of hand cannon to match-lock

1450-1500

..Large cannons in use

..Development of rifling

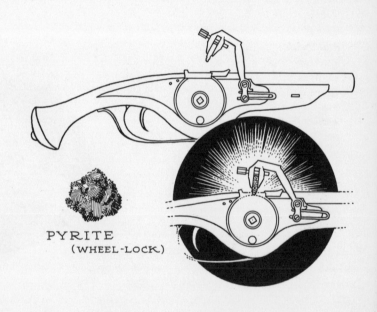

4-3. In a pan at the side of the gun barrel appears the upper edge of a serrated steel wheel. When the trigger is pulled, this wheel commences a rapid rotation. A piece of iron pyrites is pressed against it and the friction creates sparks among the powder grains filling the pan.

PYRITE
(WHEEL-LOCK)

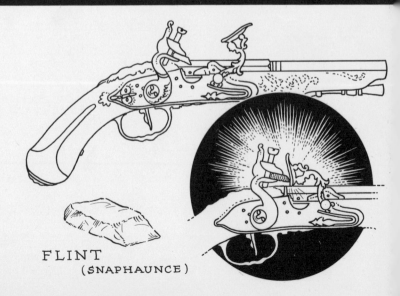

4-4. Sparks re- sulting when the flint struck the frizzen and ignited the powder in the pan; the flash from this explosion ignited the main charge in the barrel.

FLINT
(SNAPHAUNCE)

4-5. The mique-
let lock offered
nothing new in
the ignition
story, but its
unique outside
lock mecha-
nism sets it
apart from the
usual flintlock
arm.

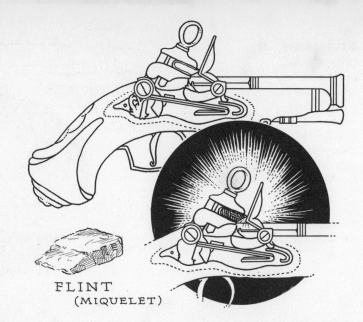

FLINT
(MIQUELET)

..First dated, rifled gun,
belonging to *E m p e r o r
Maximilian of Germany*.
(The coat of arms he
used between 1493 and
1508 is on the gun.)

..The Turin Armory had at
least one rifled iron gun
in 1476

1500-1520

..*Leonardo da Vinci,* famous artist, first sketched
the mechanism of a
wheel lock in 1508

..The wheel lock type of
ignition is believed to
h a v e b e e n developed
around 1510 to 1520

..In 1518 *Emperor Maxi-
milian* forbade the mak-
ing of wheel lock arms

..Crude "cartridges" first
made their appearance

1520-1526

..Earliest datable wheel
lock—circa 1521-1526

..Combined crossbow and
gun made for *Archduke
Ferdinand* (Bayerische
National Museum of Mu-
nich.)

..In 1522 the city of Fer-
rara, Italy, forbade the
carrying of firearms in
the city, day or night

4-6. The pic-
turesque blun-
derbuss pistol
is always an
eye-catcher to
both collectors
and laymen
alike, although
the ignition
principle is of
the regular
flintlock sys-
tem.

FLINT
(FLINTLOCK)

4-7. Lower de-
tail sketch
shows the
magazine door
open to permit
the loading of
ball and pow-
der into their
separate mag-
azines. On the
extreme for-
ward move-
ment of the
lever, with pis-
tol pointing
downward,
the ball is first
deposited in
the barrel,

followed by
the powder
charge. As the
lever comes
on around, a
priming
charge from
the little
magazine, seen
just in front
of the hammer
in the upper
illustration,
is deposited
in the priming
pan, and the
hammer is
cocked for fir-
ing.

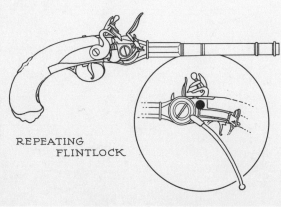

REPEATING
FLINTLOCK

1526-1545

..Earliest actually d a t e d wheel lock, 1530

..The *Duke of Florence* forbade the carrying of firearms short enough to conceal, specifically mentioning wheel locks and arms using flint

1545-1560

..First recorded use of guns in dueling

..First mention of a repeating rifle

..Repeating rifle made by *Peter Kalthoff*

1560-1580

..First appearance of the snaphaunce system of ignition

..Flash pans became a part of the lock rather than of the barrel

..Bayonets were developed

1580-1610

..M a n y a r m i e s w e r e equipped with matchlock calivers and muskets

..Advent of the u n i q u e Spanish miquelet arms

1610-1630

..Flintlock developed by *M a r i n le Bourgeoys* of France, and others

..Dog locks, locks using a "dog" behind the hammer to hold it at half cock came into being

4-8. The trigger guard forms the handle for the threaded screw-type breechblock, which when lowered permits the ball and powder to be inserted into the barrel.

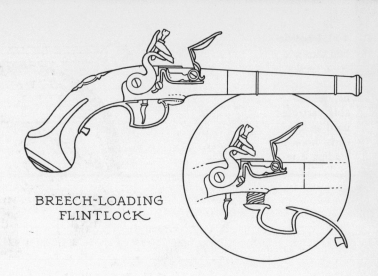

BREECH-LOADING
FLINTLOCK

4-9. Turning the "scent bottle" magazine containing loose fulminate one-half turn, deposited a bit of fulminite powder in a touchhole in its axis, which leads to the main charge in the barrel. When the magazine is returned to its original position, a spring upheld firing pin was ready for the blow of the hammer to detonate the fulminate, and likewise the main charge in the barrel.

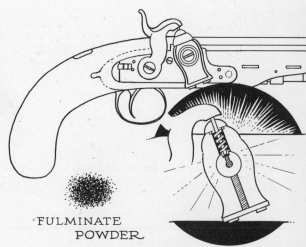

FULMINATE
POWDER

4-10. Tiny pellets, or pills, placed into the vent hole leading to the bore of the barrel, formed the detonating agent for this early underhammer pill lock arm.

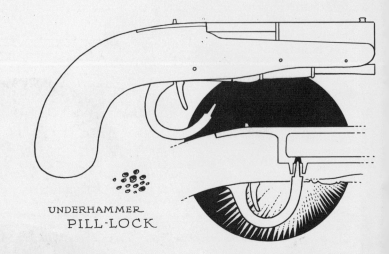

UNDERHAMMER
PILL-LOCK

4-11. Small detail shows a cross section of the metallic, reloadable cartridge used in this early breechloading arm.

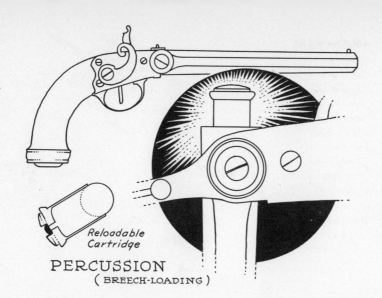

Reloadable Cartridge

PERCUSSION
(BREECH-LOADING)

4-12. A small tube containing fulminate was inserted into a slot leading to the bore of the gun. The falling hammer crushed the tube, detonating the fulminate, which flashed into the bore containing the main charge.

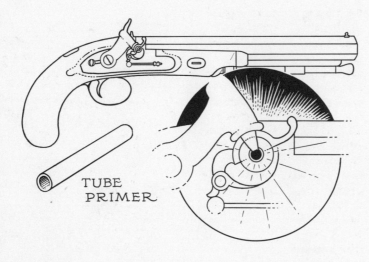

TUBE PRIMER

4-13. Similar to the modern cap-pistol cap, this early paper cap was inserted into a removable hammer nose for firing. Resulting flash entered the nipple, and through it to the bore of the gun. Removable noses provided a supply of detonators ready for instant use.

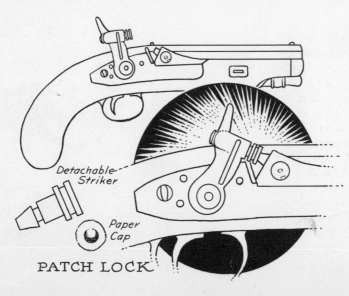

Detachable-Striker

Paper Cap

PATCH LOCK

1650-1700

..The flintlock became so much in common use that it was adopted by most of the major powers

1723

..Breech-loaded flintlocks issued to select units of the army by France

1750

..Previous to this, many of the finest gun b a r r e l s were of Spanish origin

1770

..Austria armed its Dragoons and Cavalry with breechloaders

1776

..*Patrick Ferguson* perfected a flintlock b r e e c h-loading rifle

1805-1807

..*Rev. Alexander John Forsyth,* a Scottish clergyman, invented a fulminate that would explode w h e n s t r u c k a sharp blow. Such fulminate was made originally as loose powder. Later it was developed into a pellet form

1812

..*J e a n S a m u e l Pauly,* a Swiss living in Paris, patented a breech-loading g u n u s i n g a self-contained rimmed, re-loadable, metallic, center-fire cartridge

1814-1817

..Development of the Percussion caplock by *Joshua Shaw* of Philadelphia. First caps were made of iron, later of pewter, and finally of copper or brass

1816

..*Joseph Manton* invented the pellet lock

1817

..*John H. Hall* of Portland, Maine, invented the Hall breech-loading flintlock rifle . . . first breech-loaded military rifle adopted by the U.S.

1818

..A Frenchman by the name of *Prelat* invented a percussion cap

..*Joseph Manton* of England invented the tube lock

1820

..A Frenchman, *Deboubert* by name, secured a patent for a lock using a nipple and a copper cap

1822

..*Joshua Shaw*, English artist residing in the U.S., invented and patented a percussion cap

1826

..*Dr. Samuel Guthrie,* a surgeon in the War of 1812, developed fulminate in the form of a pill. Locks using it were originally called "punch locks" . . . later more commonly known as "pill locks"

4-14. Detail il-lustrates the principle of the needle fire in which a slender needle penetrates the base of the paper cartridge containing the powder charge and detonates the fulminate at the base of the cardboard sabot.

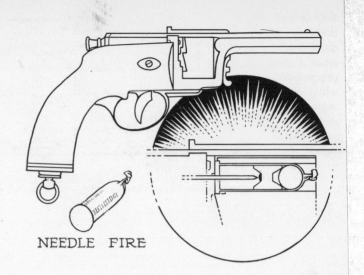

NEEDLE FIRE

4-15. Utilizing the percussion cap, this Colt revolver was the leader of pioneering American percussion revolvers. Method of loading the five chambers is illustrated in the detail sketch.

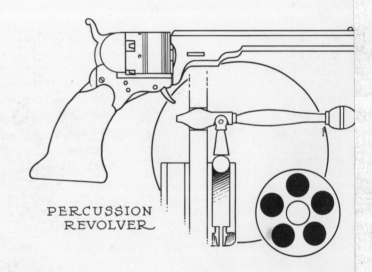

PERCUSSION REVOLVER

4-16. Enlarged detail shows a cross section of the pinfire cartridge, in which a pin is driven by a blow from the hammer into an interior percussion cap containing fulminate.

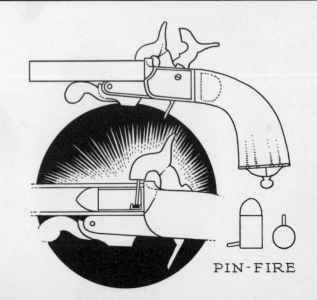

PIN-FIRE

4-17. One of the early double-action arms is this pepperbox which employs regular percussion caps as the detonating agent.

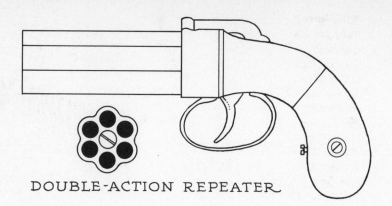

DOUBLE-ACTION REPEATER

4-18. The lower sketch illustrates how the roll of tape containing little spots of fulminate is fed across the nipple to then be detonated by the blow of the falling hammer.

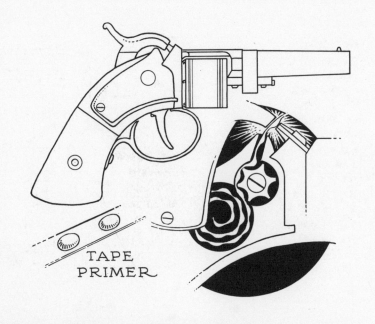

TAPE PRIMER

4-19. The principle of the regular percussion cap is shown in the lower detailed sketch. Fitting over the nipple, the sparks from it, when hit by the hammer, enter the channel of the nipple, and on into the bore of the barrel.

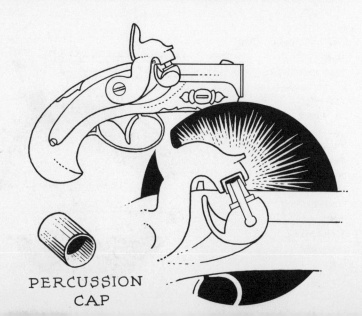

PERCUSSION CAP

1827

..*William Hart* of Fredonia, N.Y. began the manufacture of his pill lock guns

1829

..*Johann Nicholas Dreyse* invented the "needle gun," the principle of which involved a long, slender firing pin (or needle) being driven through the powder to the fulminate cap on the base of the bullet

..*Pottet* patented a center-fire cartridge

1830

..*Samuel and Charles Smith* of London secured a patent on what they called their "Smith's Patent Imperial Cap and Nipple." The cap was much larger in diameter, and flatter in height than caps then in common use. The nipple was made shorter and with a wider channel through which the flash entered the bore of the gun. This theory of faster ignition was well received by British sportsmen

1836

..*M. Lefaucheux*, a Frenchman, designed a pinfire, self-contained cartridge

..*Samuel Colt* started manufacture of his famous "Paterson" repeating firearms, with rotating cylinders

1838

..*Westley Richards* was granted a patent for a self-capper which could be used on both handguns and long arms

1840

..First issue of percussion arms to a British regiment

1842

..*Baron Heurteloup* improved his previous invention of a continuous tape primer so it would not burn beyond the part cut off

..*Westley Richards* designed a pasteboard primer covered with waterproof material

1844

..U. S. issued percussion arms to its military regiments

1845

..*Dr. Edward Maynard,* a dentist of Washington, D.C., invented the tape primer, a series of fulminate powder spots between strips of paper, not unlike the modern cap pistol rolls

..*M. Flobert* invented the BB or bullet-breech cap

1846

..Frenchman, *M. Houllier* patented a pinfire cartridge having a copper case

1848

..*Christian Sharps* perfected his famous action consisting of a block which moved up and down in a slot at the breech of the gun

1852

..Practical center-fire cartridges developed in England

..*Christian Sharps* secured a patent for a disc primer, which consisted of fulminate powder between thin discs of copper foil

4-20. A speck of fulminate between two pieces of thin copper or brass is the detonating agent of this disc primer breech-loading pistol. The thin wafer-like discs are thrown forward by the falling action of the hammer and are hit just as they are in position over the nipple.

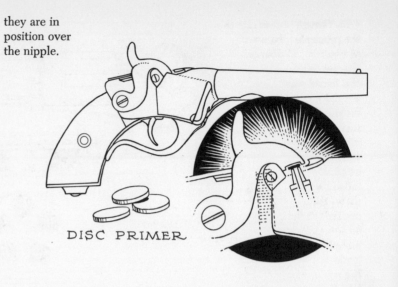

DISC PRIMER

4-21. Advanc-ing still another step forward in the arms story, this sketch illustrates the placing of the fulminate in the base of the bullet itself, thus providing a self-contained cartridge.

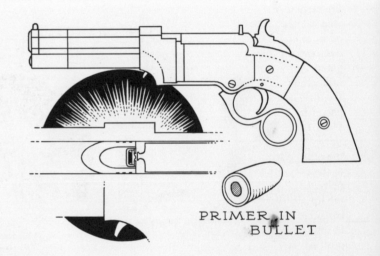

PRIMER IN BULLET

4-22. America's first revolver using self-contained metallic ammunition. This little gun fathered the trend toward the modern-day firearms. Fulminate was placed in the rim of the copper case, the hammer then striking any place on the rim would result in the detonating of the powder charge. It was pioneered by Smith & Wesson.

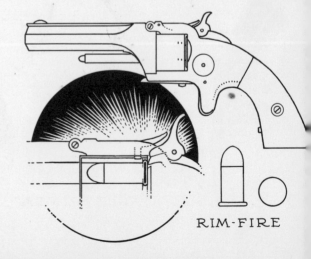

RIM-FIRE

4-23. Though the principle of two charges in one barrel was not unknown, the use of such a method in a revolver was a bit unusual. Detailed sketch shows the position of the odd-shaped bullets after loading. Right hammer falls first to detonate the forward charge.

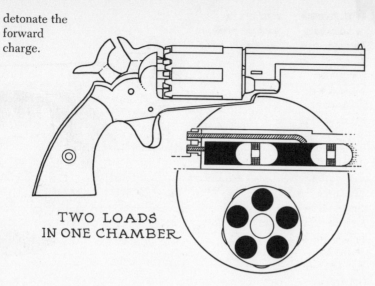

TWO LOADS
IN ONE CHAMBER

4-24. The lip- fire system was but one effort to circumvent the patent utilized by the little revolver in Plate 4-22. A slot in the the outer edge of the cylinder permitted the lip of the cartridge to fit into proper position to be hit by the hammer.

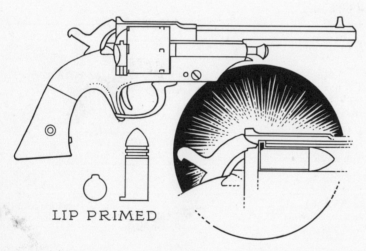

LIP PRIMED

4-25. Another effort to circumvent the breech-loading system employed by the revolver in Plate 4-22.

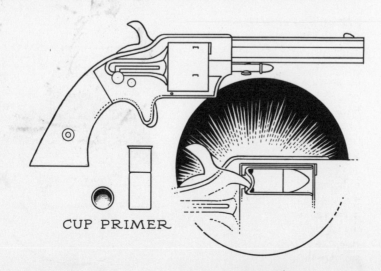

CUP PRIMER

1854-1860

.. Volcanic arms, using fulminate in the bullet without a case, were manufactured

.. *Lt. J. N. Ward* secured a patent in 1856 which consisted of the tape magazine being located in the hammer instead of the lock plate

... The Schroeder, an American needle fire military arm, was p a t e n t e d in 1856

1855

.. *Rollin White* of the U.S. was given a patent involving a cylinder bored through from end to end. Smith & Wesson acquired production rights to the patent

1857

.. *Smith & W e s s o n* produced America's first revolver using self-contained metallic ammunition

.. *Lawrence's* p a t e n t involved the use of a disc primer fed from a tube in the lock plate

.. *Lt. Col. J. Durrell Greene* secured a patent on an underhammer rifle. This rifle, having an unusual oval bore, was the first and only rifle having the hammer on the u n d e r side of the barrel to be a d o p t e d by the U.S. Army

1859

.. *Jesse S. Butterfield and Simeon Marshall* w e r e granted a patent for an "Improvement i n S e l f-Priming Locks" for firearms. Their improvement used "wafer primers" not unlike the disc primers

..*Jacob Rupertus* secured a patent for a gun having a magazine for primers in the butt

1860

..A metallic cartridge with a lip-like projection containing fulminate was patented by *E. Allen*

1866

..*Col. Hiram Berdan* of the United States perfected a primer for the center-fire cartridge

1867

..*Col. Edward M. Boxer* developed a center-fire cartridge

1884

..First controllable explosive made with nitrocellulose developed in France

1886

..France adopted the new smokeless powder

1892

..The Schonberger automatic pistol first manufactured in Austria

1893

..Invented by *Hugo Borchardt* of Connecticut, the Borchardt automatic was the first true automatic

1894

..Development of the Bergmann automatic

1897

..*John Browning* secured a patent for an automatic pistol. This patent formed the basis for the Colt line of semi-automatic arms

1900

..Smokeless powder in virtually universal use in military arms over the

4-26. Unusual front-loading cartridge with the fulminate contained in a "teat-like" projection on the head of the case. This was but another effort to circumvent the breech-loading system.

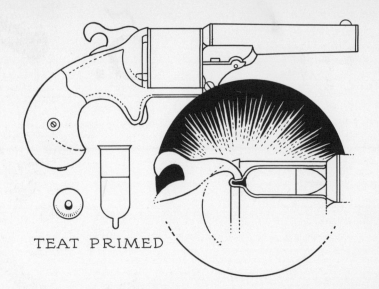

TEAT PRIMED

4-27. Illus- trated here is a cross section of a center-fire cartridge utilizing a replaceable primer containing fulminate. In use for the past ninety years, it has yet to be replaced by a better or more efficient means of detonating the powder charge.

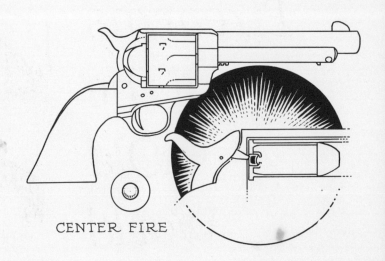

CENTER FIRE

4-28. This rim- less self-contained cartridge also employs a separate primer. With it we ring down the curtain on the evolution of firearms ignition until a more efficient method, if any, is ever found to detonate the powder charge. Modern firearms efficiency owes much to the Rev. Alexander John Forsyth, who introduced fulminate detonating powder so long ago.

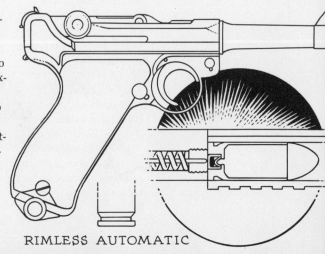

RIMLESS AUTOMATIC

5.

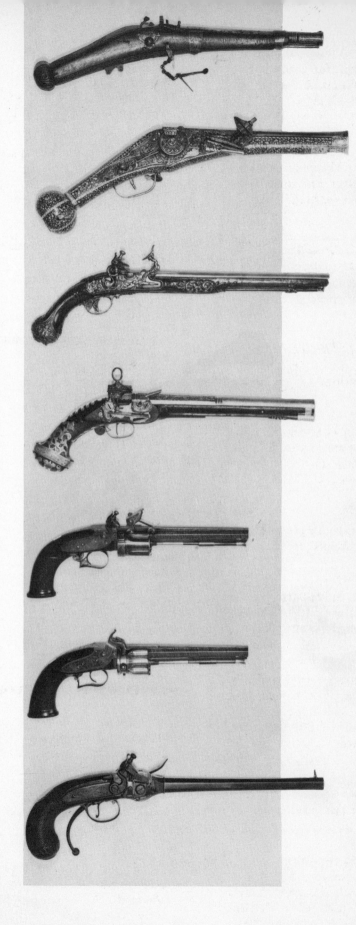

the Firearms of the Old World

5-1. From top: 1/Odd matchlock type pistol. 2/Ornate German wheel lock. 3/Italian snaphaunce. 4/Spanish miquelet. 5/English Collier flintlock with multi-chambered rotating cylinder. 6/Later Collier model designed to use percussion caps. 7/Lorenzoni or Cookson type repeating flintlock.

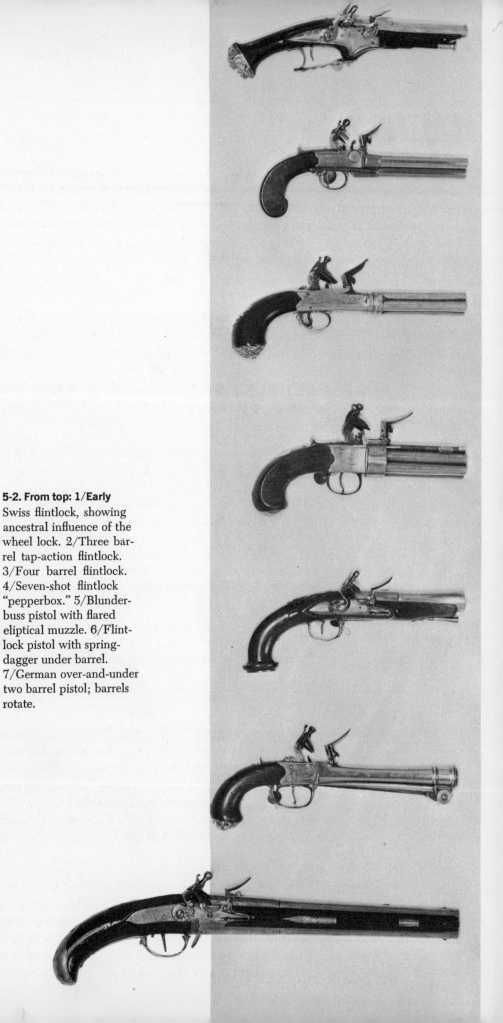

5-2. From top: 1/Early Swiss flintlock, showing ancestral influence of the wheel lock. 2/Three barrel tap-action flintlock. 3/Four barrel flintlock. 4/Seven-shot flintlock "pepperbox." 5/Blunderbuss pistol with flared eliptical muzzle. 6/Flintlock pistol with spring-dagger under barrel. 7/German over-and-under two barrel pistol; barrels rotate.

EARLY FIREARMS

The earliest firearms were without mechanism; they consisted essentially of a heavy tube closed at one end, with a small vent hole drilled from the top surface to the interior cavity just in front of the closed end. Gunpowder and one or more projectiles were placed in the interior cavity; then more powder was shaken into the vent hole. When fire was applied to the latter, the internal charge would be ignited.

THE MATCHLOCK

It was discovered that a piece of rope, soaked in a strong solution of saltpeter and dried, would burn steadily but very slowly even in wind and rain. A mechanism to adapt this to firearms consisted of a pivoted clamp whose jaws held a piece of such "slowmatch" well away from a pan adjoining a touchhole in the gun barrel. Pressing on a trigger caused the clamp to turn, bringing the burning end of the "slow match" into contact with fine priming gunpowder in the pan.

This matchlock system, originating in German-speaking lands, was widely used for about two hundred years (1500-1700) and spread westward to the Low Countries, France, and Britain, and eastward to Persia, India, and the Far East. The Occidental peoples favored a "serpentine" or "cock" working toward the shooter, while in Oriental lands the action of the cock was toward the muzzle of the gun.

One improvement was the addition of a spring action to the serpentine; it was "cocked" by being pulled away from the pan against the force of a spring until caught by a spring catch; pulling the trigger released this catch and the cock snapped to the pan. A variation was the "tinder lock;" instead of a clamp, the serpentine ended in a small ring which held a tuft of tinder, which had to be ignited from a slow match or flint-and-steel just before shooting.

THE WHEEL LOCK

The sparks struck by a wagon rim on a stony road probably inspired the next development, which avoided the smoke and smell of the Matchlock. Through the pan at the side of the gun barrel projected the top edge of a serrated steel wheel, which could be caused to turn by a strong spring. A piece of iron pyrites, held in a movable clamp was, by another spring, pressed against the edge of the wheel. When the trigger of the gun was pulled the wheel started to rotate, and its friction against the pyrites resulted in the creation of sparks right in the priming powder in the pan.

The wheel lock was sure-fire and concealable (so much so that laws were made forbidding it, though without noticeable result). The German-speaking folk made probably more wheel locks than did any other ethnic group; their product was steady and reliable. French wheel locks were, though beautiful, perhaps more delicate. Italian gunsmiths, especially those in the neighborhood of Brescia, produced masterpieces in chiseled and pierced steelwork decoration.

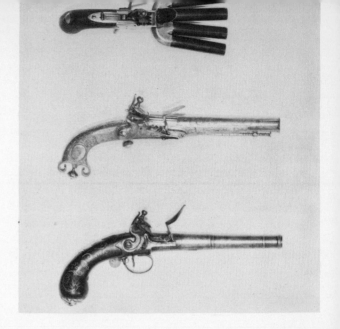

5-3. From top: 1/Four-shot "Duckfoot" flintlock. 2/ Scotch flintlock with ram's horn shape butt. 3/English flintlock of Queen Anne type.

THE FLINTLOCK

The next main development in hand firearms was the flintlock, which collectors usually divide into three principal sub-types: the snaphaunce, the standard flintlock, and the miquelet. All have the common principle that the sparks for igniting the gunpowder are derived not from the grinding action of the wheel lock but from the even older principle of the striking action of flint and steel. A piece of flint held in a movable clamp or cock is struck violently against a stationary plate of steel positioned above the priming pan. The resulting sparks fall into the pan and ignite the powder, which, through the adjacent touchhole, ignites the main charge.

In the snaphaunce locks the steel or "frizzen" is pivoted slightly in front of the pan which has a separate pan cover, usually opened automatically by a push rod actuated by the falling cock. The arm may be carried in safety by simply moving the frizzen forward out of the way of the flint.

In the standard flintlock the frizzen is integral with the pan cover, which forms a horizontal extension from it. When the flint strikes the frizzen, the latter is tilted away from the flint, uncovering the pan for the sparks to fall into it. The action of

the cock, with its flint, is caused by a strong mainspring, inside the lock plate, pressing on a cam or tumbler attached to the shaft or arbor of the cock. When the cock is pulled back, against the action of the mainspring, it is held by a spring catch or "sear," which engages a notch in the tumbler. Pulling the trigger pushes the sear out of engagement, and the cock, with its exposed flint, falls. For safety the standard flintlock has also a second, deeper notch, from which the sear cannot be moved by the trigger, the so-called "half cock" notch.

The miquelet lock is similar to the standard flintlock except that the mainspring is outside the lock plate, acting on the base of the cock near its pivot, and that there are separate sears for the full-cocked and half-cocked positions; both are inside the lock plate but act through it on the base of the cock.

THE PERCUSSION LOCK

In 1807 the Reverend Alexander Forsyth patented the idea which has been basic to all subsequent hand firearms: a mixture of chemicals (usually fulminate of mercury and chlorate of potassium) will produce a fiery explosion if struck with a hammer. This explosion is too violent for use inside a gun; the barrel would burst before the bullet

5-4. From top: 1/Irish holster or horseman's flintlock. 2/French holster flintlock. 3/Dutch holster flintlock. 4/German holster flintlock.

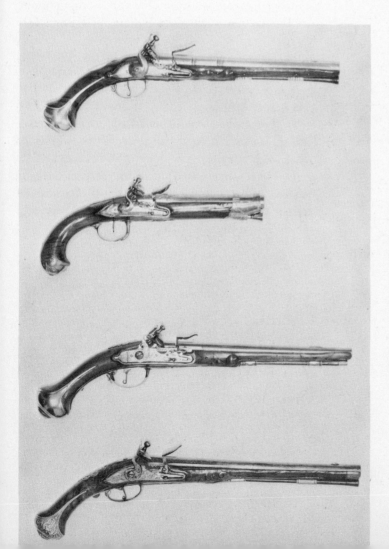

left the muzzle. However, it is excellent if only a tiny quantity is used adjacent to a touchhole. At first the detonating compound was used in the form of loose powder, then compressed pellets, with various ingenious methods of applying the chemical in the proper position.

The idea spread rapidly from Britain to Europe and to the United States, but the original form was soon superseded. The copper percussion cap is claimed as an invention of France, Britain, and America. The touchhole of the firearm was extended as a short nipple. Over this fitted a copper cap containing a bit of detonating compound. The lock action was like the flintlock, except that the cock, instead of terminating in a clamp for flint, ended as a solid hammer. On falling, it hit the cap, exploding the chemical and sending a jet of flame down the nipple into the gun.

The system worked well but required a double loading of the gun: (a) The charge of powder and projectile and (b) The percussion cap. A single cartridge, containing everything, which could be loaded at the breech, was obviously required. French and German gunsmiths brought out the needle gun, in which a needle, actuated by the mainspring, penetrated the powder charge and struck the detonating chemical in the base of the bullet.

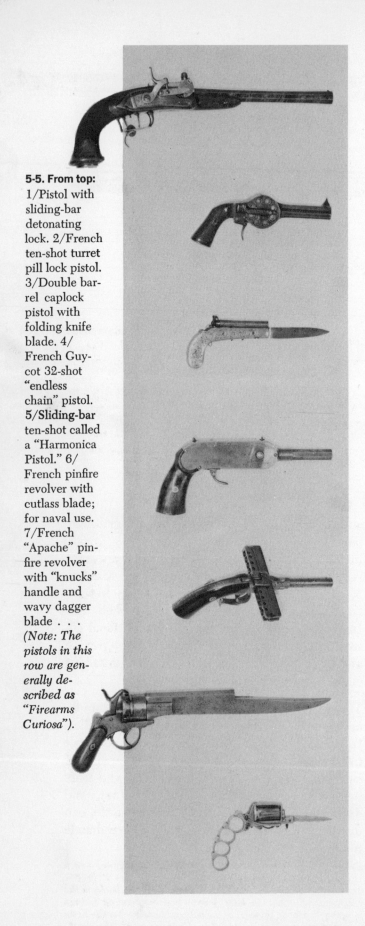

5-5. From top:
1/Pistol with sliding-bar detonating lock. 2/French ten-shot turret pill lock pistol. 3/Double barrel caplock pistol with folding knife blade. 4/ French Guycot 32-shot "endless chain" pistol. 5/Sliding-bar ten-shot called a "Harmonica Pistol." 6/ French pinfire revolver with cutlass blade; for naval use. 7/French "Apache" pinfire revolver with "knucks" handle and wavy dagger blade . . . *(Note: The pistols in this row are generally described as "Firearms Curiosa").*

Meanwhile gunsmiths were discovering that a thin copper shell, containing gunpowder and a bullet, would expand when the powder exploded, so that the gas produced would not leak backward past the shell but would all go to propelling the bullet. This made the modern breechloader practicable. It was, however, necessary to place the detonating device inside the shell. Many methods were tried. In France the pinfire cartridge of M. Lefaucheux was popular for many years: a pin projecting vertically from the side of the cartridge at its base was struck by the hammer and driven down upon a cap underneath it inside the shell. Such a cartridge can of course be inserted only one way, with the pin up. About the middle of the nineteenth century there appeared the *rimfire* cartridge, which is still used in small calibers. Before the gunpowder is placed in the shell, a little detonating compound is dropped in; then the shell is spun around rapidly. Centrifugal force distributes the compound all around the inside of the shell rim. No matter how the shell is inserted in the gun, the hammer should strike an area on the rim with detonating compound underneath it.

Finally in the 1860s the modern center-fire cartridge was produced by making the base of the shell heavy enough to contain a primer much like the percussion cap formerly used on the nipple of cap-and-ball arms. In the meantime the industrial revolution had been taking place. Firearms were no longer made in small shops staffed by a master craftsman and a few assistants, but in factories, with each machine, each operation, handled by a different workman. The product was perhaps better mechanically, but, although occasional pieces were elaborately engraved, it was as a whole less individualistic, less a work of art.

Yet even in pre-flintlock days firearms were often the product of more than one maker. Matchlocks were seldom signed. Wheel locks, on the other hand, often bore names or marks of separate makers of lock, stock, and barrel. Some of the most beautiful arms in the world had wheel locks and barrels carved by the brothers Daniel and Emanuel Sadeler of Munich or their successor Caspar Spät. The stocks for such arms were finished in polychrome enamel by David Altenstetter of Prague (for the Emperor Rudolph II) or in wood inlaid with engraved staghorn by Hierony-

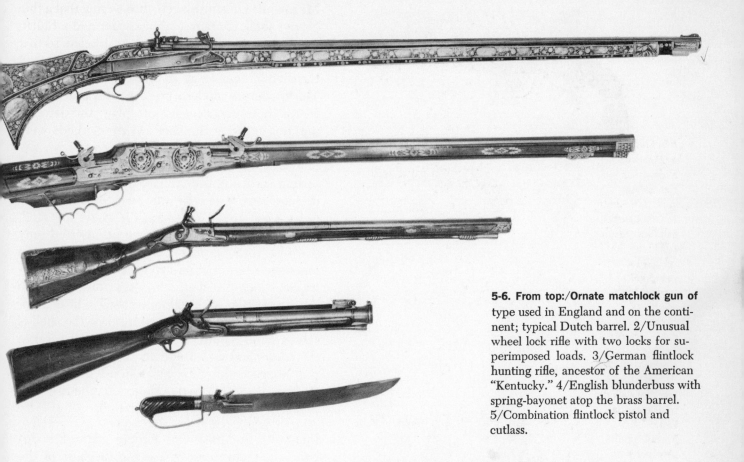

5-6. From top:/Ornate matchlock gun of type used in England and on the continent; typical Dutch barrel. 2/Unusual wheel lock rifle with two locks for superimposed loads. 3/German flintlock hunting rifle, ancestor of the American "Kentucky." 4/English blunderbuss with spring-bayonet atop the brass barrel. 5/Combination flintlock pistol and cutlass.

mus Borstoffer of Munich, Elias Becker of Augsburg, or Martin Süssebecker of Dresden. The Cominazzo family of Gardone, near Brescia, made beautiful barrels and sometimes the locks which accompanied them. Claude Thomas of Epinal is known by a single set of wheel lock rifle and pair of pistols, dated 1623; he appears to have made them entirely himself, possibly as his "masterpiece"—to prove his right to be regarded a master gunsmith.

With the arrival of the flintlock, firearms were more usually signed by a single master, and the names of these great gunsmiths are spread all over Europe and the British Isles. The Comminazzi in Italy continued to produce masterpieces of carved and perforated steel. In Portugal, Jacinto Xavier made fanciful pocket pistols, each with a concealed corkscrew in the butt, yet, despite their gadgetry, no less works of art. In Spain, Nicholas Bis, Juan Fernandez, Josef Cano, and many others made simple but very handsome arms. In Germany Bongarde of Düsseldorf, in Austria the Zellner family of Vienna, in France Piraube, Desgranges, and later Boutet, Le Page, Gauvain,

and Gastine Renette made beautiful and elaborate pistols. In England the tendency was toward meticulous workmanship and extreme accuracy rather than elaborate decoration; Egg, Manton, Mortimer, and Greener are famous names. In Scotland John Murdock, Alexander Campbell, and John Christie of Doune made the traditional all-steel "highland" pistols, with fine Celtic engraving and silver inlay. There is no space to begin the list of the other great gunsmiths of the past.

The arms they made would not fire as rapidly as modern automatic weapons, nor their bullets travel as fast or as far as those our guns shoot today. But many of these arms were capable of surprising accuracy, and the collector who truly loves fine craftsmanship, beautiful lines, and decoration in individual and consistent taste, can find deep pleasure in contemplating the handmade firearms of the Old World.

Editor's Note: *The illustrations (and captions thereto) which accompany Dr. Hoopes' text were provided by Frank E. Bivens, Jr.; photography by Dick Friske. In addition to the books in the bibliography found on later pages, two outstanding foreign language works on firearms of the old world are:* Ueber die Erste Entwicklung der Handfeuerwaffen *(German) by M. Thierbach;* and Flintlaset *(Swedish) by Torsten Lenk.*

6.

the Kentucky- Pennsylvania Rifles and Pistols

6-1. Early Kentucky of the Revolutionary War period (*circa 1780*) attributed to A. Verner but unmarked except for the initials "J.R." on the silver thumb plate. Early details are the octagon and round barrel, the flat butt plate with stock thick at butt, the broad and flat scrolled trigger, and the small amount of carving and decoration. The rear of the trigger guard is fastened with a screw—another early detail; the comb of the stock is high and relatively straight. Barrel measures 45¼ inches, caliber .56 smoothbore. Lock is unmarked and has no frizzen roller. The ample stock has little curl.

It has been said that the Kentucky rifle and the Kentucky pistol are deserving of a lasting place in American history. There is little doubt that the long rifle and its look-alike offspring, the single shot pistol, have indeed made their mark and are as safely recorded as though their names were carved in granite.

The flintlock Kentucky was an environmental development. It was designed to meet the specific requirements of hunting in a wilderness area and for Indian fighting. Its life spanned almost 100 years. The long barrel of the rifle and the small bore took less powder to charge and burned it cleaner. It made less noise on discharge, could be held steadier than a fowler or a musket, and was supremely accurate—an answer to an economic necessity of the times.

Few words can more adequately describe these famous guns than those of Captain John G. W. Dillin, the pioneer collector and author: "Light in weight—graceful in line—economical in consumption of powder and lead—fatally precise—distinctly American."

And the Kentucky was distinctly American. An evolvement of the German Jaeger rifle, it was originally made by gunsmiths of the Lancaster, Pennsylvania, area of predominately German, Swiss, Austrian and Huguenot extraction. The flintlock long rifle has been historically termed "Kentucky" although most of them were made in Pennsylvania.

Perhaps it was Daniel Boone whose explorations in 1770 west of the Cumberland mountains so captured the imagination of the people living in the East that they appeared anxious to join in the settlement of this rich area of land that was loosely referred to as "Kentucky." The territory was a major topic of discussion of the day, both by word of mouth and in the newspapers. As Boone knew, the rifle was a prime necessity to the people who hoped to establish their homes on this wild frontier. And the majority of the people who owned these long guns knew how to use them. They were usually skilled shots, for their living and often their lives depended upon a gun.

Despite the fact that these famous long rifles were largely made in Pennsylvania, it is highly doubtful that they will ever be widely known by any other name but "Kentuckys." They are mentioned as such in surviving literature as early as 1815, and the name has been accepted by most collectors and historians.

The Kentucky has made its share of history. It was not designed primarily as a military arm, and to term it "the gun that won the Revolutionary War" is to exaggerate. But it did play a significant part in this war and undoubtedly due to Washington's experience during Braddock's campaign, Congress lost no time in authorizing ten companies of riflemen in June of 1775 and directing that they report to the army at Cambridge. These companies were made up of men from Pennsylvania, Virginia and Maryland who were armed with the long rifle and knew how to use it.

As a military weapon, the Kentucky rifle was slow to load, could not handle prepared ammunition as a musket could, and was unsuited for use with a bayonet. In spite of these disadvantages, the guns made an admirable record for themselves in the Revolutionary War as well as in the War of 1812. Fatal shots made at extended ranges of up to three and four hundred yards had a devastating effect on the morale of the British, particularly since the principal targets of the riflemen were often the Redcoat officers. To speed loading in battle, an unpatched ball, cast to the size of the bore, was sometimes used; for greater range, a gun was sometimes double charged. Accurate shots at two hundred yards were not unusual with close-fitting round balls patched with greased linen. This was quite remarkable with open sights, and the Kentucky proved to be the most accurate rifle of its day.

A number of the officers of these rifle companies carried the Kentucky pistol as an auxiliary weapon. This is a fact attested to by existing records in both wars.

That the long rifle made a historical war record is indisputable. Their everyday record in the wilderness and in the opening of the western frontiers of their day—as a pioneer's hunting weapon and a defender of his home—was perhaps not as spectacular, but in reality was undoubtedly their greatest and most lasting contribution. In a day when the smoothbore fowler and musket were the only alternatives to the rifle, there could be little doubt as to the choice of the pioneer settler.

Many Pennsylvania gunsmiths were working in the eastern section of the State during and directly following the Revolutionary War. They appeared to have no difficulty in selling all the rifles they could make, and while cost depended somewhat on the amount of decoration, existing records show that somewhere between $12.00 and $18.00 "hard money" was the price of an average gun. Barrels were forged by hand from a bar of soft iron and laboriously rifled. Some makers bought bored blanks and others bought barrels that had been both bored and rifled. Stocks were hand hewn from native maple especially selected for the curl and beauty of the grain and aged for upwards of four years before shaping.

Locks were largely purchased after 1790—Dillin believed in a ratio of about 30 percent homemade and 70 percent purchased. Joe Kindig believes that except for the hand-forged locks made by the gunsmith himself, most locks came from Germany and England through Philadelphia importers. There were some Pennsylvania artisans who specialized in making locks alone.

The brass patch box and trim was an artistic achievement, without much doubt solely American in development and with artistic merit of the highest degree. The smooth flowing lines and beautiful decorative inlays of these guns appealed as greatly to the original owners as they do to the collector of today.

Delineation of styles of the individual gunsmiths and the attribution of unmarked guns to a certain workman or to a specific locality become monumental tasks for the collector. However, breakthroughs in these areas have come about through study and efforts of men who industriously probed old court records, town and county histories, and studied hundreds of existing Kentuckys. If ever a book was of prime importance to a serious collector, it is to the collector of the Kentucky.

Captain Dillin published *The Kentucky Rifle,* the first extensive work on the subject, in 1924. Since then this book has been through four editions, each time being corrected and expanded.

Early in 1960 The Stackpole Company published a well-documented and illustrated work by a native of Lancaster County and a faculty member of a Pennsylvania State Teachers College, Henry J. Kauffman's *The Pennsylvania-Kentucky Rifle.* The list of many gunmakers and their styles, with documentation, is exactly what was and is needed by the serious collector to assist in identification, relative values, and historical information.

Later in 1960 a second work was published. It is authored by perhaps the greatest student and collector of the Kentucky, Joe Kindig, Jr. His epic work is entitled *Thoughts on the Kentucky Rifle in its Golden Age* and clearly illustrates and describes the long rifle at the height of its achievement. The book was written by a serious student in love with his subject. The result is magnificent.

Too little has been written on the Kentucky pistol, but the pioneering effort on this subject was done by the astute collector, Samuel E. Dyke, and is to be found as a chapter in the fourth edition of *The Kentucky Rifle* by Dillin. Kauffman's book also contains a chapter on the Kentucky pistol. Other useful publications that have carried definitive articles of interest to the collector are the magazines The American Rifleman, Muzzle Blasts, and An-

78

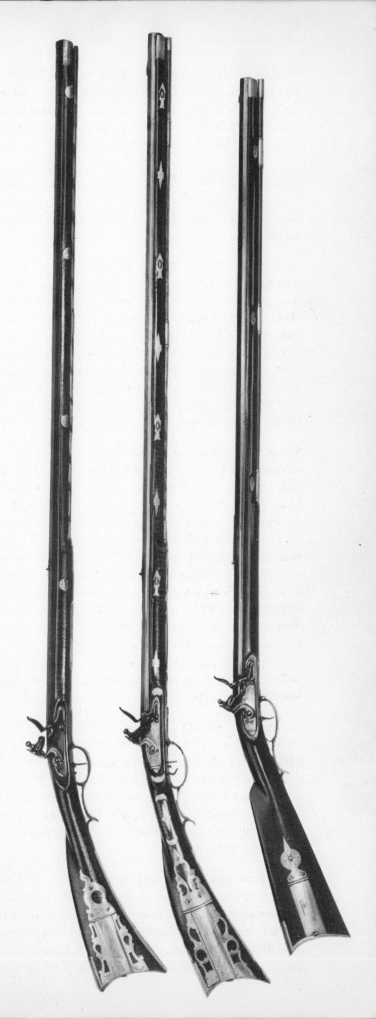

TIQUES. The collector is well advised to study every one of these publications. The material will be found most useful, particularly the illustrations.

Each gun was individualistic, even the style of a single gunsmith changed at times. Therefore, the reader will understand how difficult it is to date and to attribute Kentuckys when you compare their study with that of the military guns of a corresponding period or the machine-produced guns of a later period.

How does a collector date or attribute a Kentucky? What represents value? Will the purchase of a Kentucky rifle or pistol be a sound investment? To attempt to answer these and other questions that might come to mind, it can truthfully be said

6-2. From left: 1/A graceful, light Kentucky rifle, circa 1810, showing the progression of the curving butt plate and thinner stock. Probably made in the area of Reading, Pa. This gun is decorated with ten silver inlays and incised carving. Lock has frizzen roller and is marked "Pleasants, Philadelphia, Warranted." The full octagon barrel measures 43½ inches and is marked "G *S"; caliber is .40, rifled. Curly maple stock.
2/An extremely ornate rifle in fine original condition. Made circa 1815, this rifle has the "Roman Nose" stock attributed to the Bethlehem, Pa., area. Curved butt plate. The curly maple stock shows incised carving and is further decorated with 47 silver and brass inlays. Lock is marked "C. Bird & Company, Philadelphia, Warranted." Double set triggers. The octagon barrel measures 42¾ inches and is caliber .40, rifled; it is marked "J.D."
3/While this rifle is a "New England type Kentucky" *(circa 1820)* it is fairly typical of the end of the flintlock progression in style and shape. The 38-inch octagon barrel is shorter than earlier types and the comb of the stock is more pronounced; stock is cherry wood. Lock with frizzen roller is marked "R. Norris." Barrel is marked "M. *(Martin)* Smith, Greenfield, Mass." and is caliber .45, rifled. This gun is a fine original specimen and a good example of a rare type.

that study on the part of the collector is possibly more important in this particular field than in any other connected with guns. Buy and read all the books and articles you can. This is only sensible groundwork. Then study as many guns as you can. Learn to know what is really good and what isn't—and why.

As previously stated, the long rifle was probably a transitional development from the German hunting rifle. In the beginning it was quite crude, but it had its own American earmarks. The barrel was considerably longer than the Jaeger—it averaged around forty to forty-five inches. Calibers ranged from about .40 to .60. The early rifles that pre-dated the Revolutionary War or were made during the war often had a rather straight butt plate. The stock was usually thick at the butt end. Patch boxes were simple and the guns were very sparsely decorated. Locks were often hand-forged and lacked the roller on the frizzen spring. Early hammers were of the gooseneck style, later to be supplanted by the reinforced type.

Few of these very early pieces were signed. A reason offered for the lack of marks—that the early Pennsylvania gunsmiths feared reprisals by the British—is undoubtedly true. Another valid reason might be that, at this period in our history, most gunsmiths were well known in their own locality, if not beyond it. In consequence, there was little need for the gunsmith to mark his guns because everyone in the area knew him and his work. Another reason might be that few people along the early frontiers could read or write—sometimes including the gunsmith. Whatever the reason, it is difficult indeed to attribute these early guns.

As greater beauty of style and design evolved, the Kentucky entered its "Golden Age." Mr. Kindig puts this roughly from 1790 to 1815. During this period, the great makers produced works of art in rifles and pistols that have made their mark in history. Stocks were relief carved with rococo "C" and "S" scrolls as well as delicate moldings. Patch boxes were elaborately pierced and inlaid. These guns were not only supremely accurate weapons, but had a balance of line and symmetry that captures the eye to this day. It is quite superfluous to say that these "Golden Age" guns now represent collectors' prizes. Some were signed, and makers have been traced and their working eras have been delineated.

Astute collectors have, by the study of design and style characteristics, been able to show the area in which an unmarked gun could have been made. For instance, Mr. Kindig believes that the so-called "Roman Nose" stock to be more of a sectional than a period characteristic.

In evaluating markings on these guns, here is a word of caution: It is dangerous indeed to attempt to attribute a Kentucky with the barrel marked with initials to a known maker, unless the piece definitely embodies many familiar characteristics of his work. Likewise, the name on a lock plate rarely has any connection with the maker of the gun.

In the period following the "Golden Age," many fine guns were made, but they tended to be more elaborate and some lacked delicacy of line. As percussion ignition came into popularity, many of the early flintlock rifles were converted to this form, and the rifles built solely as percussion pieces lost their early refinements, with the exception of the Bedford area guns. Calibers decreased because of the lack of big game and many old rifles became smoothbores for shooting small game. By about 1840 the saga of the Kentucky came to an end.

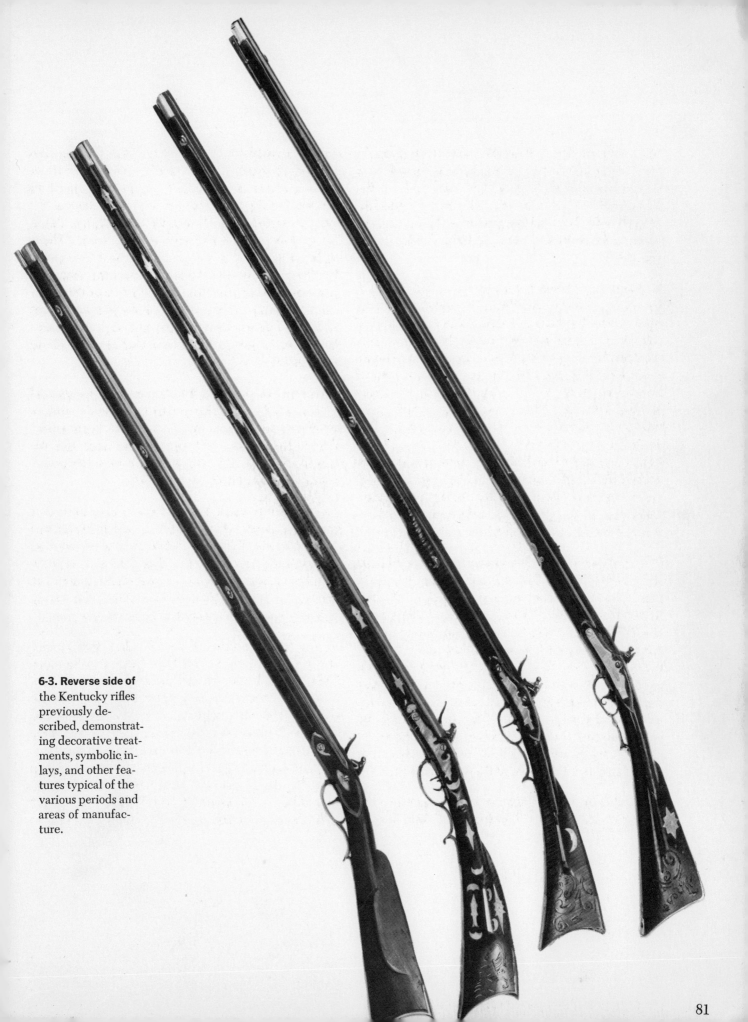

6-3. Reverse side of the Kentucky rifles previously described, demonstrating decorative treatments, symbolic inlays, and other features typical of the various periods and areas of manufacture.

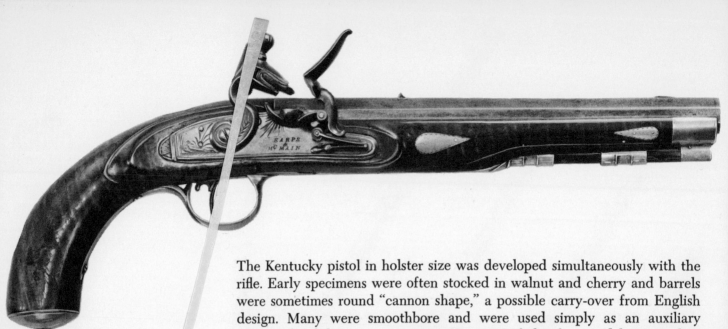

The Kentucky pistol in holster size was developed simultaneously with the rifle. Early specimens were often stocked in walnut and cherry and barrels were sometimes round "cannon shape," a possible carry-over from English design. Many were smoothbore and were used simply as an auxiliary weapon for fighting or protection. Because of this fact, and because they were useless for hunting, the pistol has come down to us largely in its flintlock state. The comments on makers' marks applying to the rifle apply with equal validity to the pistol. As the rifle developed, so did the pistol. Barrel shapes usually went from round, to octagon and round, and to full octagon over the years. Stocks of curly maple or those treated with that fine red "violin" finish supplanted the early ones of walnut. More pistols were probably mounted with silver, percentagewise, than were rifles, but silver mounts made of the coin silver of the day are still extremely scarce.

Flintlock pocket-size Kentucky pistols are rare. More of this size were made in the percussion period and most of the later pieces were rifled. Calibers ranged from about .40 to over .60 and twelve to fourteen inches was about an average overall length for the holster-size gun. Mr. Dyke estimates there was one Kentucky pistol made for every two hundred and fifty rifles; and collectors were not long in learning that these handguns represented not only a most distinct and artistic design that was solely American, but that they were items of the greatest rarity.

6-4. Matched pair of Ken-tucky pistols by Beeman, circa 1820. The 9½-inch octagon barrels are caliber .45 smoothbore. Striped maple stocks decorated with silver and brass inlays. The locks are marked "Earps & McMain," and one pistol has been converted from flint to percussion by a striker held in the jaws of the flintlock hammer and a drum and nipple at the vent area of the barrel *(not visible)*.

Now, some advice for the Kentucky collector. As in every item of value, let your motto be "Caveat Emptor" (let the buyer beware!). If you are looking for a rifle in original flintlock condition, bear in mind that Mr. Kindig believes that possibly only two guns in ten are original flint and have not been re-altered. It is always a good policy to remove the lock when buying an expensive piece, and to remove the breech plug as well, to see if the vent has recently been re-bushed. But remember that many legitimate repairs were carried out over the years on these guns—a situation that can be readily understood.

Beware of "assembled" pieces—guns made up of various old parts—with new wood or repairs carried beyond the realm of the simple restoration of a time-honored and worn piece. Frizzens were legitimately "re-steeled" and ramrods replaced. These are not matters to become concerned with. A modern cast-iron replacement frizzen that won't spark can usually be replaced.

Because of their artistic nature, the Kentuckys seem to appeal to a broader strata of collectors than do the mechanical variations in machine-made guns. They took many years to develop and they come in a great variety, two of which are rarely alike. They represent the individualistic expressions of many superb gunsmiths of their day who took great pride in their workmanship.

Kentucky rifles and pistols are in an ascending market. It is well for the collector to understand this. The top-grade, high-priced gun of today may well be the bargain of tomorrow. The supply is dwindling. The vintage Kentucky of the "Golden Age," or the very early gun of the Revolutionary period, always commands a top price. Some collectors find this hard to understand as they believe a poorly made, late gun, of more elaborate or ornate decoration, should be more valuable.

Value is based on rarity, original condition, authenticity, and period. In Kentuckys, numbers do not count, quality does.

One final word on this subject in which I would like to paraphrase one of the most astute names in the field of Americana, Mr. Albert Sack:

> In any collecting field there are only a small number of choice items that are classic examples of beauty, design, and authenticity. To the less practiced eye, the superior piece will look too similar to the average to justify the substantial price difference.
>
> Some collectors can see the difference, but settle for less.
>
> Some collectors try to beat the game by trying to discover mink for the price of rabbit. Nine times out of ten they lose and lose badly.
>
> As the investment is substantial in any case, the choice article is almost always the better buy. It is hard to find anyone who has set high standards of collecting who has ever regretted it. While premium items are more costly today (and will be equally or more so in the future), so are the average items.

Therefore, study and know your Kentuckys—and favor quality!

6-5. Photographer E. Irving Blomstrann employed a mirror to picture two sides of this fine 1760 period New York map horn in the John S. du Mont collection. Decorated powder horns were a valued loading accessory in the Kentucky rifle era.

7.
the Revolving Cylinder

Shoulder Arms

Man's search for multi-shot weapons began soon after the matchlock and wheel lock came into practical use. The lock work of the wheel lock was not well suited to employment of a rotating multichambered breech (revolving cylinder), but the matchlock was more adaptable. Specimens of early matchlock guns with a rather crude, multi-shot rotating breech exist in some museums and in a few private collections.

The lock work of the flintlock certainly offered no ideal ignition system for a rotating breech, but this did not deter Old World gunmakers from having a try at it. The snaphaunce and miquelet forms of the flintlock were employed, as well as the more common form. We find flint-fired revolving-breech arms produced by Italian, Flemish,

7-1. From left: 1/Six- chambered revolving cylinder flintlock marked "Carreaux." 2/Three-chambered French flintlock. 3/Eight-chambered snaphaunce. 4/Collier percussion smoothbore, 5-shot. 5/W. Billinghurst pill lock, 7-shot. 6/T. P. Cherington pill lock, 7-shot. 7/Kentucky-type cylinder rifle by Noble, 6-shot, percussion, offset hammer. 8/H. Volpius percussion, circa 1850, 7-shot.

7-2. From right: 1/Benjamin Bigelow two-barrel percussion gun, 7-shot cylinder. Lower smoothbore barrel fired by underhammer. 2/William Billinghurst, same as above but pill lock. 3/Colt 8-shot, Paterson Model of 1836, ring trigger rifle. 4/Colt, similar to above but with factory attached loading lever on side. 5/Colt Paterson rifle, no bridge over cylinder, odd non-factory loading lever. 6/Colt Paterson shotgun, 6-shot. 7/Colt Paterson carbine, 6-shot (*smoothbore*); 8/Nichols & Childs patent 1838, Conway, Mass., 6-shot.

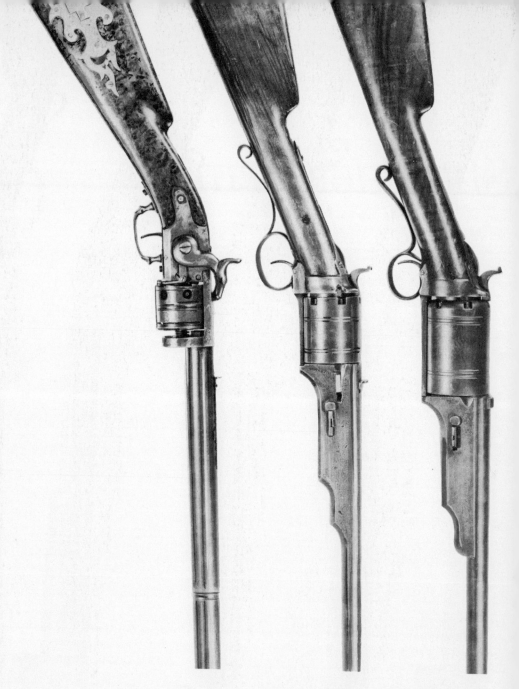

French, Irish, and English gunmakers and by a few artisans from other Old World countries.

In America, our vague claim to some recognition in the flintlock field is the sketchy data suggesting that New Englanders Elisha H. Collier, Artemas Wheeler, and Cornelius Coolidge werè associated in producing and promoting the rotating breech flintlock system on which Collier was granted an 1818 patent in England, and Coolidge an 1819 patent in France.

A very interesting account of the Collier story, along with one of the best published articles on cylinder rifles, can be found in the February, 1951, issue of *The Gun Collector*.

Collier is said to have obtained a patent on a percussion arm with a multichambered rotating breech in 1820, thus pre-dating American patents for percussion revolving-cylinder arms by some years. Helpful information regarding these Collier arms may be found in *English Guns & Rifles* by J. N. George.

Controversy as to which or who came first is apparent in quite a few areas of gunmaking and it touches the origins of cylinder rifles in America.

J. Miller is generally credited with starting the manufacture of multichambered revolving breech rifles through a patent issued in 1829. D. G. Colburn's name then finds its way into the development of the arm; and

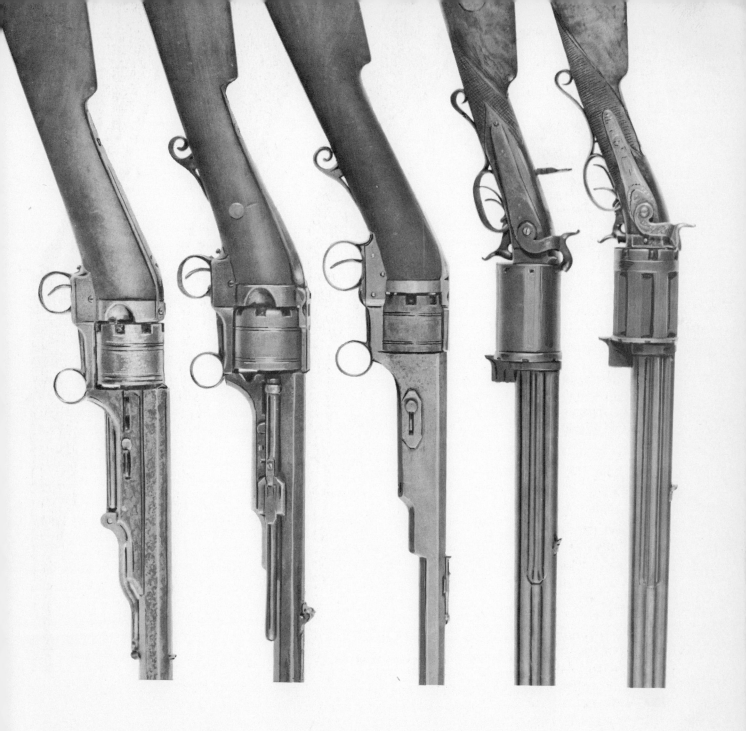

thereafter we have an interesting number of pill lock cylinder rifles, manually operated, and all of a rather uniform pattern. Among the names appearing on these guns are: Miller, Brown, Cherington, Volpius, Ormsby, Smith, Bigelow, and Billinghurst.

William Billinghurst and Benjamin Bigelow, both located in Rochester, New York, prior to 1850, are perhaps the best known in this group. They are the only gunmakers known to the writer, other than Le Mat, who made cylinder rifles with over-and-under barrels. The lower smoothbore barrel served as an axis for the cylinder and was fired by a striker on the under side. Combination guns of this style are extremely rare and command high prices if in good condition.

majority of the Miller-style hand-rotated cylinder rifles were fired by detonating pills, but a few will be found which use percussion caps. Benjamin Bigelow's personal cylinder rifle, with over-and-under barrels, employs standard percussion caps, whereas the Billinghurst gun of this same rare type, following it in the illustrations, is a pill lock. Bigelow moved from Rochester to San Francisco in 1850, sailing around the Horn in the *Palestine*. In 1852 he opened his gunshop in Marysville, California, where he resided until his death in 1888. He was probably the only commercial producer of cylinder rifles in the far West.

Contemporary with the Miller type of gun we find a few guns sometimes decribed as "Kentucky-type" cylinder rifles, their stocks usually of striped maple. They were apparently made in small shops by individual gunmakers. A gun of this type marked "Noble" was formerly in the Herman Dean collection; it has a six-shot percussion manually-operated cylinder and an odd offset hammer.

A close uniformity in cylinder rifle models was not attained until the Patent Arms Mfg. Co. of Paterson, New Jersey, employing Samuel Colt's patent of 1836, produced their ring trigger eight-shot percussion rifle with a concealed hammer. A more successful six-shot Colt gun came along in 1839, this one with an exposed hammer and simplified working parts. The Colt cylinder rifle story is too extensive for detailed treatment here; for the interested arms student details will be found in *Colt Firearms* by Serven.

Following Samuel Colt's 1836 patent, we find that O. W. Whittier, D. Leavitt, and J. W. Cochran took out patents in 1837, and in 1838 patents for multi-chambered arms were granted to Nichols & Childs, E. Jaquith, M. Nutting, and T. Strong. Rifles built from these early 1837 and 1838 patent designs are extremely scarce, and in some cases nearly nonexistent.

For all practical purposes, the cylinder rifle in America did not reach important production until the 1850s. In this decade we find various patented features built into Colt's 1855 sidehammer rifles and shotguns, the North & Savage, Warner, Remington, Allen & Wheelock, Hall, and a few others. The number of chambers ranged from four to fifteen, with five and six chambers the most common.

This was an active period, too, for gunmakers abroad and we find cylinder rifles bearing the Paris address and names of Devisme, Le Lyon, and Le Mat; the name of Herman of Belgium; and a number of English names such as Lang, Deane, Adams, Barnes, and Tranter. Some of these European guns employed unusual features; the rifle shown here with two cylinders is a good illustration of inventive ingenuity. The Le Mat gun is worthy of some special mention, too. Alexander Le Mat of New Orleans was granted patents in 1856 and 1869. A few arms of his two-barrel design were made under the name of Le Mat and Girard in England, but the majority were manufactured in France. Le Mat's loyalty was with the Confederacy and many of his arms were used by the South in the War between the States. His pistols are not easily found, and the Le Mat shoulder arms are especially rare. It is altogether likely that Le Mat was inspired by the Billinghurst and Bigelow two-barrel guns.

The multi-chambered breech was not restricted solely to a drum-like straight-bored cylinder. Several manufacturers adopted the system employed in Cochran's patent of 1837 and designed rifles with a radial multi-chambered breech shaped something like a hockey puck. These are often called "turret" guns. The Cochran gun was made by C. B. Allen at Springfield, Massachusetts, and is a very choice collector's item. In this gun the radial breech is mounted in horizontal position. The same is true of the E. H. Graham "turret" rifle. Graham was also a New Englander, residing in Maine and later in New Hampshire. Patents were granted to him in

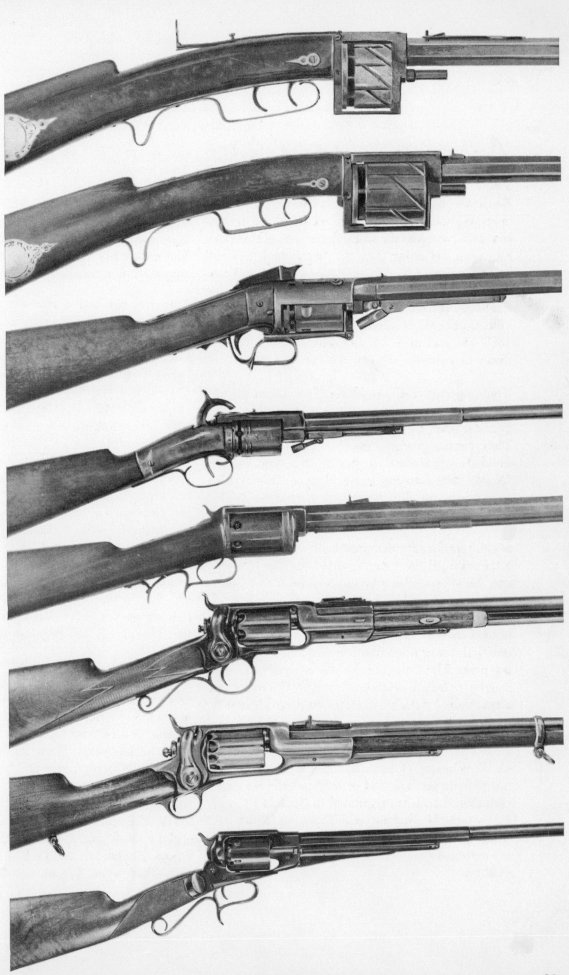

7-3. From top:
1/Whittier Model 1837 rifle, 9-shot, 2/Whittier shotgun, 6-shot. 3/ North & Savage, 6-shot. 4/James Warner grooved cylinder model, 6-shot. 5/James Warner solid frame model, 6-shot. 6/Colt Model 1855, Root sidehammer sporting model. 7/Colt military model rifled musket. 8/Remington Model 1858 rifle, 6-shot.

1851, 1855, 1856, and 1863. The Graham guns are even harder to find than the rare Cochran.

A commoner rifle with a radial rotating breech is the 1851 invention of P. W. Porter. This gun has a vertically-hung, radial multi-chambered breech. The earliest models employed detonating pills; ignition for the later models was the standard percussion cap. Some of the late-production Porter guns were furnished with an eight-shot breech rather than the usual nine-shot.

Turret guns were built abroad, too, one of the best known makers being H. Genhart of Liege. Wilkinson of London built a few beautifully finished guns of the Cochran style. But turret guns were not destined to be popular. The dangers of drum-type straight-bored cylinders were great enough, but the radial bored flat-disc type of cylinder spread the danger in all directions, including a direct line with the shooter himself. Porter tried to minimize this danger by furnishing a removable cover to serve as a safety guard over the top of the cylinder. These guards are now in themselves rarer than the gun, for few have survived and seldom is a Porter rifle found complete with the guard.

Manufacture of revolving-breech rifles continued into the 1860s, but the pace began to slow down. The Roper Repeating Rifle Co. of Amherst, Massachusetts, came out with a rotating-chambered rifle

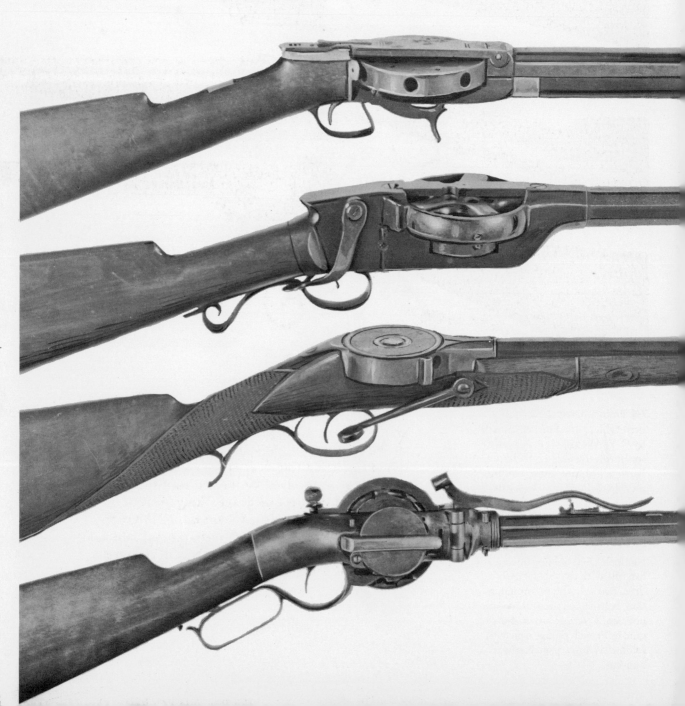

7-4. From top, left: 1/Cochran turret rifle, patent of 1837, made by C. B. Allen, 7-shot. 2/Graham turret rifle, 5-shot. 3/Genhart Brevete, 10-shot European turret rifle. 4/Porter pill lock rifle, 9-shot, shown with rare shield over radial cylinder.

Above, from top: 5/Alexander Hall's patent of 1856 cylinder contains 15 chambers. 6/English rifle with two 8-shot cylinders. Top cylinder in firing position, bottom cylinder pivots into position. 7/Roper 4-shot shotgun. 8/French pinfire rifle with folding bayonet, used for boar hunting.

and two sizes of a similar shotgun, developed from an 1866 patent. These were four-shot arms in which steel cartridges with a nipple at the rear were inserted through a trap door in the enclosed breech housing. Fins, revolved by the action of the hammer, turned the steel shells into firing position. In later production, nipples and percussion caps were supplanted by primers which were pressed into a recessed pocket at the rear of the shell. In any case, the gun was not much of a success.

Efforts to produce an efficient revolving-cylinder gun continued into the cartridge era. Remington and Colt altered some of their percussion cylinder rifles to employ metallic cartridges. France and Belgium led in new production with pinfire rifles of the rotating-cylinder type. Even Mauser of Germany and Pieper of Liege turned out a metallic cartridge revolver-rifle. Perhaps the most notable American effort along these lines, insofar as collectors may be concerned, are Smith & Wesson's revolver-rifle with detachable shoulder stock and Colt's "Buntline" Single Action Army revolver with long barrel and detachable shoulder stock.

From the start the revolver-rifle had but a modest chance of success. The multi-chambered cylinder had only a few advantages but it had important disadvantages. It was lighter than multi-barrel guns and could provide more sustained firepower, especially if extra loaded cylinders were carried. But before the introduction of metallic cartridges the cylinder rifle was always a dangerous gun to handle. Makers like Collier and Savage tried to obtain a tight lap joint between the chamber mouth and the barrel, but gas and flame leakage in revolving-breech rifles was inevitable. Sometimes this resulted in multiple discharges and if one's left hand was in the normal forward position along the barrel or forestock, it was in line for a shower of lead. Colt published instructions on the correct manner to hold a cylinder rifle. They suggested that the left hand support the rifle just forward of the trigger guard, well behind the line of fire in the event chambers on either side of the barrel should fire accidentally.

The compact Henry and Spencer magazine rifles of the 1860s wrote *finis* to the era of the rather bulky revolving-breech multi-shot guns. But theirs is a fascinating chapter in man's search for greater efficiency in firearms. Because guns of this kind were made in small numbers they are not plentiful and are relatively expensive. It is not an easy field in which to collect. A small collection here, however, can be as interesting and as valuable as a much larger collection containing commoner weapons. The extensive Lowe, Stewart, Russell, Aziz, Nunnemacher, and Renwick collections, to name but a few, are evidence that revolving cylinder guns can be found and that they offer a very fascinating field of collector interest.

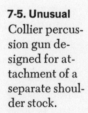

7-5. Unusual Collier percussion gun designed for attachment of a separate shoulder stock.

8.

the Muskets and Early Rifles of the U.S.

Though far and wide the rifle and the six-gun are known as the symbols of American destiny, it is the flintlock muzzle-loading smoothbore musket that did much to shape our growth and history from the War of the Revolution through the Mexican War. While the Kentucky (or Pennsylvania, if you prefer) rifle of the Revolutionary period had long captured the popular imagination, it is the common smoothbore musket that was the preferred long arm of the infantry line regiments. Its facility in loading; relative rapidity of fire; general sturdiness without excessive weight due to light, thin barrel; and last but not least, the extremely important element of the round barrel permitting the easy attachment of a bayonet; made it the principal arm of the infantry, the decisive force of armies of the day.

The prime disadvantage of the smoothbore, though it facilitated fire rapidity, was the approximate .05 inch "windage," clearance between the ball and the bore necessitated by the rough and uneven finish of the musket bores of the period. Loading the infantry musket was an intricate process requiring the use of the mouth as well as the hands. However, differing from the rifle, the loosely fitting musket ball was easily rammed home and the loading rapidly completed, permitting trained troops to fire three shots a minute. The maximum effective range was one hundred yards, with hits on man-size targets effective at most but forty percent of the time. When within effective range, the infantry fired a final round and then charged with the bayonet.

The Revolutionary War was fought with a predominance of British arms; the pinned barrel "Brown Bess" muskets had become available to the Colonials by purchase and by issue to the militia of the Colonial governments in America. The end of the war found us with a melange of arms: British muskets, remnants of almost one hundred thousand stands of French muskets acquired by purchase or by gift, and odds and ends of arms in various calibers acquired from any other source available. A small number had been made locally on orders of the various Colonial Committees of Safety. These followed the British pattern.

Inventory of public arms taken in 1793 revealed only about 31,000 sound muskets of many makes, with about half as many more in damaged condition, stored in various depots and arsenals in the United States.

In 1795, in the interest of providing adequate supplies and reserves of standard arms, the newly erected Springfield Armory began the manufacture of shoulder arms patterned on the banded French musket Model of 1763, an arm found superior to the "Brown Bess." From a modest beginning of the first year's production of 245 muskets, practically hand filed, the operations of the Armory were expanded rapidly. This production was supplemented by the output of the newly erected Harpers Ferry Armory from 1801, and with arms supplied on private contracts under the Act of 1798. Thus we were provided with stocks of standard arms for the equipment of the regular force and the militia of the several States.

Of the contracts of 1798 for 40,200 muskets placed with twenty-seven contractors, only those with twenty-four contractors were validated for a total of 36,200 stands of arms. These 1798 muskets, whether made for the Federal Government or for the States on similar States contracts, present a number of problems in maker identification, although they all followed the French 1763 pattern. This pattern, since such arms were made at Springfield Armory from 1795, we call the Model 1795. With few exceptions, such as Gilbert, Brown, and Welton on Federal contracts and Stillman, Lether, McCormick, Henry, Evans, Pratt, Miles, and Virginia Manufactory on States contracts, the majority of the contractors did not mark the arms with their names. A few marked the lock plates with their plant location; Whitney used "NEW HAVEN," Rufus Perkins used the die "BRIDGEWATER," and the Elliots "KENT."

In 1808 Congress passed an act for the arming and equipping of the whole body of militia by the Federal Government. To supplement the output of the two government armories, contracts were let for 85,200 muskets with nineteen contractors as well as with prominent arms makers such as Deringer, North, Pomeroy, Starr, Waters, and Whitney, whose armories were accorded federal recognition. The arms made under these contracts are known throughout the collecting fraternity as Model 1808, largely in that the pan was forged integral with the lock plate and was rounded at the bottom, and the hammer and frizzen ends were plain instead of ending in curlicues. There were other minor differences made to facilitate production, for by this time hand labor began to be supplanted by waterpower driven machinery. The muskets on these contracts in the main are easily identifiable, though a few puzzles in the matter of identity and classification as to model remain unsolved due to unmarked lock plates and use of old parts in transitional arms. There was but little waste in those days; serviceable older-pattern parts were used until exhausted.

The smoothbore musket with its comparative ease of loading and speed in firing, remained the standard military arm, even though rifle-armed forces of Andrew Jackson, composed largely of volunteers and frontiersmen, won a thumping victory from prepared positions over attacking British veterans at New Orleans in 1815.

In 1812 additional minor changes were made, chiefly noted in the introduction of a rounded surface hammer and elimination of the pointed tit at the end of the flat lock plate. These muskets were made at Springfield Armory and by five contractors among whom Whitney received a large contract for 15,000 muskets.

A new musket model incorporating improvements of a French Model 1777 was introduced from 1816. These arms had a sloping brass pan, rounded rear lock plate surface, browned barrel and a combless stock as principal characteristics in addition to other minor improvements beyond the scope of this chapter. These 1816 Models were made by the two national armories as well as by a number of contractors such as Evans, Waters, Wickham, Whitney, Pomeroy, Starr, and others. From 1831 browning of barrels was discontinued in favor of the old bright finish.

In 1835 a new model was introduced, recognizable primarily by a horizontal brass pan with a fence at rear and by a round instead of heart-shaped hammer hole. These arms were also made on contract principally by Nippes and by Pomeroy. Model 1835 was the last of the flintlock musket models, though flintlock muskets remained in use through the Mexican War of 1846 mainly because flints as well as powder and lead could be obtained from enemy sources; supplies of percussion caps were uncertain in this campaign. Model 1835 muskets are rare; but few survived due to later conversion to the percussion system of these otherwise serviceable and well-made arms.

Model 1842 introduced arms made on the *percussion* ignition system. These were also the last of the smoothbore muskets. The French invention and our adoption of an expanding base bullet made loading of rifled arms as rapid and facile as the old smoothbore. In 1855 a rifled arm of .58 caliber was adopted as standard for the services, which, less a tape primer and with other minor modifications, served as the infantry rifle-musket through the period of the War Between the States and finally emerged in altered form as a breechloader in 1865.

In all, over 800,000 flintlock muskets were produced by the two national armories between 1795 and 1844. The total reaches a million or so when the contractor arms are considered. Although thousands upon thousands were destroyed, converted, or exported for sale as obsolete, enough remain to make them a very worth-while object of collector interest. Collection of our historical long arms should pay big dividends from a number of angles: Historical association, variety, acquirement at relatively reasonable cost, possibility of procurement of the complete model series, and facility of repair and restoration—often with original parts. Also much has been written on

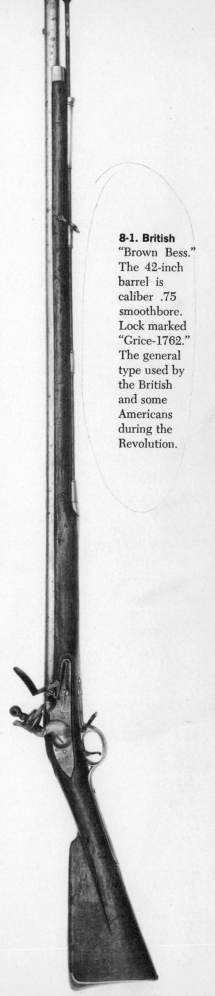

8-1. British "Brown Bess." The 42-inch barrel is caliber .75 smoothbore. Lock marked "Grice-1762." The general type used by the British and some Americans during the Revolution.

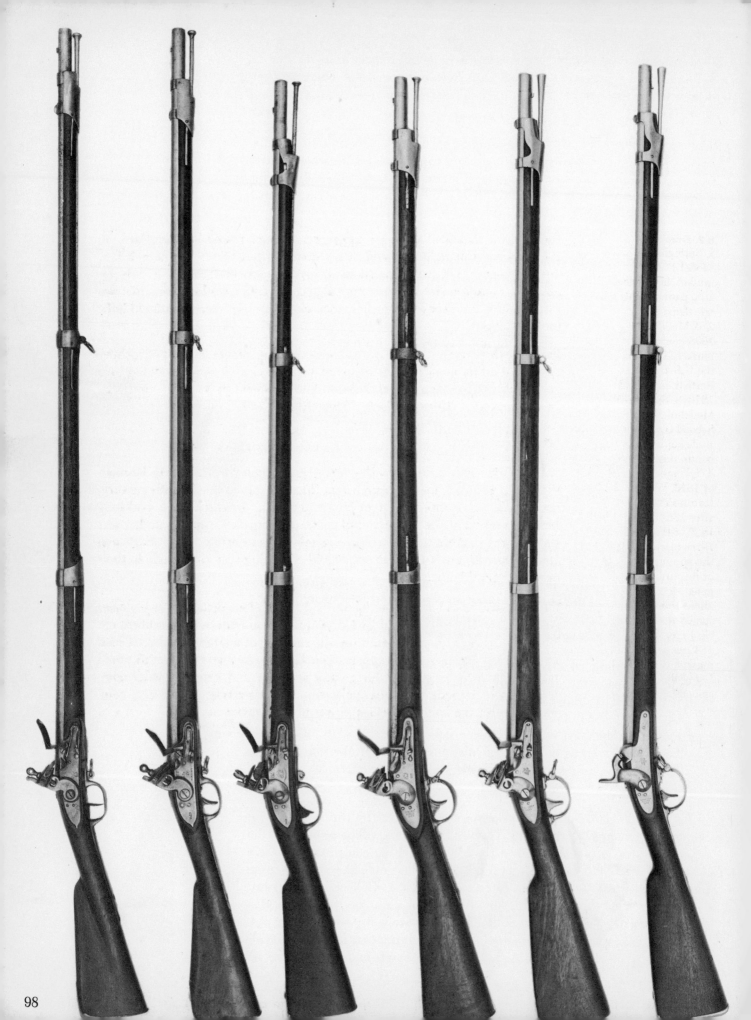

the subject. Excellent material, the result of much research, is available in the works of Fuller, Hicks, and in my own "United States Muskets, Rifles, and Carbines." Yet many questions are still unanswered and it is only by arousing more interest in our historical and romantic shoulder arms that we can hope for the necessary further research which will shed additional light on the subject.

Perhaps when you next come across one of these old pieces, instead of rushing to trade it off for a machine-made pistol, you will clean it up with loving care and be able to hear the echoes of Baron Von Steuben's passed-on commands, *"Poise Firelock," "Cock Firelock," "Take Aim," "FIRE!"*

*T*he rifle was brought to the American Colonies by the early German settlers in Pennsylvania (Pennsylvania "Deutch") in the early 18th century, about 1728. This arm, the direct progenitor of the Kentucky rifle, had long been a weapon of the chase and of marksmanship in Germany, and it was but natural that these settlers, among whom were artisans and craftsmen connected with arms manufacture, would continue to ply their trade in their newly adopted homeland.

Of necessity, to suit the dense forests and tremendous distances of Colonial America, the large caliber sturdy German rifle soon underwent modification. The caliber was reduced, permitting the carrying of a larger number of lead balls by the hunters and trappers. The barrel was made lighter to avoid fatigue and was lengthened for greater accuracy and longer powder combustion, which made for higher velocities and flatter trajectories, thus compensating for the loss of shocking power of the heavier bullet.

Many fanciful and glamorous tales have been woven on the role of the rifle in the French-Indian and Revolutionary Wars. These should be taken with a grain of salt, though undoubtedly many rifles were in use on both sides. They were much more accurate and had better range than muskets but they were three times slower to load—even slower when fouled by considerable firing. Another drawback was the fact that as property of the individuals carrying them (woodsmen, hunters, trappers) they had no provision for attaching a bayonet to their hexagonal or octagonal barrels. This necessitated the use of hunting knives and tomahawks for close-in fighting.

Historically, the Rifle Corps of the War of Revolution was formed in 1776 under Hugh Stephenson and built around nine companies of riflemen from Pennsylvania known as William Thompson's Rifle Battalion. Six of these were among the original rifle units of the Continental Army and the others were organized later. Included in the Rifle Corps were also two companies from Virginia, two from Maryland, as well as some other units. The most famous of these was one commanded by Daniel Morgan in the latter half of 1777.

After the War, in 1792, the military establishment was reorganized into a Legion, a field army in which infantry, cavalry, and artillery were associated for a specific mission. The Legion continued with the rifle unit tradition: One battalion of each of the four sub-legions (regiments) was a rifle battalion. After 1794 the four sub-legions became the First, Second, Third, and Fourth U.S. Infantry Regiments.

To furnish standard military arms to these postwar rifle units Harpers Ferry Armory began in 1804 to manufacture a standard rifle approved in 1803. This Model 1803 half-stock flintlock rifle resembled the contemporary Kentucky rifle in general outline; it had brass furniture, a patch box, a somewhat ornate trigger guard, and differed mainly in a shorter (31 to 36-inch) part-octagonal barrel more convenient for military use.

Though Harpers Ferry Armory continued the manufacture of these 1803 rifles in small numbers into 1820, in 1814 when contracts were awarded to manufacture rifles to Johnson and to Deringer, the rifle, still retaining the part-octagonal barrel, was improved by a full stock. Not many were made before the design was further modified in 1817 to contain features facilitating manufacture and handling.

The Model 1817 flintlock rifles, as they finally emerged, proved to be handsome, sturdy, banded, round-barreled, full-stocked arms which were in general service until replaced by the percussion ignition system in 1841. They were made on contract by Deringer, Johnson, North, and Starr and are easily recognized by the steel trigger guard extension which forms a handgrip with a sling swivel at end, except those of the late Deringer contract of 1840 on which the extension was omitted.

In 1812 John H. Hall of Yarmouth, Maine, adapted a breech-loading mechanism of his invention to flintlock rifles and received from Ordnance an order for one hundred Hall rifles for experimental trials in 1817. As a result of favorable reports, Hall was sent to the Harpers Ferry Armory where he perfected the arm and was given a contract in 1819. Here he was provided facilities to build machinery to manufacture the rifles and provide for uniformity and parts interchangeability. These Hall flintlock breech-loading Model 1819 rifles were also made on contract by Simeon North to augment Harpers Ferry production. In the main, these accurate, fast, and easy-loading arms were too advanced for the day. They were not popular with troops, largely because of the gas leakage at the breech, disconcerting to the firer.

Model 1819 was the last of the flintlock rifle models. It was followed by the well-known and excellent percussion rifle Model 1841, easily recognized by its browned barrel and brass furniture. These 1841s were made at Harpers Ferry and on contract by Remington, Robbins, Kendall & Lawrence, Robbins & Lawrence, Tryon, and by Whitney. They were used to arm Dragoons, Mounted Rifles, light infantry companies of militia, and volunteers; they were issued to the Mississippi Rifles, a state organization commanded by Jefferson Davis. In general, riflemen were used in battle in small detachments as light infantry and trained in sharpshooting. They did not use the paper cartridge then in universal use, but were taught to have patches sewn around balls in advance for rapid loading and to keep extra balls ready in their mouths in a fight, the moisture from saliva making for easier ramming.

In 1855, as a result of the invention of the expanding base Minié bullet, the Ordnance Department adopted a caliber .58 standard for all arms, eliminating .54 for rifles and .69 for muskets. The Model 1855 rifle-musket was designed as well as a complementary shorter-barreled 1855 rifle, both in .58 caliber. These had a Maynard-invented tape primer set into the lock, operating as a self-primer.

With the advent of the Civil War the Model 1855 arms were modified into the Model 1861 rifle-musket, primarily by the omission of the not too reliable and difficult to manufacture Maynard primer. These Model 1861 rifles were made by Springfield Armory and by a number of contractors; they were the standard infantry weapon through the war. Some with slight modifications were known as the Special Model 1861, made by Colt, Amoskeag and Lamson, and Goodnow & Yale, incorporating minor changes based on the Enfield model. In 1863, these changes were officially incorporated in the Model 1863, in which band springs were omitted, the ramrod was made without swell, and the lock case-hardened in mottled colors.

The Model 1855 rifle production was discontinued during the war. The shorter rifle was replaced in the army by the Remington Model 1862, known as the "Zouave," a handsome brass-trim, blued-barrel arm, and in the navy by the Whitney Navy Rifle Model 1861 designed by Admiral Dahlgren and known as the "Plymouth" for Dahlgren's flagship. This anachronism for some reason was produced in the old caliber .69 and took a saber bayonet or a heavy, bowie knife-type so-called Dahlgren bayonet.

8-3. From left: 1/Model 1803 Harpers Ferry rifle, caliber .54, dated 1803. 2/Model 1814 United States rifle, caliber .54, made by H. Deringer, Philadelphia. 3/Model of 1817, sometimes called the "common rifle," made for U.S. by N. Starr.

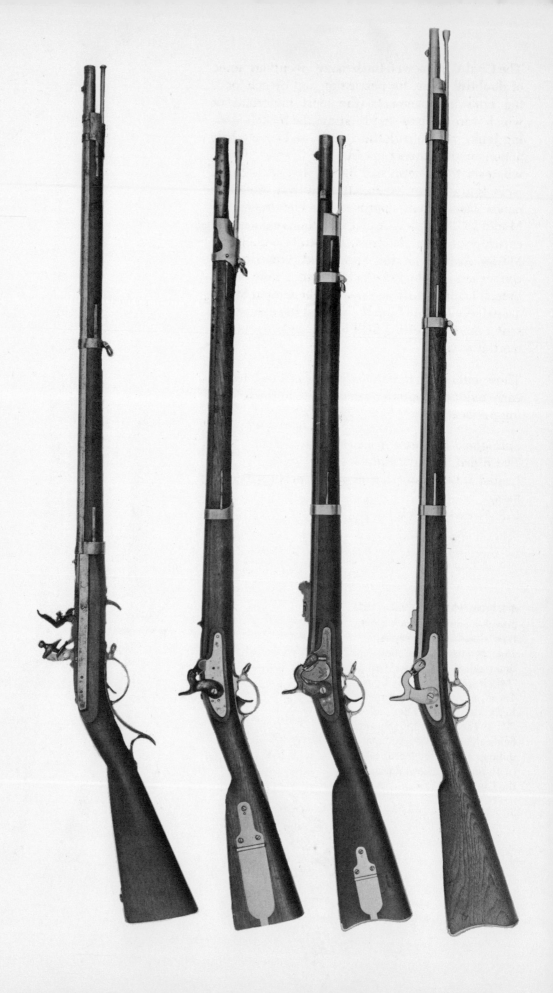

The Civil War spewed forth many inventions, some of doubtful value, for percussion and breech-loading arms improvements, the most important of which were the two-shot Lindsay; the breech-loading Jenks; the Merrill; the Sharps; and even a bolt action, underhammer, percussion Greene. These, whatever their merit, had but limited service and went into oblivion when, after the war, the Ordnance Department approved for conversion the Model 1861-63 rifles, available in thousands, to the cartridge system designed by Erskine S. Allin, Master Armorer of the Springfield Armory. This conversion, the Model 1865, started a new era of breech-loading cartridge arms of the United States armed services, but both the old and the new represent a most interesting field for the collector of our martial arms.

Those interested in *detailed* data pertinent to our early military long arms are referred to the following publications:

Springfield Shoulder Arms (Fuller)
The Rifled Musket (Fuller)
United States Muskets, Rifles, and Carbines (Gluckman)
U.S. Firearms (Hicks)

8-4. From left: 1/Hall Model 1819 breech-loading flintlock early type, dated 1824. 2/Model 1841 percussion rifle, sometimes called the "Yager" or "Mississippi" rifle, made by Tryon, caliber .54. 3/Harpers Ferry Model 1855 rifle, caliber .58. 4/The Model 1861 Springfield caliber .58 rifle, principal military rifle of the North (with minor changes) during the Civil War.

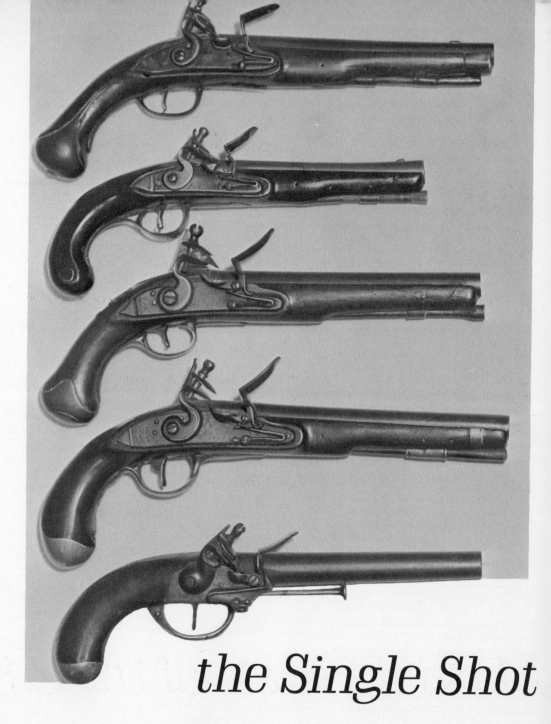

9.

the Single Shot

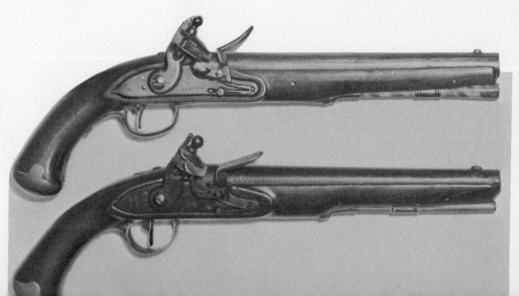

Sooner or later in any discussion of United States Single Shot Martial Pistols, whether it be between two old-time collectors of these top prizes of American handguns or a veteran hobbyist giving the benefit of his experience to a newcomer to the field, there comes a time when the question is raised, "Which are true martial pistols, which are the so-called 'secondaries' and which are merely pistols of the period?"

Technically speaking, of course, the true U.S. Single Shot Martial Pistol is one that was made by or contracted for the United States military services. In this brief outline, however, the author has taken upon himself the liberty of including a few single shot pistols which do not fall strictly within these limits, but which still have been generally considered U.S. Martial Pistols by collectors for many decades. The purist martial collector may be disturbed by this, but it has been done in the interest of a broader treatise of the subject.

For many years arms authors began the subject with the exceedingly rare North & Cheney flintlock pistol of 1799 because of the known contract and the physical evidence of a handful of surviving pistols. However, this overlooks the fact that pistols were used by American forces in the Revolutionary War and carried by the few military units in the decade and a half following the war prior to 1799. It is recognized that the majority of handguns used by American fighting men on land and sea in the Revolution were of English or French origin, and as such will not be dealt with here.[1]

Pistols were made in this country for military usage before, during and after the Revolutionary War; three representative (and rare) specimens are illustrated. Photo No. 9-1 (top, left) shows an early American-made flintlock pistol that has been variously

[1] Included are the English Heavy and Light Dragoon models, the various Sea Service pistols and the French Model 1763 and 1777 pistols. Incidentally, the author believes these to be the cheapest and most honest Revolutionary War type pistols obtainable on today's high-priced market.

Martial Pistols of the U.S.

9-1. From top: 1/Committee of Safety 1776. 2/Revolutionary Period 1770-80.
3/Rappa Forge 1780.
4/McCormick 1798.
5/North & Cheney 1799.
6/J. Guest 1807.
7/J. Henry 1807.

judged by experienced firearms collectors as being a Colonial (pre-Revolutionary) piece or a Committee of Safety pistol.[2] It made its appearance from an attic in York, Pennsylvania, and its cheap, thin brass mountings and somewhat crude workmanship indicate it might have been made under contract (and thus perhaps a Committee of Safety piece) rather than representative of the best efforts of an early gunsmith to be offered for private sale on its construction and merits alone. The lock is an early type without bridle between base of frizzen and pan. The 9½-inch part octagon and part round iron barrel is smoothbore of .60 caliber. As stated, the brass mountings are of thin brass and rather crude but still appealing to a connoisseur of American pistols. Full stock is of applewood.[3] Cavalry pistols such as this were contracted for by Congress in 1776 with various gunsmiths in Lancaster, York, Philadelphia, etc.[4]

The second pistol (P. 104) is an American flintlock pistol, probably Pennsylvania-made, typical of the Revolutionary War period. It is unmarked, as is often the case, and the 7¼-inch brass barrel is smoothbore of .46 caliber. The early hand-forged lock has the typical slashbar at the rear, squared iron pan and a flat gooseneck hammer. Note the early curl to tip of trigger. No butt cap, but the other brass mountings show a gunmaker's fine engraving. The full stock is of American walnut. This is a type of pistol rarity to watch for; even today they sometimes appear and are often unrecognized.

A third example of an American-made Revolutionary War pistol is the famed Rappahannock Forge product. Only three genuine pistols are known to exist, along with several fakes and a

couple others that may have some original parts. Both the pistol illustrated and one of the other original specimens are marked at the rear of the lock plate "RAPa FORGE" with two vertical slashes beneath. The double-curved brass sideplate is engraved "P L D – No 4 – 1 T" which presumably stands for Light Dragoons, Number 4, First Troop. Both

[2] *See Arms and Armor in Colonial America by Harold L. Peterson, Page 202.*

[3] *American apple wood stock, as determined by tests at U. S. Forest Products Laboratory at Madison, Wisconsin. Perhaps a suggestion is in order here: The author strongly recommends testing wood stocks of unmarked pistols when there is a question whether the pistol was made in America or not. The wood can be determined to be European or American grown and while this information is not the sole determining factor in deciding whether the entire pistol is American-made or not, yet this knowledge helps. For the beginner, we add that an American-made flintlock pistol is usually worth much more than that of a European piece of similar type and period.*

[4] Small Arms and Ammunition in the United States Service *by Berkeley R. Lewis, Pages 41-46.*

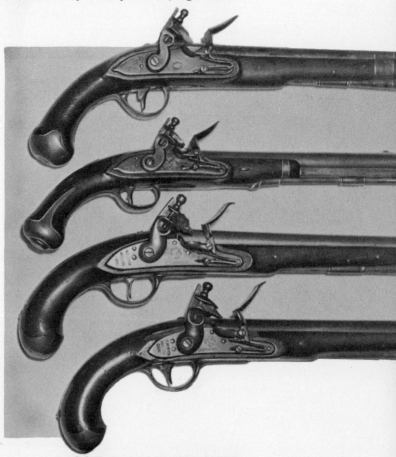

9-2. From top: 1/John Miles 1808. 2/Harpers Ferry 1806. 3/North Berlin 1808. 4/North Berlin 1811.

are marked "3 Rgt" on the heavy brass butt cap. The third known original pistol has the additional "I. HUNTER" stamping on the barrel, but bears no unit markings on sideplate or butt. The Rappahannock Forge began military operations in 1776 when James Hunter purchased the forge which had been in operation since 1732. Mainly muskets, bayonets, spades, kettles, etc., were produced, but in 1780 the General Assembly authorized outfitting Baylor's Third Dragoons, including seventy pairs of pistols for the enlisted men. It seems possible that these two martially marked pistols might be those, and the pistol simply stamped "I. HUNTER RAPa FORGE" was an earlier product. The forge was dismantled and production suddenly ceased in the spring of 1781 with the threat of a raid by Tarleton's cavalry and it is doubtful that any more arms were made there. This is an extreme rarity and about tops in Revolutionary War pistols.

Although the famed North & Cheney pistol has been claimed to be the first pistol officially contracted for by the U.S. Government, records dug out of National Archives in Washington, D.C., by ardent researchers[5] in the past ten years show that pistols like the McCormick pistol shown were assembled and fitted from government parts from 1797 through 1801. Thomas Annely, John Miles, John Nicholson, Jr., Joseph Morgan, and Robert McCormick are on record as having done this work. As a result of several articles in the TEXAS GUN COLLECTOR magazine by Harry Knode in 1954-55, seven of these pistols are known and have been described and illustrated. One is stamped "McCormick" on the stock opposite the lock and thus is presumed to have been assembled by Robert McCormick as one of the one hundred ship's pistols delivered by him to the Schuylkill Arsenal at Philadelphia on December 11, 1799. Others, such as the pistol illustrated, may have been assembled by McCormick or any of the other men mentioned above. Pistols with the fishtail butt similar to those of the later 1807-08 contracts were termed "horseman's pistols" and the "ship pistols" had the bulbous butt type shown here. Records indicate somewhat less than 1,000 pistols of both types were assembled by all the contractors. They must have seen very hard and long service as the survival rate is extremely low—about the same as the North & Cheney. The pistol illustrated is engraved "Ketland & Co" in two lines on the lock plate under the pan and stamped "United States" in a slight curve at the rear. The 9¾-inch round iron barrel is .64 caliber smoothbore and bears the eagle head over P sunken proof and is also stamped US. The full stock is stamped US V and has a brass band near the muzzle.

9-3. From top: 1/North 1813. 2/Edward Evans 1814.
3/Springfield 1807. (1818)

[5] Too much credit cannot be given to researchers like Lt. Col. R. C. Kuhn, Archer L. Jackson, Harold L. Peterson, Col. Berkeley R. Lewis, and Maj. James E. Hicks who have literally spent weeks and months in pouring over official records in National Archives, Washington, D. C.

Simeon North of Berlin, Connecticut, signed two pistol contracts, one dated March 9, 1799 for 500 pistols and the other February 6, 1800 for an additional 1,500. Delivery was completed September 11, 1802. With but seventeen known genuine specimens today (some with reconversion and restoration but for the most part original) the question is still puzzling collectors as to what happened to 99 percent of the North & Cheneys. Two reasons have been advanced that offer possibilities: Many of these pistols may have been in sea service and gone to the bottom on one or more ships of the U.S. Navy, or (and this is the author's pet theory), some day a collector doing research in National Archives may run across a document that ordered "all the old style brass frame pistols be scrapped for salvage." Be this as it may, the North & Cheney product is today considered the most desirable of all U.S. single shot pistols. Elisha Cheney was Simeon North's brother-in-law and a clockmaker by trade. He may have helped in the manufacture of small parts such as pins and screws. However, he did not sign the contracts with North and we wonder why Cheney's name appears on the pistols. Perhaps he may have acted as a bondsman to aid North in gaining the contract.

Through serial number study, the author has determined that the pistols of the first contract of 500 were marked "S. North & E. Cheney Berlin" and the pistols of the second contract of 1,500 were marked simply "North & Cheney Berlin." Both markings appear in a curve on the under side of the brass frame. The pistols were patterned after the efficient Model 1777 French pistol, some of which Lafayette had brought with him to this country during the Revolution. However no North & Cheney ever had a belt hook, which 95 percent of the French pistols had, and this is one deterrent to a faker who might attempt to change an $80 French pistol into a several thousand dollar American copy. A few 1777 French pistols were made without the belt hook, so this is not infallible detection. The North & Cheney pistols have an additional screw, a trifle larger than the forward trigger

guard screw, holding the barrel to the frame. No French pistols have been noted with the extra screw. North & Cheney barrels were 8½ inches long—an inch longer than the French barrels. However, if a cut-off Colt-Walker barrel can be skillfully restored to its original 9 inches, so can a French barrel be increased to 8½ inches. We mention these things as a warning, as it seems surprising that, with the tremendous monetary increase to be gained, we haven't seen more than five faked North & Cheneys thus far. There are more things to watch for, such as the three hidden serial numbers on the North & Cheney and the size and type of numerals. It would be well for any prospective purchaser to compare the offered piece with a genuine specimen before final purchase. Checking the wood stock could be the clincher in forming an opinion. In addition to the marking mentioned, the specimen illustrated has its barrel stamped "U-S P V" and it is serial 189 of the first contract.

Aware of a need for pistols in addition to those being turned out by the National Armory at Harpers Ferry, Virginia, Secretary of War Henry Dearborn instructed Tench Coxe, Purveyor of Public Supplies, to contract for 2,000 pairs from various Pennsylvania gunmakers in 1807. Two of these 1807 contract pistols are shown; one by John Guest of Lancaster, Pennsylvania, and one by Joseph Henry of Philadelphia. On January 2, 1808, John Guest, in association with Peter Brong and Abraham Henry, obtained a government contract for 400 pairs of pistols at $10.00 per pair. This Guest pistol is stamped "Drepert" on the lock plate under the pan and "US" behind the hammer; Henry Drepert, also of Lancaster, supplied the locks. The 10⅛-inch barrel is caliber .54 smoothbore and has the oval eagle head and P proof and is marked "I. Guest" in script. The Henry pistol is stamped "J. Henry Phila. US" on the lock plate and the barrel is also marked "J. Henry Phila." with the usual eagle head and P proof. The 10⅛-inch barrel is .54 caliber smoothbore. Another pistol of this period is shown. It was made by John Miles and is stamped in an oval on the lock plate "Miles Phila." The 10-inch caliber .62 barrel is marked "Miles Phila." and a large P. The full stock has a brass muzzle band. This was a militia pistol and one has been noted stamped "4 Va Regt" on the barrel. Other known contractors were Calderwood, Frye, Schuler, Ansted, and Deringer.

Prior to these 1807-08 contract pistols, the first handguns to be made at a national armory were the Model 1805 Harpers Ferry pistols. They were ordered on November 13, 1805, approved on February 26, 1806 and produced during the years 1806-08. Two thousand and forty-eight pairs were made and the barrels were serial numbered in pairs. They are the most graceful of our martial pistols, with eye-pleasing brass mountings which include a long butt cap spur up each side of the grip. The lock plates are stamped with the eagle, "US Harpers Ferry" and the date which was either 1806, 1807 or 1808. The 10-inch .54 caliber smoothbore barrels are stamped at the breech with the eagle-head proof, US and the serial number, which is number 50 on the 1806 dated specimen shown. Pistols dated 1806 normally carry serial numbers up to about 105 and are the rarest of the three lock dates. However, there is some overlapping and locks stamped 1806 are now found with barrels as high as 175 and 212. The 1807 dated pistols have barrel serials running as high as the mid-1800s, although the lowest serial found on an 1808 dated lock is 1592. This overlapping could be the result of honest repairs and adjustments at the armory, parts assembled by troops in the field, or a later collector's work in making a better pistol for his collection by swapping locks or barrels.

In 1808 Simeon North secured his second pistol contract and entered into a period of what was to be over twenty years of active pistol manufacturing for the government. During that time he produced 48,000 pistols, before leaving that field to concentrate on long arms and until his death in 1852. The North navy contract was of June 30, 1808, for 1,000 pairs and an additional 500 pairs were contracted for on December 4, 1810. One of these 3,000 Model 1808 pistols is

shown. The 10⅛-inch round barrel is unmarked and smoothbore, with the caliber seeming to vary from .64 to .67. Lock plates are stamped with an eagle over "U. States" between hammer and frizzen and "S. North Berlin Con." in three lines at the rear. They were provided with belt hooks and considered a good serviceable seaman's pistol.

With the success of the navy pistol, a shorter model was contracted for the army on November 18, 1811. It has an 8½-inch barrel with measured calibers ranging from .69 to .73 smoothbore and, unlike the 1808 pistols, these 1811 models have proofmarks on the barrels and inspector's stamps on the stocks. Usual barrel markings are "P" (proved) over "US." The lock plates are stamped the same as the 1808 pistols. One thousand pairs were contracted for, but before completion of the contract M. T. Wickham at the Philadelphia Ordnance Depot brought out an improved double band to hold the barrel to the stock. No records have thus far been located stating how many pistols were so changed, but it must have been few as most Model 1811 pistols seen today are those with the pinned full stock, as shown in the accompanying illustration.

On April 16, 1813 Simeon North obtained a contract for 20,000 pistols, huge by standards of those days; and that summer he opened a new armory at Middletown, Connecticut, six miles east of Berlin on the Connecticut River. The Model 1813 pistol, as shown in illustration 9-3, was the product. Even in the early days of martial pistol collecting it was felt from the few specimens encountered that 20,000 were never made.[6] Approximately 1,500 pistols was a previous production estimate and this was later reduced to an exact 1,156. Recent gleanings from records in National Archives indicate that but 626 of the .69 caliber model 1813 pistols were made for the army by February of 1817. After that date North's deliveries were all of the .54 caliber (called "rifle caliber") 1816 model. However, North had many .69 caliber pistols on hand in various stages of completion. Records

---

[6] United States Single Shot Martial Pistols *by Charles W. Sawyer; and* Simeon North, First Official Pistol Maker *by S. N. D. and Ralph H. North; both published in 1913.*

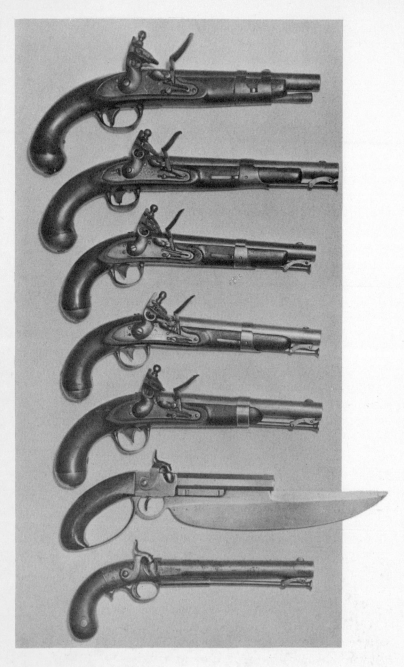

9-4. From top: 1/North 1816.
2/North 1819. 3/North
1826. 4/Evans 1831.
5/R. Johnson 1836. 6/Elgin
Cutlass 1837. 7/All Metal
Waters 1849.

indicate he entered into a contract with the Navy Department for 1,000 of these .69 caliber pistols with the addition of belt hooks. Delivery was made at New York on November 16, 1816. Plugged holes in the stocks of numerous pistols seen in collections today show these belt hooks were later removed.

As a result of many production delays at Middletown, North had renegotiated his 1813 contract for 20,000 of the 1816 model .54 caliber pistols with delivery to run until 1819. A specimen of the Model 1816 is shown in Photo 9-4 (top). Early lock markings of the 1813 pistols were an eagle with shield between the letters "U" and "S" and "S. North" in a curve above and "Midln, Con." below. A very few have been found simply stamped "US S. North." The significance of this change in marking is unknown. Barrels were stamped "P" over "US." Lock markings on the early 1816 .54 caliber pistols were the same as the 1813 model, but later a change in the abbreviation to "Midltn, Conn." occurred.

During these years the various states fulfilled their needs for arms by either a state armory or contracts with private manufacturers. An example of a private contract is the pistol (Photo No. 9-3) made by Edward Evans of Evansburg, Pennsylvania, in 1814. As North & Cheney copied the French model 1777, Evans followed the pattern of the French army pistol of 1805. The 8⅝-inch barrel is of .69 caliber, is dated underneath 1814, and shows inspector's stamps. The lock is simply stamped "Evans." No information has been uncovered as to how many were made or the unit they were made for, but these pistols are extremely rare today and but eight are known.

In 1807 production was authorized and work began in February of 1808 on the monstrous pistols known for many years to collectors as the 1818 Springfield. With parts for about 400 pistols made up at Springfield Armory, Massachusetts, someone exercised good judgment and put a stop to it and the various parts remained in storage there until 1817 when the U.S. Ordnance Department instructed the Superintendent of Springfield Armory to resume production and complete 1,000 pistols. Those locks made up back in 1807 had the old style gooseneck hammers. The newly-made locks had reinforced hammers. Being of .69 caliber with a 10⅜-inch barrel and an unwieldly 17¾ inches overall, the finished pistols went into storage and were still listed as unissued in 1850. While a very few specimens are dated 1815 on the lock plate, most all are stamped with the eagle and "US Springfield 1818" on lock plate and "P" (eagle-head) V 1818" on the barrel. As quite a number of these pistols are found altered to percussion, it is possible they were later issued for some home guard use during the Civil War or were bought up as "war surplus" and converted.

With the completion of his 1816 contract in 1819, Simeon North eagerly sought more work for his Middletown armory. A new contract for 20,000 pistols was made on July 21, 1819. An example of the model 1819 is shown in illustration 9-4. Except for the date at the rear of the lock plate, either 1821 or 1822, the marking is the same as that on the 1816 model. A few undated pistols have been found. Barrel length was increased to 10⅛ inches and the .54 caliber retained. The swivel ramrod was a practical improvement and was continued on later U.S. models, but the sliding safety at rear of the lock appeared only on this model. This was an extremely serviceable pistol. Many were later altered to percussion and used until the Civil War.

Following this, a slightly shorter model was made by North under three contracts of 1,000 each, dated November 16, 1826, December 12, 1827, and August 18, 1828. The lock plates are stamped "US S. North" and the date either 1827 or 1828. Barrels are marked "US AH" for Asabel Hubbard, the government inspector. Many of these pistols were also altered to percussion and have since been put back into flintlock to please collectors. In addition to those made by North, W. L. Evans of Valley Forge, Pennsylvania, made 1,000 similar pistols. From the markings, apparently those stamped "US W. L. Evans

9-5. From top: 1/ Aston 1842. 2/Ames 1842. 3/ Deringer 1843. 4/Springfield 1855.

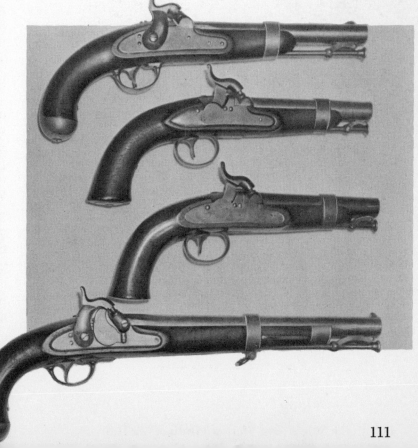

The first percussion single shot pistol was contracted for by the U.S. Navy and was a cutlass pistol which made its appearance in 1837. One of these extremely rare cutlass pistols is shown in photo 9-4. Only 150 were made by C. B. Allen and N. P. Ames, both of Springfield, Massachusetts, for a South Seas Exploring Expedition and about twenty are known to have survived today.[7] These rarities are stamped "Elgin's Patent PM CBA 1837" on top of the five-inch octagon barrel and "C. B. Allen Springfield, Mass." The serial number of the gun appears on the left side of the frame. Of .54 caliber, these pistols feel good in the hand and naval records tell of their being used by landing parties against the natives in the South Pacific. Smaller sized bowie knife pistols were also made about that time by Morrill, Mossman & Blair; and by Morrill & Blair of Amherst, Massachusetts. These were non-martial and are quite rare.

Still a question mark in collector's knowledge today is the so-called "all metal Waters" percussion pistol. About a dozen are known to exist today and although their markings indicate their origin, nothing of their contract or use is known. The pistol shown is stamped on the left side of the barrel "A. H. Waters Milbury, Mass. 1849" and also has the eagle head US P mark. The 8-inch barrel is of .56 caliber smoothbore with swivel ramrod underneath. Another model Waters pistol of this period, dated from 1844 to 1849, is known and termed the "original percussion" or "flat lock plate" Waters. It is stocked like the model 1836 and quite scarce. While these latter half-stock Waters pistols probably were militia or state guard arms, the marking on the "all metal" Waters pistol seems to indicate a U.S. martial piece.

The model 1842 percussion pistol is the most commonly found of all single shot martials, 30,-000 having been made by Henry Aston and 10,-000 by Ira N. Johnson, both of Middletown, Connecticut. The Aston pistols were made between 1846 and 1852 and the Johnson pistols are found dated from 1853 through 1855. Having an 8½-inch .54 caliber smoothbore barrel and

1830" were for the army and those marked "W. L. Evans V. Forge USN 1831" were for naval use. All had belt hooks, however. There are also pistols of this model marked simply "J. J. Henry Boulton" with no US or USN or inspector's initials. These were probably made for militia service and are the rarest of this model 1826.

With North concentrating on carbine and rifle manufacturing, two new contractors were successful in bidding on the contract of 1836. From 1836 through 1844, Robert Johnson of Middletown, Connecticut, produced 18,000 of the model 1836 pistols and Asa Waters of Milbury, Massachusetts, turned out 19,000 more. These were the last of the U.S. flint pistols. While well made and serviceable, the horse pistol was at a disadvantage compared to the five- and six-shot cap-and-ball revolvers that Sam Colt had made since 1836.

being well made and sturdily constructed, they were the best single shot military pistols of their day. Only the revolver was to improve on them.

Although termed for many years the model 1843 pistol, the box lock model produced by N. P. Ames of Springfield, Massachusetts, was contracted for much earlier. Work on this pistol was begun in November, 1841, by Ames and correspondence in National Archives tells us that 300 pistols had been completed by August 5, 1842. One of those first types with the 1842 date and the early (pointed-rear) lock plate is shown. Following this first batch, there were a few changes made including a rounded-rear lock plate, and over 3,000 more of this model were produced. A few pistols are known stamped "USR" instead of "USN" on the locks, indicating United States Revenue (Coast Guard). All are .54 caliber smoothbore with six-inch barrels and swivel rammer.

Henry Deringer of Philadelphia had a contract for 1,200 of the box lock pistols, but records in Archives indicate he experienced great difficulty in manufacture and as late as 1847 only 282 barrels had been submitted and accepted. Some of the Deringer pistols are stamped with his name and city and "US" and a very few are known marked "Deringer Philadel'a USN 1847." Because of the rarity and higher price for the Deringer pistols, a number of Ames pistols had their markings filed off a few years ago and were re-stamped with Deringer markings. Examples noted thus far are easily spotted and are quite obvious when compared with the genuine. Similar but better work was done in removing the markings on model 1842 Aston pistols and marking them as having been made by the Palmetto Armory in Columbia, South Carolina, in 1852. To avoid purchasing such fakes, it would be best to consult experienced collectors and pay for such opinions. A few Deringer box lock pistols have rifled .54 caliber barrels for reasons unknown. The variance in Deringer lock markings and in rifled or smoothbore barrels is believed caused by a termination of his contract because of his delay. Subse-

quently Deringer probably put together and sold privately those pistols he had on hand in varying stages of completion and marking. The construction of the enclosed hammer in the lock was for ease in carrying and drawing from a belt or sash.

Last of the percussion single shot martials is the Model 1855 pistol-carbine, of which 4,021 were made at Springfield Armory and a very, very few at Harpers Ferry. It was designed for use by mounted troops and when the detachable wood stock was hooked to the pistol, it shot well. However, the pistol was 18 inches overall with a 12-inch .58 caliber rifled barrel and was certainly awkward as a handgun. Its tape primer mechanism was considered an innovation at that time and used on many rifled muskets. The pistol only is shown here (see 9-5), with the brass-mounted wood stock omitted for lack of space.

Last to be included in this outline of United States Single Shot Martial Pistols are three Remington .50 caliber cartridge models. That single shot pistols were contracted for as late as 1871, with cap-and-ball revolvers showing effective use all during the Civil War, indicates a great reluctance for change on the part of the Ordnance Department. The Model 1865 Remington pistol is rare today because, of the 7,500 made through 1867, at least 6,500 were returned to the Remington factory to have barrels shortened and trigger guards added. The result was the change shown as Model 1870, with the 8½-inch barrel cut to 7 inches, a trigger guard, and a conversion from rimfire to center-fire. In 1871, 5,000 of the improved army model were obtained by the government from Remington in a swap for Remington percussion revolvers left over from the Civil War.

Thus we conclude this brief outline of single shot U.S. martial pistols covering a period of one hundred years, from pre-Revolutionary 1771 to 1871. We regret that we must confine ourselves to the primary models, but the student may find data on secondary models in some of the books listed in the bibliography found on later pages.

[7] When exact figures of low survival rates of certain martial pistol rarities are stated in this chapter, they are the result of some thirty years of gathering serial numbers and other survival data by the author.

10-1. .64 caliber Hall-Harpers Ferry percussion Model 1837 breech-loading U.S. Army carbine, early "spur lever" breech release, 18¼-inch sliding ramrod bayonet, 23-inch smoothbore round barrel, used prepared paper cartridges.

the Early Breech-loading

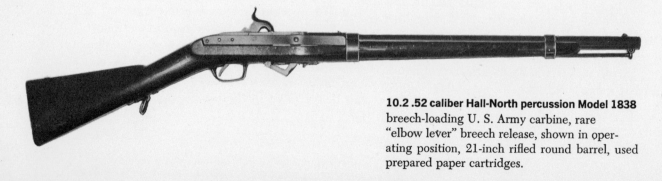

10.2 .52 caliber Hall-North percussion Model 1838 breech-loading U. S. Army carbine, rare "elbow lever" breech release, shown in operating position, 21-inch rifled round barrel, used prepared paper cartridges.

*I*f you may ask a dedicated carbine collector to explain why he collects these large-bore, stubby weapons, so important to the U.S. cavalryman, especially in the days of the Civil War and the Indian fighting, you will certainly draw forth many sound reasons for his enthusiasm. He will tell you of the romantic aspect of the carbine which made the cavalry as dashing and important in their era as mechanized forces are in today's warfare. And he would expound on the fascinating variety of some forty unique breech actions in which each inventor thought surely his was superior to that of his competitors! The crudely carved name of the former cavalryman-owner often found in the stock will bring forth the thought: "If only this old gun could talk!"

The coming of the breech-loading system brought with it first the prepared combustible or paper cartridge and later the improved self-contained metallic cartridge. Thus the efficiency of the cavalry was much improved. No longer was the cavalryman placed at a disadvantage while trying to load a muzzle-loading weapon while mounted—especially when in action—but he could now handily load his carbine in a matter of seconds!

The cavalryman usually carried his carbine at the end of a wide leather sling strap, swung across his right shoulder. A large steel swivel snap at the end secured it to the sling ring of the carbine, allowing it to hang in a balanced position behind the left leg when the cavalryman was in the saddle.

The strap was adjusted so the lowered gun barrel would clear the ground when dismounted. The strap also prevented the cavalryman from losing his carbine while charging over rough terrain. If pressed for time in reloading during the heat of battle, he had but to drop the gun to the end of the strap and draw his saber.

Making its appearance in the early 1840s was the famed Hall percussion carbine, which is given credit for being the first breech-loading carbine in the United States Service as well as the first to employ use of standardized

Carbines of the U.S. 10.

parts. Although never made in flintlock (except possibly experimentally) this interesting carbine is found in a number of different models, differing largely in four types of breechblock opening release levers. The first were the Models 1833 and 1837 fitted with a unique form of ramrod bayonet; they employed a "spur lever" release which protruded from the under side of the stock and directly below the breechblock. This sharp pointed lever proved unsatisfactory. In fact, it was capable of inflicting painful wounds to the hands or shoulders of the cavalryman.

From suggestions of Inspector N. W. Patch, the Model 1838 "elbow lever" design of breechblock release was adopted. In the writer's opinion, this was the most practical of all the systems. The lever pivoted back against the face of the trigger guard when not in use, to form a smooth underside to the forearm.

The Model 1840 followed in form of a "fishtail" lever which lay reasonably flat to the underside. The last system was the Model 1843, using a "side-lever" release; it was used in considerable numbers until the manufacture was discontinued in 1852.

Hall carbines were carried by the U.S. Dragoons in the early California expeditions as well as in the Seminole Indian War; some of the Model 1843s were even used in the Civil War.

In strong competition to the Hall in this pre-Civil War period, was the trim and well-designed "Wm. Jenks" percussion carbine—forerunner of the later Merrill carbine of Civil War fame. It had a very efficiently designed breech action, remarkably free from the usual breech gas leakage of the period.

The Jenks featured an unusual "mule ear" or "sidehammer" striker in which the annoyance and danger of flying cap particles was kept at a minimum. The beautiful brown lacquer finish on the barrels—the formula of which seems to be lost to the ages—was a very durable one as evidenced on remaining specimens found today.

Although originally designed for the U.S. Navy and Coast Guard Service with usual breech markings of "U.S.N." and accompanying dates in the 1840s, a few are known with "U.S.R." markings, designating use by the "United States Revenue Marine Service"—the predecessor of the present-day United States Coast Guard. These are considered exceptionally rare. In 30 years of collecting carbines, the writer has been able to acquire only one.

10-3. .54 caliber rare "Wm. Jenks" percussion breech-loading U. S. Revenue Marine Service carbine (breech marked "U.S.R., 1844"), side "mule-ear" hammer, 24¼-inch rifled round barrel, used prepared paper cartridges.

The Spencer cartridge carbine, with its seven-shot magazine, has the claim to being the most popular carbine of the Civil War and its popularity continued into the Indian Wars. With a total of 94,196 purchased by the Federal Government during the Civil War at a cost of $2,393,633.82, the Spencer is further recognized as being the leader in numbers purchased, in spite of the fact it did not make its appearance until the second year of the war.

The Civil War Model Spencer in .52 caliber and with a 22-inch round barrel, should not be confused with the more common postwar so-called Model 1865 "Indian War" carbine of .50 caliber and in 20-inch barrel length.

The .52 Spencer was extensively used in the Battle of Gettysburg by the famous "Iron Brigade"; also, by famed General George C. Custer's Michigan Cavalry.

Ranking second in numbers used in the Civil War, with 80,512 of the Models 1859 and 1863, the Sharps was also a very popular carbine; various models are eagerly sought by the collector today.

Undoubtedly heading the Sharps' list is the earliest model, known as the "Model 1851 Box Lock," in which the hammer is swung inside the lock plate in contrast to outside hammers of later models. Its design was the first military carbine to incorporate the famed Maynard tape primer patented in 1845, in which paper fulminate caps —much like those of toy cap pistols today—were fed over the nipple by the cocking action of the hammer.

The first production of this model was made for the Government; up to the observed serial number range of #235 all bear "U.S." markings at the breech end of the barrel as well as inspector's marks. Higher numbers (#1064 is the highest observed) do not bear these markings and some appear to have been made without the saddle ring assembly for civilian sale. Other models of the Sharps, both percussion and cartridge, also find great favor with collectors.

Third in numbers used was the Burnside percussion carbine, made in four distinct models; 55,-567 were purchased for use in the Civil War. The rarest is the first model of which it is estimated only a few hundred were made. They are easily recognized, as they were made without the wooden forearm and with General Burnside's own design of curved breech opening lever under the hammer, in contrast to the improved G. P. Foster's patent lever-locking device found on the later models. The first model also features a tape primer magazine. Unlike Dr. Maynard's famous tape primer, which utilized the primer in roll form, the Burnside system used it in straight form.

Since today's collector interest in military carbines seems to center on models used in the Civil War, the new collector will be wise to concentrate first on the basic models of which he can plan to acquire approximately a dozen exceedingly interesting specimens. Fortunately, these are comparatively easy to come by at this time and are frequently found on dealers' lists or at the various gun shows now becoming popular throughout the nation.

10-4. .52 caliber Spencer rimfire early model repeating U. S. Civil War carbine, 7-shot tubular magazine in stock, 22-inch rifled round barrel, chambered for the .56-52 Spencer cartridge. A principal carbine of the Civil War.

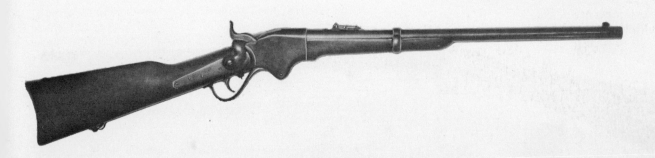

For guidance, a checklist follows, indicating the importance of each make in reference to numbers purchased by the U.S. for Civil War use:

Type of Weapon	Purchases 1861-1866
.52 RF. Spencer, 7-shot magazine carbine	94,196
.52 Percussion Sharps Breechloader, Models 1859 & '63	80,512
.54 Percussion Burnside Breechloader, Fourth Model	55,567
.50 Percussion Smith Breechloader	30,062
.54 Percussion Starr Breechloader	25,603
.50 Percussion Gallagher Breechloader	22,728
.50 Percussion Maynard Breechloader	20,202
.50 Rimfire Remington "Split-breech"	20,000
.54 Percussion Merrill Breechloader	14,495
.52 Rimfire Joslyn Breechloader	11,261
.50 Percussion Cosmopolitan Breechloader	9,342
.50 Rimfire Warner Breechloader	4,001
.52 Percussion Hall Breechloader	3,520
.54 Rimfire Ballard Breechloader (also .44 RF. cal.)	1,509
.52 Percussion Gibbs Breechloader	1,052
.50 Rimfire Ball, 8-shot magazine carbine (received too late for Civil War use)	1,002
.50 Rimfire Palmer Breechloader (received too late for Civil War use)	1,001
.58 Percussion Lindner Breechloader	892
.44 Rimfire Wesson Breechloader	151

Included in the above figures are 5,000 each of the .54 Starr and .50 Gallagher carbines in cartridge form. Also, 5,000 of the Remington "split-breech" in .46 rimfire caliber. Thus, these three variations must be considered "Civil War Contract Carbines." We find a total of 22 carbines contracted for, which gives the collector a goal of sorts. He has a vastly extended field of interest if he projects his collecting to include prewar, postwar, or experimental models.

The progress of the U.S. military carbine may be dramatically shown by placing the massive 7-shot lever-action, black powder Spencer alongside the trim, light 15-shot .30 M1 automatic carbine of World War II fame—a striking contrast which illustrates 100 years of arms-making development in America.

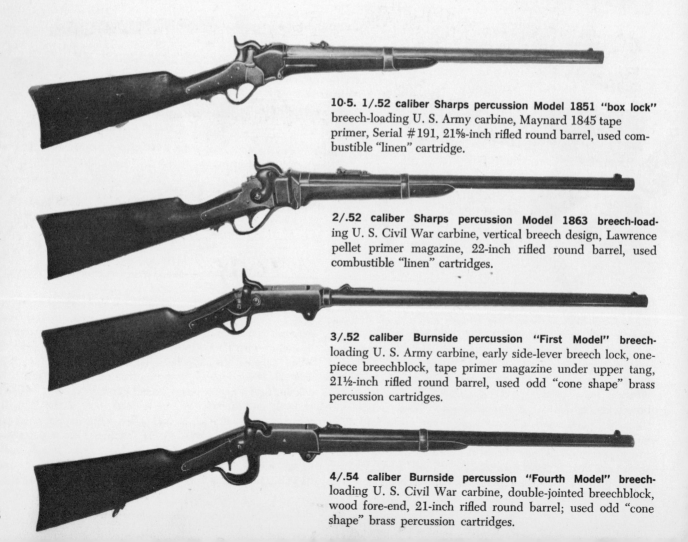

10-5. 1/.52 caliber Sharps percussion Model 1851 "box lock" breech-loading U. S. Army carbine, Maynard 1845 tape primer, Serial #191, 21⅝-inch rifled round barrel, used combustible "linen" cartridge.

2/.52 caliber Sharps percussion Model 1863 breech-loading U. S. Civil War carbine, vertical breech design, Lawrence pellet primer magazine, 22-inch rifled round barrel, used combustible "linen" cartridges.

3/.52 caliber Burnside percussion "First Model" breech-loading U. S. Army carbine, early side-lever breech lock, one-piece breechblock, tape primer magazine under upper tang, 21½-inch rifled round barrel, used odd "cone shape" brass percussion cartridges.

4/.54 caliber Burnside percussion "Fourth Model" breech-loading U. S. Civil War carbine, double-jointed breechblock, wood fore-end, 21-inch rifled round barrel; used odd "cone shape" brass percussion cartridges.

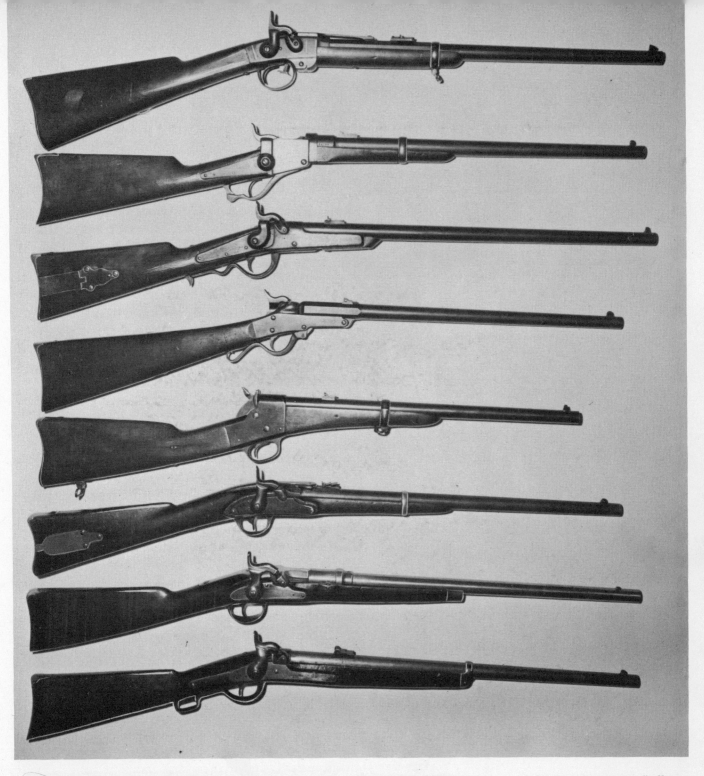

10-6. From top: 1/.50 caliber Smith percussion breech-loading U. S. Civil War carbine, "top break" action, well designed breech sealing, 21½-inch rifled round barrel, used paper wrapped brass percussion cartridges. 2/.54 caliber Starr percussion breech-loading U. S. Civil War carbine, lever action, two-piece breechblock, 21-inch rifled round barrel; used combustible "linen" cartridges. 3/.50 caliber Gallagher percussion breech-loading U. S. Civil War carbine, lever action with barrel sliding forward in frame and tipping up to load, 22¼-inch rifled round barrel; used paper wrapped brass percussion cartridges. 4/.50 caliber Maynard percussion breech-loading U. S. Civil War carbine, lever action, "tip-up" barrel, 20-inch rifled round barrel, used reloadable brass percussion cartridges. 5/.50 caliber Remington rimfire "split-breech" U. S.

Civil War carbine, forerunner of the later Remington "rolling block," 18-inch rifled round barrel, chambered for the .56-50 Spencer rimfire cartridge. 6/.54 caliber Merrill percussion breech-loading U. S. Civil War carbine, developed from the Wm. Jenks carbine, top lever opening breech design, 22⅛-inch rifled round barrel; used prepared paper cartridges. 7/.58 caliber Lindner percussion breech-loading U. S. Civil War carbine, breechblock tips up to load, one of the desirable types of the Civil War; 20-inch rifled round barrel, used prepared paper cartridges. 8/.52 caliber Gibbs percussion breech-loading U. S. Civil War carbine, lever action, barrel slides forward in frame and tips up to load, a Civil War rarity, 22-inch rifled round barrel, used prepared paper cartridges.

the
Federal
Civil
War
Revolvers

The revolvers of the Civil War would naturally include any revolving handgun used in that war—and that would include so many pieces that the subject would hopelessly flounder.

Many soldiers of the Civil War carried commercial pocket revolvers and there were untold revolving hand-arms of sundry commercial sources that although of military size were not what we would consider "issue" arms.

As it was, there were many different issue pieces that must be considered. The U.S. Government bought about any practical arm they could find. They even purchased second-rate pieces for no other reason than to keep them out of the hands of the Confederacy.

In this chapter only handguns that were contracted for, or purchased by the U.S. Government, will be discussed.

It must be kept in mind that although we have records available to us today as to how many of this or that were purchased during the Civil War, these records are not always complete or accurate. There are a number of reasons for this. The best available information comes from a book known as "Executive Document 99." This book purports to include *all* U.S. Government purchases of *all* military arms. In scanning the pages one sees everything from cannon and shot to cartridges and sabers. The government did not get the same item always from the same source. A few came from this man and a thousand of the same thing from another man.

When the plethora of purchases was gathered together for the records there was a problem of terminology. Sometimes the contract or purchase stated so many "Colt's pistols" or "revolving pistols," or "Army revolvers" and just exactly what these arms were is hard to say. Scholars have worked with "Executive Document 99" and have come up with figures that at least give us an idea. In some instances the figures are wrong but they are wrong only in that they do not include *all* of the stated items that were bought and used.

As an example of how word usage can be confusing, consider the purchase from W. & H. Burkhardt of Franklin, Tennessee on July 22, 1862. These two men, or company, or whatever, sold to the U.S. Government "13 Navy pistols with appendages" for a total amount of $325.00. This was an open purchase and the Burkhardts were paid by the government on July 15, 1863. Today we wonder just what those "Navy pistols" were. They may have been Colt 1851 revolvers, or they may have been Whitney revolvers—or they may even have been single shot percussion pistols.

As long as we are pondering, we might ask ourselves why two men in Tennessee were selling arms to the Union.

Another facet of the problem of who purchased what— and who used what—is the fact that many arms used by Union troops were not paid for by the Union Government and therefore are not included in "Executive Document 99." Many state military units were outfitted by that state's treasury. In practically all cases where state troops needed arms the U.S. Government provided them, but if they *had* arms, so much the better—and off they went to war.

In some few cases the arms used were purchased by private funds and again these purchases are not included in "E. D. 99." This last situation usually occurred when the arms the unit had were obsolete to the point that their officers all but refused to take them into battle. If the Federal Government was unable to supply proper arms, the officers took it upon themselves to equip their men with arms that were bought with private funds. The actual monies in these cases came from civilian subscription, cities and towns, and from the officers and men themselves.

This generalizing with "arms" and how they were put into the hands of the troops does not apply only to revolvers; indeed much of what has been stated above applies directly to the long arms as carried by the Union. We can understand, however, that problems with shoulder weapons and how they were procured must apply, in some degree, to the revolver situation.

The figures used for the various purchases of revolvers in this writing will be those figures that have been compiled from "Executive Document 99." Due to private purchases, state purchases, and obscure terminology, they may be incomplete. We can say, however, that *at least* that many of each *were* purchased.

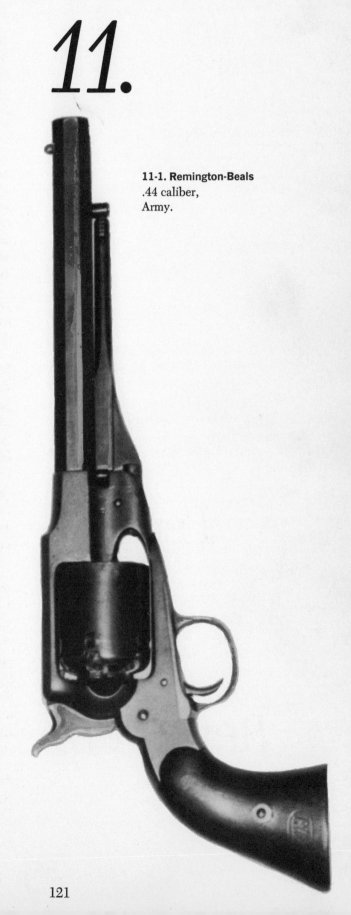

11.

11-1. Remington-Beals
.44 caliber,
Army.

All but one of the revolvers shown here are from the collection of Lieutenant Colonel R. C. Kuhn, United States Air Force, Retired. The Colonel is not only a serious and avid collector but he is also one of the gun world's leading researchers. When Roy Kuhn says that a Joslyn revolver is a "Navy issue Joslyn" as against an "Army issue Joslyn," collectors respectfully listen and remember.

In photo 11-2, all the revolvers in the picture are Colts. Understandably there were other Colts used in the Civil War but these seven comprise the vast majority of the purchased Colt revolvers. Records show that there were 129,730 "Colt's Army Revolvers" purchased, and 17,010 "Colt's Navy Revolvers" purchased. This does not mean that the U.S. Army or U.S. Navy had that many Colt revolvers. The names "Army Colt" and "Navy Colt" refer to the style and caliber of the arm regardless of what military force used or purchased it. The "Navy Colt" was a .36 caliber revolver of the so-called 1851 Model and/or possibly the 1861 Model. Even though they were termed "Navy" the U.S. Army bought more of them than did the U.S. Navy. Conversely the U.S. Navy bought some of the 1860 "Army" revolvers that were of "Army size," i.e., .44 caliber.

To determine whether a given gun was purchased by the Army or Navy a study of the details of the arm itself and the inspectors marks will usually provide an answer.

The second photograph (see 11-3) displays a variety of Remington-Beals, Remington, and one Whitney revolver. The compilation from "E. D. 99" states that 2,814 Remington-Beals revolvers were purchased. There were .36 caliber Beals revolvers called "Navy" by collectors and there were .44 caliber Beals called "Army" by collectors. The number 2,814 presumably includes both calibers and it is doubtful that anyone knows how many of each were bought.

The Remington revolvers were divided in the listing as to "Navy" and "Army" and again this refers to .36 "Navy" size and .44 "Army" size regardless of the purchasing organization. There were 125,314 Remington "Army" revolvers bought and 4,901 Remington "Navy" revolvers bought. The Remington revolver situation is further complicated by the knowledge that not all revolvers were the same

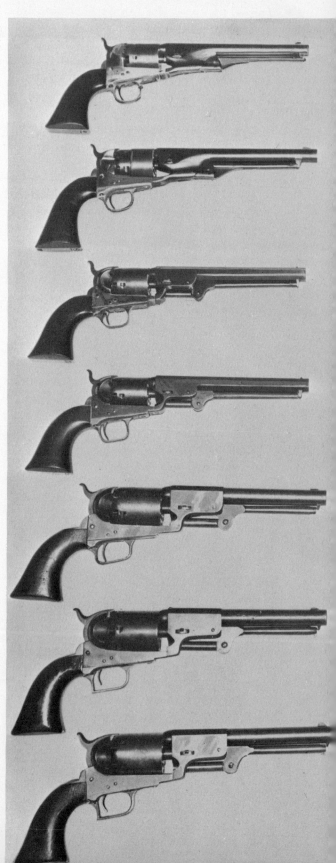

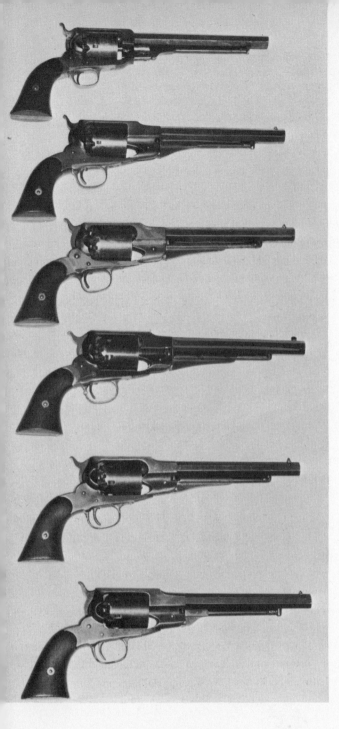

11-3. From top. 1/Whitney .36 caliber
U. S. Navy. 2/Remington .44 caliber
Model 1861, Army. 3/Remington .44
caliber Model 1861, Army (variation).
4/Remington New Model (1858) .44
caliber, Army. 5/Remington New Model
(1858) .36 caliber, Navy. 6/Remington-
Beals .36 caliber, Navy.

model, and that within each model classification there will be found variations that interest the serious Remington student.

Most collectors are familiar with the Remington "New Model." It is the most commonly encountered U.S. Military Civil War Remington revolver. There is confusion about this model within collectors' ranks and some mistakenly believe that the "New Model" was the final design produced by Remington for the Civil War. Actually the "New Model" preceded the final design. The 1861 revolver (and so marked) came after the "New Model." When a manufacturer elects to use the name "New Model" he can't very well call a subsequent product a "New New Model" as this could lead to a ridiculous series of names. Remington simply dropped the "New Model" and marked the 1861 Model with the company name and the year it was patented.

Any time a factory changes over from one model to another there is often not a clear demarkation from the old to the new. Collectors have found Remington revolvers of the "New Model" which have aberrant features and likewise they have found variations of the 1861 Remington. Remington arms will be discussed in somewhat more detail elsewhere in this book.

There were at least 11,214 Whitney Navy revolvers purchased by the U.S. during the Civil War period. The Whitney was a serviceable weapon that was made by the Whitneyville Armory at Whitneyville, Connecticut. The Whitney was well enough liked down South that it was copied by the Confederate firm of Spiller & Burr.

Plate 11-4 contains some revolvers that were manufactured in the northern United States. At the top is the Allen & Wheelock percussion revolver of which only 536 are reported as having been purchased. The martially marked specimen illustrated is serial number one. This Allen & Wheelock big center-hammer design was also made on a smaller scale and some in the various sizes were modified to use lip-fire metallic cartridges.

The two Starr revolvers shown are both .44 caliber and were used by the U.S. Army. They differ in that one is simply a single-action revolver and the other employs a cocking device so that the pistol operates

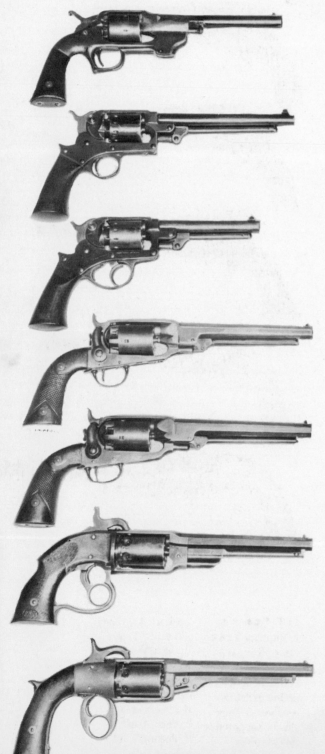

as a double-action arm. Starr also supplied a .36 caliber Navy revolver that had the self-cocking mechanism. The records show that 47,952 Starr revolvers were purchased, without giving detail as to how many were of what feature or caliber. A closer look into "Executive Document 99" discloses that only 1,250 Starr "Navy" revolvers were purchased directly from the Starr Arms Co. This does not rule out the possibility that such Starr "Navy" revolvers were bought from somebody else. To reinforce such a possibility it can be pointed out that not only were Whitney revolvers purchased from the Whitney Co. but they were also supplied by arms dealers like Schuyler, Hartley & Graham of New York and Philip S. Justice of Philadelphia.

The Joslyn Fire-Arms Co. of Stonington, Connecticut, supplied .44 caliber percussion revolvers to both the Army and the Navy. The Navy version is easily identified as having the normal iron strap in the center of the butt separating the wood of the grip. The Army revolver has an oval plate on the bottom of the grip that is held in place by two screws.

The records indicate that 1,100 Joslyn revolvers were purchased without drawing any distinction between those for the Army and those for the Navy.

During the Civil War the Army bought the vast bulk of the arms. There were times when the Navy was so in need of small arms that they sent officers out into the cities to buy outright suitable arms that could be found in dealers' stocks. These arms are commercially produced pieces that usually bear a large "P" for "Proved" or possibly "Purchased." It is not known if these "purchased" arms are included in the figures from "Executive Document 99" or not, but it is thought that they are not included.

There were two distinct models of the Savage Arms Co. revolver as purchased by the government. The first type is called the "figure eight" Savage by collectors because the cocking lever and trigger resemble the number "8." This "figure eight" version is by far the rarer specimen and was manufactured in several variations using different styles of frame and grip and employing different metals. The "figure eight" Savage shown here from the R. C. Kuhn collection is the only one known to this writer that bears U.S. martial inspector's marks.

The records show that all Savage revolvers of all types come to the total of 11,284. This figure is probably low as it is known that some Savage revolvers were over-the-counter purchases by naval officers in search of small arms. The Savage being a .36 caliber revolver might well have found favor with the Navy Department.

The three revolvers illustrated at the top of photo 11-5 on this page are all weapons of foreign make.

The top specimen is a Raphael that was manufactured in France. It used a self-contained metallic cartridge that was advanced for its day. "E. D. 99" contains an entry that one George Raphael sold the government "106 breech-loading revolvers" and later "806 revolvers." If all of these were the Raphael system arm, the total of 912 still falls short of the 987 Raphael revolvers reputedly bought by the Union. It may well be that someone else supplied the additional Raphael revolvers.

The same George Raphael also sold the U.S. 138 Lefaucheux revolvers. The Lefaucheux was another French revolver and according to the records 12,374 of them were purchased. The Lefaucheux also used a fixed self-contained metallic cartridge from which the firing pin extended at right angles from the base. It is called "pinfire" and was so successful that it is used in a limited way to this date.

The revolver in the photo 11-5 just underneath the Lefaucheux pinfire is the English "Kerr" revolver. There is some controversy over the use of this pistol. On this particular specimen there is a plain stamp (on the inside of the butt curve) "U.S." and an anchor. The U.S. bought sixteen Kerr revolvers and considering the incompleteness of "Executive Document 99" it would not be surprising if Kerr revolvers were purchased by the U.S. Navy with private funds and therefore would not be included in "E. D. 99." There is a belief among some that Kerr revolvers were also bought and used by the Confederacy.

The Adams revolver shown in photo 11-5 is normally considered to be an English product—and normally it is. The Government is said to have purchased 415 Adams revolvers—which undoubtedly they did. But that is not the whole story. There were at least a thousand Adams revolvers used by Union troops but many of them were purchased with state funds and are not included in the U.S. Government records. Further, revolvers of Adams design were manufactured right

11-5. From top: 1/Raphael 12mm center-fire cartridge revolver. 2/Lefaucheux 12mm pinfire cartridge revolver. 3/Kerr .44 caliber percussion revolver (marked U. S. and anchor). 4/Adams .36 caliber made by Massachusetts Arms Co. 5/Roger & Spencer .44 caliber, Army. 6/Freeman .44 caliber, Army. 7/Pettingill .44 caliber, Army.

here in the U.S.A. by the Massachusetts Arms Company of Chicopee Falls, Massachusetts. The pictured revolver (see 11-5) is a pristine example of the Adams Navy pistol as made by the Massachusetts Arms Co., and a rare specimen it is!

As far as anyone can tell, all of the Rogers & Spencer percussion revolvers were bought from the Rogers & Spencer Company. The records show that a total of 5,000 of them were purchased and examination of the dealings with Rogers & Spencer disclose that they supplied all of the 5,000. The purchases were late, starting in January of 1865 and ending in September of that year. The odds are that none of them saw service in the Civil War. It is known that the bulk of these revolvers remained in storage for many years. Often when encountered today they are in very fine original condition.

The Freeman revolver shown just under the Rogers & Spencer is a much rarer arm. The Rogers & Spencer organization obtained the use of the Freeman revolver patents and no Freeman revolvers were manufactured after the Rogers & Spencer Company started operations.

There are no records of the Freeman ever having been bought by the U.S. but martially marked specimens have been observed, so undoubtedly Freeman revolvers were used to some small extent.

The last specimen in photo 11-5 is the Pettingill percussion revolver. The listings in "Executive Document 99" tell us that all of the 2,001 Pettingills were purchased from Rogers & Spencer between October 20, 1862 and January 17, 1863. The Pettingill was also available through commercial channels and will be found without martial markings. Also the Pettingill was made in a smaller size. These pocket-size Pettingill revolvers were probably carried by some Union soldiers but were not official sidearms of the Union.

Other revolvers not shown in the photographs were bought and used by the U.S. Government, but not many. One that is missing here is the Perrin, another foreign product that used a center-fire, self-contained, metallic cartridge. Two hundred such Perrin revolvers were purchased.

Civil War revolvers will undoubtedly continue to hold a fascination for many gun collectors. The number and diversity of these arms are a challenge to even the most avid collector; a few years and quite a few dollars may be spent in the quest.

Editor's Note: *The problems of interpreting government records, involving a great number of contracts, purchase orders, and other data are great. Consequently we find in published works some varying conclusions as to purchase totals. It is not felt necessary in this brief outline to undertake extensive analysis to reconcile minor differences. The totals provided here—and from the other sources— will be found helpfully indicative of the relative number of each type arm purchased by the U. S. Government.*

the Arms of Ethan Allen

and Associates

*E*than Allen, son of Nathaniel and Lucy Allen of Bellingham, Massachusetts, would almost certainly have gained a greater and more lasting place in American history had he not been named for the unrelated but heroic leader of Vermont's Green Mountain Boys in the Revolutionary War battle of Fort Ticonderoga. History can rarely do justice to more than one man under a single name, so Ethan Allen the gunmaker was destined to relative obscurity despite his many unique accomplishments that would have brought fame to a less familiar name.

Commencing with the manufacture of saw-handled underhammer percussion pistols as a side line to shoemakers' cutlery sometime between 1832 and 1834, Allen soon found that there was a wider market for pistols than for his highly specialized line of knives. For several years this very distinctive "bootleg" pistol was practically the sole product of Ethan's arms making. Produced in a variety of sizes, this gun was sold almost exclusively in pairs which were numbered alike. Most were marked on the flat top plate: "E. ALLEN GRAFTON MASS." and "POCKET RIFLE CAST-STEEL WARRANTED" though even at this early time, some were especially marked for large arms dealers, establishing a practice which became far more common in later days of production.

The demand for this arm grew so rapidly that by February of 1837, Allen saw the need of expanding his business and inserted the following advertise-

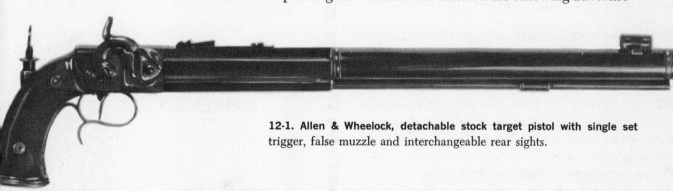

12-1. Allen & Wheelock, detachable stock target pistol with single set trigger, false muzzle and interchangeable rear sights.

ment in the *Massachusetts Spy:* "*A man with a small family to take charge of a boarding house. Wanted on the first of April next, a number of Gunsmiths or Machinists to work at the manufacturing of Pocket Rifles. Liberal wages will be given, and references as to good moral character required. Enquire of E. Allen, New England Village, or at this office.*"

12.

Very soon thereafter, to provide additional executive help, Ethan prevailed upon his sister's husband, Charles Thurber, to give up his academic life as master of the Latin Grammar School of Milford (Massachusetts) Academy to form the partnership of Allen & Thurber.

Here it may be well to introduce a list of the various firm names and places of manufacture for the Allen factories, since this information can serve the collector as a means of ascertaining a broad chronology of the Allen arms.

E. Allen	Grafton, Mass.	1832-1837
Allen & Thurber	Grafton, Mass.	1837-1842
Allen & Thurber	Norwich, Conn.	1842-1847
Allen & Thurber	Worcester, Mass.	1847-1854
Allen, Thurber & Co.	Worcester, Mass.	1854-1856
Allen & Wheelock	Worcester, Mass.	1856-1865
E. Allen & Co.	Worcester, Mass.	1865-1871
Forehand & Wadsworth	Worcester, Mass.	1871-1890
Forehand Arms Co.	Worcester, Mass.	1890-1902

These several firms constitute a family dynasty founded by Ethan Allen. A second brother-in-law, Thomas P. Wheelock, long an employee of the Allen & Thurber firm, was to become a silent partner as the "& Co." added to the firm name in 1854. Wheelock became a full partner upon the retirement of Mr. Thurber in early 1856. By the time of Thomas Wheelock's death in May of 1864 Allen's two sons-in-law, Sullivan Forehand and Henry C. Wadsworth, became the "& Co." of the new E. Allen & Co., thus perpetuating the family interest beyond the death of the founder himself.

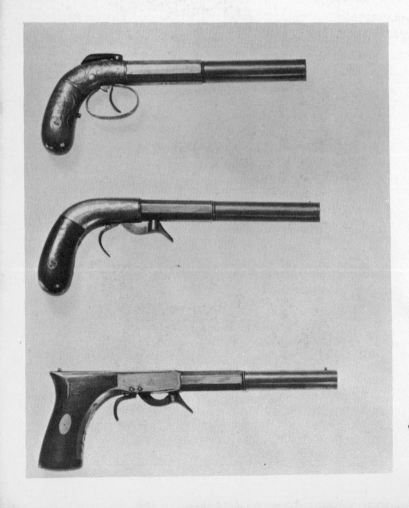

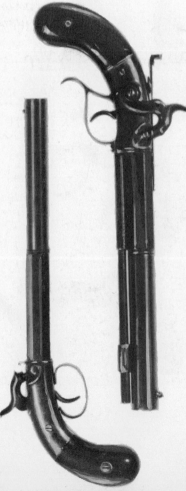

12-2. Far left, from top: 1/ Allen & Thurber, Norwich bar hammer. 2/ Allen & Thurber, Worcester under-hammer. 3/E. Allen, Grafton "Pocket Rifle." Left: 4/Allen & Wheelock, "box lock" belt pistol. 5/ Allen & Thurber, Worcester bag-grip target pistol.

12-3. Right, from top: 1/Allen & Wheelock, stud trigger center hammer. 2/Allen & Thurber, Grafton "1837 Patent Model." 3/Allen & Thurber, Grafton early bar hammer. Far right, from top: 4/Allen & Thurber, Worcester muff pistol. 5/Allen & Wheelock, bar hammer pistol. 6/Allen & Thurber, Worcester double-barrel pistol.

The production of the Allen & Thurber firm during its Grafton period is marked by the introduction of the odd double-action single shot sidehammer pistol (see photo 12-3) whose mechanism was also the basis for the first of twenty-six patents granted to Ethan Allen by the United States Government. This model was relatively short-lived and was replaced by the characteristic bar hammer mechanism, which was to become the hallmark of Ethan Allen arms.

Within a short time after establishment, the Grafton factory was producing the interesting six-barrel "pepperbox" pistols which were the cornerstone of the long-lived Allen success. While vastly less accurate than Samuel Colt's patented single barrel revolver, the Allen pepperbox made up for this shortcoming through three very distinct advantages over the Colt pistol. Its six barrels offered more "fire power" than the contemporary Colt five-shot cylinder, and these six charges could be fired more rapidly than the Colt's five shots; and, most importantly, the Allen could be purchased for less than one-fourth the Colt price!

Fortunately for the Allen & Thurber firm, Colt managed to create a wide and growing demand for multi-shot pistols, but his company could not begin to meet the demand. Although $300,000 of invested capital was poured into the Patent Arms Manufacturing Co. which produced arms under Colt's patent, it went into receivership in 1841, having produced a total of about 2,000 revolving pistols in almost six years of operation.

Thus, temporarily left with a virtual monopoly of the American market for rapid fire multi-shot pistols, the Allen & Thurber business expanded so rapidly that it moved to Norwich, Connecticut, to take advantage of that city's better transportation facilities. During the year 1847, which saw Allen & Thurber's production interrupted by the removal from Norwich, Connecticut, to Worcester, Massachusetts, the company still managed to manufacture and sell something over 8,000 six-shot pepperboxes, and nearly 1,500 single shot bar hammer pistols!

With the establishment of the Allen & Thurber fac-

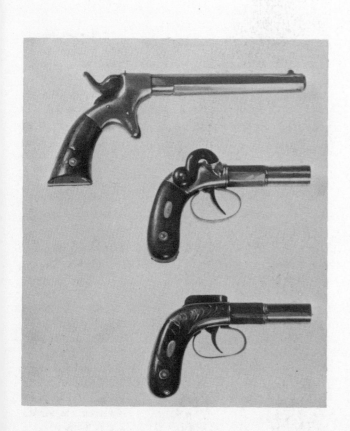

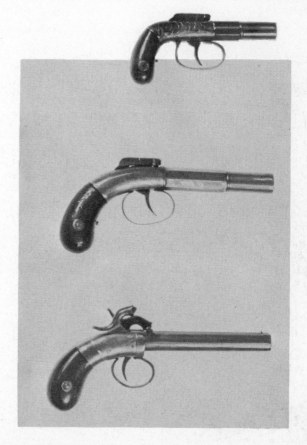

tory in Worcester in July of 1847, the company entered into an era that saw rapid addition of variety to their output. Within a year or two they had added the lightweight sidehammer target pistol and the "inside hammer" single shot pistol in barrel lengths from three inches to ten inches as well as exceptionally fine sportsman's target pistols fitted with a false muzzle, available with or without detachable shoulder stock (see photo 12-1) and the double-barreled single trigger pistol. All of these new models continued without significant change through the span of the Allen & Thurber and the Allen Thurber & Co. production, and well into the period of Allen & Wheelock manufacture.

This period also saw rather dramatic changes in the pepperbox line. While the earlier pepperboxes had a "rib" running the length of the cylinder between each two barrels, those of later Worcester manufacture had these ribs omitted, leaving a "fluted" barrel cylinder. A five-shot pepperbox of this style was also added to the line, and continued into Allen & Wheelock production without change.

By the time the firm had become reorganized as Allen & Wheelock, the American arms-making industry was anxiously anticipating the expiration of Colt's extended patent on the single-barreled revolver. Undoubtedly Allen & Wheelock started experimental development of this type of revolver in advance of the expiration of the Colt patent in 1857. Still, the multi-barreled pepperbox was so very popular that the firm added a four-shot pepperbox and continued the production of both five- and six-shot models concurrently with manufacture of their newly introduced single-barrel revolvers.

Allen & Wheelock's initial step into the single-barreled revolver field was a five-shot bar hammer "transitional" revolver which retained the double-action principle and bar hammer of the pepperbox.

Still lacking a satisfactory sighting arrangement, it was hardly an improvement in accuracy over its five-shot pepperbox counterpart. Nonetheless it was produced in two sizes for a considerable time.

The first really effective competition to the contemporary Hartford Colt revolver produced by Allen & Wheelock was the sidehammer percussion revolver which was developed in the intermediate (or belt) size (see 12-4), and subsequently in pocket model and holster model as well. This line was, in fact, a copy of the Root model Colt pistol, and was often spoken of by Allen employees as their "Colt pistol."

Allen & Wheelock's entry into the field of cartridge revolvers presented a seven-shot .22 caliber rimfire in July of 1858. Within the following five years, the firm was producing .32 caliber revolvers in both regular and long cylinder cartridge models and finally the series of exclusively Allen lip-fire revolvers, commencing with a .32 caliber adaptation of the earlier rimfire arm. The .44 caliber lip-fire of this series was the largest American cartridge revolver of its time and it was followed by a scaled-down model in .36 caliber. The last of the Allen & Wheelock cartridge revolvers to make its appearance was the .25 lip-fire seven-shot which is only rarely found bearing the maker's name.

Rollin White, in defense of his patent of April 3, 1855, covering a cylinder bored through for loading cartridges at the rear, instituted a suit against Ethan Allen on behalf of the Smith & Wesson firm, late in the year 1859. However, this suit was allowed to languish in the courts for almost four years before an injunction was finally obtained on November 12, 1863, restraining Ethan Allen and his firm from the manufacture or sale of this class of arms. Thus barred from further production of any cartridge revolvers, Allen & Wheelock found

12-4. Left row, from top. 1/Allen & Thurber, Grafton "Dragoon" pepperbox. 2/Allen & Thurber, Worcester " '49er dragoon" pepperbox. 3/Allen & Thurber, Worcester thumb-hammer (single action) pepperbox. 4/Allen & Thurber, Worcester standard 6-shot pepperbox. 5/Allen & Thurber, Norwich ring-trigger "hammerless" pepperbox. 6/Allen & Thurber, Worcester "hammerless" pepperbox. 7/Allen, Thurber & Co., 5-shot pepperbox. 8/Allen & Wheelock, 4-shot pepperbox.

Right row, from top: 1/Allen & Wheelock, small 5-shot "transitional" revolver. 2/Allen & Wheelock, large 5-shot "transitional" revolver. 3/Allen & Wheelock, .28 caliber side-hammer revolver. 4/Allen & Wheelock, .31 caliber side-hammer revolver. 5/Allen & Wheelock, .36 caliber side-hammer revolver. 6/Allen & Wheelock, .44 caliber center-hammer "Army." 7/Allen & Wheelock, .36 caliber center-hammer revolver. 8/Allen & Wheelock, "Providence Police Model" revolver.

it necessary to fall back on a newly introduced line of percussion revolvers which had been introduced to meet the demand for personal side arms for soldiers and officers in the Civil War.

The massive .44 caliber, center-hammer, percussion revolver is often considered by collectors as a martial arm. However, the few of this model that were purchased by the government were all bought on the open market from various wholesale and retail dealers and sporting goods stores, and none was produced under government contract. The writer has never heard of one of these "martial" pieces bearing any martial stamping and it is certain that the Allen & Wheelock .44 percussion revolver (12-4) was of only secondary importance as a martial arm.

The .36 caliber center-hammer percussion revolver was more popular than the massive .44, and this model (12-4) is far more commonly found on the market today. The last model of percussion revolver to be introduced by the Allen & Wheelock factory was the so-called "Providence Police Revolver" which is almost always found without maker's mark.

Single shot cartridge pistols in both .32 and .22 calibers were produced in large quantity while the firm was banned from the production of multi-shot cartridge arms. A sequence of three varieties of Allen & Wheelock .32 caliber single shot pistols is illustrated along with a representative Allen & Wheelock single shot .22 pistol.

Only a single new model of percussion single shot pistol was introduced by the Allen & Wheelock firm. This pistol made use of a wide variety of barrels which had been manufactured for other models, thus utilizing "salvage" materials and making this

one of the cheapest guns of its time.

The death of Thomas P. Wheelock in May of 1864 brought to a close the nine-year period embraced by the partnership that bore his name. The Allen & Wheelock period must be considered the golden age of the Allen enterprises, during which more than a score of new handgun models was introduced to the market.

The firm of E. Allen & Co. resumed the manufacture of cartridge revolvers immediately upon the expiration of the Rollin White patent in 1869, continuing the .22 and .32 rimfire models of the pre-injunction Allen & Wheelock production. Ultimately, these and the single shot cartridge pistols were dramatically changed in form as is shown in the illustrations of a late E. Allen & Co. .22 revolver and the series of round-gripped single shot pistols.

Perhaps it is the writer's personal bias, but it seems that with Ethan Allen's death, a certain aggressive spark was lost to the continuing enterprise under Sullivan Forehand and Henry Wadsworth. Nonetheless, the business continued to flourish for a considerable time but, with fewer new models being introduced, the Allen line went into a slow decline.

No other 19th Century American firm produced a wider variety of firearms than did the series of factories dominated by Ethan Allen. While this chapter has dealt solely with the more popular handguns, the diligent collector will find Allen-made long arms, both percussion and cartridge, in almost unbelievable variety. Certainly the Allen line of arms offers something of interest to every general collector of American antique guns, and provides a field of specialization which has given the writer more than a quarter century of fascinating and enjoyable gun collecting activity.

12-5. Left, from top: 1/Allen & Wheelock, first model 7-shot .22 revolver. 2/Allen & Wheelock, late model .22 revolver. 3/E. Allen & Co., .22 revolver with bird-head grips. 4/Allen & Wheelock, first model .32 revolver. 5/Allen & Wheelock, .32 long-cylinder revolver with bronze frame. 6/ Allen & Wheelock, .32 single shot of late production. 7/E. Allen & Co., .32 single shot of early production. 8/Allen & Wheelock, .32 single shot of intermediate vintage. 9/Allen & Wheelock, .32 of early production.

Middle row, from top: 1/Allen &. Wheelock, second model 7-shot .22 revolver. 2/E. Allen & Co., early .22 revolver with square grips. 3/E. Allen & Co., bird-head grip .32 pistol of late manufacture. 4/E. Allen & Co., short-cylinder steel frame .32 revolver. 5/Allen & Wheelock, .32 revolver of relatively early date.

Right row, from top: 1/Allen & Wheelock, .44 caliber lip-fire revolver. 2/Allen & Wheelock, .36 caliber lip-fire revolver. 3/Allen & Wheelock, .32 caliber lip-fire revolver. 4/Allen & Wheelock, .25 caliber lip-fire revolver. 5/Allen & Wheelock, .22 rimfire single shot pistol. 6/E. Allen & Co., early .22 rimfire single shot. 7/E. Allen & Co., late .22 rimfire with bronze frame. 8/E. Allen & Co., tiny bronze framed .22. 9/E. Allen & Co., .41 caliber rimfire derringer.

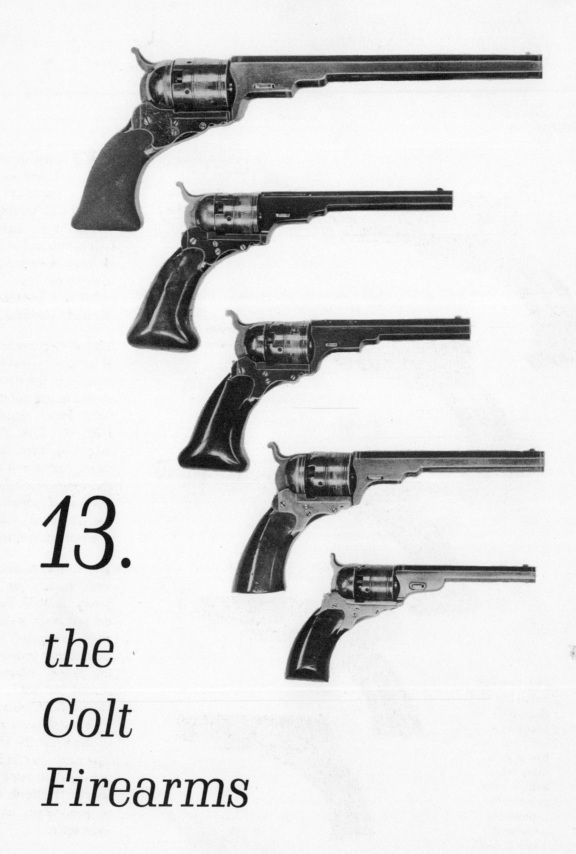

13.
the
Colt
Firearms

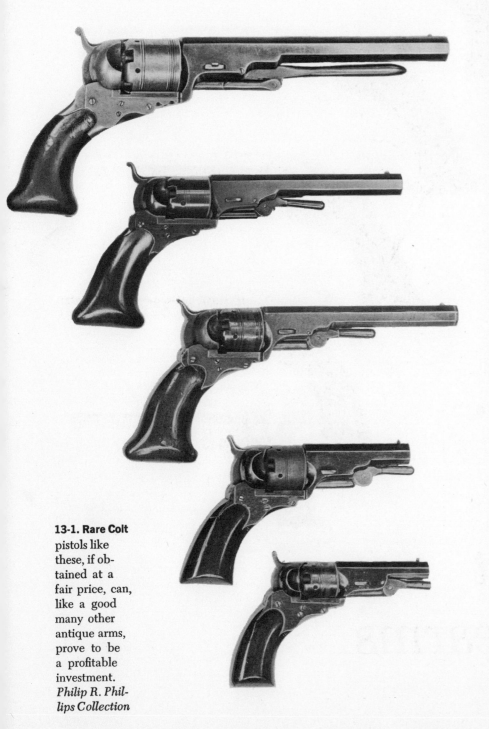

13-1. Rare Colt pistols like these, if obtained at a fair price, can, like a good many other antique arms, prove to be a profitable investment. *Philip R. Phillips Collection*

There are many reasons why Americans show keen interest in Colt firearms. Samuel Colt invented the first truly successful repeating pistol; more Colt pistols and more different models have been produced than those of any other manufacturer; the Colt pistol is a popular symbol in our dramatic national history.

Samuel Colt's personal story is one of the most colorful in the annals of American industry; it is ably recorded in suggested reference books listed later. Samuel Colt died in 1862; the Colt Patent Fire Arms Mfg. Co. then came under new management and eventually under changing ownerships. But the production of popular Colt pistols at the Hartford, Connecticut, plant was not interrupted.

The first Colt pistols came off the workbenches at Paterson, New Jersey, in 1836. From 1843 to 1847 no weapons were produced, the stock company formed to make Colt patent pistols at Paterson having failed. Manufacture was resumed in 1847 at Whitneyville, Connecticut, when the big "Walker" Colt pistols were made there under contract for the U. S. Government. The next year (1848) Samuel Colt managed to establish his own factory at Hartford, where the wheels of production have been turning ever since.

Let us first give attention to the Colt cap-and-ball models, from the folding trigger original pattern made at Paterson, New Jersey, to improved Colt pistols manufactured through the Civil War.

The sire and king of the Colt pistol line is the folding trigger five-shot model marked on the barrel "Patent Arms M'g. Co. Paterson N. J. Colt's Pt." These pistols were made in three major sizes and in different calibers and barrel lengths. Some were put up in fine hardwood boxes in which were included the loading tools and an extra cylinder. Values now run from a thousand dollars sharply upward. The most popular of the sizes is the so-called "Texas" model of .36 caliber; these usually have a 7½-inch or 9-inch barrel.

In addition to pistols, the Patent Arms M'g. Co. made Colt shoulder arms at Paterson. While these are actually in smaller supply than pistols, they have never been as much in demand nor have they brought near the price of pistols. Actually, more records of prominent use are credited to the carbine than any other Paterson-made weapon. Some were used by the early Texas Rangers; they were issued to a select group of skirmishers aboard ships of the Pacific Squadron in 1846; famous trader Josiah Gregg carried one down the Santa Fe Trail; William Lewis Manly toted one in his heroic rescue of the Argonauts stranded in Death Valley. At the present ratio of quoted prices, Paterson-made shoulder arms are especially desirable.

The next Colt endeavor was to produce, in Mr. Eli Whitney's manufactory near New Haven, a big four-

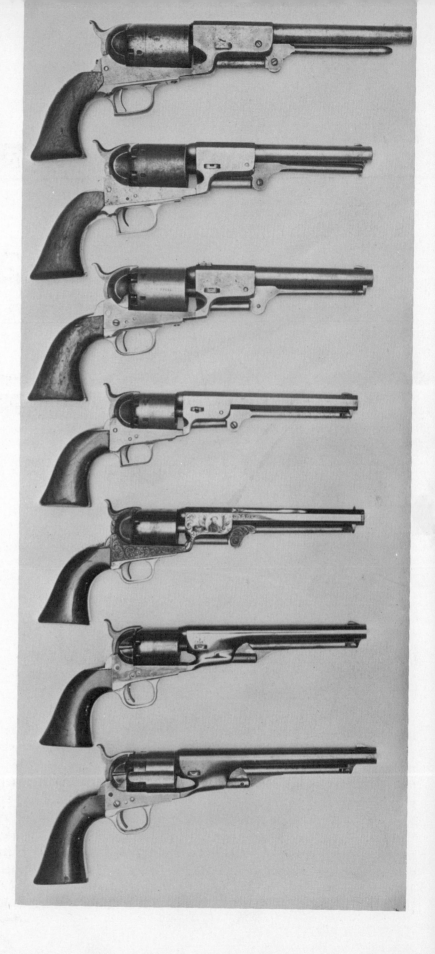

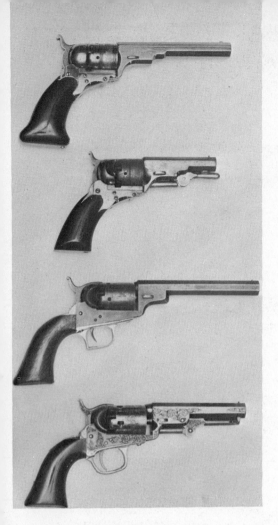

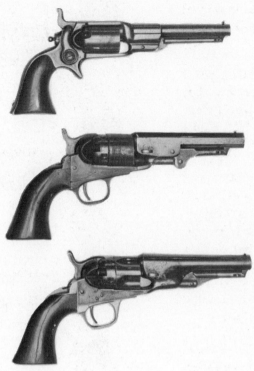

13-2. Left, from top: 1/Whitneyville-Walker 1847 Colt Dragoon. 2/Whitneyville-Hartford 1848 Colt Dragoon. 3/Third Hartford model Dragoon, designed for attachable shoulder stock. 4/Model 1851 Navy pistol, first model with straight-back trigger guard. 5/Model 1851 Navy pistol round guard, presentation engraved. 6/ Model 1861 Navy pistol, round barrel with rachet loading lever. 7/Model 1860 Army pistol; early type with full-fluted cylinder.

pound Dragoon pistol of .44 caliber, with a 9-inch barrel marked on the right side "U. S. 1847." This was the first Colt "six-shooter" and credit goes to Captain Samuel H. Walker for helping Colt redesign the old Paterson model, making the newer model sturdier, easier to load, and possessing more firepower. About 1,100 were made at the Whitney plant.

Moving his scene of operations to Hartford, Samuel Colt soon had found the resources to start a small factory in that city. Here, using some leftover (or rejected) parts from the Whitney contract along with new parts, Colt produced the prototype from which his famous Dragoon pistols would take their final form. Only a few hundred pistols of this first output (known as Whitneyville-Hartford Dragoon pistols) were made. They had a 7½-inch barrel and are recognized primarily by features of the trigger guard; the serial numbers run approximately in the 1100 to 1400 range. Obviously these pistols are rare and quite valuable. Replicas and fakes are found in specimens of the high-priced Paterson, Whitneyville-Walker Dragoon, and Whitneyville-Hartford Dragoon designs. The inexperienced collector should always have such high-priced weapons authenticated before buying.

Three .44 caliber Colt Hartford Dragoon pistol models followed, varying little, gaining popularity with mounted troops of the U. S. Dragoons and with westerners generally. Although they retailed around $25 apiece at the factory, they often sold for as high as $150 in the California gold fields. These big four-pound weapons have always rated very high in popularity and in value among arms collectors.

Along with the big .44 caliber Dragoon holster pistols, Colt designed a small .31 caliber pocket pistol in 1848. These first pocket pistols were made with barrels 3 to 6 inches long that had no attached loading lever. The trigger guards, resembling the early Dragoon design, had a straight back. Later models of both the Dragoon and pocket pistols were fitted with trigger guards which were rounded front and back.

Thus in 1848 began at Hartford a long line of Colt pocket pistols. Soon these were accompanied by a size loosely described as "belt pistols," but which were in effect a size between the big .44 caliber holster pistols and the small .31 pocket pistols. Most Colts in this class were made in .36 caliber.

Following the pocket model of 1848, there soon came the 1849 model which had an attached loading lever under the barrel. This loading lever became a standard feature on all but a special few of the Colt percussion pistols made thereafter. In practically all Colt percussion models you will find certain variations that set some specimens apart as rarer than others. Obviously we do not have space here for extensive details, but collectors are urged to study these features in the books which do describe them, for they often have important influence on desirability and value.

One of the least successful of Colt's pocket pistols was a sidehammer pistol known as the Root 1855 model. This design is credited to Elisha K. Root (who followed Samuel Colt to the Colt Co. presidency). The pistol had a sheath trigger, without guard. It was made in .265 and .31 calibers with a five-shot cylinder (sometimes round and sometimes fluted). There were various other structural variations, but none of these pistols had the ability to stand very hard use. Al-

though the Root mechanical principles worked reasonably well in the larger-frame revolving cylinder rifles and shotguns made at the same time, the center hammer and standard lock design of the previous models were the more reliable for pistols. This standard center-hammer lock system was even used for the famous Single Action Army cartridge model, a rugged revolver manufactured right to this day.

A truly effective pocket pistol known as the "Pocket Pistol of Navy Caliber" came on the market soon after the Root model. Navy caliber is .36, and we'll get to Navy belt pistols soon. These .36 caliber pocket pistols are sometimes erroneously referred to as the Model of 1853. They have a rebated five-shot cylinder and an octagon barrel. With a short barrel they were true pocket pistols, but with their long 6½-inch barrels they were small belt pistols. The next model of this same class (the final design of all Colt percus-

13-4. Left row, from top: 1/Thuer cartridge conversion of the Colt model 1861 Navy pistol. 2/Single Action Army model of 1873, called the "Peacemaker" or "Frontier." 3/Bisley target model, flat-top frame. 4/"Lightning" model Colt DA. An unusual variation in .32 caliber with long barrel and target sights. 5/Scarce variation of the Colt DA Army and Frontier model flat-top frame, target sights. 6/Colt DA Marine Corps revolver of 1905; swing-out cylinder, caliber .38. 7/One style of the Colt "Officer's Model" target revolver. Right row: 1/All-metal .41 rimfire "No. 1" Colt derringer. 2/Caliber .41 "Cloverleaf" Colt, four-shot cylinder, scarce 1½-inch octagon barrel. 3/Colt's early "open-top" .22 pocket revolver, desirable variation with integral ejector housing on barrel. 4/"New line" .38 police revolver, figures of cop and thug in the stock pattern. 5/Single Action Army Colt in "store-keeper's model" or "house pistol" style—short barrel without ejector. 6/Colt's first model automatic pistol, caliber .38, Browning's patent of 1897. 7/Model of 1903 Colt .38 automatic pocket pistol. *Philip R. Phillips Collection*

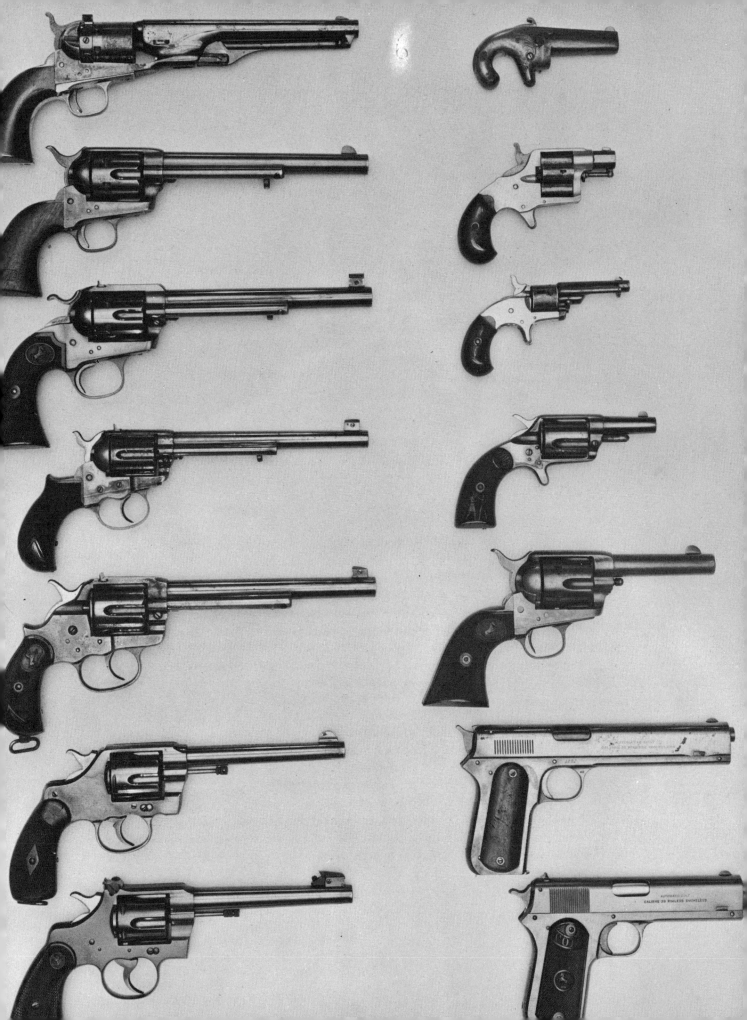

sion pistols) is known as the Police Pistol of 1862. These are also of .36 caliber and can be easily identified by their semi-fluted five-shot cylinders, round barrels, and improved ratchet-type loading levers. A rare variation of this pistol has a short barrel and no loading lever. These pistols have the most beautiful streamlining of any Colt percussion model; they are very popular with collectors.

Soon after the 1849 pocket pistols were moving out well, Colt had turned his attention to designing an in-between pistol, a pistol that did not have the weight and bulk of the big .44 caliber Dragoon but possessed more power and accuracy than the .31 caliber pocket model. True genius went into this work, for Colt's model 1851 Navy pistol was destined to become the most widely used of any percussion repeating pistol ever manufactured. It had a 7½-inch octagon barrel, a round six-shot cylinder bearing a naval scene, and was of .36 caliber. The balance and grip were especially pleasing; it was dependable, had good range and accuracy.

Early models of the 1851 Navy were fitted with straight-back trigger guards. The first type had a notched cylinder pin (not slotted as on later models) and the wedge screw was under the wedge slot rather than in the usual position above it. Any of

these early Navy pistols with *original* straight-back guards (and appropriate low serial numbers) are scarce and valuable.

After ten years of manufacture (in which a rounded trigger guard early became the standard), the octagon barrel was replaced by a round barrel which had a rachet-type loading lever instead of the old hinged type. In this form the pistol became known as the Navy Belt Pistol of 1861.

A year earlier Colt had redesigned the big .44 Dragoon holster pistol, reducing weight and making it more streamlined. This became the Army Holster Pistol of 1860. A few early 1860 Army models retained the Navy size grip, but this was soon changed to a longer grip with the same general contour. Most of the first pistols were made with a fluted six-shot cylinder. After somewhat over 5,000 were made, the fluted cylinder was abandoned in favor of a rebated cylinder. Hence the fluted cylinder models are relatively scarce and valuable.

Model 1849 pocket and model 1851 Navy percussion pistols were also made for a short time (1853-1857) at a London armory operated by Colt. These pistols will be found to have a London address on the barrel and British proofmarks on barrel and cylinder. Some pistols made in the United States for sale in Great Britain also bore a London address. These will sometimes be found without any proofmarks.

There are many Colt percussion pistols of special interest and merit. Some are attractively cased with their appropriate accessories; some are beautifully engraved and fitted with fancy stocks; others bear presentation inscriptions; a few are equipped with attachable shoulder stocks which transform a pistol into a carbine. (More spurious or replica shoulder stocks are to be found than the original Colt-made products, and one must be wary when buying.)

The war years 1861-1865 brought about rapid development of the metallic cartridge. Smith & Wesson held a very important patent which reserved for them until 1869 the use of the straight bored-through revolver cylinder. Colt got around this patent by a system developed by one of their most talented workmen, F. Alexander Thuer. Thuer's system was designed to accommodate tapered front-loading cartridges. Any of the center-hammer Colt percussion pistols could be quickly converted to use the Thuer metallic cartridges by an interchangeable cylinder and conversion ring. Pistols so equipped are extremely rare and quite valuable. They are so rare and valuable that an enterprising dealer in Mexico has manufactured a large number of replica cylinders and rings, which have made the purchase of a Thuer conversion pistol very risky unless authenticated by a qualified expert.

When the Rollin White patent held by Smith & Wesson was no longer an obstacle, the Colt company converted many of their percussion models so that they might be chambered for .38 and .44 metallic cartridges, either rimfire or center-fire. This period was merely a lull after the storms of war, wherein Colt managed to use up a lot of parts on hand and work on designs of pistols specifically planned for the metallic cartridge. It is an interesting period, however, and the collector will find many Colt variations. The .44 rimfire model, with no conversion ring and a raised rear sight on the barrel (ancestor of Colt's "Peacemaker") is actively sought by collectors and has good value.

Among the first of Colt's new models in the cartridge line were their single shot derringer pistols. These were all .41 caliber. The first was marked with the Colt company name and address and "No. 1" on the barrel; it is all metal. The second bore a "No. 2" marking and has wood stocks. The third was designed by F. A. Thuer, had a side-swinging barrel action instead of the swing-down system of the first two, and was simply marked *COLT*. Colt resumed production of a derringer similar to the Thuer model in recent years, but it is .22 caliber rather than the original .41 rimfire.

Another early cartridge model is the house pistol of 1871, called the "Cloverleaf" because of the odd shape of the four-shot cylinder. A similar pistol, but with a round five-shot cylinder, was also produced. Rarest variations are the "Cloverleaf" pistols which are fitted with short 1½-inch round or octagon barrels.

Closely following the "Cloverleaf" pistols in the early 1870s came a series of rimfire and center-fire pistols of pocket size. There is an "open-top" model in .22 rimfire, notable only because the type with an integral ejector housing is quite scarce. The "New Line" pocket pistols had a solid frame and screw-in barrels. Most of them had a rounded "bird-head" grip, sheath trigger, and fluted cylinder. Calibers were .22, .30, .32, .38, and .41. From this basic design came a model of especial interest to collectors—the police and house revolvers with a flat instead of a rounded butt. The police revolvers were chambered for .38 center-fire cartridges and were fitted with hard-rubber stocks on the lower section of which were the figures of a "cop and thug." These police pistols and the companion flat-butt house pistols are good collector items.

Just as Colt had really produced a winner in the 1851 percussion Navy model, they came up with another "all-time great" in their Single Action Army cartridge revolver of 1873. This revolver has been continually manufactured from 1873 to the present except for the period 1941-1955.

Many collectors seek nothing but this one model. It can be found in many different calibers, various barrel lengths, with or without cartridge ejector, in standard or target model, and with a variety of finishes and stocks.

The .22 rimfire and .44 rimfire specimens, few in number, are actively sought as are the target models with flat-top frames. Specimens with A, B, or C quality engraving and carved ivory stocks are in good demand and bring substantial prices.

This is the revolver which has dominated all others in western use for many years. Modern TV shows would have a hard time getting along without this good old "Frontier," sometimes also called the "Single Action," or the "Peacemaker."

A companion piece of similar mechanical design is known as the Bisley model. The major differences are that the Bisley has a broader hammer and trigger, and the grip has a longer, humpbacked contour. The Bisley model was also made in many calibers and various barrel lengths, and in standard or flat-top target frame design. See photo 13-4.

Self-cocking revolvers had been on the market back in the percussion days and were a subject of great interest to Colt designers. By the first of 1877 Colt had a self-cocking model ready. Collectors call this the "Lightning" model. About the greatest claim to fame this model has is that Billy the Kid is said to have used one, a rather dubious distinction. Gunsmiths hate to work on these "Lightning" revolvers and collectors give them very little attention. One model, however, is as scarce as hen's teeth, and that is a .32 caliber *target* model. Most of the standard models were chambered for .38 and .41 center-fire cartridges.

Larger self-cocking Army and frontier pistols, with bird-head grip like the smaller "Lightning" pistols, came along and are known as models of 1878 and 1902. They were not very popular. The best collectors' pieces are the rare target model and the so-called "house" model which is made with a short barrel and no ejector.

We pass now into the extensive realm of Colt revolvers with swing-out cylinders. The models are many. Some, like early Marine Corps revolvers, are rather scarce and desirable. In general, collectors will find the target models and engraved specimens good collector material. Others, of which production was small, will also have appeal.

The early Colt automatic pistols are popular among those who find interest in automatic weapons. There is good material here for the collector, as a study of the different models will reveal; many are the product of John Browning's genius. See photo 13-4.

Colt long arms, too, are worthy of the collector's interest—from the Paterson or Hartford cylinder arms through the Civil War Colt rifled muskets, the Franklin, the Berdan, the double rifles, the lever and pump action rifles, and the Gatling guns.

One fact the Colt collector must be willing to accept—he can never find every variation of all the Colt models ever made. There are too many models and too many variations. Furthermore, values on Colt arms of interest to collectors are now so high that one need only consider the average $500 price tag on a Dragoon Colt to realize he could have thousands of dollars tied up in variations of that one model alone.

Many collectors are wisely selecting one particular period of manufacture or one model of Colt firearm, devoting their energies to searching out every variation in that period or of that model. Others satisfy their Colt collecting desires by assembling good representative specimens of the less expensive models. It is indeed a very rich field for specialization. But unless you are a millionaire, it may be frustrating and hard on the bank account if you try to collect all the rare and high-priced models. It can be good fun just collecting the lower-priced pieces and adding a rare one now and then when chance brings one your way at a modest price.

Much has been written about Colt firearms that will interest and inform the collector. A few of the books you will find helpful are: *Colt Firearms* (Serven), *Colt's Variations of the Old Model Pocket Pistol 1848-1872* (Shumaker), *Colt, the Man, the Arms, the Company* (Mitchell), *The Peacemaker and Its Rivals* (Parsons), *The Story of Colt's Revolver* (Edwards).

the Pepperbo

14.

The common name for one type of multi-shot pistol is quite intriguing—the Pepperpot, or Pepperbox. After one gains experience in collecting these pistols, the name gains more significance and seems very appropriate. Pepperbox pistols appear to have been used mostly as a close-up weapon and were pointed rather than aimed. The multiple shots made it possible to "sprinkle" shots at the target.

In man's search for a multiple-shot weapon, the Pepperbox made an important contribution. By combining three or more barrels around a central axis and revolving these barrels, either by hand or by mechanical action, the desired multiple shots from one loading were obtained. The transition to the early form of revolver, like the Colt, was fairly simple; it can be broadly stated that the barrel group of the Pepperbox was shortened and a single barrel attached in front of the shortened barrel group which thus became a cylinder.

Apparently, the first weapons of the Pepperbox type date far back in the history of firearms even though not many have survived to become valuable gems of collectors. Once in a great while a really old revolving matchlock Pepperbox of three barrels or more is found. No doubt there are specimens which could be called Pepperboxes from the wheel lock and snaphaunce eras.

There were so many types and variations in Pepperboxes manufactured in the 19th century, in this country and abroad, that a collector usually can find plenty to absorb his interest and draw on the capacity of his pocketbook. Many of these pistols are percussion, but there are a few that employed the needle fire and other firing systems. The cartridge era also saw many Pepperboxes manufactured, of which a few are illustrated here.

In the flintlock period, English gunsmiths had made some very fine flintlock revolving pistols, or Pepperboxes. A beautiful pair of 7-barrel flintlock Pepperboxes by H. Nock, of London, is shown. There are many surviving examples of this type by English gunsmiths. Some students of firearms believe that most of them were actually manufactured by the Nock firm of London. Although several exceptions are known, flintlock Pepperboxes usually are hand revolved; all barrels are loaded at one time, but it is necessary to prime for each shot. This disadvantage was overcome in the per-

Pistols

14-1. Matched pair of "H. Nock—London" flintlock Pepperbox pistols, seven shots, formerly owned by the editor and now in the extensive Frank R. Horner collection.

cussion period which followed. However, enough of these early revolving flintlocks have survived that many are represented in general as well as Pepperbox collections.

Following the flintlock period, there were many different types and varieties of Pepperboxes manufactured in this country and in Europe. In the following paragraphs we shall discuss briefly the more usual types and call attention to some of their interesting features. While the Pepperbox attained its greatest popularity during the percussion period, its popularity carried over for quite a while into the cartridge, or so-called modern era.

In the United States, you are more likely to find Pepperboxes where the multiple bores are fashioned from a solid block of metal. In European firearms, you find a great many Pepperboxes where there are separate barrels joined together. Later old-world makers, particularly in England, followed the usual American system and manufactured many Pepperboxes from a solid block of metal through which the bores were drilled. You will find single-action and double-action mechanisms, the hammer on top or underneath the barrel and sometimes concealed; some with self-cocking hammers, others with double hammers and multiple hammers; revolving firing pins; nipples extending out from the rear of the barrel at a right angle or some other angle; some with a nipple shield to prevent multiple discharge and others without; barrel releases of various types; and many varying features too numerous to discuss in an article of this length.

Incidentally, "Revolving Pistol" is the name used in advertisements and found in instructions with cased sets to describe pistols of this type. The term "Pepperbox," is one applied by the public and not by the manufacturer.

Generally speaking, American Pepperboxes have a different look than those made in Europe. Their composition is simpler; there is less engraving or the engraving is not as fine as European work; and grips are usually plain. Many American Pepperboxes were made by Allen, or under one of his patents. Since this book has a section devoted exclusively to Allen products, we shall refer here only briefly to those made by Allen, or under his patents.

Of the pistols other than Allen, some that have been generally believed to be made by Darling, are brass-barreled Pepperboxes. Doubt has been expressed by a few collectors as to whether these types were actually made by the Darling brothers. Research on this subject is being carried out as this book is being written and it may result in an interesting story for Pepperbox collectors in the future. Regardless of who made them or where they were made, these brass-barrel pistols are not plentiful but in the past a person could always find one and add it to his collection if he was willing to pay a somewhat higher price than that of the average Pepperbox. The usual types are four and six barrels but there is one known specimen of three barrels. Generally, the markings are J. Engh, A.C.S., A.I.S., I.E.H., and J.E.H., although not all of them are so marked. Illustrated is a brass-barrel Pepperbox of six shots.

In recent years, a few B. & B. M. Darling Pepperboxes of the known April 13, 1836 patent design, with an all-iron barrel group and quite different mechanism than the brass-barrel type, have been found and added to collections. It appears that this 1836 type Darling Pepperbox is one of the most valuable as well as one of the most difficult firearms to acquire. Not too much information has been discovered as to the background or activities of the Darlings.

Other interesting American percussion Pepperboxes were made by Pecare & Smith, Leonard, Stocking, Bacon, Robbins & Lawrence, and Blunt & Syms. They are relatively scarce and hard to obtain, especially the first two mentioned. Other percussion Pepperbox names to look for, most of which resemble the Allens, are: Allen & Wheelock, J. G. Bolen, A. W. Spies, Young & Smith, Tryon, Lane & Reed, Manhattan, Washington Arms, Phenix Armory, Union, Marston & Knox, Sprague & Marston, and W. W. Marston. Among the cartridge Pepperboxes you will find such makers' names as Bacon, Continental, Remington, Rupertus, and Sharps.

One American Pepperbox which invites speculation is the fifth from top, right row, in photo 14-2. As you will notice, it has an underhammer, the barrel revolves by hand, and it has a grip very

14.2. From top, left row: 1/"**G. Leonard, Jr., Charlestown**" 4-shot, caliber .31, overall 6⅝ inches unusual cocking lever and firing trigger—striker revolves. 2/"Pecare & Smith's Patent 1849" 4-shot, caliber .32, overall 7 inches; sights on each barrel—brass frame. 3/"J. P. Tirrell Maker —North Bridgewater" 6-shot, caliber .26, 7¼ inch O.A., smooth bronze barrel, probably experimental. 4/Brass frame and barrel pistol. 5/"Bacon & Co., Norwich C.T." 6-shot, SA, caliber .30, O.A. 7⅝ inch, unusual under- hammer. 6/"Pecare & Smith's Patent 1849" 10-shot, caliber .26, O.A. 8 inch, concealed hammer, barrel cover, iron frame. 7/"Blunt & Syms New York" 6-shot, caliber .31, O.A. 8-inch, first model, no shield over nipples, Ger- man silver grips. 8/"Robbins & Lawrence Company— Leonard's Patent 1849" 5-shot, caliber .30, O.A. 9¼ inch, barrels unscrew for loading, barrel block breaks down to cap. 9/"American" 18-barrel block, caliber .34, O.A. 9½-inch, inner ring 5 barrels, outer ring 13 barrels, hand revolved. 10/"American Primitive" 4-shot, caliber .75 O.A. 11½-inch shotgun-type barrels, crude and unusual.

From top, right row: 1/Blunt & Syms unmarked 6-shot caliber .37, O.A. 11¼-inch, later model, saw-handle grip, dragoon size. 2/"Allen & Thurber Worcester Patented 1837," .34 caliber 9½-inch O.A., called "49er," spur trigger guard. 3/"Tryon" and "Allen & Thurber—Nor- wich C.T."—"Allen's Patent" 6-shot, .36 caliber, 9¼-inch O.A. 4/"Stocking & Co. Worcester" 6-shot, SA, caliber .30, O.A. 8½-inch, operated by lever hammer, extra spur trigger guard. 5/Unmarked rare underhammer, 6-shot, caliber .30, 8¼-inch O.A. frame, grip hammer like New England underhammer single shot pistols. 6/"Hyde & Goodrich New Orleans" and "Allen's Patent" 6-shot, .31 caliber, 6¾-inch O.A., slotted hammer for sighting. 7/ "Manhattan 3-shot, caliber .32, O.A. 6." 8/Allen & Wheelock "Allen's Patent" 4-shot, caliber .32 O.A. 5⅞-inch, no nipple cover. 9/"Rupertus' Patent Pistol Mfg. Co.—Philad." 8-shot, .22 caliber R.F., 5⅞-inch O.A., unusual loading and safety device. 10/"Continental Arms Co. Norwich, Conn." 5-shot, S.A., R.F., .22 caliber, O.A. 5¼ inches.

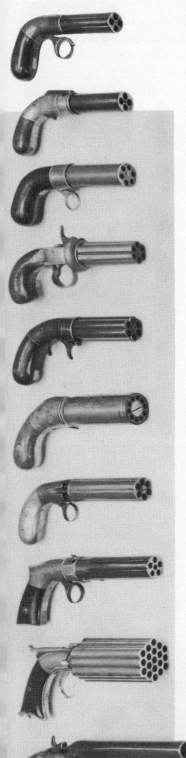

similar to underhammer, single shot pistols. There are only a few known specimens and there is no marking.

Of the old world Pepperboxes, the better known are the Belgium and French makes with several barrels attached together, and the English with the block type of barrel. The Belgium and French types are most generally known as the Mariette and the number of barrels most commonly seen are four, six, and eight, but quite a variety were made. While many bear the typical Belgian ELG proofmark, there are others which bear names of gunsmiths from other countries.

Germany also used the separate barrel type of assembly. Among German makers, Herman seems to be the best known. Some of his unusual barrel and firing arrangements are seen in plate 14-3, left row. They also seem to be of a better quality than the usual assembled-barrel groups from Belgium and France.

The English gunsmiths developed some very beautiful firearms. Grips are generally finely checkered, frames are usually engraved, and the barrels are of good quality. Among the types with four bores in the same block are the orthodox revolving systems and there are those which have two hammers and the barrel is hand-revolved for 180 degrees so that the two barrels may be fired, one succeeding the other. The six-bore in one block is the most usual type found, produced by a large number of makers. Many of these pistols are beautifully cased; at least one maker, Parker Field & Company, furnished a loading flask similar to that of the Paterson Colt—the charges in all barrels can be deposited at the same time.

English gunsmiths also made a number of cartridge-type Pepperboxes. Some were made with 12 to 18 barrels, all contained within one cylinder block.

Included in the classification of Pepperboxes are the multiple firing weapons such as the Sharps 4-barrel, and similar pistols where the barrels do not revolve but the firing pins do. Although there are not so many makers of this type, a great many pistols were manufactured.

Reference may be made to Lewis Winant's book, *Pepperbox Firearms* for additional information on weapons of this general style. An interesting article by Sam Smith devoted to Darling Pepperboxes appeared in the old *The Gun Report* magazine, Vol. III, No. 3, January, 1942.

Up to the time of this writing, collecting Pepperboxes has been reasonably easy because fewer collectors have been interested and because it has not required a large investment. Many ingenious devices for firing will be found in Pepperboxes and it is not difficult to find a hundred or more variations in arrangement and number of barrels, size of bore, methods of revolving barrels or firing pins, arrangements of nipples and nipple shields, loading, priming, etc. If you are already a collector or join the group of Pepperbox collectors, a lot of pleasure is in store for you, so here's to happy hunting!

14-3. From top, left row: 1/English "James Harper," large, 5-shot, .58 caliber, O.A. 11 inches, cap box in butt heavily engraved. 2/Italian "G. Pilla," large 6-shot, .60 caliber, O.A. 10½ inches, double-action, concealed hammer. 3/Belgian "Mariette Brevete" 18-shot, .32 caliber, O.A. 8 inches, 18 separate barrels, 6 on the inner circle and 12 on the outer circle. 4/Unmarked, probably Herman, 8-shot, .34 caliber, O.A. 9½ inches sight on frame, concealed hammer. 5/German-Belgian "J.J.H. Brevete," 8-shot, caliber .50, O.A. 9 inches unusual arrangement of barrel group, probably Herman. 6/English "Manton & Co.—Calcutta," 4-shot, .50 caliber, 9¾ inches O.A., two hammers, two triggers, revolved by hand 180 degrees. 7/English "J.R. Cooper—Maker" early 6-shot, .34 caliber, 8½ inches O.A., unusual barrel release. 8/Unmarked English 6-shot with bayonet, .36 caliber, 7½ inches O.A., 12⅞ inches O.A. with bayonet—from cased set. 9/German-Belgian "Herman Brevete," 4-shot, caliber .48, O.A. 9½ inches, unusual double action with 4 hammers like a player piano.

From top, right row: 1/Irish "Wm. Norman—Dublin" 6-shot, .44 caliber, 8-inches O.A., unusual sighting and firing mechanism. 2/English "Smith—London" 7-shot, SA, .32 caliber, 7⅝ inch O.A., hand revolved to right, large nipple shield. 3/English "Budding —Maker" 5-shot, .32 caliber, 8 inches O.A., bronze barrels and frame, unusually simple firing mechanism. 4/English "Samuel Nock—London" 4-barrel, .50 caliber, 8¼ inches O.A. 5/Irish "W. & J. Rigby—Dublin" 6-shot, .38 caliber, 7 inches O.A., buttons release cylinder. 6/French "Boissy" 5-shot pinfire, .41 caliber, 8⅛ inches O.A., animal head hammer. 7/"Rissack Patent" 4-shot needle fire, caliber .36, O.A. 7 inches, SA barrels revolve by hand to right. 8/English "Chas. Lancaster—161 New Bond St., London" 6-shot .30 caliber, 6½ inches O.A., finely made. 9/English "F. Hill & Son— Sheffield" 12-shot, DA-RF, .22 caliber, 5 inches O.A.

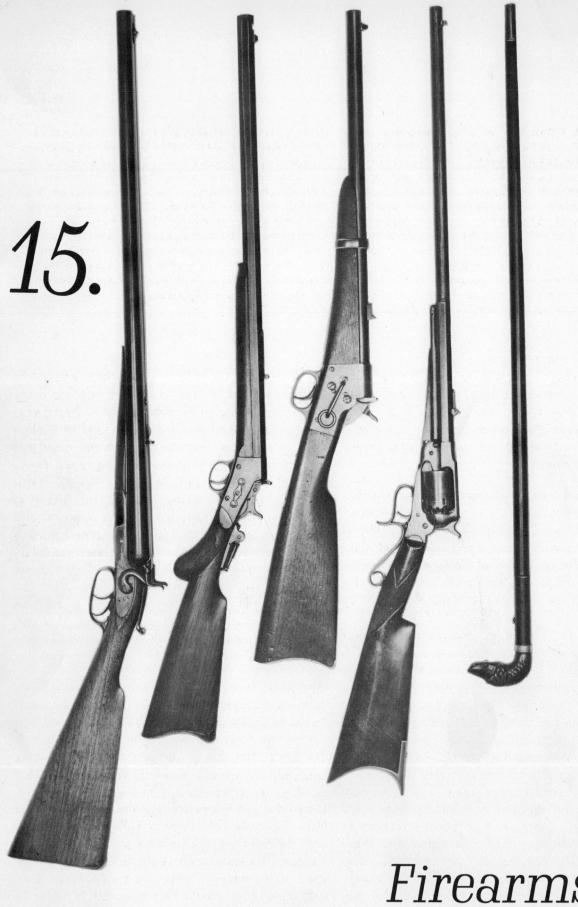

the
Firearms of
Remington

Eliphalet Remington (called by some the father of American gun manufacturing) had a well-established business at Ilion, New York, by 1856. After about forty years of endeavor, his fame had spread throughout the United States and his gun barrels were in great demand.

Remington had proved his manufacturing capability with the completion of a government contract for Jenks carbines. His shop at Ilion was a Mecca for young inventors who came to work out their ideas. With the expiration of Colt's patent protection in 1857, Eliphalet Remington set about producing handarms. The first revolvers produced by Remington were small impotent .31 caliber percussion revolvers. They were manufactured under patents issued to Fordyce Beals on June 24, 1856 and May 26, 1857. Fordyce Beals was no newcomer to Ilion, having been there in connection with the Jenks contract in 1846. The strangest part of the Beals invention was the fact that the hand and the activating arm were on the outside of the weapon. This revolver was manufactured in some quantity and was numbered in batches or series; it was introduced with a small trigger guard and was easily concealed on the person or in a hand. About 5,500 were produced. There are four distinct versions of this model, indicating that Remington and Beals were constantly working on improvements. The second model was produced without the trigger guard, a sheath trigger was added and the grip shape was changed. The outside activating arm changed in shape and was now round. It has been estimated that 1,000 were produced in this series, but very few are known to have survived.

On September 14, 1858, a patent was granted to Fordyce Beals that was to be the basis for many thousands of handguns produced by E. Remington & Sons. This patent covered a new kind of loading lever, so arranged that the cylinder pin could not be withdrawn without the loading lever being dropped. The first weapon produced under this patent was what is known to collectors today as the Beals pocket, third model. This was the first Remington revolver to have an attached loading lever. The third model was also manufactured in .31 caliber. It had the sheath trigger of the second model but the cylinder was longer than either the first or second model. The grips took a different shape and were checkered gutta-percha. This arm still had the outside pawl which was round like that found on the second model.

War clouds were looming on the horizon and Remington had secured contracts for rifled muskets and for the remodeling of muskets. The government was buying revolvers and Remington wanted some of this trade, but the government was buying only large caliber weapons. Almost at the same time that Remington's third model pocket was produced, Remington put into production the Beals .36 caliber Navy. This was what might be called a conventional arm; the revolving mechanism was placed inside the weapon. The first models of the Beals Navy had the same single wing cylinder pin as the Beals third model pocket revolvers. This gave way to the more conventional double wing pin found on all Remington percussion revolvers produced later. With the introduction of the Beals Navy, the production of the small first, second and third models ceased.

In 1859 another inventor came on the Remington scene; he was Joseph Rider. Rider was granted a patent on a breech device for a single shot pistol. This device held the percussion cap and was removable. It utilized the fulminate of mercury in the cap as the total charge. No powder was used. The weapon fired a .170 caliber ball. It was marketed by Remington as the "parlor pistol," and was made of brass. Only twenty-one specimens are currently known to exist. In the same year Rider obtained another patent for a self-cocking or double-action revolver. This was produced in .31 caliber and apparently replaced the pocket revolvers designed by Beals. This revolver is referred to by collectors as the Rider DA with the "mushroom" cylinder, the terminology coming from the fact that nipples are set into the rear of the cylinder at a peculiar angle, giving it the appearance of being expanded.

Fixed ammunition was now becoming popular but patents held by Smith & Wesson made manufacture almost impossible without specific licensing. By 1860 another inventor had come on the scene at Ilion. Patents were granted to William Elliot for a small pepperbox-type pistol that utilized fixed ammunition; it is commonly called the "Zig Zag" pistol. It consisted of six barrels revolved around a center pin by the action of a stud riding in grooves cut into the side of the barrels. The hammer was concealed.

On April 13, 1861, Eliphalet Remington died and Ilion mourned the loss of their leading citizen. But business continued as usual under the direction of Eliphalet Remington's three sons—Philo taking over the management of the plants, Sam taking over sales, and Eliphalet III doing the accounting for the firm.

Still another pocket pistol was introduced into the Remington line a short time later. This was the .22 caliber vest pocket pistol. This single shot arm was manufactured under a patent that had been granted to Elliot on October 1, 1861. A portion of the patent claimed the hammer served as a combination breech and hammer. This little pistol enjoyed continued production for many years.

In a desperation attempt to secure government con-

tracts, Remington introduced the .44 caliber Remington-Beals Army revolver. This was a larger copy of the Beals Navy which had enjoyed popular acceptance, approximately 14,000 having been produced. At this time the line being produced was the Rider DA .31, the Zig Zag .22 RF, the vest pocket .22 RF pistol, and the Beals .36 caliber Navy revolver.

A patent had been issued to William Elliot on May 29, 1860, for another pepperbox-type pistol with stationary barrels using a revolving firing pin. This gun was not produced until late in 1861. Again Elliot's patent, October 1, 1861, was a part of the design. The pistol was produced in a .32 caliber RF four-shot model and in .22 caliber five-shot model. Production was briefly brisk but these little weapons disappeared from listings soon after the Civil War.

The introduction of the Beals .44 caliber Army was to change the tide of things to follow. The Beals Army was introduced in a form identical to the Navy except that the rammer shape and the overall size were increased. This was a six-shot weapon with an 8-inch barrel. The barrel stamp contained the familiar Beals patent date, September 14, 1858. The first type had a short production run; after about 2,000 revolvers were produced the overall pattern was changed to Elliot's patent, dated December 16, 1861. This patent was intended to improve the arm by employing a cylinder pin which could be drawn without dropping the loading lever. This was done by channeling the lever and then grooving the cylinder pin so that it would slide in the lever channel.

The Remington firm received their first government order for 1,000 pistols and shipped the .44 Beals Army revolvers. These proved satisfactory and negotiations were completed for the purchase of more .44 revolvers and also some .36 Navy revolvers. Remington's response to this was to ship the newly patented '61 Models. (This was referred to by some writers as the "Old Model." We do not feel this is the correct terminology and would prefer to call it the '61 Model, due to the date and the barrel marking of the weapon.) The total production of the '61 Models was about 8,000 in .44 caliber and 6,000 in .36 caliber.

The arm took on a new look. It became more streamlined; the square corners of the loading lever were rounded. The cylinder pin wings had a sweep that suggested streamlining. The result of this so-called "improvement" could have been very damaging for the Remington concern had this not been a time of war. The method of withdrawing the pin without the loading lever being lowered was a good theory, but forgotten was the fact that with the gun in a holster, the muzzle pointing down, the pin could work itself out and the cylinder could fall out when the gun was withdrawn from its holster. This could be disastrous under battle conditions.

Remington called in most of these weapons and inserted a screw into the channel of the rammer so that the pin could not be withdrawn unless the loading lever was dropped. The Model '61 was quickly dropped from production and was replaced by the original Beals model (patented September 14, 1858). However, the streamlined lines of the '61 rammer were retained. It is our contention that Remington numbered all Beals Army and Navy revolvers and '61 Models consecutively.

An interesting area awaits the collector in the .44 Beals Army field; within the serial number range of 10,000 through 15,000 all parts used to manufacture the '61 models were used up and we find many interesting combinations. Around serial number 15,000 the transition to the New Model was complete but the barrel marking "New Model" did not appear until serial numbers 23,000. The same transitions were evident in the .36 Navy revolvers.

Lack of sales of the New Model .36 revolver eventually led to the development of the Rider double-action .36 Belt Model, manufactured under Rider's patent of 1859. It has the same outward appearance of the New Model Army or Navy but is scaled down. A full fluted cylinder on some specimens represents a variation from the standard round cylinder. This arm was also produced under Beals'

patent in single-action, known as the Single-Action .36 Belt Model. Sales on these lagged some and Remington went back to the .31 caliber revolvers to capture the home trade. Remington's new .31 revolver was a very small version of the big New Model, scaled down and produced with a sheath trigger. There was a favorable reception and a goodly number was produced.

Remington had further ideas; next from their workbenches came an intermediate size weapon. Collectors refer to it today as the Police Model. It was .36 caliber and a complete scaled-down version of the New Model Army or Navy models.

Early in 1865 split-breech pistols were put into production. They were manufactured in .30 RF and .41 RF. Remington applied this split-breech action to carbines, and about 20,000 were purchased by the government. A few split-breech pistols were fitted with skeleton stocks (these are referred to by collectors as Buggy Rifles). The split-breech was manufactured under patents issued to Elliot and Rider.

In 1865 the firm of E. Remington and Sons was incorporated under the same name. In April, Lee surrendered to General Grant and the war was over. The government set about canceling all orders. This brought about a serious situation at Ilion. The local bank went into receivership and was closed. People were out of work. The Remington firm had overextended themselves. But the Remington family at this time was a family of considerable means, and personal fortunes were poured back into the business to save it.

On December 12, 1865, Elliot was granted a patent for an improvement on a multi-barreled firearm. This particular model enjoyed the longest production run of any Remington pistol. Under this patent all of the double derringers were produced. The first model was produced without any extractors. About 2,000 were produced like this; then an extractor was provided that extended across the face of the breech with a slide on the left side of the arm. From this period forward, all of the derringers were equipped with this extractor. Production commenced in 1866 and extended until discontinued by Remington in

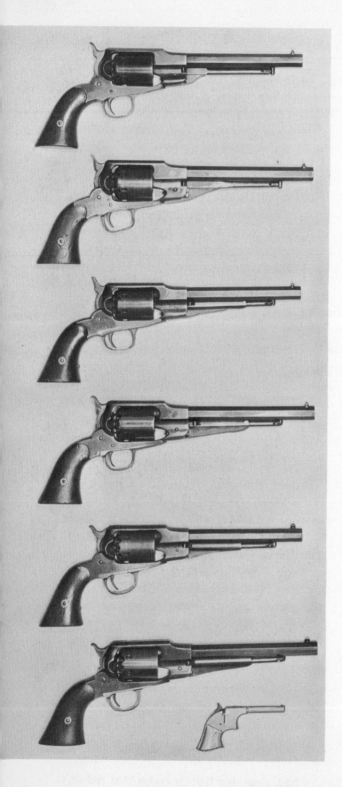

1935. During this time it is estimated that 150,000 double derringer pistols were produced.

The arm that was to change life in general at Ilion was the rolling block pistol. The rolling block action was based on a patent issued to Leonard Geiger on January 27, 1863. In November 1866 the government purchased 5,000 single shot .50-caliber rimfire pistols with spur triggers and 8½-inch barrels; this order was increased to 6,500 in 1867. This model is referred to by collectors as the 1865 Navy.

In 1870 the government issued an order for these single shot pistols to be altered to .50 caliber center-fire, trigger guards were to be added and the barrels cut down to 7 inches. These cut down versions are sometimes referred to as the 1867 Model; actually they are converted 1865 models. In 1871 the government placed an order for another 5,000 single shot pistols in .50 caliber, these known as the 1871 Army. This model had a different sweep to the frame, the grip was longer, and the grip strap was bolted through both sides of the grip frame with a single bolt. Remington also sold many of these single shot pistols to the general public, using the '65 Model frames.

On August 22, 1867, Elliott was granted a patent under which E. Remington & Sons manufactured the single shot .41 derringer, sometimes referred to by collectors as the "Mississippi Derringer."

Many of the cap-and-ball pistols were returned to the factory for installation of metallic cartridge cylinders. This helped to turn the tide of depression that had befallen Ilion. The rolling block action, fitted to carbines and rifles, started business on the upswing and Ilion again headed toward prosperity.

In 1871, Rider was granted a patent for a magazine-fed repeating pistol, but this arm was produced only in limited numbers. The reason for its production here eludes us at this writing, except that it was a repeater and not a revolver.

15-2. From top: 1/.36 caliber Beals Navy. 2/.44 caliber Beals Army. 3/.36 caliber 1861 Model *(this pistol and the .44 immediately below are also referred to as the OLD MODEL but that classification is confusing).* 4/.44 caliber 1861 Model. 5/New Model .36 caliber. 6/New Model .44 caliber. 7/.170 caliber Parlor Pistol, showing contrast between this midget among Remington arms and the big .44 above it.

On October 21, 1873, a patent was issued to W. S. Smoot and E. Remington & Sons for a cartridge revolver that combined a solid frame and barrel arrangement. It was also equipped with an integral ejector for ejecting spent cartridge cases. This revolver was produced in various forms until the company failed in 1888. The first model was a .30 caliber rimfire arm. It had a distinguishing revolving recoil shield to close off the loading gate when the arm was loaded. The second model was .32 rimfire, and this one had a fixed recoil shield. The third model Smoot was a larger version of the previous models and had a saw handle grip. The second issue of this model was produced with a bird-head grip. It also departed from the original patent in that the barrels were screwed into the frame. This model was available in both center-fire and rimfire ammunition. The fourth model was a stubby affair and was produced in limited numbers in both .38 center-fire and rimfire, and in .41 center-fire and rimfire. An ejector was not included in this model. A smaller version in .22 caliber was introduced and is referred to by collectors as the "Iroquois" Revolver. Many were marked Iroquois.

In 1875 Remington introduced their "New Model Army" in .44 Remington caliber; a single-action revolver that was to compete with Colt's single-action Army model. Many of these arms were exported, but production never got far off the ground; it has been estimated that 25,000 were produced. The export market had now run out of steam and again Remington faced a crisis. This time they were not to recoup as they had done in 1865. In 1888 the firm went into receivership, and a corporation with Marcellus Hartley at its head was the purchaser. The new corporation was known as the Remington Arms Co.

Many pistols and revolvers in general were removed from the line. The single-action was one handgun that was put on the market in a slightly revised form and it is known today as the 1890 SA. The principal difference between its earlier version was the reduction or cutting away of the web under the barrel.

Rolling block pistol parts were left over, and in 1891 a model was introduced with a 10-inch barrel known as the "Target

15-3. From top: 1/Beals Pocket First Model .31 caliber. 2/Beals Pocket Second Model .31 caliber. 3/Beals Pocket Third Model .31 caliber, first with loading lever. 4/Rider Double Action Pocket .31 caliber. 5/New Model Pocket .31 caliber. 6/Rider D.A. Belt Model .36 caliber (with full fluted cylinder). 7/Single Action Belt Model .36 caliber. 8/Police Model .36 caliber with 6½ inch barrel, also called the "Slim Jim" (also available with 3½ inch, 4½ inch, and 5½ inch barrels).

153

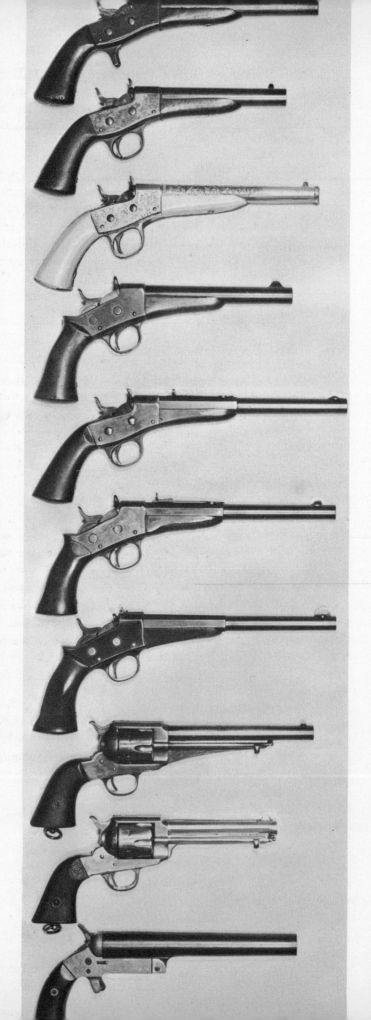

15-4. From top: 1/1865 Model Navy .50 caliber rimfire, 8½ inch barrel, stud trigger. 2/Converted 1865 Model, barrel cut to 7 inches, trigger guard added, changed to .50 caliber center-fire, incorrectly referred to as 1867. 3/1867 Model .50 caliber rim or center-fire, 8½ inch barrel, this is a transition arm. *(Engraved pistol pictured is one of a cased pair).* 4/1871 Model Army .50 caliber center-fire, 8 inch barrel. Note the new sweep to the grip and the frame change. 5/1891 Target Model .22 caliber rimfire. This is a very rare version of this model as it utilizes an 1865 Model frame. 6/1891 Target Model .32 S & W cartridge, barrel is 10 inches; this one uses the more conventional 1871 Model frame. 7/1901 Target Model .22 caliber, grips checkered, rear sight mounted to the frame *(also made in other calibers).* 8/1875 Single Action or New Army Revolver, 7½ inch barrel, .44 caliber Remington *(also found in .44 caliber W.C.F.).* 9/1890 Single Action Revolver, .44 W.C.F., has a 5¾ inch barrel; can be distinguished by the cut away web under the barrel and composition grips with monogram; it is signed Remington Arms Co. *(do not be fooled by reworked 1875 Models).* 10/Mark III Flare Pistol, 10 gauge 9 inch barrel, brass frame, used in World War I.

15-5. From top: 1/Elliot's .22 caliber Zig Zag Revolver. 2/Vest Pocket Pistol .22 caliber. 3/5-shot .22 caliber Pocket Pistol. 4/4-shot .32 caliber RF Pocket Pistol. 5/Split Breech Pistol .30 caliber *(also other rimfire calibers up to .41).* 6/Double Derringer .41 caliber rimfire. 7/Elliot's SS .41 caliber Derringer *(also called "Mississippi" Derringer).* 8/Rider Magazine Pistol, .32 caliber extra short rimfire. 9/First Model Smoot .30 caliber rimfire *(revolving recoil shield).* 10/Second Model Smoot .32 caliber rimfire *(fixed shield).* 11/Third Model Smoot .38 caliber rim and centerfire *(also made with saw-handle type grip);* all First, Second, and Third Model Smoots have extractors. 12/Fourth Model Smoot .41 caliber rim and center-fire *(no extractor).* 13/Remington Iroquois .22 caliber. 14/Remington Automatic Pistol .32 and .380 caliber *(also .45 ACP for government tests— the tests were not successful).*

Pistol"; its last appearance was in 1901 catalogs. This model had checkered grips and fore-end, and was finely finished. It is referred to by collectors today as the 1901 Target Model. The only other pistol in production at this time was the double derringer.

In 1912 Remington Arms Co. merged with the Union Metallic Cartridge Co. and was known thereafter as Remington Arms Co.-UMC. With the approach of World War I, rifles were manufactured in greater numbers than ever before. Pistol manufacture was limited to the Mark III Flare Pistol. This was a single shot ten-gauge weapon with a 9-inch barrel, brass frame, and plain wood grips. Also, Colt Model 1911 caliber .45 automatic pistols were produced for the government under a subcontract.

Early in 1918 development started on an automatic pistol, based on patents issued to John Pedersen, and it was marketed as the Model 51. The Remington automatic was manufactured in .32 ACP and .380 ACP calibers. In 1919 several were made up in .45 ACP caliber and submitted for governmental trial; they proved unsatisfactory. Manufacture ceased in 1934. The only remaining arm to tie the past to the new company was the double derringer. This derringer was produced in limited numbers until 1935. No pistols or revolvers were then produced until the introduction of the XP-100 in 1963. The single shot XP-100 shoots the new .221 "Fireball" cartridge. It is the first handgun produced by Remington since 1935 when the double derringer was dropped from the line. The XP-100 is a bolt-action arm, has an overall length of 16¾ inches, a weight of 3¾ pounds, and has a molded nylon stock. This gun was introduced at the National Rifle Association convention in Washington, D. C., on March 23, 1963. The overall appearance resembles a Buck Rogers Special, but it fits into the hand like a tailored glove. It is a weapon made for shooting, designed by shooters.

In conclusion, we can state that the Remington story is not over. Through all kinds of ups and downs, Remington guns have continued to appear on the market. One hundred and forty-seven years after Eliphalet Remington started building guns, Remington weapons are still coming off the workbenches.

Those collectors who are attracted to weapons only by their grace of line, quality of manufacture, and physical beauty, read no further—Confederate arms are not for you. This subject is for the more imaginative. It is for those who can sense the ingenuity, resourcefulness, and urgency behind apparent crudity, and for those who prize raw courage, devotion, and steadfastness to duty over mere physical attributes.

The reward of owning one of the comparatively few remaining Confederate guns lies not in their beauty but in wonderment at how twisted iron was made to substitute for steel, brass for iron, lead for brass, and so on down the line. Even the substitutions were not commonplace items. Brass was obtained from melted church bells, gladly donated throughout the South. The lead was from bullets salvaged from the battlefields, from roofing, and even in some cases from children's toys. Household knives and utensils were melted for their metallic content. Holding one of these arms one has the reasonably sure knowledge that it was actually handled by a gray-clad soldier; in addition, there is the very strong possibility that it was actually fired northward in anger. In this respect the Confederate arm is unique, for despite the remarkable efficiency of its Ordnance Department under the able general, Josiah Gorgas, the South was continuously faced with a shortage of materiel with which to wage war. Thus the interval between manufacture of a gun (sword or pistol) until placed in the hands of the waiting soldier, was dependent only upon the speed of transportation from armory to arsenal to field of battle. Indeed the lack of arms was so desperate in the early part of the war that many men were supplied only with six- or eight-foot poles tipped with iron—a weapon more antiquated than the flintlock rifle would be today.

Why such difficulty to produce war materiel? As opposed to the North, center of all kinds and types of manufacture, let us remember the culture of the South was geared only to an agricultural complex whose few industries were slanted accordingly. With the war, these were converted as quickly as possible to the making of revolvers instead of cotton gins, etc. In the specific case of the Nashville Plow Works, the ancient Biblical injunction was reversed and the firm henceforth produced only swords. With this in mind, let us examine the source of the weapons which enabled the South to resist overwhelming odds for four long and bloody years.

16.

16-1. From left: 1/First Model, Virginia Manufactory pistol. 2/Second Model, Virginia Manufactory pistol. 3/LeMat revolver, imported for use by Confederate forces. *(From collection of William A. Albaugh III)*

The ill-starred and ill-fated Confederacy was composed of the following eleven states: Virginia, North Carolina, South Carolina, Georgia, Tennessee, Alabama, Mississippi, Arkansas, Texas, Louisiana, and Florida. Varying quantities of weapons were made in all but the last named. We will discuss this manufacture in the given order of these states.

VIRGINIA

Virginia had had previous experience in the manufacture of arms. With remarkable foresightedness an armory had been established in Richmond and was in operation by 1802. The Virginia Manufactory, as it was known, operated only until 1821 but during this time it turned out large quantities of arms for her State Militia. With the gathering of the dark war clouds in 1860 the old armory was completely refurbished and it was here that the machinery and equipment taken from the U. S. Harpers Ferry Armory and Arsenal was set up after its seizure as "State property" on the eve of Virginia's secession from the Union, April 18, 1861.

Such State seizure was commonplace throughout the South and upon the secession of each, all federal property was seized and claimed by that state within whose boundaries it lay. As a matter of fact it was the refusal of the federal government to turn Fort Sumter, at Charleston, over to South Carolina that actually precipitated hostilities. While the actual amount of arms so gained was disappointingly small, the establishments themselves later proved valuable.

Harpers Ferry, however, was a real prize, for despite its attempted burning by the Federals, many thousand stands of arms and parts were taken, along with fine machinery for making the Model 1855 rifle and rifle-musket. These were promptly placed at the disposal of the newly formed government on loan "for duration of war" and upon being set up in Richmond became the largest small arms plant in the South as well as the heart of Confederate Ordnance. Here were produced thousands of rifle-muskets, carbines, and related items. The operation continued full blast until burned to the ground at the evacuation of Richmond in April, 1865—the end of the war.

Close by the Armory was the breech-loading Carbine Factory. Here, first under the private own-

the Confederate Firearms

ership of S. C. Robinson and later under government control, were manufactured some 3,000 imitation Sharps until the factory was removed to Tallassee, Alabama in 1864. Also close by was S. Sutherland, gunsmith, and many others of the same trade who were engaged principally in converting old flintlock arms to the then modern percussion type of ignition.

Wytheville was the site of another less modern type of conversion. Here, J. B. Barrett assembled guns from parts salvaged at Harpers Ferry and from the barrels of Hall rifles, but in so doing, converted them from breech to muzzle-loaders. Why? Simply because of the urgent need for any type of arm, and they could be made faster in such manner. Keen Walker & Co., Danville, made similar conversions and also the Read brass-framed carbines which vaguely resemble those of Perry, Maynard, and Tarpley.

J. D. Bennett, C. Bilbers, and G. H. Hall, all of Pittsylvania Courthouse, each received contracts to alter and make muskets. Their products have never been identified. In Norfolk, Thomas Cofer managed to turn out some 100 specimens of his distinctive brass-framed revolver before the Yankees inconsiderately but effectively put an end to such activity by capturing the city.

NORTH CAROLINA

The Model 1855 rifle machinery taken at Harpers Ferry was forwarded from Richmond to Fayetteville and set up in the former U. S. Arsenal at this point, and manufacture was continued there until the end of the war. Products of this Armory were equal in all respects to those of the U. S. Government, and the operation was a sizable one. Also in Fayetteville was M. A. Baker, who altered flintlocks and made sharpshooter's rifles and a few guns from Harpers Ferry parts. Lamb & Brother and Mendenhall, Jones & Gardner, both of Jamestown, were awarded state contracts for 10,000 Mississippi (Model 1841) rifles. Only a small quantity

16-2. From top, left: 1/Leech & Rigdon revolver. 2/Rigdon-Ansley (with L & R type cylinder). 3/Griswold & Gunnison revolver. 4/Kerr's Patent, London Armoury revolver (imported). From top, right: 1/Rigdon-Ansley revolver (12 cylinder notches). 2/Unmarked copy of Colt's 1851 Navy model. 3/Spiller & Burr revolver.

of these was delivered. At Greensboro, J. F. Garrett, a former hat manufacturer, produced some 500 single shot brass-frame pistols from old 1842 Model pistol barrels and later a limited number of carbines on the Confederate patent (February 14, 1863) of Jere H. Tarpley. Asheville was the site of a private armory which in the fall of 1862 was purchased by the government and a year later was removed to Columbia, S. C. Jointly it is estimated that approximately 500 rifles and/or carbines were produced.

SOUTH CAROLINA

South Carolina also had some slight experience in arms making. Sensing the need to increase arms over those furnished by the federal government, in 1852 she awarded a contract to William Glaze of Columbia and Benjamin Flagg of Massachusetts for 6,000 muskets, 1,000 rifles and 2,000 pistols. The contract was fulfilled at the Palmetto Armory in Columbia which was owned by Glaze. Thereafter it returned to more peaceful activities and never resumed gunmaking. However its rifles, muskets, and pistols all went to arming South Carolina troops during the war. In 1864 a Confederate Armory was established in Columbia with machinery and equipment from the Asheville (North Carolina) Armory. Only a very few Enfield-type carbines were produced before Columbia was burned by the Federals in 1865.

Until the spring of 1862 George W. Morse, was superintendent of the Nashville (Tennessee) Armory. With the loss of that city, Morse went farther south and at Greenville established an extensive armory, the State Rifle Works. Here, under State contract, were made 1,000 brass-framed breech-loading carbines which required metallic cartridges, the only one of its kind in the South; but the inability to produce these cartridges in sufficient quantity made them impractical for field or general use. The State Rifle Works also made a limited number of muskets, peculiar in that their locks are concealed within the stock.

GEORGIA

Georgia was second only to Virginia in production of arms. In Atlanta was a large C. S. Arsenal which supplied the armies operating south and west of North Carolina. Near the Arsenal was the pistol factory of Spiller & Burr, who produced some 760 brass-framed copies of the .36 caliber Whitney

revolver before being bought out by the government. At this time (January 1864) the plant was removed to Macon and continued production for an additional 600. Also in Macon were extensive ordnance works, although no other arms were made there aside from a few cavalry carbines by W. C. Hodgkins. Some twelve miles east of Macon was Griswoldville. Here, prior to the war S. Griswold and A. W. Gunnison (foreman) manufactured cotton gins. With the war, the product was changed to a .36 caliber brass-framed imitation Colt. Over 3,600 were produced until the town was burned by the Yankees in November, 1864. Today, the possession of a Griswold and Gunnison revolver is considered a real prize.

Cook & Brother chose Athens for the site of their private armory after their forced removal from New Orleans, Louisiana early in 1862 and continued manufacture of rifles and carbines. They are particularly attractive to today's collector because their lock markings include a Confederate flag, the firm name, address, date, and serial. Serial numbers indicate that some 8,000 were made. A musket factory was located at Tilton, but details as to its operation and production are lacking.

At the state capital, Milledgeville, the penitentiary was converted into an armory, and Mississippi (1841 Model) rifles were produced on a limited scale, all stamped "Ga. Armory, 1862." Columbus was the location of Greenwood & Gray and J. P. Murray, makers of carbines and rifles. Here also, L. Haiman & Brother, better known for swords, made approximately 100 imitation Colts, .36 caliber under the name of Columbus Firearms Manufacturing Co. before being bought out by the government with the unrealized anticipation of continuing the product.

Greensboro was the final location of Leech & Rigdon's revolver plant following its removal from Columbus, Mississippi. (Original operations began in Memphis, Tennessee.) Today, these 1,500 imitation Colts with firm name and "CSA" are eagerly sought. The partnership ended in the fall of 1863. Thereafter, Leech remained in Greensboro while Rigdon went to Augusta after securing a new partner, J. A. Ansley. Operations in both cases continued, Leech on a small scale while Rigdon produced an additional 1,000. The Augusta Machine Works, a C. S. establishment, also made a small but undetermined number of revolvers with 12 cylinder stops, a feature also peculiar to those of Rigdon-Ansley.

TENNESSEE

Tennessee was lost to the Confederacy as far as manufacture was concerned after the first year of the war, but during this first year, George W. Morse at the Nashville State Armory supposedly turned out a few muskets. Records also indicate arms making at Gallatin but to date such activities have not been tied down. Memphis was the first location of Leech & Rigdon and in the same city Schneider & Glassick made a very few imitation .36 caliber Colts. At Pulaski, a few rifles were made of hybrid nature which combined the features of both military and sporting arms.

ALABAMA

Records as to arms making in the State of Alabama range from meager to nonexistent. In Montgomery was the State Arsenal where a number of flintlock arms were converted to percussion. Here also was the Alabama Arms Manufacturing Co. (H. M. Gilmer Sr.) whose activities extended little beyond the planning stages but are nevertheless reported to have made "excellent Enfield rifles." Also in Montgomery were the Winter Iron Works (George Todd) and C. Kreutner both of whom made rifles under State contract. Wallis & Rice (Daniel Wallis) and Lewis G. Sturdivant of Talladega also held State contracts for rifles. Neither fulfilled same. Sturdivant removed to Selma after rejection of 280 rifles by State authorities and Wallis' plant was destroyed by Federal raiders in August, 1864. Dickson, Nelson & Co., originally of Dickson, made fine rifles under State contract but due to frequent relocations, to keep one step ahead of the enemy, their production appears to have been held to 645 rifles for which they were paid an average of $80.00 each. Their contract called for 5,000 rifles and bayonets. Their last location was at Dawson, Georgia and they were going full blast when the war ended.

A. C. Suter of Selma, under contract with the State, delivered at least 50 rifles prior to the expiration of his contract in November, 1864. Selma incidentally was a very large heavy ordnance center but few small arms were made there. Davis & Bozeman, Central, working on a State contract supplied at least 749 rifles and 89 carbines between October, 1863 and November, 1864.

MISSISSIPPI

The Mississippi State Arsenal was located at Panola. Later it was removed to Brandon and still later to Meridian. The extent of its activities are not known but in December, 1862, $20,000 was appropriated for "additional tools and machinery to enlarge the State Gunshop at Brandon." It is not known that Mississippi had other arms making activities.

ARKANSAS

As of January, 1861 the U.S. Government had on hand in forts and arsenals within Arkansas: 1,130 muskets and 54 rifles, the bulk of which was contained in the U.S. Arsenal, Fort Little Rock. This was seized by the State on February 8, 1861 and in May the same year was "loaned" to the Confederate government for duration of the war. Shortly thereafter a C.S. Armory was created at Arkadelphia. A few rifles were made there and are best described by a Confederate General as "no better than shotguns." Meanwhile at Little Rock, main ordnance activities appear to have been the repairing of shotguns, rifles, and pistols. It is possible also that a few rifles were made. On September 7, 1863, Little Rock was abandoned to the Federals after all ordnance stores and supplies had been sent to Arkadelphia, and thence to Tyler, Texas.

TEXAS

J. S. Short, Tyler, Texas, under contract with the State of Texas for 5,000 Mississippi rifles, supplied one prior to October, 1863, when the establishment was purchased by the Confederate government and manufacture continued through March, 1865. Records show a total of 2,223 guns and 331 bayonets were made under the supervision of Col. G. H. Hill. Of these, only four are known to be extant. Elsewhere in Texas, Dance Brothers of Columbia made less than 350 imitation .44 caliber Colts for the State. Tucker, Sherrard & Co., Lancaster, secured a contract with the State for 3,000 revolvers. Few, if any, were delivered. N. B. Tanner, Bastrop, under contract with the State, produced some 265 muskets. Whitescarver, Campbell & Co. of Rusk, and Billings & Hassell of Plentitude, secured State contracts for 900 and 1,200 rifles, respectively. The first delivered some 700. The output of the latter is unknown. The arms of both went to arm Indians loyal to the Confederate cause.

LOUISIANA

New Orleans, key city of Louisiana, fell early to the Federals in April, 1862. At the time, Cook & Brother were located in this city and were busy making rifles under contract for the state of Mississippi. They were able to remove before being captured, and eventually located in Athens, Georgia, there to continue gun manufacturing endeavors. Shreveport was ordnance headquarters for the Trans-Mississippi Department but no arms were made there. The point served only as a distributing center.

FLORIDA

Records do not indicate that any arms were made in Florida.

MANUFACTURE ABROAD

In addition to domestic manufacture, the Confederacy was supplied by direct contracts with two foreign firms. The London Armoury of London, England, was under direct contract with the Confederacy for both long arms and revolvers made under the "Kerr Patent." However, they were also under contract with the English government at the same time and the problem remains as to which went where. Despite this, it can be said with certainty that most London Armoury weapons in the American Civil War were used by the Confederates.

Another revolver which is definitely Confederate is the LeMat. This most interesting weapon fea-

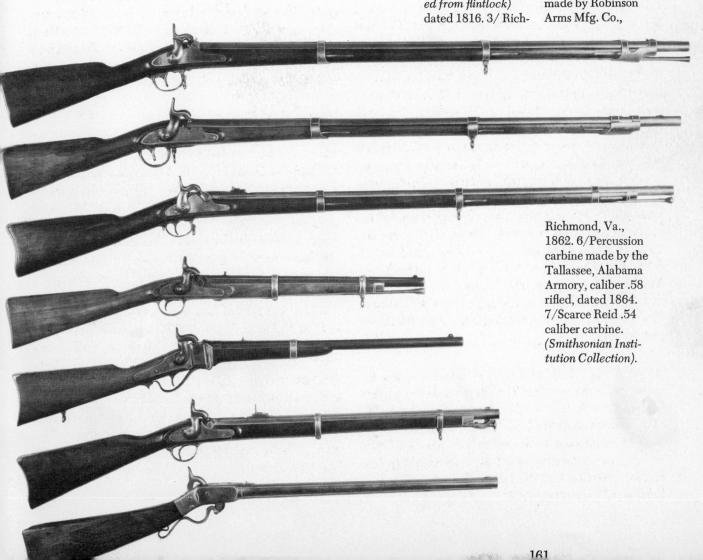

16-3. From top: 1 Percussion musket marked Palmetto Armory, S.C., 1852. 2/Percussion musket made by Virginia Manufactory, Richmond, Va., *(converted from flintlock)* dated 1816. 3/ Richmond Armory .58 caliber rifled musket, dated 1863. 4/ Percussion carbine by Cook & Brothers, Athens, Ga., dated 1864. 5/Imitation of Sharps carbine, made by Robinson Arms Mfg. Co., Richmond, Va., 1862. 6/Percussion carbine made by the Tallassee, Alabama Armory, caliber .58 rifled, dated 1864. 7/Scarce Reid .54 caliber carbine. *(Smithsonian Institution Collection).*

tured a nine-shot cylinder which revolved around a "grape-shot" barrel and was invented by Dr. Jean Alexandre Francois LeMat of New Orleans, Louisiana, who first patented this formidable arm in 1856. Approximately 300 were made prior to the war (probably in New Orleans), when LeMat, whose loyalty lay entirely with the South, received contracts from both the Confederate Army and Navy for his revolvers. Operations were removed from New Orleans to Paris, France, and still later to London, England. Despite misleading serial numbers the total output amounted to some 3,000. As all but the original 300 were made under exclusive contract for the C.S. Army and Navy, there is no question as to their Confederate "nationality" despite having been made abroad.

This review touches only the broad aspect of small arms production in the Confederacy. A book on each person and establishment named is entirely possible. At any rate, these are the persons, the places, and the establishments which supplied Confederate armies that were ill fed, inadequately equipped, and poorly armed—but magnificently manned.

Crude these weapons may have been, but if anyone questions their effective employment a review of Union casualty lists will dispel any such doubts.

The subject of Confederate firearms is pursued in greater detail for the student in *Confederate Handguns*, by Albaugh, Benet and Simmons; *The Original Confederate Colt*, by Albaugh and Steuart; *The Confederate Brass-Framed Colt & Whitney*, by Albaugh; *Confederate Edged Weapons*, by Albaugh; and *Firearms of the Confederacy*, by Fuller and Steuart. Additional titles by Albaugh are: *Tyler, Texas, C.S.A.*, and *A Photographic Supplement of Confederate Swords*. There is also *Confederate Arms* by Albaugh & Simmons.

17.

the
Derringer
Pistols

17-1. Left: Historic pair of Henry Deringer pocket pistols, rare straight-back trigger guards. Made for Col. G. Talcott, one-time Chief of U.S. Ordnance.

Top right: Typical H. Deringer pistol with plain butt. The 2½ inch barrel was given Deringer's famous striped brown finish. Bottom, right: Imitation of the above pistol marked "J. Deringer" *(no relation to Henry Deringer).*

In the mid-1800s the small pistols produced by Henry Deringer, Jr., of Philadelphia, became so representative of an efficient pocket pistol that all small, concealable pistols were popularly called *derringers*. Thus, by a slight deviation in spelling, the Deringer name became the noun *derringer* with generic meaning, a distinction accorded few manufacturers.

Small pocket pistols, which we shall now call derringers, certainly were nothing startlingly new. We find small hand cannon, pocket sized flintlocks, and small percussion pistols made in Europe by many gunmakers. Ethan Allen made a great variety of small percussion pocket pistols here in America, as shown elsewhere in this book. Henry Deringer's pistols, however, were different in form from other single shot pocket pistols of the day. They were light, compact, handsomely custom finished, and of a relatively large bore which made them deadly at close range. A pair of these beautiful little pocket pistols gave the man so armed a definite sense of security.

Henry Deringer, Jr., arrived in Philadelphia and started his gun business in 1806, after serving a period of apprenticeship to a Richmond, Virginia, gunsmith. Flintlock pistols, rifles, and 1,200 box lock percussion pistols were turned out in the Deringer shop, but these must occupy the background. The little H. Deringer pocket pistols, coming on the scene somewhere around 1830 and a household word by 1850, are the weapons by which Henry Deringer will always be remembered.

After 1850, California became a rich market for derringer pistols. They were of little interest to frontiersmen, but as the western settlements grew into towns and cities, thickly

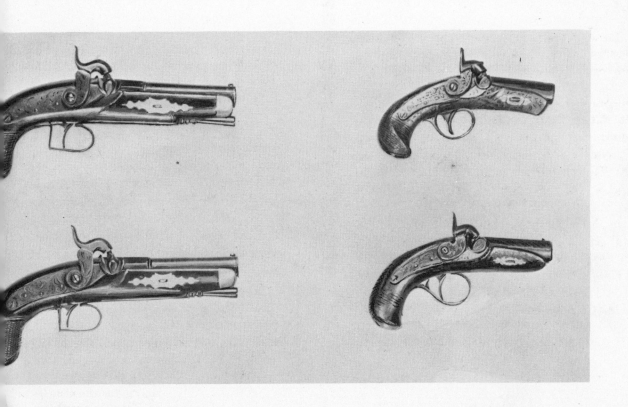

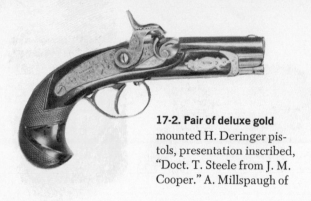

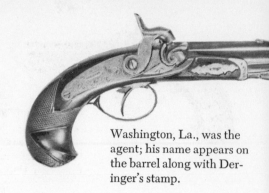

17-2. Pair of deluxe gold mounted H. Deringer pistols, presentation inscribed, "Doct. T. Steele from J. M. Cooper." A. Millspaugh of Washington, La., was the agent; his name appears on the barrel along with Deringer's stamp.

populated but still not truly civilized, it was a practical precaution to be adequately if inconspicuously armed. Pairs of derringers were common armament in the pockets of public officials, editors, gamblers, and businessmen in various fields. Even peace officers found a little "hide-out" derringer a very handy firearm. And ladies of the night sometimes carried a derringer pistol in their reticule or on their person to protect their earnings if not their virtue.

Residents of our Southern states were quick to recognize the compact efficiency of a derringer; a reliable source records that three times as many pairs of Henry Deringer pocket pistols were sold in the South as in the Northern states.

Gun dealers throughout the nation soon became aware of the increasing demand for derringer pistols, and Henry Deringer's modest manufactory, where all work was done pretty much by the old hand-fitting methods, was hard put to keep up with the demand.

An interesting custom developed among Deringer's customers. Although the great majority of genuine Deringer-made pistols bear only the H. Deringer name and an abbreviated Philadelphia address, quite a few may be found which also bear the name of a dealer on the top flat of the barrel. This provides collectors with quite an area in which to find interesting marking variations to add to their collections. Some dealers' names to be found on barrels are: C. Curry, N. Curry & Bro., A. J. Plate, W. C. Allen & Co., and A. J. Taylor, all of San Francisco.

There were M. W. Galt & Bro. of Washington, Wolf & Duringer of Louisville, F. H. Clark & Co. and Lullman & Vienna of Memphis, W. H. Calhoun & Co. of Nashville, A. B. Griswold & Co. or Hyde & Goodrich of New Orleans, A. Millspaugh of Washington, Louisiana, and others.

The popularity of Henry Deringer pistols, built on their efficient adaptability in general use and on quality workmanship, soon found imitators seeking to share in this active derringer pistol demand.

Henry Deringer had no patents or legal rights to protect him against those who made pistols of his pattern. A few unscrupulous gunmakers went so far as to attempt to capitalize on the Deringer name and reputation. Some spurious copies were marked "Deringe." Another competitor took as a silent partner a man named J. Deringer (no relation to Henry), so they might mark their pistols "J. Deringer."

From the collector's standpoint, some of Henry Deringer's competitors not only made pistols equal in quality but production was less and these pistols are therefore relatively harder to acquire. The barrels of Henry Deringer pistols were made of wrought iron, whereas most of his imitators used steel, claiming their barrels to be superior.

There must be a line of distinction drawn between those who produced spurious copies of Henry Deringer pistols and are generally classed as unscrupulous imitators and those who produced similar but

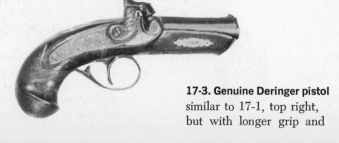

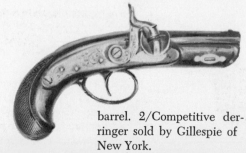

17-3. Genuine Deringer pistol similar to 17-1, top right, but with longer grip and barrel. 2/Competitive derringer sold by Gillespie of New York.

Pair of H. Deringer pistols, 6 inches overall, engraved silver hardware, cap boxes in butts, sold by N. Curry & Bro., San Francisco agents.

the Derringer Pistols

165

honestly marked competitive pistols.

The most serious competitor in terms of volume was a firm which adopted the name Slotter & Co. It was made up of a group of old Deringer workmen who left Deringer's employ in 1859. The ethics of this firm are not altogether above censure on several counts, but they did produce pistols of good quality, many of them honestly marked "Slotter & Co. Phila." A. J. Plate, R. Liddle & Co. and Wilson & Evans of San Francisco sold many of these Slotter pistols.

Others who made creditable pocket pistols of the H. Deringer pattern were: Tryon, Krider, Robertson, Constable, Wurfflein, Evans, Lins, Spang & Wallace, Grubb, Foehl, and a few others, all of Philadelphia. There were Bruff, Gillespie, Seaver, Spies, and Syms, all of New York City. A few other makers were J. Bitterlich & Co. of Nashville, H. E. Dimick of St. Louis, Schneider & Glassick of Memphis, and C. Sutter of Alabama.

Departing from the true Deringer single shot pistol, but employing a basic weapon of the same general appearance, Frederick Beerstecher's patent of 1855 provided for a movable striker on the hammer, two nipples, and two charges in the one barrel. The principle of a double charge in one barrel was similar to that used on the better known Lindsay pistol, although the Lindsay used two hammers.

Another innovation of 1855 was J. S. Butterfield's patent derringer pistol. These pistols were fitted with a special priming device integral with the

lock. It is very doubtful that either Beerstecher's or Butterfield's "improvements" gained any degree of popularity.

The Henry Deringer type of pistol was of a rather uniform over-all pattern, but with enough variation to send a collector on long, hard searches. Barrels varied from a snub-nose $2\frac{7}{32}$ inches (exclusive of the breech plug) to a long 4 inches. The most popular barrel lengths were $1\frac{1}{2}$, 2, $2\frac{1}{2}$, and 3 inches. Loading rods were sometimes attached under the longer barrels. A few pistols were fitted with cap boxes set in the bird-head butt. Stocks were uniformly of walnut, nicely checked, and fitted with engraved silver hardware; a very few special pistols were made up with an ivory or metal stock. Calibers varied from about .34 to .50, with .42 a good average—that was the caliber of the H. Deringer pistol used to kill President Lincoln. Locks were of the "back-action" variety, usually stamped with the maker's name and address.

While the little percussion derringers were primarily a weapon of defense, they provided their share of human drama. Duels were even fought with them—some tragic and some comic, as in the "across the table" duel in Southern California between a pompous Colonel and an equally pompous doctor.

The seconds, feeling the matter not serious enough for bloodshed, secretly loaded the pistols with ground cork instead of lead. The actions of the participants in the resultant bloodless duel clearly

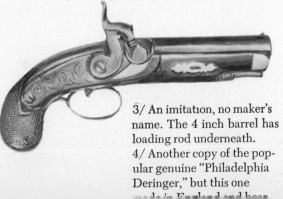

3/ An imitation, no maker's name. The 4 inch barrel has loading rod underneath.
4/ Another copy of the popular genuine "Philadelphia Deringer," but this one

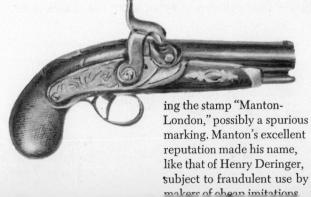

ing the stamp "Manton-London," possibly a spurious marking. Manton's excellent reputation made his name, like that of Henry Deringer, subject to fraudulent use by

revealed, however, which man had the greater courage.

When the war between the States ended, the heyday of the percussion derringer was over. One of the fruits of that tragic struggle was development of the metallic cartridge, and thus entered the derringer-size pistol with fixed ammunition.

Our treatment here of the percussion derringer pistol has given dominant attention to the weapons of Henry Deringer and his competitors; this is the field in which collectors express primary interest. But a reminder seems in order that throughout the entire history of firearms many pistols were made of derringer size other than the "Philadelphia Deringer" pattern. These, too, have virtues of their own to attract the collector.

As we enter the cartridge era, we find that the small pocket arms generally referred to as "derringers" take on broader scope. Unlike most derringers of the preceding era, cartridge derringers as often as not were multi-barrel affairs. In fact, the Sharps four-barrel pistol, patented January 25, 1859, was a pioneer in this field.

Perhaps the theory of the multi-barrel derringer was that four .22, .30, or .32 caliber cartridges would be as effective or possibly more effective than one large ball over .40 caliber in size. This theory, however, was not accepted by all. One big caliber "stopper" remained the favored derringer ideal of many. Thus we find, coming along as the Civil War was about to end, a .41 caliber rimfire all-metal derringer which Daniel Moore had patented in 1861. Here we have the beginning of a long line of .41 caliber rimfire derringers, and a number of fine collections have been built on pistols of this type alone. Second only to the .41 rimfire caliber as a collecting favorite are little derringer pistols in .22 rimfire caliber.

The illustrations accompanying this brief commentary will provide some idea of the variety to be encountered. Space here does not permit comment on all the varied types and calibers but a few observations relative to cartridge derringers of .41 caliber may prove useful.

The all-metal .41 derringer of 1861, mentioned previously, was produced first by Moore's Patent Fire Arms Co., which later became the National Arms Co., and which in turn was purchased by Colt in 1870; the all-metal pistols thereafter were marked with the Colt name and "No. 1," possibly indicating their pioneer appearance in the field. They were very effective also when held in the hand in such a way as to be used as "knucks." As in the case of the "Philadelphia Deringer," Moore's derringer soon had plenty of competition. In the excellent studies made by John E. Parsons he has very properly divided these cartridge derringers into seven classes, each with a different principle of mechanical operation. These varied mechanisms have the following characteristics: (1) *Barrel slides forward*, as on the Williamson derringer patented in 1866. This derringer, having a full stock of walnut, most closely resembles the "Philadelphia Deringer." An interesting feature capable of converting the pistol from the usual .41 rimfire cartridge was an auxiliary metal cartridge case, which could be loaded with loose powder, a ball, and a percussion cap. The Sharps, of course, also employed the sliding barrel principle. (2) *Hinged barrel that rotates down to the side*, as on the Moore, National, Colt No. 1 and Colt No. 2.

Hammond's Patent "Bull-dozer" pistol (.44 RF) had a somewhat similar action, the breech swinging to the left and backward. (3) *A fixed barrel with a breech formed and locked by a rolling motion involving the hammer.* Remington produced several types, each patented by Wm. P. Elliott. In the split-breech type with flat grip, pistols were made for calibers .22 to .41 and called "vest-pocket pistols." (4) *Tip down barrel.* Starr's patent of 1864 and Ballard's 1869 patent were the most prominent adherents to this principle. Marston was another manufacturer who liked this hinged barrel system. Marston pistols of this character were designed with three superposed barrels, and their small caliber does not rightly put them in the same category as the .41 caliber models which are our immediate subject. (5) *Barrel pivots sidewise.* For this principle there were quite a few supporters. Colt's No. 3 derringer patented by F. Alexander Thuer in 1870 was one example which was very popular—in fact, Colt has now returned to making these (in .22 caliber). If they had not resumed manufacture, no doubt some replica-maker would be turning them out, just as they are now copying the Remington over-and-under double derringer. Others who favored the side swinging barrel were Allen (1865), Marlin's derringers called the "Victor" and the "Never Miss" (1870), a similar XL derringer made by Hopkins & Allen, and the "Southerner" (1867) made by the Merrimack Arms & Mfg. Co. and Brown Mfg. Co., both of Newburyport, Massachusetts. (6) *Rotating double barrel.* The chief exponents of this system were American Arms Co. (1865-66) and Frank Wesson (1868-69). Wes-

17-4. From top, left row: 1/Starr (button trigger). 2/Ballard. 3/Marlin "Victor." 4/Marlin "O.K." 5/Southerner. 6/National Arms Co. "No. 2." 7/National Arms Co. "No. 1." 8/Conn. Arms Co. (Hammond's Pat.).

Center row: 1/ 1/Marston superposed 3 barrels (4 inches). 2/Same but 3 inch barrels. 3/Marston's small .22 caliber size. 4/American Arms Co., superposed 2 barrels. 5/F. Wesson superposed 2 barrels with knife blade. 6/Same without knife blade. 7/F. Wesson baby .22, sometimes called the "watch fob" pistol.

Right row: 1/Allen & Wheelock .32 rimfire. 2/Merwin & Bray .32. 3/F. Wesson .22. 4/E. Allen .22. 5/E. Allen baby size .22. 6/Star vest pocket .22. 7/Rupertus double-barrel .22. 8/Terry vest pocket .22.

son went his competitor in this field one better. On some pistols he included a retractable knife blade, assumed to finish up any business two bullets failed to accomplish. (7) Last of the major cartridge derringer principles is the one which survived in greatest prominence; this is the *hinged barrel* derringer made up principally by Remington under patents of the 1860s and continuously in their line until 1935. As stated before, various manufacturers now produce copies of this design.

All derringers, of course, did not follow standard principles. One of the great oddities (and exceptionally rare) is the Perry & Goddard "double-ender" of 1864. The novelty of this was that it could be loaded at either end. When one cartridge was fired, the barrel was swiveled so the muzzle became the breech. In theory, the ball from the cartridge loaded in what had been the muzzle, when fired, would in its passage from the barrel blow out the empty cartridge case, thus eliminating any need of extracting a spent cartridge! This was really giving a victim the works—not only a ball, but a shell casing along with it!

Another system tried with little success was one that, like the Perry & Goddard, was patented in 1864. It was James Warner's "trap-door" derringer which had a side-swinging hinged breech similar to that best known as the Snider system. The Warner derringers are understandably scarce.

The derringer, in its generic sense, has been the subject of much fact and fiction in American literature. It is indeed a fascinating field for the collector. An outstanding source of information on both the percussion and cartridge types of large bore derringers is John E. Parsons' *Henry Deringer's Pocket Pistol—A History of the Famous Percussion Pistol and Its Cartridge Sequels.*

18.

the

Stories

in

Cased

Firearms

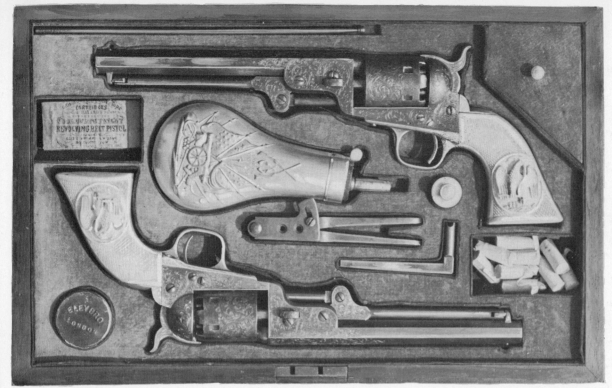

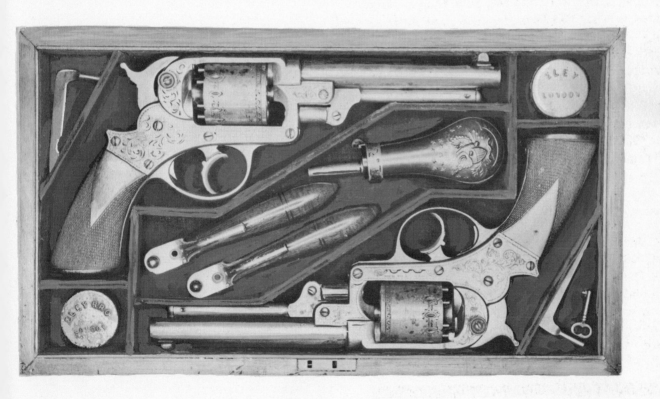

The avid collecting of cased arms is of relatively recent date. Until the mid 1930s the collector removed the arm from its case and hung it decoratively on the wall. The gun student and author, Charles Winthrop Sawyer, greatly influenced this as many of his articles were devoted to the decorative display of arms. His published work in book form and magazine articles were about the only literature available except for Bannerman's catalog to the collector of that era. My earliest recollections of gun collectors circa 1925 are most vivid of walls loaded to the ultimate with arms but the empty cases were stacked in closets or cellars if not discarded in the trash. I say this with authority as one of the very few collectors who valued even the commonest cased Colt 1849 pocket revolver for the establishment of the correct accessories back in the 1920s. I might note one other contributing cause to the removal of guns from their cases when added to collections. Blame it on the spool cabinet! These general store repositories for milady's sewing thread were common at the turn of the century. All makers of sewing thread had these available for the shop-keeper, fancifully embellished with trade names such as Clark's O.N.T. etc. The shallow drawers wouldn't accommodate a case, so out came the gun and away went the case when it became the fad to house your collection in the common spool cabinet.

Casing of arms and their accessories was essential in the period prior to machine standardization to ensure the preservation of the correct bullet mold, powder charger, correct sized flints, finished bullets, and the tools for use of the arm. Loss of the mold or the charger resulted in the questionable accuracy of the arm. Thus the case was important as the vital storage point for accessories. In addition it protected the arm from exposure to weather and the wear and tear of exposed storage. Common usage of a case for firearms seems to be in the early 1700s. The protection of casing has brought many arms through the ravages of time in a well-preserved state to the modern collection. That was a prime reason for my devotion to cased outfits as compared to the dusty, rusty, wall-hung specimens of my early collecting days.

The early cased set had its place in the home of the wealthy and in the cabin of the ship's captain. The traveler resorted to holster, muff, or sash for the keeping of his arm. With the advent of the matched pair, such as duelers, this basic concept continued with the exception of the officer's or gentleman's traveling case of arms. Such cased outfits will be found with the arms equipped with sash or belt hooks, a clip-like affair on the left side of the arm, and later with lanyard ring in the butt. Cases were commonly of oak, walnut, pine, and mahogany in this utilitarian period. Hinge and lock design are clues to the period of the case.

The dueling pair used in affairs of honor emerged as an important casing in the late 1700s. Justly famous makers of precision arms such as Wogdon

cased their flint duelers and proudly pasted their label in the lid of the case. The label was an interesting early advertising form. As the gentleman of the period idly examined his host's duelers, he noted they were by such a maker as Mortimer, who also proudly stated he was gunmaker to his majesty the King of England. Or on a visit to the ship of a fellow captain, the guest might note that the cased elliptical-mouthed mutiny gun complete with shoulder stock, bullet mold to cast twelve nasty slice-of-pie-like slugs, loader, etc. had an ornate label with the royal lion and unicorn shield and garter of England and "James Wilkinson and Son, Gunmakers to His Majesty, to the King and Prince Royal of Persia, and the Honorable East India Company." He probably also noted the address No. 27 Pall Mall, London, and made a mental note to drop by and buy such a set. That same house of Wilkinson became sword makers and today are noted for their stainless steel razor blades. That label helped preserve their company for posterity. Today these labels are significant in locating the early manufactory of arms and the various places of business of the early dealers. Joe Manton, probably the most celebrated of English makers, is so traced from Hanover Place to Leicester Square; and we note his brother John, to whom the trade was referred when they could not afford Joe's prices, was located nearby. Later such labels assist in identifying the work and location of two other famous brothers, James and Philip Webley.

So far we have only thought about the utilitarian casing of arms. How were they contained in the box? Two schools of casing emerged that for ease of identification are referred to as the English and French, though both types were found in either country as well as all other countries where arms were cased.

The English style is by partitioning, thin pieces of wood usually covered with material dividing the case into sections for arm, bullet mold, flask, etc. The French style is accomplished by inletting or carving from a block the shape of the items to be cased and lining the entire interior with material.

This inletted style was usually a tighter fit and kept down the friction wear of the loose partitioning style, but rusting will be found more prevalent where the contact of piece to material makes such tight quarters. Always remove the arm and examine the side that contacts the case material before you mentally evaluate the outfit.

Prior to the 1930's the American collector preserved arms in their original casing in two general classes, the *pair* or the *presentation* item. Pairs were chiefly of the dueler or gentleman's pistol type. The presentation-type arm by its special treatment deserved to be left intact in its case rather than hung on the wall or put in the spool cabinet. We class as presentation, in this collecting era, those arms that received special treatment of engraving, stocking, inlaying, cast or chiseled trigger guards, butt caps, etc., that were prepared either for the élite's own armory or as a valuable gift or memento to some important personage. Typical examples are the work of Boutet of France. His work as armorer to the King of France and more importantly as the designer of exquisite gift sets for Napoleon, Emperor of France, are truly works of art. If they were to be presented to a famous admiral the motifs of the sea were cast and chiseled in superb detail by this artist and his workmen. Each case on the French style was inletted for each highly embellished accessory. Such a presentation set is a collection within itself. A later example of presentation casing would be that of Schuyler Hartley and Graham of Maiden Lane, New York, in the mid 1860s. Again the French style was employed and the casing style is distinctive and recognizable, even without the label inside the lid. By the same token presentation sets from Abraham Lincoln to the Kings of Sweden and Denmark are tastefully done in the English style of partitioning. With the presentation set we find new woods introduced such as ebony, rosewood, bird's-eye maple, and the case received treatment equal to that given the contents, with escutcheons, carrying handles cleverly inletted, and brass-bound corners. The presentation-type casing appeared about 1800 and developed to

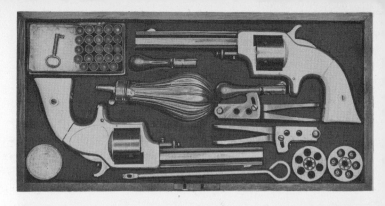

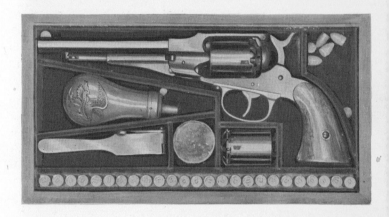

18-2. From top: 1/Plant pistols showing tools, cup-primer ammunition and the alternate cartridge and percussion cylinders. 2/Smith & Wesson double casing. 3/Remington double-action caplock pistol showing tools and the conversion cylinder, available when metallic cartridges could be used. 4/Seldom found cased is the Savage Navy pistol.

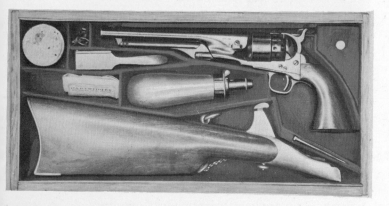

18-3. From top: 1/Alsop pistol showing tools and extra cylinder of different type. 2/English casing of Colt .44 Army pistol with accessories including shoulder stock.

own sturdiness to house such collector items as Smith and Wesson first models, Smith and Wesson revolving pistol rifles, Plant front loaders, and many others. The quality of the ordinary case varied as to the class of arm and the type of competition. The large brass-plate keyhole in square or shield design of the early Colt dropped down to a wooden insert for the pocket revolver competing with Remington, Manhattan, Nepperhan, Bacon, et al, and in the larger revolvers to a shape-of-the-keyhole brass insert or keyhole liner. There were patents issued on hinges, locks, and in corner design. The best known is Kidder's Patent, April 1854, corner locking design as it was so stamped on the top of the back section of the case proper. Cases, originally sold as an extra at a profit, became the cardboard box costing pennies that was written off as packaging. No one ever imagined their present-day value.

Why are cases valuable? We have discussed the preservation on vital accessories, the clue-yielding labels, and the presentation value. My first real appreciation of original casing came with the quality of the condition of a cased piece, then came the realization that herein lay the answers to identification of accessories. At this late date the latter has assumed the prime importance. What did the cleaning rod of a Colt Paterson revolver, or a Colt 1855 Sidehammer revolver, look like? The first is easily identified by numerous pictured cased outfits but the rod for the Sidehammer model as well as the tool for adjusting the breech clearance could be recognized only by finding them first in a cased set. How about the barrel wrench for the Robbins and Lawrence pepperbox to open the barrel for powder and ball? The wrench with its two lugs would be unknown except for its appearance in cased sets. The Lindsay bullet mold, the Wesson and Leavitt Dragoon mold, and most importantly the LeMat mold casting one conical bullet and two buckshot, owe their identification to the same source. Original cased sets lend identity to otherwise unknown accessories.

its peak in the years just after the Civil War in America. Thereafter we find casing of precision arms such as, for example, Gastine Renette target pistols or Smith and Wesson metal-cased target pistols, ending the cased-arm picture as an expensive part of the arm.

From the era of the relatively expensive wooden case with hinges and lock, we find a deterioration of the utilitarian feature to finally a simple two-piece cardboard box with perhaps a cloth hinge for the lid or not even with that refinement. In this period we find leather used as an outer covering on wood, cloth on wood, cloth on cardboard, and the introduction of the plastic or gutta-percha case, and finally cardboard alone. Leather or patent leather type covering appeared circa 1840, the leather outer case for carrying about 1875, and gutta-percha, first by Smith and Wesson (their cost $9.50 per dozen for the cases) about 1860. The cardboard covered by cloth was used in the 1870s and usually the inside is a flannel-type material. Such cases are preserved more because of their contents than their

With the advent of machine-produced arms we find the lid of the case not only bearing the address and name of maker or dealer but also, most important, instructions on handling the arm, loading, disassembly and assembly for cleaning, etc. This printed data provides valuable information for the student. Simple clues like the label in a cased Kerr caliber .36 stating "either double- or single-action" became my first clue that two types were possible and later permitted the identification of Belgian imitation Kerr Navy Serial # 1 as intermediate in the evolution since it was double-action, but lacking the bolting (safety lock) feature.

Occasionally there is found loose in the case other valuable printed material. Labels on cap boxes, bags of caps, or packets of cartridges are examples, plus the possible find of a printed circular of the manufacturer and a price list neatly folded in a compartment. In my collection is a cased 1862 Colt .38 caliber Conversion that contained the original 1872 price list (4 page) of Colt's Patent F. A. Mfg. Co., picturing the Colt Peacemaker, the old-line seven-shot .22 with ejector, the Colt derringer (.41 cal., third Model), and the Colt National derringer in first and second models, thus closely dating and tying in the acquisition of National Arms Co. and Moore's Patent arms. This unpublished price list has many valuable clues to the state of production circa 1872. So add another value to cased arms in the printed material available.

In this day and age it is well to dwell for a moment on originality. The original owner could have easily added an item or two that he found useful but were not the maker's original. Such things as nipple pricks, nipple primers, spring vises, palm rammers, and replaced flasks can sometimes throw the student off the track. Then, the item could have been lost from the case and a replacement added at a later date.

I recall a superb cased Boutet pair, presented by Napoleon, that had a replaced flask, not correct but satisfactory. There are many ways one may be led down an erroneous path. Grubb of Philadelphia assembled certain American items and sent them to Belgium where fine arms engravers and gunmakers created superb cased outfits. A Hartford arm and a Philadelphia flask could well reappear as a superb Belgian finished outfit with special trigger guards, and the Philadelphia Grubb label. Study and care should be exercised in conclusions on any cased set as early exigencies may have created strange bedfellows.

Now we come to the danger point for the eager collector of cased sets. With their demand and value so enhanced by the collecting foibles of the day and the increased number of collectors we find the faker preying on the unknowing. There are many genuine examples of American arms that were cased at the period of their manufacture in an older European case. This is particularly true of the presentation type where a suitable case was redone with a suitable interior. Beware of the one just done a week ago to satisfy your demand. There is quite a study to be made on case design and the writer has concentrated down to even the correct screws to hold the hinges. There is no substitute for experience, knowledge, and comparison but a bill of sale stating the case is original and contemporary to the period of the arm is good protection. A very dear friend during the depression in the 1930s had some cases made of Philippine mahogany in the style of corner fastening current to the 1850 Colt era. He used them to case and preserve some of his fine specimens and also sold them through advertising not as fakes or originals but only to provide a casing. I recall they sold lined and unlined, partitions included, for about $8.00 to $12.00 and I have two examples here in the collection still in the raw unfinished state. It is saddening to see these same cases now bringing hundreds of dollars as original circa 1850-60 cases! Knowledge of patina and a feel for age is important with modern manufacturing going all out to satisfy a demand from eager easy-money novices. There are many modern-day amateur attempts at casing of arms, the wildest of which I saw some years ago by a collector who manufactured metal electrical switch boxes with a black mottled finish as a livelihood—and used these to case his firearms!

Some years ago a new collector visited me and proudly brought in his collection of five cased sets, three of which were of very recent workmanship. When we went up to the gunroom he was taken aback by seeing over one hundred fifty cases arrayed in racks. I couldn't resist telling him the story of a gentleman who was considered by some the Dean of American Collectors from 1910-1930. A collector with a gun to sell would visit him and offer it for sale as one he didn't have. This gentleman would examine it casually, toss it down on his large

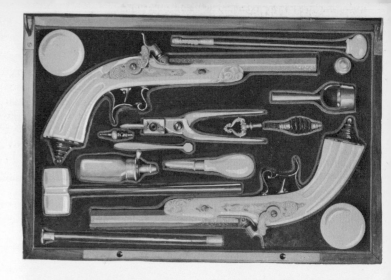

teakwood table and point to a pyramid of cases on one side of the room, saying something like "there is a brand new engraved model of this in the fourth case over in the second level of that pile of cases." The collector, thus deflated, eventually sold the piece very cheaply to this shrewd gentleman so he "could give it to a friend." When this shrewd collector died it was discovered that only the top six cases in the pyramid contained arms! All the rest were just empty boxes. The new collector didn't have the temerity to go digging through mine to see if they were empty. However, the lovely wife of one of my dealer friends, on hearing the story, dug in with vim and vigor so that it was several weeks before my cased sets got back in their racks, and one has never found a place! They were all filled and I trust original, but as some one has said, "I don't worry about the fakes I recognize, it's those I don't recognize that bother me!"

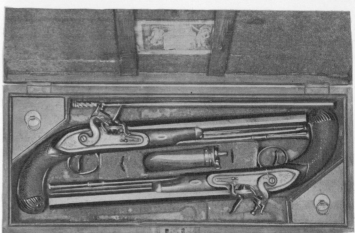

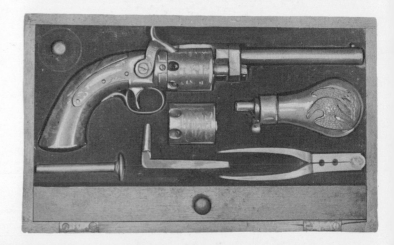

18-4. From top: 1/Ivory stocked caplock pistols with typical French style recessed casing. 2/Flintlock pistols by Mortimer of London with typical English partition-type casing. 3/Wesson & Leavitt pistol, showing tools and extra cylinder. 4/Maynard Rifle with tools, ammunition and extra barrels.

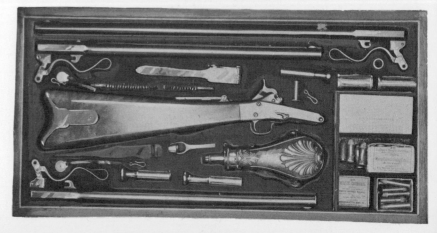

18-5. From top: 1/French
casing of two caplock
pistols by Devisme of
Paris. 2/Elaborate casing
of derringer pistols showing
the various tools and
loading implements.
3/Robbins & Lawrence
pepperbox with distinctive
flask and tools.
4/Allen pepperbox com-
plete with the needed
accessories.

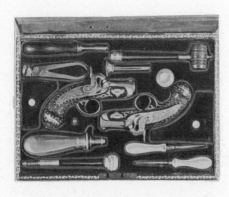

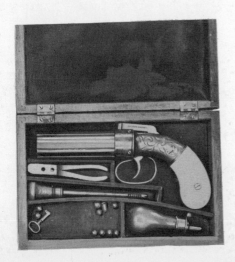

19-1. From top: 1/ Christian Sharps' first model, made at Mill Creek, Pa. It has an odd circular capper forward of the lock. **2/**The second model Sharps varied mainly in the priming, this model having Dr. Maynard's tape-primer device incorporated in the lock. Caliber .40. **3/**The next sporting model was made at Hartford, Conn., and has a sloping breech and disc priming device.

4/A heavy Model 1874 "Buffalo" rifle, made at Bridgeport, Conn. **5/**Creedmoor-type long-range target model with vernier rear sight which could be used at tang or at the heel of the stock. Guns of this type were used in International Matches. **6/**Target model of the 1878 Borchardt Sharps with concealed hammer, one of the finest of all single shot actions.

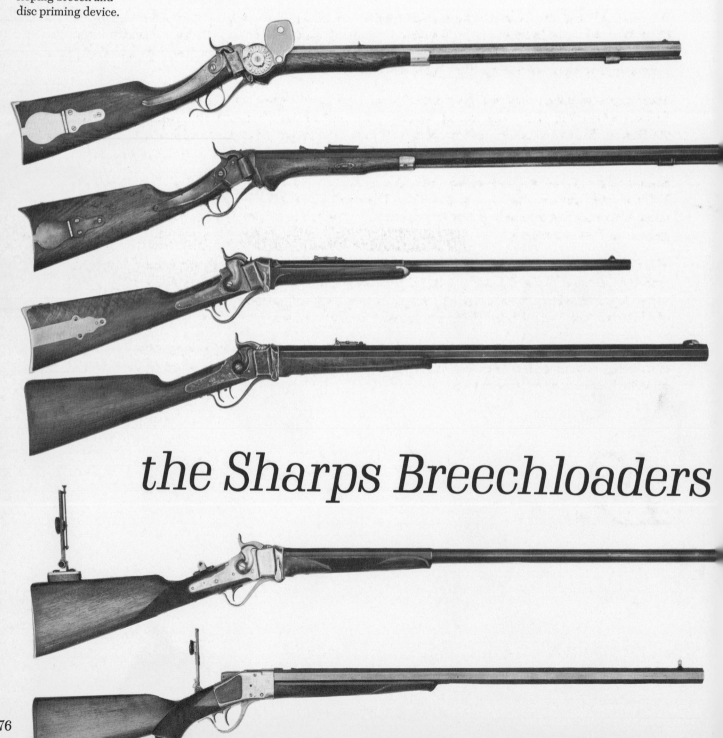

the Sharps Breechloaders

The name Sharps is one that brings to mind important weapons used in the war between the states, weapons used in our Indian wars, those superb weapons which won world supremacy on thousand-yard targets, and those big Sharps buffalo guns—the dominant weapon in bringing almost total extinction to the largest concentration of big game the world has known. We think of Christian Sharps as the inventor also of little four-shot pocket pistols. But these arms were made by an entirely different firm than that which made the big rifles, and they will be discussed later.

Collectors are attracted to big Sharps firearms because they are not only historic military weapons but their record as frontier and sporting weapons is equally impressive; the Sharps and the Remington were America's first popular long-range cartridge rifles, prominent at International Matches on the famous Creedmoor target range, and highly valued on the western prairies.

We are told that the Federal forces purchased 9,141 Sharps full-stock military rifles during the Civil War. Colonel Berdan's sharpshooters were armed with the Model 1859 Sharps military rifles which used a .52 linen cartridge. Sharps carbines proved the more popular, however, and 80,512 were manufactured for use by the Union forces.

Some captured guns and privately-owned Sharps were used by the Confederate army, too. The S.C. Robinson Arms Mfg. Co. of Richmond, Virginia, made at least 3,000 carbines which closely resembled the Sharps. Richmond-made carbines of Sharps design were poorly constructed and often dangerously defective. Now, one hundred years later, they are considered a great prize for the collector.

Sharps carbines were popular with hunters as well as the military, but their principal use was in the U.S. mounted service. They saw action with "The Army of the West" in Indian fighting. They were carried by Pony Express riders and by stagecoach guards. For a time they were the official saddle gun of the Texas Rangers.

The first carbine model was the box lock of 1851. Then came the slanting-breech model of 1852; next the so-called "John Brown" model, sometimes called "Beecher's Bibles"; then the 1855 model with Maynard primer, which almost ruined the Sharps Co. financially. The vertical breech model of 1859, and the "New Model 1863" saw much Civil War service.

When we get into the cartridge carbines we find transition models, the Models of 1869 and 1870, and enough others of varied designs and calibers (including the concealed hammer Borchardt Model of 1878) to keep collectors very busy.

19.

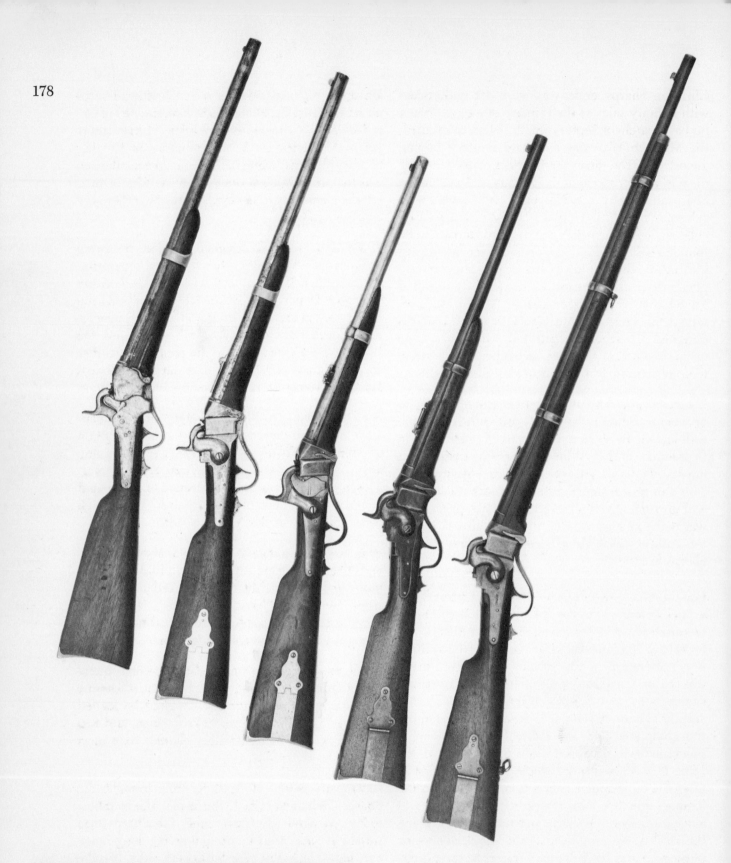

19-2. From left: 1/First of the Sharps military arms, the carbine
model of 1851, made by Robbins & Lawrence at Windsor, Vt.
2/Sloping breech model of 1852, made at Hartford, Conn. 3/
Model 1855 Sharps carbine with Maynard primer. This model put
the Sharps Rifle Mfg. Co. on the rocks financially. 4/The Sharps
"New Model 1859." Many were used in Civil War. 5/Not many
Sharps military rifles were made in comparison to the carbines.
This is the "New Model 1863" rifle, somewhat similar to the .52
caliber guns issued to Berdan's sharpshooters.

Christian Sharps' endeavors were not undertaken with military sales as the primary objective. When his basic patent of September 12, 1848, was granted, the Mexican War was over and military buying almost nil. The first Sharps rifles were sporting models, and production of 700 was undertaken for Sharps in 1850 by A. S. Nippes of Mill Creek, Pennsylvania (near Philadelphia). These now are a rare collector's prize. Possibly not over a dozen are to be found in collections. As shown in the accompanying illustration, the first model has an odd circular capping mechanism forward of the lock; it is called Model 1849. The second design, Model 1850, retained the same long curving lock plate, but was designed to accommodate Dr. Maynard's tape primer instead of the circular capper. These rifles, too, are extremely scarce and desirable.

Meager finances handicapped Christian Sharps, so he went to New England and made a deal with the well-known Robbins & Lawrence gunmaking firm to produce (at their Windsor, Vermont, factory) an improved Sharps gun known as the Model 1851. This gun was designed with a box lock mechanism and also employed the Maynard tape primers. It was made in sporting rifle style and also as a military carbine, this carbine becoming the first *military* Sharps firearm.

For the Sharps-Robbins & Lawrence undertaking, a stock company known as the Sharps Rifle Manufacturing Co. was organized. Christian Sharps was to serve as "technical advisor" and receive royalties. A consideration in the various agreements made was that an arms factory would be built at Hartford, Connecticut, and Robbins & Lawrence would operate it. There at Hartford, as soon as the factory was completed and under direction of Richard S. Lawrence, was produced a new Sharps—the Model 1852. It was a slanting breech pattern, the first to resemble our popular conception of a Sharps sidehammer gun. For some reason, a patent primer was always a feature of Sharps percussion models, and this 1852 system employed a tube-like device which pushed up and fed fulminate wafers to the nipple. It is believed many shooters just stuck to the old reliable percussion caps, manually applied for each shot.

Unhappy with his sideline role, Christian Sharps withdrew from the Sharps Rifle Manufacturing Co. in 1853 and returned to Philadelphia. Thus his short personal activity in the manufacture of the big Sharps rifles was terminated. His main contribution was that he developed the basic ideas. Sharps then left the manufacture and development in other very capable hands.

A different lock was designed in 1855, returning again to the Maynard mortise for rolled tape priming, a system then popular with the U. S. Army Ordnance Department. Financial troubles had been piling up, and losses resulting from delays, changes, and cancellations of Model 1855 orders put the Robbins & Lawrence Co. on the rocks; on October 26, 1856, they failed. Two days later the Sharps Hartford factory was forced to suspend operations.

Somehow the Sharps Rifle Manufacturing Co. managed to survive the ensuing lawsuits and disruption of their manufacturing contracts, and got going again under leadership of Richard S. Lawrence. This inventive genius soon proceeded to design and manufacture a new "vertical breech" rifle which became known as the Model of 1859.

War was now imminent and the Sharps workmen and machinery were soon busily turning out carbines and military rifles for the federal government. There was a "New Model 1859," "New Model 1863," a conversion model of 1866; and thus we are brought to the metallic cartridge era.

While the Sharps rifle was far from the first to employ a sliding or dropping breech system, it was one of the simplest and strongest. It could be loaded and fired rapidly, was easy to keep clean, and was capable of containing stronger charges than most other guns of the day.

Lawrence's patent of April 6, 1869, brought the Sharps sidehammer rifle to the form we know it best today. At about the same time, the Sharps firm turned its attention to designing big long-range cartridges, including new bottleneck cases like the .44-77. Collectors will find the field of Sharps cartridges a most interesting auxiliary branch of their hobby.

Having now established a very efficient design for Sharps long-range hunting and target guns, Richard Lawrence retired. Two years later, in 1874, Christian Sharps died. On August 1, 1874 the litigation-weary stockholders of the Sharps Rifle Manufacturing Co. decided to liquidate the company.

A group of farsighted Bridgeport, Connecticut, businessmen, led by E. G. Westcott, purchased the patents, machinery, and other assets. Early in 1876 operations were moved to Bridgeport and there, under a slightly shortened name (Sharps Rifle Co.), manufacture of the sidehammer Sharps rifle was energetically resumed. The Sharps Model 1874 rifle became one of the most popular guns of the day. Soon after the move to Bridgeport, the Sharps Rifle Co. adopted the "Old Reliable" trade-mark.

There was big demand now for a long-range rifle on the western prairies where the buffalo harvest was well under way. And the international rifle matches with England and Ireland at Creedmoor aroused American sporting blood.

Reports of the heroic stand by a few buffalo hunters at Adobe Walls, down in the Texas panhandle, stirred the nation. This small group of hunters, all armed with big .44 and .50 caliber Sharps rifles, held off nearly a thousand charging savages.

With their fine 1874 action, the new Sharps Rifle Co. extended their line of sporting rifles to include short-range, mid-range, and long-range models. There were "hunters" models, "business" models, and "Creedmoor" target models. There were different types and lengths of barrels with many different calibers. So here the Sharps rifle collector comes to an area where he will find many different specimens.

One of the rarest of the metallic cartridge Sharps rifles is the Model 1875. This gun has a flat-sided breech with a different type integral lock. It was quickly superseded by the Model 1878 Borchardt with paneled flat-sided breech and concealed hammer.

Last of the *sidehammer* Sharps rifles (and one of the rarest) is the Model 1877. This has a smaller, curved lock plate, smaller hammer, and other refinements; it is practically custom-made.

The Model 1878 Borchardt carbines and rifles are relatively well-known. Many of our famous barrel makers like Pope, Zichang, Schoyen, and Peterson used the Borchardt action when building their fine target rifles. Military models were made primarily in .45-70 caliber (a few .45-75); sporting models were available in several calibers. There was a variety of barrel lengths and barrel weights, different quality in stocking, a wide selection of sights, and the finish could be plain or embellished with elaborate engraving on appropriate metal parts.

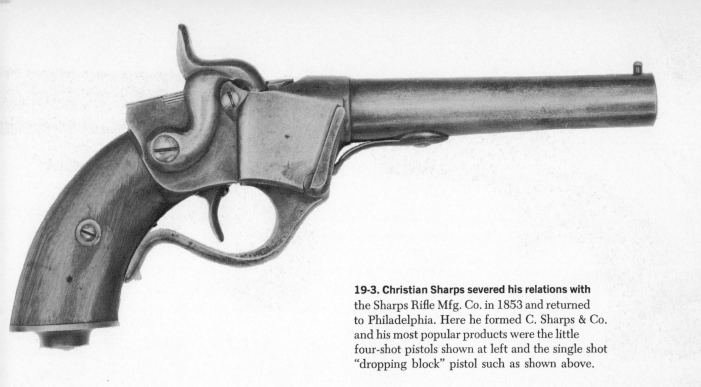

19-3. Christian Sharps severed his relations with the Sharps Rifle Mfg. Co. in 1853 and returned to Philadelphia. Here he formed C. Sharps & Co. and his most popular products were the little four-shot pistols shown at left and the single shot "dropping block" pistol such as shown above.

Additional interest for Sharps collectors may be found in the various conversions made on the basic Sharps actions. The work of Frank W. Freund of Cheyenne, Wyoming (later at Jersey City, New Jersey) is especially important in this field, and his name will be found on Sharps rifles altered by his various systems.

In 1881, thirty-three years after the Sharps rifle had been patented, the last Sharps-made gun came off the workbenches at Bridgeport. These had been a busy, and sometimes hectic, thirty-three years. But during these years the loud voice of the Sharps was heard wherever American history was being made. Today many interesting specimens await the collector. Some are scarred by hard usage on the buffalo range; others have heroic identity with the soldier; and still others reflect the great beauty and craftsmanship that went into fine target rifles. All in all, it is a fascinating field of collecting.

Although the weapons are not associated in the sense of common manufacturing interests, some Sharps collectors extend their collecting to include the arms manufactured at Philadelphia subsequent to Christian Sharps' withdrawal from the Sharps Rifle Manufacturing Co. in 1853.

These arms were primarily the products of a new firm formed by Sharps and known as C. Sharps & Co. Among the arms produced, models of special interest are a dropping-block single shot percussion pistol and a light sporting rifle built on the same action. There was also a pocket-size percussion revolver which is a scarce and desirable collector's piece.

The most popular of Sharps' pistols made in Philadelphia were his four-shot pocket pistols; they were made in .22, .30, and .32 rimfire calibers. These little pistols are to be found with a number of variations, some involving important mechanical changes but most of the variations were minor.

Sharps formed a partnership with William Hankins in 1862, and this arrangement lasted for four years, during which Sharps and Hankins turned out four-barrel pistols along with a not-too-successful carbine and rifle which has an action that permits the barrel to slide forward for loading. One rather unusual feature found on many of the Sharps & Hankins carbines is that the barrel is encased in leather.

Sharps gave up the gun business in 1871 and died three years later at the age of 63. He died a poor man in worldly goods, but rich in prideful accomplishment.

The collector will find help and interest in these publications: *The Sharps Rifle* (W. O. Smith), *Fourteen Old Gun Catalogs* (Satterlee—Reprint by Gun Digest Co.), *Single Shot Rifles* (James J. Grant), *The Rifle in America* (Phil Sharpe), and AMERICAN RIFLEMAN MAGAZINE (April, 1962).

the Products of Smith and Wesson 20.

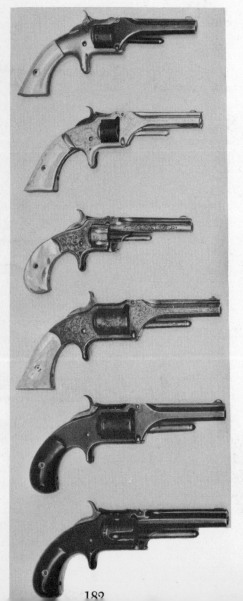

20-1. From top, left: 1/Model 1 Series 1, .22 caliber. 2/Model 1 Series 2, .22 caliber. 3/Model 1 Series 3, .22 caliber. 4/Model 1½ Old Model, .32 caliber. 5/Model 1½ Transition Model, .32 caliber. 6/Model 1½ New Model, .32 caliber. From top, right: 7/Model 2, .32 caliber. 8/Plant-Merwin & Bray patent infringement.

Any study of Smith & Wesson firearms must of necessity begin with a consideration of the early patents which were to be the building blocks of this great American industry.

As is the case in many rags-to-riches stories, the success of Smith & Wesson was born of failure. In 1849 Lewis Jennings, by modifying several earlier patents, produced a tube-fed magazine rifle utilizing self-contained bullets ignited by an external priming system. The rifle lacked sufficient firepower to be competitive with the muzzle-loaders, so the idea was abandoned. B. Tyler Henry, an employee of Robbins & Lawrence who had manufactured the Jennings rifle, saw some merit to the mechanism and sought to perfect the weapon.

In the early 1850s Horace Smith was an unknown but skilled gunsmith in Worcester, Massachusetts, at that time a center of the infant American firearms industry. In the fall of 1850 Smith was approached by Tyler Henry with an idea for further improving the Hunt-Jennings rifle to a level of practical use. In August of 1851 a patent was accordingly issued to Horace Smith for an improved magazine firearm but there is no record of firearms production of the association of Smith & Henry. At some time prior to 1854 the two were joined by Daniel B. Wesson, a brother of Edwin Wesson, the inventor of the Wesson & Leavitt revolver.

Until this time the supremacy of Colonel Colt's revolver was well established, both in public acceptance and in court decisions involving patents. Daniel Wesson, as heir to Edwin Wesson's patents, had the rights to both a mechanically operated cylinder as well as to the "break-open" system of removing the cylinder for reloading. Because of

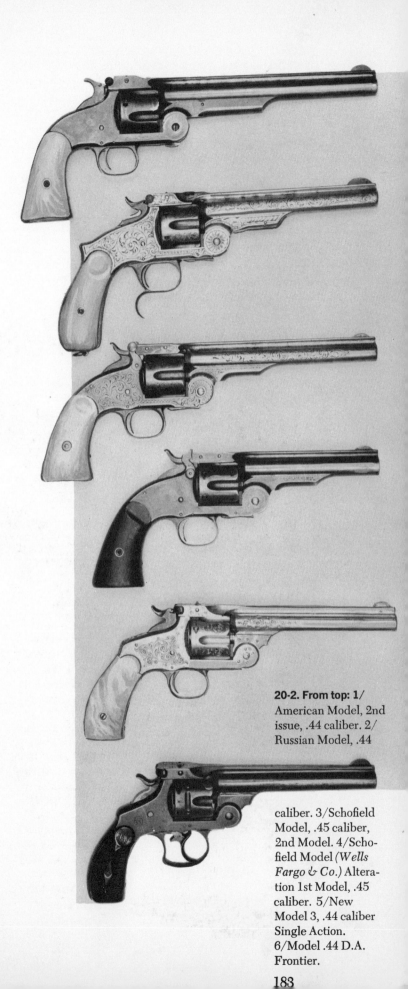

20-2. From top: 1/ American Model, 2nd issue, .44 caliber. 2/ Russian Model, .44 caliber. 3/Schofield Model, .45 caliber, 2nd Model. 4/Schofield Model (*Wells Fargo & Co.*) Alteration 1st Model, .45 caliber. 5/New Model 3, .44 caliber Single Action. 6/Model .44 D.A. Frontier.

patents issued to Colonel Colt, Wesson could not employ the Colt principles. Wesson's attraction to Smith and Henry may have resulted from his desire to meet Colonel Colt on more favorable fields of competitive arms manufacture.

Through the combination of the inventive genius of Smith, Wesson, and Henry, there evolved the Smith & Wesson and eventually the Volcanic repeating pistols and rifles. Both are similar in mechanical principle, there being a toggle mechanism in the receiver activated by the lever-like trigger guard which feeds cartridges from a tubular magazine beneath the barrel into the breech. In general, two pistol models are known, both of varying barrel lengths. Three barrel markings are seen, each representing a transition in the company. They are as follows:

(a) "Smith & Wesson, Norwich, Conn." This represents the original production of iron frame 4-inch and 8-inch barrel pistols in .30 and .38 caliber (1854-1855).

(b) "Volcanic Arms Company, New Haven, Conn." This was the production of the Volcanic Repeating Arms Company of New Haven (1856-1857) and included the brass-frame pistols in both sizes, together with a stocked pistol, rifles, and carbines.

(c) "New Haven, Conn. Patent Feb. 14, 1854." The final transition to the New Haven Arms Company producing both size pistols and the carbines from 1858-1860. According to Colonel B. R. Lewis, minor differences in the caliber of the three types of Volcanic types will be seen, varying from bore diameters of .302 inches to .396 inches.

All of the Volcanic-type arms depended upon the self-contained cartridge consisting of a conical lead ball into whose base was placed a small amount of fulminate of mercury acting as both primer and propellant. The self-limiting firepower of this cartridge, although adequate for low velocity target shooting, offered little competition to Colonel Colt's "man stopper." This feature, together with the corrosive effects of the fulminate of mercury on barrel life and the dangers peculiar to the manufacture and handling of the cartridge, lead to the early demise of the Volcanic-type arms. It was undoubtedly a direct result of the defects in the Volcanic cartridge that led Daniel Wesson to his experiments that were to result in the development of the rimfire cartridge.

Oliver Winchester, in the tradition of the Connecticut Yankee, negotiated with Smith & Wesson the transfer of the repeating arms patents along with an agreement to manufacture and sell all cartridges under the past, present, and future patents of Horace Smith. This master stroke at the bargaining table was apparently done through the efforts of Tyler Henry, then associated with Winchester.

The partners, Smith and Wesson, their pockets now lined with Oliver Winchester's gold, moved to Springfield, Massachusetts, to perfect a revolver that was to accommodate Daniel Wesson's rimfire cartridge.

The Colt revolving cylinder patent was not to expire until the fall of 1857. The .22 rimfire cartridge was still experimental and the revolver to use it had not yet evolved. In this developmental phase of the organization, a patent search led them to the name of Rollin White, a Hartford, Connecticut, inventor-gunsmith, who in 1854 had been issued a patent for a revolver with the cylinder bored through from front to rear. There was at the time of submission of the patent no provision for a cartridge for the arm. White, thinking only in terms of loading, backed the powder charge and ball with paper wadding.

The next step was obvious. Smith & Wesson had the cartridge and with the Rollin White cylinder, the modern cartridge revolver was about to be born.

In November of 1856 an assignment of Rollin White's patent of April 3, 1854, was made to Smith & Wesson. The price was $500 and 25¢ for each and every arm produced with the bored-through cylinder.

The die was now cast. Smith & Wesson began to assemble the skilled gunmakers, machinists, and suppliers necessary for firearms production. By November of 1857 the first revolvers were ready for delivery.

The "toylike" first model S&W .22 revolver may be considered by collectors as a rarity of the first order. This diminutive arm, the forefather of modern cartridge revolvers, measured less than 5 inches over-all. The oval brass frame was characterized by a circular brass plate on the left side, secured by the hammer axis screw, which allows access to the inner workings of the trigger and hammer assembly. The barrel was octagonal with a top rib and approximately 3¾6 inches in length. All barrels bore the rolled stamp *Smith & Wesson, Springfield, Mass.* The barrel was joined to the frame in front of the top strap and held on the bottom by a spring latch which was released by upward pressure. The trigger mechanism of the spur variety operated directly from the hammer. The hammer and cylinder stop mechanism were peculiar to the arm. The upper portion of the hammer being jointed in a jaw-like arrangement, engaged a spring-loaded projection from the top strap as the hammer fell, this arrangement thus locking the cylinder at the point of firing. The cylinder was bored for seven cartridges and engaged to the frame by a projecting knob through the recoil shield. The cylinder was marked *Patented April 3, 1855.*

The need for improvement was obvious in the production progression of the arm. At least six variations are known, largely through the research efforts of Herschel Logan and Carl Kountz. The six variations all carry the two-piece hammer and the round side plate.

The first variation, by far the most rare, has a simple flat spring-type barrel latch and a recoil shield held in place to the frame by a dovetailed key. Very few specimens of this variation are known. The remaining five variants are characterized by the improved "uplift" barrel catch, together with improvements on the recoil shield mechanism, this simplification being a reflection of a continuing improvement of the cartridge. It has been estimated by some that approximately 68,000 of the "oval frame first model" were produced. The first and second models were numbered consecutively, with a total production of the two models in the neighborhood of 126,000. The survival rate of the first model is sufficiently low to make the author suspicious of the first figure. It would seem logical to agree with Herschel Logan's figures of the first model production ending in the 11,000 to 12,000 serial range.

In 1860 a new model of the No. 1 was offered to the public, known to collectors as the No. 1-2nd issue.

It featured a flat brass frame with the round side-plate being replaced by an irregular plate offering improved access to the inner workings. The jointed hammer was eliminated, with slight improvements to the cylinder stop. The serial range continued through 126,249. This model is frequently seen in presentation grades, indicating its popularity as a pocket weapon during the Civil War period. Perhaps one of the few concessions to quality is to be found in the first model, 2nd issue revolver. During the Civil War, when the demand had far exceeded the supply, a limited number of pistols, defective in appearance but not in function, was placed on the market. These pistols were marked on the left barrel flat just in front of the cylinder with a clear stamp "2nd quality." The specimen in the author's collection has a flaw in the brass sideplate with a hole ¹⁄₃₂ inch in diameter completely penetrating the plate. Certainly the circumstances of demand must have been quite dire to allow the release and sale of these arms.

In June of 1861 Smith & Wesson, acceding to the demands of the public for greater firepower, began delivery of their "Model 2" pistol. This revolver of .32 caliber physically resembles the "Model 1-2nd issue" with several variations. The "Model 2" was a 6-shot, .32 caliber, rimfire revolver, the frame was of iron, and barrel lengths of 4, 5, or 6 inches were available. The recoil shield had been eliminated and the revolving ratchet was an integral part of the cylinder. Two distinct models are known, their differences being so small as to be overlooked by the average collector. The earlier No. 2 guns have only 2 pins in the frame over the cylinder holding the cylinder lock, while the later Model 2 has 3 pins. The earlier gun has the serial stamped with a smaller size die than does the later model. The earlier serialed cylinder will not fit the later serialed gun. The Model 2 represents truly a collector's bonanza. If we tire of minor mechanical differences, we can seek out the presentation pieces with the strong Civil War attachment, or perhaps even better advance to a collection of Model 2 pistols with various selling agents names stamped thereupon. The models sold and stamped with the names of B. Kittredge, John Krider, H. E. Dimick, J. W. Storrs, Webley, J. C. Jane, or Tiffany & Co. are a story within themselves. The popularity of this revolver was world-wide. The author has seen more models of foreign copies of this revolver than of any weapon that Smith & Wesson manufactured. Included in this group are the usual Belgian imitations but also high quality English, German, and Swiss weapons that are direct copies of the Model 2. Total production reached serial #76,502 and ended in 1874. The Civil War production ended in the 22,000 range. The popularity of the weapon in the war is well documented; the limited cartridge supply prevented far greater acceptance.

At this point it might be well to consider a marking system used on the earlier Smith & Wesson revolvers that seems to be confusing to some collectors. Great doubts are currently placed on the validity of an antique firearm with "so-called mixed numbers." This stems from the fact that the earlier arms makers identified all of the major parts, i.e., cylinder, barrel, frame, etc. with a serial number corresponding to the master number of the gun itself. Smith and Wesson did not adopt this system until the production of the Schofield model. On most of the earlier S & W's, an assembly code was all to be found that would interrelate one major part with another. This code consisted of a single letter or number or combination of letter or symbol and number that was placed on the gun in three places. On the breech portion of the barrel, visible as the gun is "tipped open," on the front surface of the cylinder, adjacent to the pivot knob, and on the frame beneath the grips. The serial stamped on the butt of the gun was also stamped into the wooden grips. Consideration of these points will remind the collector that in corresponding marks may be found some assurance that a particular weapon has persisted in parts as it was originally assembled. When we consider the fact that S & W was a pioneer in the interchangeability of parts, it is easy to understand how the unscrupulous might well produce desirable collectors' items from the parts bin.

With the end of the Civil War in 1864, S & W was ready to branch out into further improvements and introduced their "Model 1½." This was a five-shot .32 caliber revolver that was a hybrid number somewhere between the No. 1-2nd issue and the No. 2 model pistol. The arm featured an improved cylinder stop pivoted to the bottom of the frame and operating off the hammer tumbler. Some 25,224 were produced before production was stopped in 1868. An improvement in the Model 1½ appeared in the making in 1867. This pistol, designated the New Model 1½, featured bird-head grips, a rounded

barrel, and a fluted cylinder. The new pistol also had the familiar top spring cylinder stop with the wedged hammer. By this time, either through production economy or manpower availability, S & W subcontracted parts manufacture outside of the parent plant. The correspondence with these subcontractors has brought to light a very interesting and little known revolver, which collectors identify as the "Transition Model 1½." At first glance this arm would appear to be a poor fake or at best a manufactured joke, consisting of the frame of the New Model 1½ with its bird-head grips and the plain unfluted cylinder and the flat barrel of the old Model 1½. Perhaps a thousand of these left the factory. The serial range is consecutive with the old and new models and they appear between 27,576 and 28,196. This economy move in utilizing otherwise unsalable parts has led to an unusual collector's piece. Here the assembly code is particularly useful in identifying the authentic transition model. Production of the orthodox New Model 1½ continued through 1875 with a serial range in excess of 120,000.

In 1868 Smith and Wesson produced the last of the No. 1 models with improvements corresponding to the New Model 1½. This .22 caliber 7-shot revolver featured the rounded barrel, the fluted cylinder, and the bird-head grips. Production continued through 1879 with a total production slightly in excess of 131,000.

This period in the life of Smith & Wesson was destined to become somewhat turbulent. The popularity of the Smith & Wesson rimfire revolver was loudly attested by their agents' inability to supply the public demands. Ingenuity coupled with the desire for profit led a surprising number of manufacturers to tool up and produce a wide variety of arms that were either a direct infringement of the Rollin White patent or at best a clever evasion thereof. The story of these revolvers is a chapter in itself; suffice it to mention here only the names of Allen and Wheelock, Bacon Arms Co., W. L. Grant, Manhattan Firearms Manufacturing Co., Moores Patent Firearms Co., Lucius W. Pond, E. A. Prescott, James Reid, Plant Mfg. Co., and Deringer of Philadelphia. The reader is advised not to consider these a cheap imitation of the "suicide" variety, but in many instances they equalled or surpassed the original Smith & Wesson revolver in

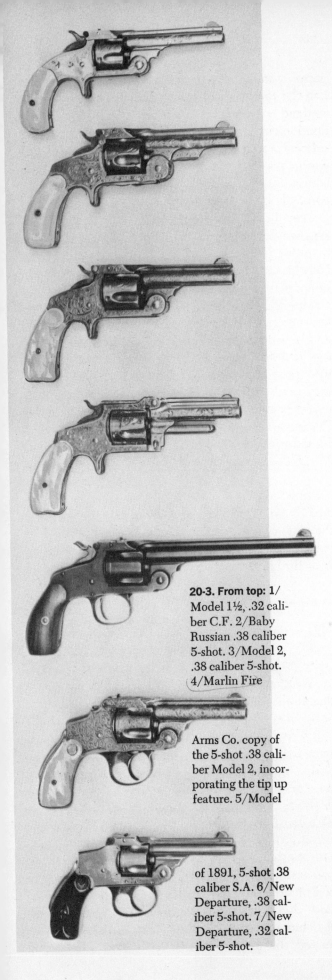

20-3. From top: 1/ Model 1½, .32 caliber C.F. 2/Baby Russian .38 caliber 5-shot. 3/Model 2, .38 caliber 5-shot. 4/Marlin Fire Arms Co. copy of the 5-shot .38 caliber Model 2, incorporating the tip up feature. 5/Model of 1891, 5-shot .38 caliber S.A. 6/New Departure, .38 caliber 5-shot. 7/New Departure, .32 caliber 5-shot.

design and quality of manufacture. The litigations involved in the patent suits to force these manufacturers to cease production were resolved in the Federal Courts in 1863, with Smith and Wesson emerging triumphant. As a result of this action, a number of the arms bearing the imitator's name may also be inscribed, "Manufactured for Smith & Wesson."

In 1869, with the Rollin White patent about to expire, Daniel Wesson set about conquering new fields. The firepower of the previous revolvers had been limited by the "tip-up" mechanism to .32 caliber. If the company was to prosper, Wesson reasoned that it would be necessary to produce a larger caliber weapon. With assignments from W. C. Dodge on a revolver frame pivoted at the frame with the barrel and held in place by a top latch, and another from C. A. King for a cogwheel mechanism for ejecting all of the spent cartridges from the cylinder simultaneously, the new No. 3 pistol was launched.

The .44 caliber "American" was the first large caliber revolver to use metallic cartridges. A six-shot weapon with an eight-inch barrel, this massive weapon now answered all of the challenges of the Colt and the Remington revolvers of the same percussion caliber along with outdistancing them in the simultaneous cartridge ejection system. The "American" held this distinction until 1874 when the Colt single-action entered the field. Two models are known. Of the first model a few over 1,000 were supplied to the U.S. Army. These are distinguished by the "U.S." marking on the top strap just in front of the cylinder, along with inspectors' stamps (P & A) on the cylinder and frame. The first model carried a plain hammer, the second issue being characterized by a notch which engaged the barrel latch as the hammer is depressed. Those of the first issue, with serial numbers under 1500, are characterized by a small oil vent in the bottom of the ejector housing. The second model "American" incorporating the notched hammer-barrel catch safety feature was introduced after serial number 6000 and continued to the termination of the model.

The association with the military of the first model "American" led to interest on the part of Colonel George Schofield in the development of another S & W. Schofield was not only a soldier but also somewhat of a firearms inventor and accordingly sought to improve on the Model 3. S & W, anxious to further their military contracts, sought Schofield's suggestions on the development of a second military arm. The result of this association led to the development of the Schofield model. A .45 S&W caliber six-shot revolver, differing largely from the No. 3 American in two variations of the barrel latch and in the mechanism, allowed more ready removal of the cylinder. Approximately 8,000 of these pistols were delivered to the government; the "U.S." stamp is to be found on the butt with inspector's marks on the frame and cylinder. By now Colt and Remington had entered the government supply race and a lack of interchangeable ammunition led to a premature demise of this fine old Schofield model. An unknown number of Schofields were sold as surplus property to Wells Fargo & Co. as issue weapons for the Overland Stage. This weapon, highly prized by collectors, has the barrel cut at the factory to 5 inches along with the stamp "W.F. & Co. Ex." stamped on the right side of the ejector housing. The front sight has been repinned and the U.S. on the butt remains unaltered.

In 1870 Horace Smith, apparently tiring of the firearms business, sold his interest to D. B. Wesson, but the firm continued with the original name. In 1871 Smith and Wesson began a series of contracts with the Russian government that were to result in the ultimate delivery of 150,000 revolvers and was to insure a period of prosperity for the Springfield gunmakers. Several models are known to collectors. The first or the O.O.M. (old, old model) Russian differed little from the No. 3-2nd model American. The barrels of this series were stamped in cyrillic. A few of the factory overruns were sold in the U.S. and it is not unusual to find a Model 3 American bearing the top strap inscription "Russian Model." All of the Russian series were chambered for the "Russian cartridge," an improvement on the old American cartridge. This new cartridge of .44 caliber represented a muzzle energy of 316 foot pounds and its popularity was to extend into later S & W production.

In 1873 the firm began production of a modified Russian design. This model incorporated a saw-type handle with a knuckle on the frame, a 7-inch barrel and a finger rest spur on the trigger guard. A large number of these were produced for the Russian Government, all bearing the cyrillic inscrip-

tion on the barrel. The gun was also produced unchanged for the domestic market, marked in English, *Smith & Wesson, Springfield, Massachusetts*. The bulk of those sold on the domestic market were sold through Schuyler, Hartley & Graham and their mark "SH" together with the date 1874, may appear on the butt adjacent to the serial number. The popularity of the model may be attested by its copyists; a "Tula Model" is known to be of good quality, an exact Russian copy manufactured at the Tula Arsenal. It carried the cyrillic markings together with an inspector's stamp "OOP" on the left side of the knuckle on the frame.

Ludwig Loewe Co. also supplied a number of exact copies of the N.M. Russian. These bear the cyrillic markings along with the German marks. These pistols may also be seen with the "OOP" & "1874" inspector's stamp. The die for both stamps in all probability had been fabricated in the S & W plant. Rimfires in both the OOM and the N. M. Russian were supplied to both Turkey and Mexico. These arms are of sufficient rarity and value that the consideration thereof is usually left to the advanced collector.

During this period of foreign activity for Smith & Wesson, Colt was busy flooding the American market with a number of smaller revolvers designed for the protection of home and person.

In 1874, S & W sought to regain their domestic prestige with the development of a smaller, automatic ejecting pistol. Accordingly Daniel Wesson developed the .38 caliber S & W cartridge with a 150-grain bullet charged with 14 grains of powder. By 1876 the first model .38 caliber single action was in production. The first model known as the "Baby Russian" was a 5-shot fluted cylinder revolver characterized by the enlarged ejector housing beneath the barrel and similar in action to the extractor mechanism of the .44 American and the Russian. The spur trigger was a prominent feature, although certainly not contributing to its safety features. In 1880 a second model appeared, incorporating changes in the extractor mechanism but retaining the spur trigger and the general outlines of the first model. Hard rubber grips are seen on both models, the earlier mark being a simple "S & W" on the crown portion, the later models showing the entwined "S & W" trademark carried through to the present day. A third model .38

appeared in 1891 and bore the barrel stamp "Model 91" together with the S & W mark and patent dates. This improvement carried a trigger guard and was available in .22, .32 and .38 caliber single shot barrels which were interchangeable with the 3½-inch barrel and cylinder for converting the arm to a pocket revolver.

Simultaneously there appeared a .32 caliber center-fire self-ejecting revolver. Reverting in design to the old bird-head grips, this model featured the first "rebounding hammer," so arranged to prevent the hammer from coming into contact with the cartridge head except at the moment of impact. This model was produced and sold competitively with a great number of copyists and the so-called "suicide special" variety, and its production continued through 1892 to serial range 97,000.

Somewhat content with the addition of the .38 and .32 caliber auto ejectors to the line, S & W went back to improvements on their .44 caliber revolver. This led to the design of the No. 3 New Model. This was a streamlined, large frame revolver designed to capture the imagination of the military as well as the civilian. Chambered originally for the proven and popular .44 Russian cartridge, the arm was later to appear in .44-40 target, and .38-44 target and .32-44 target, plain wood or hard rubber stocks and improved ejector gear. This single-action revolver found its greatest popularity with the target shooters of the day. Several collecting rarities exist in the New Model 3 series; a "Frontier model" chambered the .44-40 Winchester cartridge was produced as a companion piece to the Winchester rifle. The cylinder was ⅛-inch longer than the standard model with a corresponding increase in the length of the top strap. New Model 3 revolvers were also supplied to the Australian Colonial Police and bore the broad arrow stamp on the butt as well as on the shank of the extension shoulder stock that was supplied with the piece. Another interesting mark is that of the Japanese Navy seen stamped on the base of the frame beneath the cylinder, an anchor crossed with two wavy lines. These represent a small shipment of less than 600 revolvers. Rimfires in the New Model 3 were also produced, largely for shipment to Turkey.

In 1881, S & W adapted the double-action principle to a large .44 caliber revolver known as the D.A.

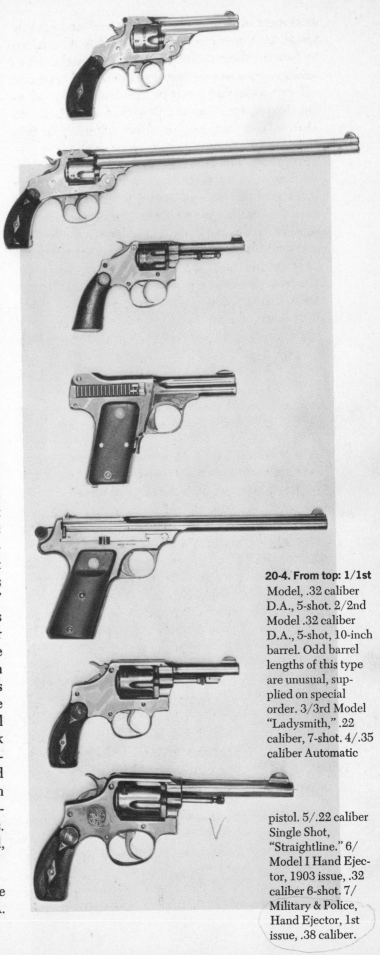

20-4. From top: 1/1st Model, .32 caliber D.A., 5-shot. 2/2nd Model .32 caliber D.A., 5-shot, 10-inch barrel. Odd barrel lengths of this type are unusual, supplied on special order. 3/3rd Model "Ladysmith," .22 caliber, 7-shot. 4/.35 caliber Automatic pistol. 5/.22 caliber Single Shot, "Straightline." 6/ Model I Hand Ejector, 1903 issue, .32 caliber 6-shot. 7/ Military & Police, Hand Ejector, 1st issue, .38 caliber.

New Model 3 Navy. This weapon was chambered for the .44 Russian, the .44-40 WCF, or the .38-40 WCF and was a well-made revolver that somehow failed to achieve any great public acceptance. It saw some military usage in South America and was modified as a target arm called the "Wesson Favorite."

Shoulder stocks for S & W revolvers appeared with the Model 3 American at this time, apparently as an afterthought. All models cut for stock show two notches in the butt, the first obliterating the final serial numbers, indicating that the stock notches were added after the serial had been applied. Shoulder stocks were also available for the Russian and the New Model 3.

In 1877 there appeared the S & W revolving rifle. Upon external appearance, this gun looked like the New Model 3 with an elongated barrel. Supplied with 16-, 18-, or 20-inch barrels, it was chambered for the .32 S & W revolving rifle cartridge. The gun was supplied with mottled orange-red hard rubber grips and fore-end together with a detachable walnut stock. Less than 1,000 were produced and today they represent the virtual top of any S & W collection.

At this phase in the chronology of Smith & Wesson we enter upon the modern era. In 1880, S & W announced their double-action revolver. The double-action principle, long known through the percussion period, was applied to a metallic cartridge revolver by Colt in 1877. The first S & W double-action revolver was chambered for the .38 caliber S & W cartridge and has several distinctive characteristics; the first was the square-backed trigger guard; the second, a double series of notches in the cylinder with a second circular groove; and thirdly, the square cut sideplate departing from irregular shape of all previous models. The sideplate was changed to the irregular shape in the second model and three subsequent models were made, all em-

bodying minor mechanical changes and except for the first two changes, identified by their serial range.

Concurrently with the .38 double-action, a .32 was produced. The first model having the double cut cylinder and the irregular sideplate; the second and third models changed to a single cut cylinder with improvements in the cylinder stop and are externally indistinguishable. The .32 D.A. is distinguished chiefly by the fact that it had the longest serial run of any previous S & W revolver, terminating in 1919 at 327,641.

The closing paragraphs of the S & W story so far as we have space to carry it here, must in passing mention the later refinements that are indeed illustrative of the inventive productivity of this fine American tradition. The "New Departures" with their safety hammer feature, designed as the perfect, safe house pistol and so well made that it failed by only a fraction of passing an Ordnance test that would have made it an Army side arm. The Perfected and the Olympic single shot target pistols held many American and foreign records. In the same vein, the "Straight Line," which but for a faulty hammer mechanism might well remain in production today. All of these arms, together with the early automatics and the diminutive "Ladysmith," the "finest American industrial example of miniaturization," represent the inventive ingenuity and high standards of Smith & Wesson workmanship which bring great pleasure to both the collector and the shooter.

The reader is referred to the more definitive works on the Smith & Wesson story by McHenry & Roper and by John E. Parsons as well as to the many articles appearing in the *American Rifleman* by Herschel Logan, Colonel B. R. Lewis, Carl Kountz, and Colonel R. C. Kuhn. Special thanks is expressed to Ralph Tidd and to M. R. Waddell for a number of personal observations mentioned in this chapter.

the Winchester Guns

21.

In 1866 the first Winchester was introduced, and within the next two decades Winchester firearms had become world famous. T h e i r greatest popularity was attained in the western U n i t e d States. Winchester is as much a part of the American scene as the famous Kentucky rifle, Sharps breechloader, or the Colt six-shooter. Today the old lever-action Winchesters are actively sought in the collector's market.

In almost one hundred years of gun production, many models of Winchesters have been made; this outline highlights just a few of these. The forerunner of the first Winchester was the Henry rifle; this was patented in 1860 and manufactured by the New Haven Arms Company of which Oliver Winchester was president. By 1862 enough Henrys had been made to make the public well aware of them. The Henry was a lever-action rifle with a sixteen-shot capacity, which made it a remarkable firearm of its day. Unfortunately, it had one serious drawback—that was the open slot along the lower side of the magazine tube; this wasn't too practical. Some of the first Henrys were made with an iron frame and the acquisition of one of these is most pleasing to the collector. The common frames were brass and are still a collector's prize.

A great deal of time and effort was put into designing an improved rifle. In 1866 a patent was issued to Nelson King for a loading port in the side of the receiver.

21-1. Model 1873 rifle, a deluxe model with selected and checkered stock, barrel marked "1 of 1000."

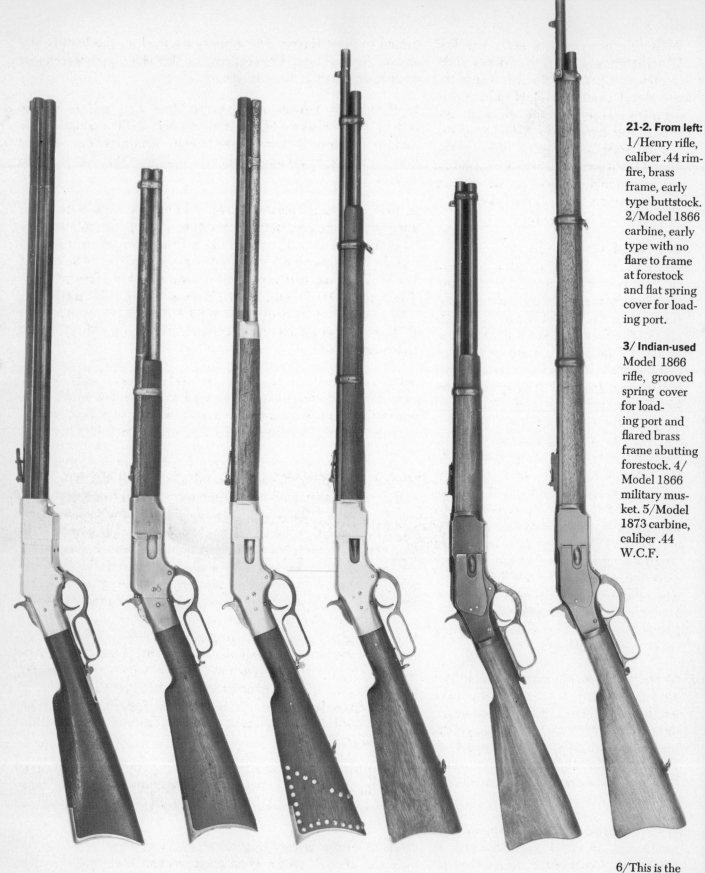

21-2. From left:
1/Henry rifle, caliber .44 rimfire, brass frame, early type buttstock. 2/Model 1866 carbine, early type with no flare to frame at forestock and flat spring cover for loading port.

3/ Indian-used Model 1866 rifle, grooved spring cover for loading port and flared brass frame abutting forestock. 4/ Model 1866 military musket. 5/Model 1873 carbine, caliber .44 W.C.F.

6/This is the military model of the 1873 gun. (See 21-1)

With this new development, the first Winchester was born, the Model 1866. Confident of greater sales, because of the new development, it was decided to re-organize and enlarge the company and change the name to the Winchester Repeating Arms Company. Deliveries of the Model 1866s were not made to the public until the summer of 1867, at which time the Henry was discontinued with some 14,000 having been made.

The Model 1866 Winchester was numbered on from the Henry, production of the two guns overlapping. Some Henry rifles known were numbered in the 14,000 serial range and Model '66s in the 12,000 range. The first '66s had a flat receiver, similar to the Henry, which was brass, made without shoulders to butt against the wooden fore-end. The spring cover for the loading port was also flat; it did not have the concave shape which was put on later ones. Some two to three thousand were made in this manner. In the latter part of 1867, the second type or "New Model" 1866 appeared with the receiver and spring cover for the loading port made in the familiar concave manner. The first type is sometimes called the "Improved Henry" and in old company records is referred to as the "Old Model" while the second type is called the "New Model." There seems to have been a very few early '66s made without a spring cover for the loading port.

At first, the name Winchester did not appear on the guns, but after some nine or ten thousand Model '66s had been made, the practice of putting the name on the barrel was established; this was early in 1869. The first Model 1866s were made both in rifle and carbine style; late in 1869 the musket style was added.

With the introduction of the Model 1866, production facilities were moved to Bridgeport, Connecticut, where they remained until 1871 at which time they re-turned to New Haven. The address stamped on the barrels was always New Haven, Connecticut, as the office and warehouse were maintained in New Haven.

In 1870, 3,000 muskets and 3,000 carbines were sold to France and in 1870-71 some 45,000 muskets and 5,000 carbines were sold to Turkey. It was these foreign contracts that helped Winchester over a financial hurdle and put the company on its feet.

In 1891, component parts of the Model 1866 that were on hand for many years were used in the assembly of about 1,000 rifles and carbines and chambered for a .44 caliber center-fire cartridge. This was the ".44 Henry center-fire" and was similar to the .44 Smith and Wesson American cartridge. These were shipped to a firm in Brazil. The standard Model '66s, like the Henrys, were chambered for the .44 rimfire Henry cartridge. The Model 1866 was discontinued in 1898 with some 156,000 manufactured, allowing for about 14,000 Henry rifles made.

Some of the choicest Model '66s, by collectors standards, are the early ones with the flat spring covers for the loading port, Indian guns which were decorated with brass tacks and, of course, gold- or silver-plated engraved specimens that were signed by Conrad or John Ulrich.

With a demand for a more powerful rifle, Winchester introduced a new model chambered for a .44 caliber center-fire cartridge. This was the Model 1873; it was this model that made the name Winchester synonymous with "lever-action rifle." In the course of its long period of production, 1873 to 1924, the '73 was chambered for .38 and .32 center-fire cartridges and .22 rimfire, but the .44-40 remained the most popular. This chambering was so popular that in 1878 Colt chambered their famous Single-Action Frontier for the same cartridge. Western folklore has often said that many a western baby cut its teeth on a saddle ring of a Winchester Model '73 carbine. This model was made in rifle, carbine, and musket style. Also available were extras, such as various barrel lengths, fancy woods, engraving, etc. For nearly half a century Buffalo Bill used the '73 both on the western plains and in his "Wild West" traveling show. This model was a favorite with everyone, from the Indian to the "Lawman."

It was the introduction of the Model 1873 Winchester that brought about the designation of the first Winchester as the Model 1866. Until that time the guns had just been referred to as "Winchesters."

With its center-fire cartridge, iron and later, steel receiver, the '73 was a great improvement over the '66. For a time in 1874 and early 1875 the

Model '66 production was stopped, but because the cost of a '66 was lower and customer demand continued, production was resumed again in the fall of 1875.

Some of the most interesting and worthwhile collector's Model '73s are the ones marked "1 of 1000" or "1 of 100." This designation was put on the barrels either in script or numerals. These

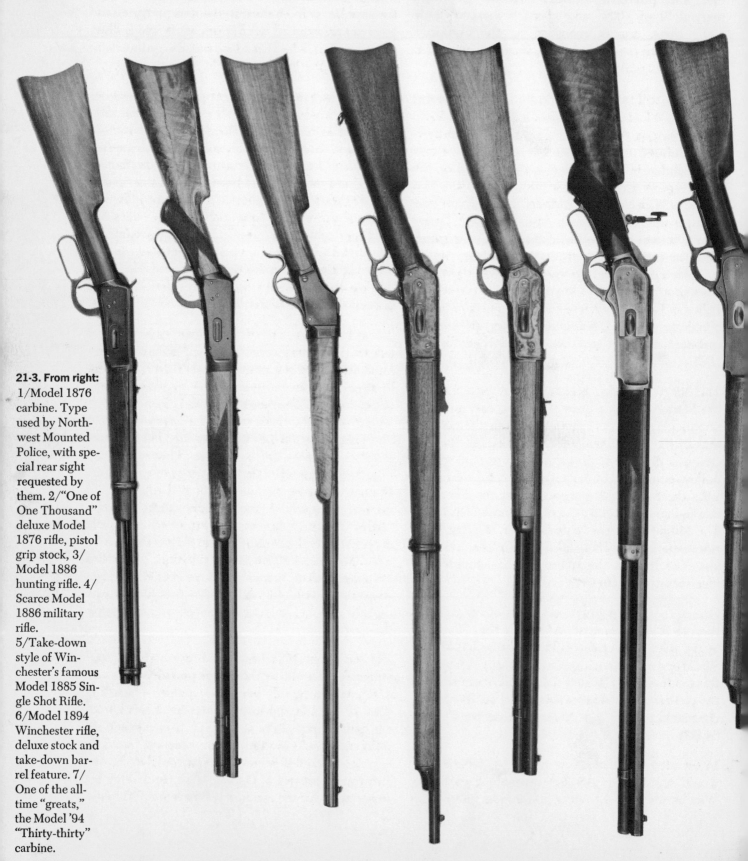

21-3. From right: 1/Model 1876 carbine. Type used by Northwest Mounted Police, with special rear sight requested by them. 2/"One of One Thousand" deluxe Model 1876 rifle, pistol grip stock, 3/ Model 1886 hunting rifle. 4/ Scarce Model 1886 military rifle. 5/Take-down style of Winchester's famous Model 1885 Single Shot Rifle. 6/Model 1894 Winchester rifle, deluxe stock and take-down barrel feature. 7/ One of the all-time "greats," the Model '94 "Thirty-thirty" carbine.

particular guns were picked for their accuracy. The most accurate was marked "1 of 1000" and the next was marked "1 of 100"; they were made up in a super-grade type, fancy wood, checkering, etc., and priced accordingly. About 133 were marked "1 of 1000" and about 8 marked "1 of 100"; these are so recorded in the company records. Like the Model '66, Ulrich-engraved '73s are also desirable.

To meet a still further demand for a more powerful repeater, Winchester brought out the Model 1876, also known as the "Centennial Model" because it was exhibited at the Centennial Exposition held in Philadelphia in the summer of 1876. Based on the same type of toggle joint lever action as the two previous Winchesters, the Model '76 was larger and stronger and could handle cartridges with longer range. It was more suited for hunting big game. Like the previous models of Winchesters, the '76 was available in rifle, carbine, or musket style with the various extras. The Royal Northwest Mounted Police in Canada adopted the carbine style, chambered for .45-75, as their official firearm. It was this carbine that helped put down the Riel Rebellion in 1885.

The .45-75 cartridge was developed especially for the Model 1876 and gave a striking energy of approximately 1,400 foot pounds, or more than double that of the .44-40 Winchester caliber. An Express rifle was listed in a .50 caliber, using a 300-grain, hollow-point, lead bullet with copper tube inserted. Like the Model '73, a very few of the '76s were marked and recorded as "1 of 100" and "1 of 1000." The Model 1876 was fairly popular as a big game rifle, especially in England, India, Africa and Canada. The '76 was the last of the "old toggle-joint lever-action Winchesters."

One of the most popular cartridges of the day was the .45-70 Government. Although the '76 was a heavy rifle, the action could not quite handle the .45-70 or similar cartridges satisfactorily. Therefore, this model never attained the popularity of some of the contemporary single shot rifles. The '76 was discontinued in 1897 with a total production of about 64,000.

In an attempt to make a repeating firearm that would handle the .45-70 Government cartridge, Winchester brought out a bolt-action rifle, which

was invented and patented by Benjamin B. Hotchkiss. This model was first introduced in 1879, later revamped and called the Model 1883. As a military firearm it was received favorably by the U.S. and foreign governments. As a sporting rifle it wasn't too popular, as the American shooters preferred the lever-action type of mechanism with which they were familiar. The Hotchkiss was discontinued in 1899; an approximate total of 84,500 were made.

In 1879 a patent was issued to John M. Browning of Ogden, Utah, for a single shot lever-action rifle. Rifles made under this patent were remarkably strong and accurate. Having heard of their merits, the Winchester Company purchased manufacturing rights about 1883 and brought out a new model in 1885 called the Winchester Single Shot Rifle. Because of the year of introduction, these rifles are somtimes called the Model 1885 and occasionally the Model 1879 because of the patent date. In announcing the new model the company stated "This gun has the old Sharps breechblock and lever and is as safe and solid as that arm."

As with previous models, various styles, barrel lengths, and extras were available. The barrels were numbered from one to five, number one being the lightest and five the heaviest. A number 3½ was added in 1910. The Single Shot was chambered for almost all of the older standard calibers from .22 Short rimfire to .50 caliber center-fire. Three different sizes of frames, the high wall and low wall, were used to accommodate the wide range of cartridges. Frames were case hardened until 1901, then bluing became standard. A special lightweight carbine, "Baby Carbine," is a very worthwhile collector's piece. Another interesting Single Shot is the special .22 caliber musket for target practice, called the "Winder Musket" in honor of Colonel C. B. Winder, who contributed to its design. The Single Shot was equally popular for target practice and big game hunting.

For some time Winchester had been giving considerable thought to the development of a lever-action repeating rifle that was capable of handling some of the more powerful center-fire cartridges of the period, especially the .45-70 Government. In 1886 such a rifle was introduced; this was based on a patent granted some two years earlier to the Browning brothers of Ogden, Utah. In making arrangements for the manufacturing rights, Winchester agreed that part of the payment would be made in rifles. This would explain why barrels of some of the Model 1886s that come to light occasionally are marked, "Browning Bros., Ogden, Utah." The Model 1886 was available in rifle style, an extra-lightweight rifle (first listed in 1897). Carbines were listed in 1887, and a very small number of muskets (approximately 350) were made.

The first '86 carbines had the same type of forearm as the Model '76 carbine; the forearm was practically the full length of the barrel. The changeover to the standard type of carbine forearm was made in 1889. The usual extras were available. Although the '86 was available in twelve different chamberings, the best known were the .45-70, .50 Express and .33 Winchester. The '86, known for its smooth and fast action, continued in production until 1935; approximately 160,000 were made. Collectors are interested in the early carbines with the '76 type forearm, muskets, and, of course, the fancy engraved ones.

The same year the Model 1886 production was discontinued, the action was revamped and brought out as the Model 71, chambered for .348 Winchester. Production of this model continued until 1957, thus making 71 years of production for the '86 action.

In 1892, the Model of that year was introduced. This was a "little '86" with the same type of action, but chambered for the same line of cartridges as the Model 1873. Variations of the Model 1892, in rifle style, were the Models 53 and 65 introduced in 1924 and 1933 respectively and discontinued in 1935 and 1947. The last of the Model 1892s, in carbine style, were made in 1941, rifle style having been discontinued in 1932.

By the mid-1890s there was an increasing demand for the new, high-powered, smokeless-powder cartridges. In 1895, Winchester brought out a rifle produced under a Browning patent that was capable of handling such cartridges. This was a lever-action repeater with a nondetachable box magazine. The Model 1895 was chambered for such cartridges as the .30 U.S. Army, .303 British, .405 Winchester and .30-06 Government. The Model '95 was used exten-

sively by big game hunters. About the first 5,000 Model '95s were made with a flat-sided receiver and one-piece lever, which are now collector's items. Late in 1897 the two-piece, jointed lever and receiver with cut down sides was introduced. An exceptionally small number of the Model '95s had case-hardened receivers, another collector's item. The usual extras were available. Carbine style was not introduced until 1898. A few Model 1895s were used by the U.S. Army during the Spanish American War. In 1905 an N. R. A. musket was brought out. This style musket was accepted by the National Rifle Association of America as conforming to the regulations governing arms for admission to military shooting matches. The '95 was one of several Winchesters carried by Theodore Roosevelt on his famous African safari. This same rifle was brought to Winchester in 1961, by Roosevelt's grandson, to be reconditioned. After it was thoroughly checked, the only thing needed was a new rubber recoil pad.

The model '95 was discontinued in 1931; about 426,-000 were made, including some 300,000 sold to Russia in 1915-16.

A story of Winchester lever actions wouldn't be complete without the famous "thirty-thirty" Model 1894. This model, introduced in 1894, was the first lever-action repeating sporting rifle designed for smokeless powder cartridges and has the distinction of being the first Winchester to pass the one million mark. That particular gun was presented to President Calvin Coolidge in 1927. Since then the Model '94 has gone over the 2½ million mark and is still holding its popularity. The 1½ millionth '94 was presented to President Truman and the 2 millionth to President Eisenhower. The '94 is a strong connecting link with early Americana.

Collectors do not limit their activity now to the lever-action Winchesters. They are finding interesting and some relatively rare specimens among Winchester's slide-action models, the bolt-action models, and the semi-automatic self-loading guns. Shotguns in all Winchester action types are also coming in for a share of interest. The collector will find helpful and interesting information in the old Winchester catalogs, and in these publications: *The Winchester Book* by George Madis, *Winchester—The Gun That Won the West* by H. F. Williamson, and *The First Winchester* by John E. Parsons.

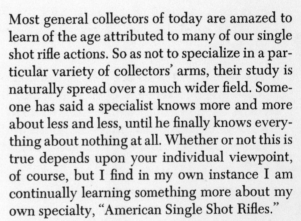

22-1.
F. Wesson
Mid Range
No. 2 Rifle,
caliber .42
Wesson
Special.

the *Single Shot Rifles*

22.

Most general collectors of today are amazed to learn of the age attributed to many of our single shot rifle actions. So as not to specialize in a particular variety of collectors' arms, their study is naturally spread over a much wider field. Someone has said a specialist knows more and more about less and less, until he finally knows everything about nothing at all. Whether or not this is true depends upon your individual viewpoint, of course, but I find in my own instance I am continually learning something more about my own specialty, "American Single Shot Rifles."

I think most general collectors have come to realize when we say "Single Shot" rifles we mean a single loader taking a metallic, self-contained round. Of course various flint and percussion system rifles are also single loaders, and no one in the arms field today confuses these with the "Single Shots"; but those outside our fold are continually confusing them.

To get back to our original idea, that of the age and origin of our single shots, certain manufacturers such as Sharps, Remington, Maynard, etc., had their beginnings in the percussion period and continued into the metallic cartridge era, but for the most part, this type rifle came into being during and after the Civil War. These rifles very soon evolved into certain distinctive specialized types, each of which soon carved a niche for itself in the everyday use on the target

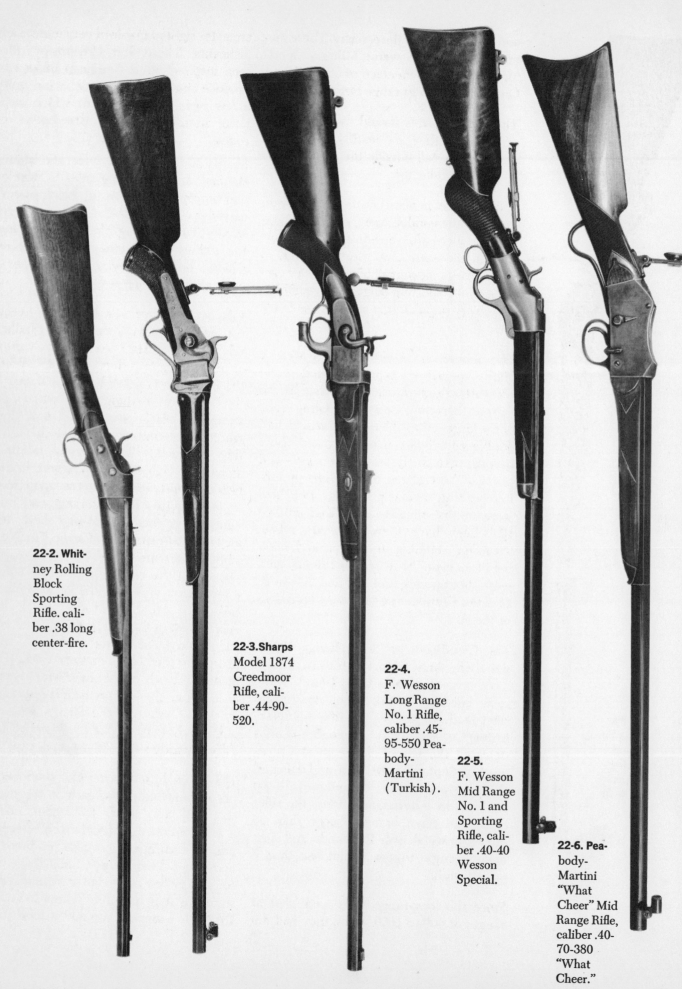

22-2. Whitney Rolling Block Sporting Rifle. caliber .38 long center-fire.

22-3. Sharps Model 1874 Creedmoor Rifle, caliber .44-90-520.

22-4. F. Wesson Long Range No. 1 Rifle, caliber .45-95-550 Peabody-Martini (Turkish).

22-5. F. Wesson Mid Range No. 1 and Sporting Rifle, caliber .40-40 Wesson Special.

22-6. Peabody-Martini "What Cheer" Mid Range Rifle, caliber .40-70-380 "What Cheer."

22-7. Winchester Single Shot Sporting Rifle, caliber .30-40 Krag.

and game ranges of the country. These several classifications were: Military, sporting or hunting; Schuetzen or offhand; and Creedmoor or long-range target arms.

The military arms should require no description as they are readily identifiable and actually fall outside the realm of the single shot collector.

Sporting rifles in plain hunting grades were made by all manufacturers, and since there were no successful repeating rifle mechanisms in the early days strong enough to handle large, powerful, black powder cartridges, the sporting single shots soon became very popular among big game hunters.

The Schuetzen or offhand rifles were a highly specialized type patterned somewhat after the percussion rifles used by the various Swiss and German shooting clubs of the larger cities. These rifles usually had double-set triggers, palm rests, and heavy barrels, with finely adjustable sights and pronged butt plates. Some clubs prohibited set triggers and palm rests, but these were in the minority and most offhand rifles seen have these necessary refinements for "standing on your feet and shooting like a man." Most rifles in this category were shot on ranges of 100 and 200 yards at paper German ring targets or variations of these.

The Creedmoor or "Long-Range Rifles" got their name from the famous Creedmoor target range on Long Island. These soon became famous when long-range rifles made by the Sharps Rifle Manufacturing Co. and by E. Remington & Sons defeated the Irish Rifle Team at Creedmoor on September 26, 1874, and defeated them again at Dublin, Ireland, in 1875. To conform to international rules, the rifles could not have barrels longer than 34 inches, or weigh over 10 pounds, and must have a single trigger of not less than 3 pounds pull.

Since the long-range rifles were shot at ranges of 400 to 1000 yards, they had micrometer sights capable of very minute adjustments. These first Creedmoor rifles soon inspired other American makers to produce similar target models; and quite a few were made, most of which were never actually used at Creedmoor, of course.

Sharps and Remington were also among the first American companies to develop and supply large, powerful, black powder cartridges and these loads, used in the strong Sharps falling block and Remington rolling block rifles, assured success whether on the 1000-yard target ranges or when shooting at large game.

John M. Marlin of New Haven, Connecticut assumed manufacture of the Ballard rifle in 1875. It had been made by various others since its introduction in 1861. While the Ballard was possibly not as strong as the Sharps or Remington, it was amply strong for black powder and lent itself readily to a foundation for a very beautiful rifle. It quickly found many admirers among the Schuetzen clan, where it soon became the standard target weapon. Marlin made quite a few mid-range and long-range target models also and these, too, are beautiful pieces. The Pacific, Far West, and Hunters model rifles were also very popular in the game fields. Marlin made a very heavy version of the Pacific Ballard called the Montana Model, which was chambered for the Sharps .45—2⅞-inch cartridge and was designed to compete with Sharps for the buffalo hunters' trade. This model evidently did not have wide acceptance among the hunters, as it is just about as scarce today as the Sharps with an original chambering for the so-called Big Fifty Cartridge—the .50—3¼-inch case.

The Massachusetts Arms Co., producer of the Maynard rifle, was early in the single shot field also. Their 1873 rifles, taking a self-contained, thick-rimmed, Berdan-primed cartridge, were also produced in Sporting, Schuetzen, and Long-range patterns; very few of the latter were made, it seems, as they are quite scarce today. In 1882 this company adopted a more conventional cartridge case in an attempt to popularize their rifles. They even chambered some of their rifles for the cartridges developed by others, such as the .32/35 Stevens and the .38/50 Ballard. These rifles were very well made and very accurate, but the company was absorbed by Stevens and that company discontinued their manufacture.

Stevens rifles, made by the J. Stevens Arms and Tool Co., also of Chicopee Falls, Massachusetts, were early in the single shot rifle field, starting as the J. Stevens Arms Company in 1864. This company made many models of tip-up rifles as well as falling block models and were one of the very last to abandon manufacture of single loaders, only doing so upon the advent of World War I. They produced many sporting and Schuetzen models of great beauty and popularity, but no long-range target models.

Peabody rifles as made by The Providence Tool Co. were also early birds in this category, appearing about the last year of the Civil War in military forms. A few sporting rifles were made in the very early seventies, mainly from leftover military receivers, but they evidently did not have acceptance or else were not pushed very vigorously by their makers. The hammerless version, known as the Peabody-Martini, appeared about 1872 or 1873. The What Cheer target range near Providence, Rhode Island, opened October 25, 1875, and it is for this target range the What Cheer Mid Range and What Cheer Long Range Peabody-Martinis are named. Some rifles are also marked Creedmoor Mid Range and Creedmoor, but it is not likely any were actually used at Creedmoor. Like the Maynard, Peabody-Martinis used their own special ammunition; and for this reason, and perhaps others, were never very popular. A few sporting rifles were made using the then common .45/70 Government cartridge, but these are also quite scarce. These Martinis are very finely made rifles, but since they were hammerless models in a hammer gun era, did not catch on with the public. The company made thousands upon thousands of military arms on this action for several European powers. They were all discontinued early in the eighties.

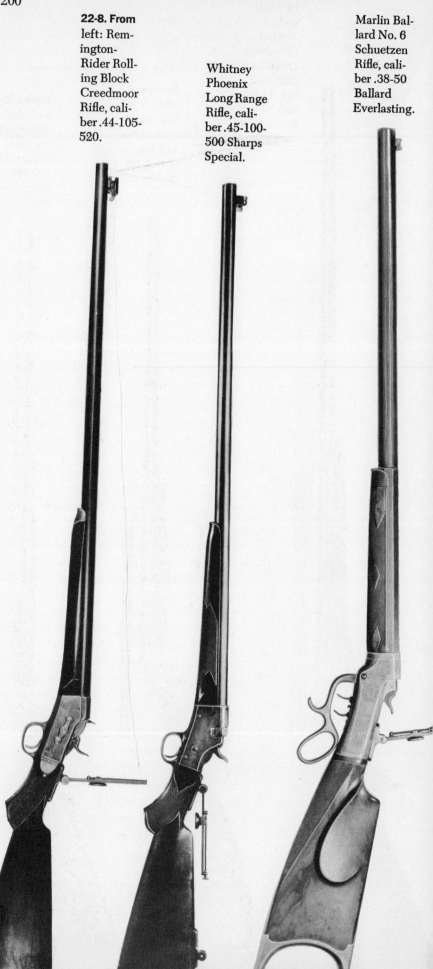

22-8. From left: Remington-Rider Rolling Block Creedmoor Rifle, caliber .44-105-520.

Whitney Phoenix Long Range Rifle, caliber .45-100-500 Sharps Special.

Marlin Ballard No. 6 Schuetzen Rifle, caliber .38-50 Ballard Everlasting.

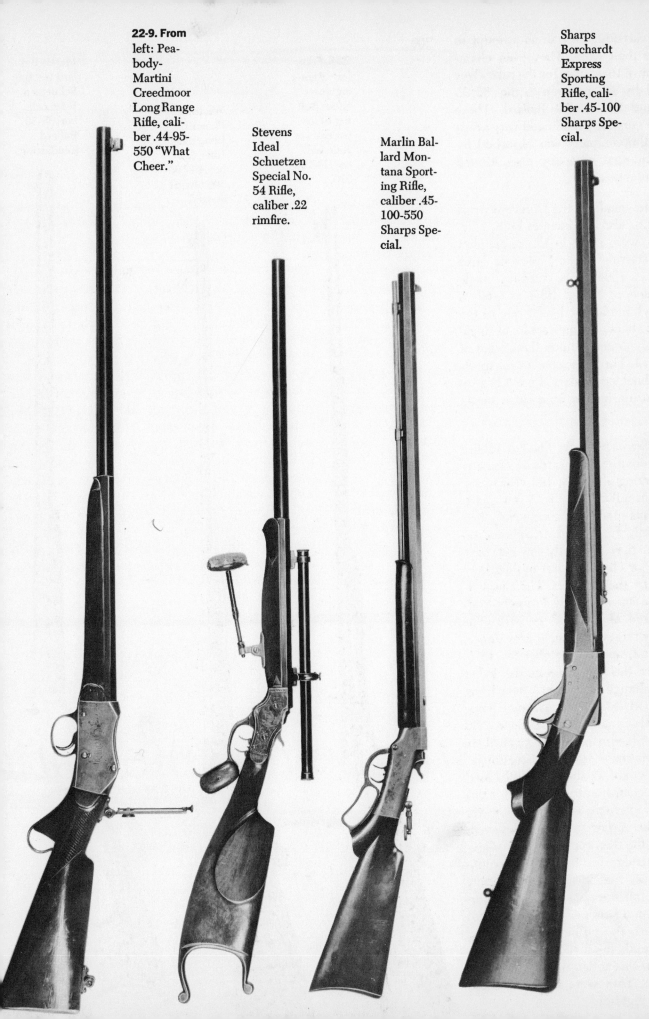

22-9. From left: Peabody-Martini Creedmoor Long Range Rifle, caliber .44-95-550 "What Cheer."

Stevens Ideal Schuetzen Special No. 54 Rifle, caliber .22 rimfire.

Marlin Ballard Montana Sporting Rifle, caliber .45-100-550 Sharps Special.

Sharps Borchardt Express Sporting Rifle, caliber .45-100 Sharps Special.

22-10. Maynard 1882 Offhand Rifle Model 16, caliber .32-35-165.

We shall mention here that The Whitney Arms Co. of Whitneyville, Connecticut, among a wide variety of other arms, produced single shot rifles on the Whitney rolling block and Phoenix swinging block actions. The rolling block rifles are found on two different actions, one being very close in design to the Remington. Both the rolling block and Phoenix systems were used on plain sporting, Schuetzen, and Mid Range and Long Range models.

Contemporaneously, Frank Wesson of Worcester, Massachusetts, was turning out a variety of single shots, his tip-up barrel models being the most numerous. Mr. Wesson was rather careless about numbering these, as several serial number "1" tip-up rifles have been found. He was very much more particular in the manufacture of his falling block models and made three varieties of these, two with sidehammer falling block actions and one center-hammer falling block style. These are just about all Mid or Long Range rifles, though a very few with offhand or Schuetzen butt stocks were made, generally on the Model Number 2 Wesson action.

Falling block Wessons are among the most eagerly sought collector's items today. They are usually found in odd, special Wesson calibers.

About 1885 Winchester Repeating Arms Co. got into the single shot rifle game by acquiring from the inventor, John M. Browning, his 1879 patent falling block rifle design. This was based on the old Sharps falling block design, and Winchester made a few minor changes before going into production on it. Over a period of approximately forty-five years, Winchester produced a great many rifles on this action in several variations and in many models. There were the usual popular sporting models in calibers from .22 rimfire to .50 caliber, and several Schuetzen models were made. They even made express models in three or four special, large express calibers, which did not prove too popular. The low wall version of the Winchester single shot rifle was introduced to accommodate the many men who wanted a lighter, smaller caliber piece. One special model made on this action was the light carbine in .44/40 caliber with 15-inch barrel. Another spe-

the Semi-Automatic

23.

23-1. 1/Borchardt Model 1892, caliber 7.65mm.

2/Bergmann pistol made in Belgium, special 7.65mm caliber, early model.

22-11. Maynard 1873 Sporting Rifle, Malcolm Telescope Sight, caliber .44-100-430.

cial model was the 20-gauge shotgun made on the regular high wall action, which was a mistake as the action did not lend itself readily to easy loading or unloading of a shotshell. About the only model not available on a Winchester single shot action was a Long Range or Creedmoor pattern rifle of which none was produced, the main reason apparently being the action came along too late. The single shot was made by Winchester along with various repeaters as late as the 1920s.

The Winchester Model 1886 rifle was the first really successful Winchester mechanism handling large, powerful cartridges comparable to those used in single shot rifles made by various makers. This 1886 rifle became very popular among hunters of heavy game, but Winchester, along with Remington and Ballard, continued to make single shot target and sporting rifles for several years after the success of this model. Remington side-lever Hepburn models and the popular Ballard in several models were still selling well. A few other more or less obscure makes like Bullard were still in busi-

ness as late as 1890. The Stevens fancy Schuetzen rifles were the last ones to leave the scene. They were a casualty of World War I and of course manufacture of these models was not resumed after the war ended. Marlin dropped the Ballard from manufacture in the early 1890s, since they were pushing their new repeaters very strongly by this time and no doubt Ballards by then were not selling too well. However, the popularity of this action and the demand for it persisted and still persists today, so it can hardly be called dead.

By 1920 all the great single shot rifles were history. They required much fine handwork, which was becoming too expensive for our mass production factories to continue; and shooting habits had changed. The repeaters had won out, but now in the 1960s, one hundred years after most of these single shot rifles first appeared on the American scene, the fine single shots are appreciated by the collectors of today as much as by their fathers and grandfathers, who shot them on the target ranges and game fields of their own day.

Editor's Note: Extensive treatment of this subject will be found in James J. Grant's two fine books, *Single Shot Rifles* and *More Single Shot Rifles.*

Pistol

3/Mannlicher Model 1905, made at Steyr, Austria, caliber 7.63mm Mann.

There are several milestones in the development of firearms which marked vital steps forward. Especially important after the production of gunpowder itself was the fulminate cap, based on Dr. Forsyth's 1807 discoveries; this cap, now called a primer, is used in all modern small arms ammunition. Another milestone of great significance after development of the metallic cartridge was the successful directing of energy from the exploded cartridge to reload, recock, and in some cases discharge the weapon. Thus we came to the era of the full automatic or the semi-automatic, both self-loading weapons which were to bring radical changes in warfare and in arms manufacture.

The self-loading or "auto-loading" system owes its first practical application to Sir Hiram Stevens Maxim, an American engineer who became a British subject. Maxim's first patent was granted in 1883. Although he had been preceded a few years by the experiments of Orbea, Pilon, Curtis, Plessner, Lutze, and a few others, the Maxim guns became the first weapons to reach significant production. In the years that followed, they were used by a number of nations.

Maxim's principal efforts were in automatic weapons other than pistols. While a few pistols were made under Maxim patents, it remained for John M. Browning of Ogden, Utah, to make the self-loading principle efficiently applicable to every type of firearm.

Nations like to claim the honor for major inventive or scientific steps forward, so the picture is often clouded by conflicting claims as to who or what came first. We are told that Major Rubin of the Swiss Army in the years 1886-1888 developed the jacketed bullet combined with smokeless powder and a solid-drawn rimless brass cartridge case. This provided efficient ammunition and made the self-loading principle truly workable.

The Schonberger pistol made at Steyr, Austria, under Laumann patents in 1892, was one of the first practical pistols. Andrea Schwarzlose in 1893 and thereafter devoted his talents to self-loading pistol design. At about this same time, another personality appeared on the scene, a man from Connecticut named Hugo Borchardt. Finding interest in self-loading pistols greater in Europe than in America, Borchardt traveled to Germany where pistols of his design were produced by the Deutsche Waffen- und Munitionsfabriken. The Borchardt is said to have been the first self-loading pistol to attain popularity in Germany and the first to be sold in England. From the Borchardt principle of a locked breech with a rising toggle joint came the world famous Luger pistols.

In quick succession, following the Borchardt pistol, came Mannlicher, Bergmann, and Mauser pistols. The 7.63 Mauser pistol, patented in 1896, is claimed to be the first self-loading pistol to enjoy widespread military service. It was used in the Boer War (1899-1903) and thereafter was sold around the world to many nations for military and police use. The 9mm military Mauser made its appearance during World War I.

England produced their Webley-Fosbery recoil operated revolver in 1901, the rare Mars pistol in 1900-1902, and the Webley & Scott self-loading pistols a few years later; but it was on the European continent where manufacture really flourished. John M. Browning took his ideas to Belgium where he began a long association with the organization known as Fabrique Nationale d'Armes de Guerre. Here were built the F. N. Browning 9mm pistol of 1903 and subsequent models of 1922, 1935, and so on. The first Bergmann pistols, called the "Simplex," were also made in Belgium, where Liege was a great arms-making center. Melior, Pieper, Clement, Martigny, Warnant, Jeffico, Le Rapide, and Delu are other pistols of Belgian origin.

Pioneers in French self-loading arms development were the Clair brothers of St. Etienne. The Societe Francais de Armes et Cycles of St. Etienne produced France's appropriately named "Le Francais." Others were the Pistole Automatique, Union Automatic Pistol, Fiel, and Vernez Carron.

In Austria, G. Roth was one of the leading designers. We find the Roth-Steyr, the Roth-Frommer, and the Roth-Sauer. There were other Austrian designers, too, but it was in Germany where produc-

23-2. 1/Steyr-Hahn
Model 1911, caliber 9mm Steyr, dated 1915.

2/Roth-Steyr Model 1908, caliber 8mm Steyr.

tion really got in high gear. We have mentioned the Military Mauser, the Borchardt, and the Borchardt's successor the Luger. There are enough variations in the Luger that some collectors seek no other make. Several books have been written on the subject. The Mauser also enjoys the distinction of extensive editorial coverage, as does the Mannlicher. Among the German names to be found are the Bergmann-Bayard, Dreyse, Walther, Sauer, Schwarzlose, Langenhan, Lignose, Chylewski, Beholla, Menta, Leonardt, Jager, Liliput, Kolibri, Haenel-Schmeisser, Simson, Stock, Mann, and a few others.

Italy had its Glisenti, Beretta, and Galesi types, while Poland favored the Radom, and Russia the Tokarev. Czechoslovakian types included their Pistole 9mm of 1924, a 1927 Pistole 7.65mm, another Pistole 9mm of 1938, and the Praga.

Spain takes the lead when it comes to a variety of names and models. While the Spanish pistols were usually of inferior quality, they were manufactured in great quantities. In *Automatic Weapons of the World* by Johnson & Haven, you will find a listing of forty-four names for Spanish pocket pistols. Star and Astra were especially prominent. Another book which contains an interesting review of semi-automatic pistols is R. K. Wilson's *Textbook of Automatic Pistols*. These books treat with automatic and semi-automatic weapons around the world, including the Nambu models of Japan. Additional books of interest to the "automatic" pistol collector will be found listed in the bibliography.

There are three basic types of self-loading pistols —the military models, the pocket models, and the target models. Each type has its devotees, and here in the semi-automatic pistol field, as in most fields of the vast world of guns, the collector will usually choose to specialize, building his collection by maker or type.

In Europe calibers are usually designated by millimeters (1 millimeter = .03937 inch). The smallest we find is the baby 2mm Kolibri, closely followed by the 4.25mm Liliput. The 9mm was a favorite in Europe, various and different cartridges of this caliber being employed. In England, the Webley pistols were chambered up to .455 caliber.

The method of pistol cartridge designation in America was somewhat different, our standard calibers being .25, .32, .380, .38, and .45, often followed by the letters ACP (Automatic Colt Pistol). Several United States manufacturers chambered their pistols for the European 9mm cartridge. Let us now review the development of semi-automatic self-loading pistols in the United States.

John M. Browning of Utah is, of course, the name which looms big in pioneering self-loading weap-

7/Model 1912 German Military Mauser pistol, caliber 7.63mm, used with wooden holster which also served as an attachable shoulder stock.

6/Walther Model P-38, caliber 9mm, used in World War II.

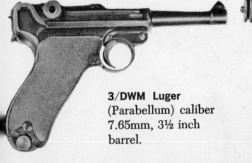

3/DWM Luger (Parabellum) caliber 7.65mm, 3½ inch barrel.

4/"New Model 14" Japanese Nambu, caliber 8mm, small trigger guard.

5/Similar to pistol at left, but with large trigger guard.

**23-3. From top,
left:** 1/Colt
Model 1900 Navy
pistol, caliber .38.
2/Similar to
above, but later
and with differ-
ent marking. 3/
Colt Model 1900
with slide
grooves at front
rather than rear.
4/Colt Model
1902, sporting
model, rounded
hammer without
the safety provi-
sion for hammer
as on pistols
above. 5/Colt
Model 1903,
pocket model,
caliber .38.

From top, right:
1/Colt Model
1906, caliber .45,
cartridge indica-
tor on slide,
squeeze safety on
grip. 2/Colt
Model 1905, cali-
ber .45, no
squeeze safety,
rounded hammer
spur. 3/Colt .45
made for govern-
ment trials of
1906-7, grip
safety, improved
slide catch, de-
sign of slide
changed at muz-
zle. 4/Standard
Colt Model 1911
bearing relatively
scarce *U.S. Navy*
marking, caliber
.45. 5/Imitation
of Colt's Model
1911 pistol, 9mm
caliber, one of
many copies of
popular American
arms made in
Spain and Bel-
gium.

23-4. From top, left:
1/Savage .45 of type submitted for U. S. trials. 2/ Savage Model 1917 pocket pistol, .380 caliber. 3/Savage Model 1907 pocket pistol, .32 caliber. 4/Remington Model 51 pocket pistol, .380 caliber.

Center: Harrington & Richardson, .32 caliber pocket pistol, patterned after the English Webley & Scott.

From top, right: 1/ Ruger Mark 1 target model, .22 caliber. 2/Another .22 caliber Ruger pistol with shorter 5 inch barrel. 3/Hi-Standard Model G, .380 caliber. 4/Reising .22 target pistol, Patents of 1916-21, stocks picture a bear with words "Reising—It's a bear."

ons. And 1900 can be chosen as the start of the "automatic" era. Browning patented a self-loading pistol on April 20, 1897, and soon thereafter brought his ideas to the Colt Patent Arms Mfg. Co. of Hartford. This was but the first of a number of such patents issued to Browning. The right to use the Browning principles was divided between Colt and Fabrique Nationale d'Armes de Guerre of Belgium.

A majority but not all of the Colt automatic pistols were developed from the Browning patents. Colt pioneered the American market and long dominated it. First was their .38 caliber of 1900. Slightly different sporting and military models followed in 1902; 1903 brought the first pocket pistol, and 1905 the first .45. The .25, Colt's smallest pocket pistol, was introduced in 1908, and in 1915 there began a long line of Colt .22 models best known today as the "Woodsman." You will find these Colt models described and illustrated in *Colt Firearms, 1836-1960* by Serven and *Colt Automatic Pistols, 1896-1955* by Bady.

Among the most interesting of the Colt semi-automatic pistols is the group which begins with the .45 caliber Model 1905 and shows developments which led to Colt's successful bid for a big government contract prior to World War I. The late Albert Foster owned one of the finest collections of these pistols, and you will find some illustrated.

The U. S. Ordnance Board conducted a series of tests to determine which of the available self-loading systems was best suited to military needs. In 1906-1907 trials were held at Springfield Armory. Among pistols considered were the Colt, Luger, Savage, Knoble, Bergmann, White-Merril, Webley-Fosbery, Schouboe, Phillips, and Remington. By a process of elimination the competition narrowed down to Colt and Savage. It is a matter of history that the Colt was chosen, and from this series of tests came the Model 1911, a .45 "automatic" used around the world to this very day. During World War I subcontracts for the Colt Model 1911 pistol were awarded to Remington and quite a number of other firms, including The North American Arms Co. of Quebec, and Caron of Montreal. Some were made at Springfield Armory. One will find interesting variations in the Model 1911 in addition to the markings, and this is a fertile field for the collector.

The second-place Savage, designed by E. B. Searle, was one of the biggest and sturdiest of the experimental .45 caliber arms tested, and enough pistols were produced that determined collectors can usually find one. A similar appearing Savage pistol, reduced in size to .32 caliber for pocket use, is known as the Model 1907. A variation in the striking piece or the grip is noticeable in the later Models of 1915 and 1917, made in .32 and .380 calibers.

Remington produced some pocket self-loading (or auto-loading pistols, however one wishes to regard them) in 1918. These were designed by J. P. Pedersen and were known as the Model 51; they fit well in the hand, but like the Savage "automatics" their life was relatively short and they were discontinued in 1934.

The Smith & Wesson .35 caliber model of 1913 and the .32 caliber model of 1925 are favorites among collectors. The .35 is not especially difficult to find, but the .32 is a scarce item. The Smith & Wesson system employed a design similar to the Belgian Clement pistol; it was beautifully made and finished but never achieved great popularity. These early Smith & Wesson pistols were discontinued in 1937 and for a number of years the company made only revolvers. Now they are back in the self-loading pistol field with several fine models.

Harrington & Richardson decided to enter the semi-automatic pistol race and, like Smith & Wesson, they adopted a design similar to that of a foreign make—the Webley & Scott. Manufacture of their .25 and .32 caliber pistols was short-lived, but their relative scarceness makes them desirable collector's pistols.

Among others which came briefly on the scene were the Phoenix, Warner-Schwarzlose, Davis-Warner "Infallible," and the Union Arms Co. pistols. One of the most interesting of the obsolete pistols is the rare Grant-Hammond .45, made in New Haven, Connecticut. It was submitted for government tests in 1917 but was unsuccessful and few were made.

Colt's "Woodsman" .22, first appearing as the .22 Target Model in 1915, became popular with serious target shooters and those who just liked to do some inexpensive plinking. This brought competition into the field in the 1920s from the Reising and the Hartford .22 pistols, the former made by New Haven Arms Co. and the latter by Hartford Arms & Equipment Co. Both failed to stand before the Colt competition and were soon discontinued. However, the Hi Standard Arms Co. of New Haven and Sturm, Ruger & Co. of Southport entered the race; and these Connecticut firms now are strong competitors to their neighbors, Colt and Smith & Wesson, and produce a wide range of semi-automatic pistols.

It is obvious that, in this or in any other of the short outlines prepared for this work, space does not permit complete and definitive treatment of the subject. The objective here is to provide in a few words and pictures a foundation of basic information; the detailed story is left for books devoted to that purpose—most of these books are listed in our bibliography.

Having a general knowledge of many fields in gun collecting, the collector may better decide if he will devote his efforts to collecting "automatics" or to some other type of weapon.

the Rare

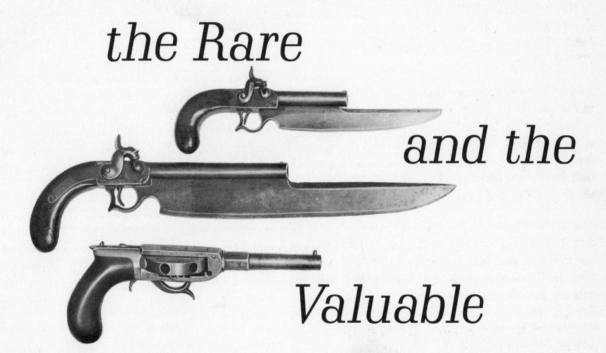

and the

Valuable

24.

24-1. From top: 1/Morrill & Blair bowie knife pistol. 2/Morrill, Mossman & Blair cutlass pistol. 3/ Allen & Cochran turret pistol.

In collecting arms today, one of the most interesting and certainly economically important things for the collector to know is which pieces have been considered firearms rarities over the years. Collecting guns can be fun and should be just that, but it behooves the collector to give some thought as to which arms have always been considered most desirable. Knowing this and actively searching for and obtaining some rarities, he will have the pleasure of favorable comment on his collection by his fellows, the satisfaction of building a collection with a fair number of rarities, and the knowledge that he has also built up a part of his estate that could be sold at a profit.

Much of our thinking here is concerned with the "general collector." While the saying still holds that the long-time collector will eventually specialize, often this trend results in several specialties. However, even the collector who specializes in one maker, such as Colt or Smith & Wesson, or one type of arms, such as wheel locks or pepperboxes, needs to know something of the background history of not only his specialty but the general field of antique weapons. The past twenty-five years have witnessed the publication of 95 percent or more of the arms books today available to collectors of firearms. Likewise, nearly all of our gun collectors associations in existence today have had their beginning in the past quarter century. It isn't difficult for a collector to determine which are the most high-priced guns offered today; he merely needs to attend a number of gun meetings and send for dealers' catalogs and price lists. But to determine which are merely demand items of the day and which are real rarities and have long been considered as such is something else.

There are still quite a few collectors who can remember back to the depression-ridden 1930s when $10 or perhaps $20 would buy a rarity. If somehow one had $100 —well, which Paterson Colt do you want? The big-time collectors of the 1920s and before have left us, but we can read their thoughts on rarity from the prices realized at the New York City auction houses of Walpole, Anderson, and others. A few dealers like F. E. Ellis, Thos. Spencer, G. R. Moore, Stephen Van Rensselaer, and the ageless F. Theodore Dexter put out lists. And then there were the Bannerman catalogs which were literally thumbed through for hours at a time. We shall use this material in going back to about the turn of the century to determine some of the American pistol and revolver rarities in the past 60 years.

A study of the bound catalog of the A. E. Brooks collection of Hartford, Connecticut, published in 1899, reveals that while there were a number of handgun rarities in the collection, no especial attention was drawn to them in group headings or text. Perhaps the reason for this was that it was a descriptive catalog and not a sales catalog. Indeed it seemed to be the pattern of those collecting days to place more significance on where the arm was found than its rarity. This was caused to a great extent by the fact that rarity, as has been determined today by data, study, and research, was not fully understood at that time. Rarity then often meant obtaining a gun which your neighbor collector didn't have.[1]

Colt revolvers have had more interest, and thus greater demand and resulting high prices, than any other single make of collector's guns. The explanation is two-fold: There were so many hundreds of thousands of Colt revolvers made that enough have survived for nearly all collectors, regardless of finances, to obtain several. There were also so many models and variations, from the Paterson on through the resumption of production of the Single Action Peacemaker, that there was always a challenge for the collector to go as far as his interest and pocketbook would permit.

Although the Colt collecting specialist knows there are more rare variations, three Colt models have always been recognized as most desirable. They are the Paterson, the Walker, and the Dragoon. More than 2,000 Paterson revolvers were made at Colt's first factory in Paterson, New Jersey, from 1836 to 1842. In the past 60 years of gun collecting, demand has so outdistanced supply that Paterson values have risen from less than $100 to several or more thousand dollars, the latter depending, of course, on the model, finish, and cylinder engraving, and whether the piece is cased with original accessories. Generally speaking, if the condition is equal, the big Texas model Paterson is in greater demand than the smaller Belt Model or the Baby Paterson sizes. This is in spite of the fact that collected data and serial numbers show that more of the Texas model were originally manufactured.[2] It is interesting to note this statement in the November 1911 issue of *The Magazine Of Antique Firearms*: "The chances for a collector getting a Paterson is about the same as being struck by lightning."

Size, if nothing more, would always make the Walker Colt a desirable collector's piece. With their nine-inch barrels and over four-pound weight, the Walker was Sam Colt's answer to the military men who desired a revolver more suited to martial use than the Paterson. Slightly more than 1,000 were made in 1847.[3] Since the beginning of the twentieth century when they were recognized and their rarity understood, the Walker has occupied a top spot in the martial percussion revolver field. Immediately following the Walker was the Dragoon model which was in production between 1848 and 1860 with more than 20,000 made. Three models appeared

---

[1] *This was told the author as a young collector many times by such older collectors as R. D. Steuart, D. L. Ingalls, Chas. Gilbert, Harold Croft, Dr. Thos. Snyder, S. A. Ingraham, N. E. Carter, C. B. Shiffer, and others.*

[2] *"COLT FIREARMS" by James E. Serven, p. 29.*

[3] *A particularly fine and original Colt Walker with C Company markings and belonging to Lt. Col. R. C. Kuhn is illustrated.*

with a few hundred equipped with detachable extension stocks. An original stocked Dragoon is indeed a rarity. In spite of the greater number of Dragoons made as compared with some later Colt rarities, the Dragoon has continued in greater demand over the years than the admittedly rarer but smaller-sized Colts. If a collector is fortunate enough to find, or financially able to buy, more than one Dragoon, he seems to take pleasure in adding

several more to his collection. Recent values have proven this to be a wise investment.

A huge dragoon-sized percussion revolver which might well have become a serious competitor to the Colt Dragoon, had not its production ended because of a patent infringement suit, was the big .40 caliber Wesson & Leavitt Patent made by the Mass. Arms Co. It appeared between 1849 and July of

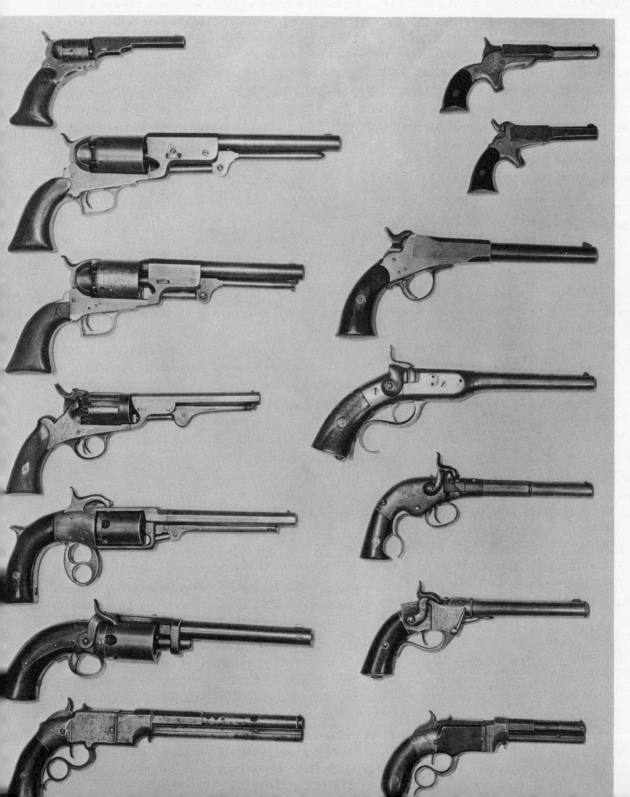

24-2. From top, left: 1/Colt Paterson Belt Model. 2/Colt Walker 1847. 3/Colt Dragoon, serial 1827. 4/Walch 12-shot, .36 caliber. 5/ North - Savage "figure-eight." 6/Mass. Arms Co., Wesson & Leavitt. 7/ Smith & Wesson magazine pistol.

From top, right: 1/Lindsay two - trigger pocket. 2/ Lindsay single-trigger pocket. 3/Lindsay big Army Model. 4/Perry B/L pistol. 5/Marston B/L pistol. 6/Sharps B/L pistol. 7/Smith &Wesson magazine pistol.

1851 when the famed Colt vs. Mass. Arms Co. lawsuit resulted in a jury verdict in favor of Samuel Colt.[4] Production of this .40 caliber model as well as the smaller .31 caliber pocket revolvers ceased with about 1,400 of both having been made. Because its distinctive huge size and scarcity was noted during the years, the "big Wesson & Leavitt," as collectors commonly call it, has long been a recognized rarity. The demand and price of the big Wesson & Leavitt has clung close to that of the Colt Dragoon in the eyes of gun collectors.

Even more rare and desirable to collectors, but until recently not as high priced, are the North-Savage "figure-eight" revolvers and the Walch, 12-shot, Navy revolver. Scanning the old New York auction catalogs of such houses as Libbie, Merwin Sales, Scott & O'Shaughnessy, and Walpole from 1906 through the 1920s shows that the big Wesson & Leavitt, "figure-eight" Savage and the 12-shot Walch were among the most highly regarded percussion revolver rarities in the sales. Even including the various models of the "figure-eights," such as the brass and iron frames and the flat and rounded-frame types, the total production was only a few hundred. The 12-shot Walch was even less.[5] Both were made in the years immediately prior to the Civil War. A few of the brass-frame "figure-eight" Savages were bought by the U.S. Government in 1858 and improvements resulted in the awkward 2nd model Savage Navy purchased during the Civil War. The Walch revolver never received much consideration and the fouling of its double-loaded cylinder spelled its early demise. Several thousand smaller .31 caliber ten-shot Walch revolvers were made later, but the quantity kept them from becoming an important collector's rarity.

The double-loading principle which the Walch revolver embodied was also used in a single-barrel percussion pistol patented by James P. Lindsay in 1860. The large so-called "army model" Lindsay and the two-trigger first model pocket Lindsay are both exceedingly rare.[6] Strangely enough their rarity has only been realized for about the last 25 years. This is probably due to the fact that only a handful of both models were known prior to the Great Depression of the 1930s and because they didn't appear, they received no publicity. What we now know as the more common 2nd Model Pocket Lindsay, however, was featured every time it appeared in the auction house catalogs or on dealer's lists. Thus what used to be considered a rarity is that no more. There were more than 1,200 produced of these pocket "Double-Derringers" as the Lindsay advertisements of the day called them. This was enough for them to appear quite regularly for sale with the resulting publicity and continued demand. Even today they are highly desired, but it is the two-trigger pocket and the army model Lindsay pistols that are the great rarities.

Three single shot, breech-loading, percussion pistols form a triad that has long been known and actively sought. Rarest and most valuable of the group is the Perry pistol.[7] They were made by the Perry Patent Arms Co. in Newark, New Jersey, for a year or two under Alonzo D. Perry's 1855 patent. Four sizes of the pistol were manufactured, including one with a shotgun barrel ranging from 18 to 27 inches that might best be termed a buggy pistol or game getter. Wm. Marston of New York obtained a patent in 1850 and used it on a breech-loading pistol produced shortly thereafter. Both brass and iron-frame types appeared in a variety of barrel lengths. Most numerous, though, were the Sharps breech-loading pistols that were similar in action to the very popular and effective Sharps rifles and carbines. Although attempts were no doubt made to interest the military forces in purchasing these single shot pistols, no contracts were obtained nor government purchases made. The three Colt revolver models previously mentioned made their appearance before these pistols did and the single shot was doomed by the revolver. However each of the Perry, Marston, and Sharps pistols have at various times been termed Secondary Martial Pistols by various authors and this has helped to continue a desirability and value for them which goes back to gun collecting at the turn of the century. Perry carbines and Sharps rifles and carbines did, of course, see military service, but the Marston long arms were simply sporting rifles and shotguns. They, too, are rare—more so than the Sharps and Perry long arms.

Until fairly recently, Smith & Wesson handguns did not enjoy great collecting popularity. This statement would even include the rare First Model .22 revolver with round frame and flat spring barrel catch, a model which did not seem particularly desirable to gun collectors until about the last ten years. An exception, however, was the Smith & Wesson magazine repeating pistol. Prices on these did not go up appreciably until affected by the Volcanic-Henry-Winchester collecting wave that hit the country after World War II, but the rarity of the S & W magazine pistols has long been known. Dealers like Dexter, Van Rensselaer, Smoots, and Serven commented on the rarity of these pistols for years, but most collectors paid little attention until prices suddenly rocketed. Four barrel lengths and a number of slight variations were made, but the early books and articles on Smith & Wesson gave them little space, perhaps because of a lack of knowledge of their rarity.

An easily recognized revolver because of its attractive brass frame and large unwieldly appearance is the Butterfield, which was patented by Jesse S. Butterfield and manufactured in Philadelphia just before the Civil War. High production costs, poor marketing, and a lack of confidence of the buying public in a weapon using a flip-top disc primer—all this produced a low sales volume and finally resulted in manufacture ceasing, with less than 700 revolvers having been made. It used to be that many Butterfields were found by collectors in the Philadelphia area, an indication of a lack of acceptance by the public, resulting in local close-out sales by the dealers. Prices on Butterfields have always seemed to equal that of a Colt Dragoon over the years.

Although the LeMat percussion revolvers were a foreign import and not proven a primary Confederate weapon until recent years, the LeMat has, nevertheless, always been eagerly sought. All Confederate weapons, especially the revolvers, experienced a sharp increase in prices for about 12 years following World War II. They have since leveled off somewhat but remain at figures which indicate continued demand. The Civil War Centennial publicity is also a factor and it has undoubtedly brought many new collectors into the field. A Texas-made Confederate that has always had great appeal because its size approximated that of the Colt Dragoon is the Dance Bros. .44 caliber army model made at Columbia, Texas, in 1862-63. Other Confederate revolvers in the rarity class include the Leech & Rigdon, Rigdon & Ansley, Leech & Co., Spiller & Burr, Griswold & Gunnison, Columbus Fire Arms Co., and the Cofer. One could say that

any authentic Confederate revolver is a rarity, with the emphasis on authentic. Fortunately many fine books and articles have been written on C.S. weapons and the collector has much to guide him in this field of collecting.

An indication of the rarity of the St. Louis-made Shawk & McLanahan revolver is found in the description of one offered for sale in the October 20, 1914, Merwin Sales Co. catalog of the Jacob Steiner collection: "Excessively rare and we believe it to be the only specimen known to collectors." Searching over the years has turned up but six more and it is truly an American rarity. It is one of quite a few percussion revolvers made by firms that never really got into production. Other examples may be found in the products of Nichols & Childs, Rupertus, Brettell & Frisbie, Frederick Newbury, Charles Buss, Jaquith's Patent made by the Springfield Arms Co.,[8] and so on. Of the three examples selected for illustration, the Newbury revolver of the 1860 patent is the rarest. But four specimens by this Albany, New York, maker are known and each piece is considerably different from the other. The Springfield Arms Co. two-trigger, .36 caliber, navy-size revolver made under the Warner Patent is a rarity sought by the Civil War revolver collector who has fairly easily gathered all of the standard makes and models. With World War II as an approximate dividing line, it seems as though arms collectors prior to then placed greater interest in the revolvers made during the 1850s to circumvent Colt's patents. Perhaps all that is needed to again fan this interest and create a big demand for the Warner and Springfield Arms and Mass. Arms Co. products is for someone to write a book on them similar to the fine work by Waldo E. Nutter on *The Manhattan Firearms*. The first of the Whitney

[4] *The book "COLT vs. MASS. ARMS CO." published in 1851 was later republished by Martin Rywell of Harriman, Tenn. It is excellent reading for contemporary facts of arms making during and prior to 1851.*

[5] *The 12 shot Walch revolver was described in 1899 A. E. Brooks catalog as one of the rarest pistols in the collection.*

[6] *"U. S. SINGLE SHOT MARTIAL PISTOLS" by Chas. W. Sawyer, 1914. Speaking of the large Lindsay pistols, "It is questionable whether there are any other army ones besides those in U. S. Government museums."*

[7] *"U. S. SINGLE SHOT MARTIAL PISTOLS" by Chas. W. Sawyer, 1914. Speaking then of the Perry pistol, "Today Perry arms are rarely seen."*

[8] *Walpole Galleries catalog of Dec. 6, 1921 sale described the Jaquith revolver, "Excessively rare revolver, being one of two known specimens."*

revolvers is the "hooded cylinder" model which is another example of a long-recognized rarity. Almost as scarce but not yet achieving the high prices of this first Whitney are some unusual models that followed. These include the iron-frame two-trigger type and the baby Walking Beam in .28 caliber.

Cyrus B. Allen of Springfield, Massachusetts, made a number of firearms that are rare Americana; in fact it might almost be said that everything C..B. Allen made is a rarity. His work with John W. Cochran in producing the Allen & Cochran turret pistol is a fine example. "The Monitor" as a few of the old auction house catalogues aptly described this extreme rarity[9] was made in very limited numbers in 1837. Turret rifles of similar construction were also made. About the same time a cutlass pistol was made that has created attention and great demand ever since. C. B. Allen fulfilled a U.S. Navy contract for 150 cutlass pistols under George Elgin's 1837 patent. A few other cutlass pistols of varying lengths were made by Morrill & Blair and Morrill, Mossman, & Blair in Amherst, Massachusetts, during 1836-39 and all have qualified as rarities. Two of them are illustrated; the larger one is 18½ inches overall length, serial number 36, and is the biggest specimen known. The smaller one is a marked "Morrill & Blair Amherst, Mass." piece and is serial number 8. It is but 12 inches overall length and more of a bowie knife pistol.[10]

In the U.S. Single Shot Martial Pistol line, the two National Armories at Harpers Ferry, Virginia, and Springfield, Massachusetts, the early models from Simeon North's armory at Berlin, Connecticut, and the pistols from a number of the private contractors, have all rated in the arms rarity class for many years. The Jacob Steiner sale of 1914, previously referred to, described the North & Cheney model

1799 pistol as "excessively rare; not more than five known to collectors." Nearly 50 years of additional searching have increased the number of known specimens to only 17 and should a newly discovered specimen turn up it would certainly be subject to a thorough examination before being added to the list. The later Berlin Norths of 1808 and 1811 were also accorded the "rare" label and rightly so. Normal military use can be severe and few pistols survived the War of 1812 service. Although four times as many Harpers Ferry pistols were made in the years 1806-08 as the Springfield 1818 monster, each has about the same rarity. This can be explained because the Harpers Ferry pistol saw service in the War of 1812 and was somewhat frail in construction, whereas the Springfields still had not been issued for service in 1850 and many may never have seen martial use. However, both pistols have the rarity tag over the years. The Harpers Ferry is called our most graceful and attractive martial pistol; the Springfield 1818 comes close to being the most awkward.

In addition to providing the Virginia State Troops with pistols, the Virginia Manufactory at Richmond, Virginia, has given arms collectors a very rare secondary martial for which to search. Two

24-3. 1/North & Cheney Model 1799. 2/North Berlin Model 1811. 3/Harpers Ferry dated 1806. 4/Virginia Manufactory dated 1807.

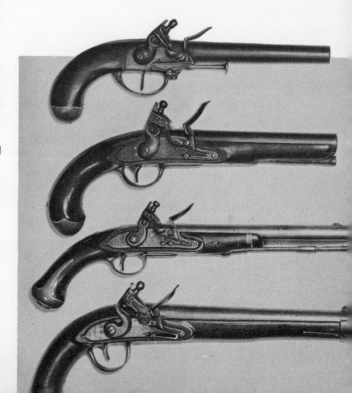

214

models were made: the first type, dated from 1805 through 1811, was a huge pistol utilizing musket parts. The second model Virginia is found dated 1812 through 1815 and closely follows the Harpers Ferry pattern of a brass mounted half-stock pistol, but with the addition of a swivel ramrod. Also highly prized in martial pistol collections are those made under federal or state contracts in the 1807-1814 period by Calderwood, Deringer, Henry, Miles, Evans, Frye, and others. They were made in small numbers and hard and long use has given them an unusually low rate of survival. The old-time collectors prized them highly and one has but to watch for an occasional one appearing on dealers' lists today to see how highly they are now valued. Seldom indeed is one found from private sources anymore; they merely pass on from one collection to another.

In conclusion it is obvious that in a single chapter little attempt can be made to give complete descriptions of very rare pistols or revolvers or to fully discuss the men or firms that made them. All we have attempted to do is bring to mind some handgun rarities that have stood the test of more than a half century as being rarities worthy of a place in any collection.

[9] *At the previously mentioned Steiner sale of 1914 and then at the Robert Gilfort sale conducted by Scott & O'Shaughnessy in 1919, the Allen & Cochran turret pistol was termed "The great American rarity." The specimen sold in 1919 brought $200 at auction—a tremendous price in those days.*

[10] *With the exception of the Colt Walker and the Smith & Wesson magazine pistols, all guns illustrated are from the author's collection.*

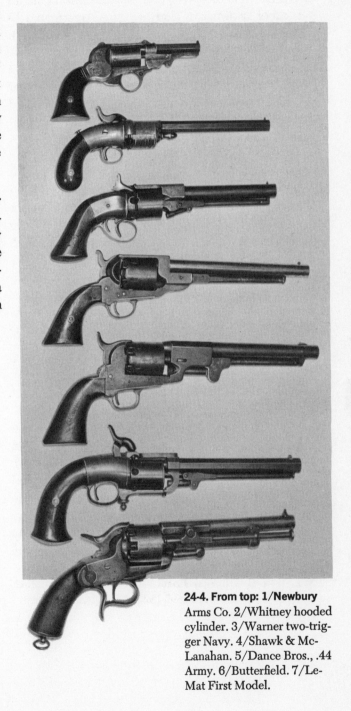

24-4. From top: 1/Newbury Arms Co. 2/Whitney hooded cylinder. 3/Warner two-trigger Navy. 4/Shawk & Mc-Lanahan. 5/Dance Bros., .44 Army. 6/Butterfield. 7/Le-Mat First Model.

25. the Chronology of the Cartridge

Oliver Winchester once said: "A gun is a machine to throw balls." While most of us are primarily interested in the "machine," a growing number of collectors are also becoming very interested in the all-important projectiles and the propellants used—the ammunition, to use a general and all-inclusive term.

The variations in cartridges are almost as countless as stars in the sky, and definitive treatment would require many pages and many illustrations. Through this illustrative chart, drawn by Mr. Herschel C. Logan and shown by courtesy of Mr. Ray Riling, we can strive only to give the collector a general idea of cartridge chronology.

For those who wish to pursue the subject studiously, well regarded books are: *Cartridges* by Herschel C. Logan, *Small Arms and Ammunition in the United States Service* by Colonel B. R. Lewis, *Cartridge Identification* by White and Munhall, and *The American Cartridge* by Charles R. Suydam. Some of the magazines which feature firearms also have excellent sections devoted to cartridge collecting.

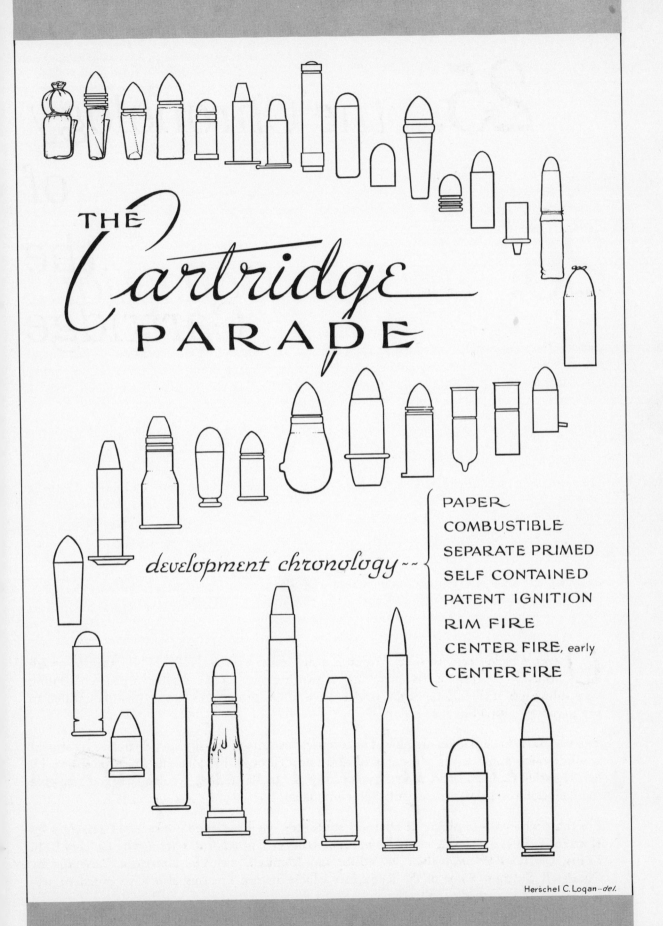

THE *Cartridge* PARADE

development chronology -- {
PAPER
COMBUSTIBLE
SEPARATE PRIMED
SELF CONTAINED
PATENT IGNITION
RIM FIRE
CENTER FIRE, early
CENTER FIRE
}

Herschel C. Logan ..del.

$26.$ *the Gun Collections*

Any collector or student of firearms likes to look at as many specimens as he possibly can. The more he sees, the more he learns. The variety of mechanisms, shapes, finishes, and decoration is almost infinite. No one has yet "seen them all," and even the most advanced student continually finds some new feature to reward his examination of such arms as he is able to find. Consequently collectors the world over are constantly on the alert for collections, both private and public, to which they can obtain access.

Fortunately there are literally hundreds of museums throughout the world which include firearms in their collections. Some of them are large; some are small. Some are of general interest; some will appeal only to the specialist. The following list includes the most important museums for firearms collectors in the United States, Canada, and Western Europe. Judging the importance of a collection of guns is a highly individual matter. The big and especially fine collections are obvious, but to a specialist a single rare specimen may make a museum worth visiting, even if it means traveling a considerable distance. The short descriptions following each entry are intended to help the reader decide from his own standpoint whether a visit might be worth the effort it will entail.

It will be noted that the coverage is much more extensive for the United States than for foreign countries. This has been done because most Americans are more interested in the arms produced here than those made abroad. Foreign museums have therefore been judged for inclusion by a more rigid standard than American institutions. In a few instances, however, museums in frequently visited cities have been listed even though they may have relatively few guns. Such instances are noted in the descriptions with the thought that the touring collector who finds himself in these cities might want to know that at least a few arms are available for his scrutiny. In the European countries also, visiting hours may vary an hour or so between the winter and summer seasons. In these instances the summer hours have been given here since this is the time when most collectors will be traveling.

of Merit in Museums

ARIZONA

Seligman

Museum of the Old West
Open: Daily   *Admission:* Free
The collection offers a relatively large miscellaneous assemblage of firearms including some fine pieces. The Colt revolvers are especially good.

Tombstone

Birdcage Theatre, 6th and Allen Streets
Open: Daily, 9:00-5:00   *Admission:* Adults, 50¢, children 6-12, 25¢
As a part of the museum exhibits in this historic theater there is an extensive collection of guns related to the history of the Old West.

Tombstone Courthouse State Monument
Open: Daily, 9:00-5:00   *Admission:* 25¢
In the jail of this courthouse, built in 1882, is a collection of firearms related to the history of the area, some of them associated with specific people.

Tucson

Arizona Pioneers' Historical Society, 949 E. Second St.
Open: Monday through Friday 8:00-4:00; Saturday 8:00-1:00   *Admission:* Free
An interesting collection of pioneer weapons, military equipment, and other material associated with the Southwest.
There is also a small display of firearms at the Arizona State Museum, on the University of Arizona campus, only a block away.

ARKANSAS

Berryville

Saunders Memorial Museum
Open: Monday-Saturday 9:00-5:00, Sunday 1:00-5:00
Admission: Adults, 50¢; children under 15, 25¢
C. Burton Saunders formed his collection during the first part of the century. He was especially interested in Colts and cased sets and in arms associated with famous or notorious individuals. Unfortunately he made no record of the source or authentication of most of his association pieces.

CALIFORNIA

Anaheim

Disneyland
Open: Daily, hours vary according to season.   *Admission:* Once the general admission to Disneyland has been paid, there is no additional charge for the gun exhibition.
There is a collection of guns related to American history in the "Frontierland" section of Disneyland. It is a representative and worthwhile group for those with a general interest in American arms.

Buena Park

Knott's Berry Farm
Open: Daily, 11:00-9:00   *Admission:* Free
Among the various exhibits at this celebrated eating place is an excellent collection of firearms related to the history of the West.

Los Angeles

Los Angeles County Museum, Exposition Park
Open: Daily except Monday, 10:00-5:00   *Admission:* Free
Most of the museum firearms collections specialize in guns related to the history of California and the Southwest. There is also the extensive Otis Collection of miscellaneous types. Because of limited exhibition space only a portion of these arms is ever on display at one time.

San Francisco

M. H. de Young Memorial Museum, Golden Gate Park
Open: Daily, 10:00-5:00   *Admission:* Free
The firearms collection is medium sized and miscellaneous in nature.

Wells Fargo Bank, 22 Montgomery Street at Market Street
Open: Monday through Friday, 10:00-3:00   *Admission:* Free
The firearms collection is small but interesting, featuring weapons used by the Wells Fargo Company or otherwise related to the history of the West.

COLORADO

Denver

Colorado State Historical Museum, 14th Avenue at Sherman Street
Open: Monday through Friday, 9:00-5:00; Saturday, Sunday, and holidays, 10:00-5:00   *Admission:* Free
The firearms collection is general but with an emphasis on guns used in the West or by Colorado men. Many are in storage.

Fort Garland

Open: May 1-October 1, 9:30-4:30   *Admission:* Free

Fort Garland has been restored as a branch of the Colorado State Museum. It contains a small representative collection of the weapons in use during the active period of the fort.

CONNECTICUT

Hartford

Connecticut Historical Society, 1 Elizabeth Street

Open: Monday through Saturday, 9:00-5:00   *Admission:* Free

There is a small general collection of firearms with an exceptionally good group of martial pistols made by Simeon North, including an unusual variant of the North & Cheney. There is also a pair of dueling pistols made by North.

Connecticut State Library, Capitol Avenue, across from the Capitol Building

Open: Monday through Friday, 9:00-4:00; Saturday, 9:00-1:00   *Admission:* Free

In Memorial Hall is the famous Colt Museum (formerly the Arthur Ulrich Museum) which was donated to the State Library by the Pratt & Whitney Company Foundation, Inc. Not only does it contain a superb collection of Colts (including experimental models) but there are also many other arms of interest.

Wadsworth Atheneum, 25 Atheneum Square N.

Open: Tuesday through Friday, 10:00-5:00; Saturday, 9:00-5:00; Sunday, 1:30-5:30   *Admission:* Free

The Atheneum possesses a small general collection of arms and armor as well as Samuel Colt's personal collection of firearms and some important Colt revolvers, including the original Paterson model and Samuel Walker's revolver.

New Haven

Winchester Museum, Olin Mathieson Chemical Corp., 275 Winchester Avenue

Open: Monday through Friday, 1:00-4:00   *Admission:* Free

This is an extensive general firearms collection covering world-wide production in all periods. Of especial interest are the predecessors of the Winchester, including the very rare Hunt.

GEORGIA

Fort Oglethorpe

Chickamauga-Chattanooga National Military Park

Open: Daily, 8:00-5:00   *Admission:* Free

The famous Claud E. Fuller Collection of U. S. Military long arms and Confederate firearms is exhibited in a special wing of the Visitor Center. It is probably the best and most complete assemblage of its kind in the country. Most guns are exhibited with their bayonets. Other guns in the museum include General Longstreet's Colt Navy revolver.

ILLINOIS

Chicago

Chicago Historical Society, North Avenue at Clark Street

Open: Monday through Saturday, 9:30-4:30; Sunday, 12:30-5:30   *Admission:* Free, except Sundays and holidays

There are firearms related to the history of Chicago scattered throughout the museum. The Kendall collection of Kentucky rifles forms a special group as do a fine selection of Civil War arms.

George F. Harding Museum, 86 E. Randolph Street

Open: The museum is in the process of moving into new quarters. The gun collection will be shown by appointment to serious students.

The firearms collection is small in numbers but high in quality with some fine examples of highly decorated European arms. There is also an important group of early *hakbuchsen*.

Rock Island

The John M. Browning Museum, Rock Island Arsenal

Open: Wednesday through Sunday 11:00-4:00   *Admission:* Free

There is a fine collection of American military arms of all types.

INDIANA

La Porte

La Porte County Museum, Court House

Open: Tuesday through Saturday, 9:00-noon; 1:00-5:00   *Admission:* Free

The W. A. Jones Collection of firearms is a large general assemblage, but it contains many fine arms, including some scarce Colts. There are 850 guns in the group.

LOUISIANA

New Orleans

Louisiana Historical Association, 929 Camp Street

Open: Tuesday through Saturday, 10:00-4:00   *Admission:* Adults, 50¢; children, 25¢

The collection is small and primarily devoted to Civil War arms, but there are some very interesting pieces. There are also a few weapons from the War of 1812.

Louisiana State Museum, the Cabildo, Jackson Square

Open: Daily, 9:00-5:00   *Admission:* Adults 25¢, children free

The collection is miscellaneous and scattered throughout the museum. Featured are arms of the War of 1812 and the Civil War, with some very good Confederate weapons. There is also an excellent World War I collection.

MARYLAND

Aberdeen

Ordnance Museum, Aberdeen Proving Ground

Open: Monday-Friday 8:00-4:00; Sunday 1:00-5:00   *Admission:* Free

The Ordnance Museum in Building 314 houses a tremendous collection of Ordnance materiel from all over the world. It is particularly strong on the weapons of the 20th century, but there is also a good representative assemblage of earlier U. S. firearms and related ordnance equipment.

Annapolis

U. S. Naval Academy Museum

Open: Monday through Saturday, 9:00-5:00; Sunday, 9:30-5:00   *Admission:* Free

Both small arms and heavy ordnance are included in an exhibit devoted largely to the arms used by the Navy and

Marine Corps. Included are the remains of a rare brass-mounted U. S. flintlock musket recovered from a shipwreck. There are also excellent swords and naval dirks among many association pieces.

Baltimore

Fort McHenry National Monument and Historical Shrine
Open: Daily, 9:00-5:00   *Admission:* Adults 25¢, children, free
One of the barracks of the historic fort houses the E. Berkley Bowie Collection of American firearms. It is a large general group with some good Confederate pieces and a strong military section.

Maryland Historical Society, 201 W. Monument Street
Open: Monday through Friday, 9:00-4:00; Saturday, 9:00-1:00. Closed Saturdays in August   *Admission:* Free
The collection of arms is small and devoted primarily to arms associated with the history of Maryland and its citizens. There is, however, a rare Rappahannock Forge pistol.

MASSACHUSETTS

Boston

First Corps Cadet Armory, 105 Arlington Street
Open: Monday through Friday, 9:00-5:00   *Admission:* Free
The basic collection in the Armory museum consists of American military arms, but there are also some very important American colonial arms on loan from the Massachusetts Historical Society.

Plymouth

Pilgrim Hall, Court and Chilton Streets
Open: April 15 through November 30, weekdays 9:30-5:00, Sunday 1:15-5:00   *Admission:* Adults 50¢, children 25¢
The arms collection is small, but it includes the swords of three of the Pilgrim Fathers plus John Thompson's dog lock pistol and a few pieces of armor.

Salem

Essex Institute, 132 Essex Street
Open: Tuesday through Saturday, 9:00-4:30, Sunday 2:00-5:00   *Admission:* Free
The arms collection of this noted museum comprises a small general assemblage plus special groups related to the Colonial Period, the Revolution, and the Civil War.

26-2. The Winchester Museum at New Haven, Connecticut, contains one of the most comprehensive and best displayed collections of American weapons in America. Collectors will find the curator very capable and informative.

26-3. A look through the doorway into one of the display rooms at Springfield Armory.

Springfield

Springfield Armory Museum
Open: Tuesday through Saturday, 1:00-4:00   *Admission:* Free
The firearms collection is extensive with the emphasis on arms manufactured or designed at the Armory. There are also other military arms, however, including Rappahannock Forge wall rifles and other Revolutionary War pieces, plus an original Blanchard stock-making lathe.

Sturbridge

Old Sturbridge Village
Open: Daily April through November 9:30-5:00
Admission: Adults $2.50, juniors (12-17) $1.00, children (7-11) 60¢
The Harrington Gun Shop houses a collection of American firearms, principally of the flint and percussion eras plus some gunsmithing tools. There is a rare civilian Hall breechloader.

Taunton

Old Colony Historical Society, 66 Church Green
Open: Monday through Friday, 10:00-noon; 2:00-4:00; Saturdays 10:00-noon   *Admission:* 25¢
There are very few firearms in the collection but among them is the early 17th century long fowler brought to Plymouth by John Thompson.

MICHIGAN

Dearborn

Henry Ford Museum, Airport Drive and Oakwood Boulevard
Open: Monday through Friday, 9:00-5:00, Saturday and Sunday, 9:00-5:30   *Admission:* Adults 85¢, children under 12, 40¢
The museum has a growing collection of American and European firearms, including some important and fine specimens. There is also a reconstructed gunsmith's shop.

MISSOURI

St. Louis

City Art Museum, Forest Park

Open: Tuesday, 2:30-9:30; Wednesday through Sunday, 9:00-5:00   *Admission:* Free

The museum has a small collection of exceptionally fine European firearms.

Missouri Historical Society, Jefferson Memorial Building, Forest Park

Open: Daily 9:30-5:00   *Admission:* Free

The collection is related primarily to the history of Missouri and its citizens. There are good fur trade specimens and excellent plains rifle material, including gunsmith's tools.

NEBRASKA

Lincoln

Nebraska State Historical Society Museum, 1500 R Street

Open: Monday-Saturday 8:00-5:30; Sundays and holidays 2:00-5:00   *Admission:* Free

The Historical Society has just been given the Walter Charnley collection of some 800 firearms ranging from fine early European pieces to modern cartridge arms. Most of the better pieces are on display.

NEVADA

Reno

Harold's Club

Open: 24 hours a day for adults; children admitted with adults 7:30-1:30 Monday through Friday except holidays *Admission:* Free

Built around the noted Ray Stagg Collection, this is one of the finest gun exhibits in the Far West. It is a general collection, but the emphasis is American and Western.

NEW JERSEY

Morristown

Morristown National Historical Park

Open: Tuesday through Sunday 10:00-5:00   *Admission:* Adults 25¢, children free

There is a good collection of Revolutionary War arms, including the only known example of the enlisted man's Ferguson rifle as used in that conflict.

NEW YORK

Fort Ticonderoga

Fort Ticonderoga Museum

Open: Daylight hours, mid-May to mid-October   *Admission:* $1.00

The extensive firearms collection is devoted primarily to arms of the Colonial and Revolutionary War periods, but there are notable exceptions, including a large group of early 19th century Kentucky rifles.

Newburgh

Washington's Headquarters

Open: Monday through Saturday 9:00-5:00, Sunday 1:00-5:00   *Admission:* Free

Most of the arms relate to the Revolutionary War era, but there are a few others associated with residents of Newburgh. The extensive musket collection is especially notable as is the rare cartridge cannister of the Revolution.

New York City

Metropolitan Museum of Art, Fifth Avenue

Open: Tuesday through Saturday 10:00-5:00, Sundays and holidays 1:00-5:00   *Admission:* Free

The Museum has an extensive collection of finely decorated firearms from Europe and the Orient, including some with unusual mechanisms. There are also a few Kentucky rifles and Colt revolvers.

New York Historical Society, 170 Central Park West

Open: Sunday through Friday 1:00-5:00, Saturday 10:00-5:00   *Admission:* Free

There is a medium-sized collection of firearms, principally those used in New York or by New Yorkers. Included is a fowler believed to have been used by Joseph Brant. Because of limited space much of the collection is in storage.

West Point

West Point Museum, U.S. Military Academy

Open: Daily 10:30-4:30   *Admission:* Free

The West Point Museum offers an extensive collection of firearms, both artillery and small arms from all nations. Featured are a number of association weapons belonging to such individuals as George Washington, George McClellan, and George S. Patton, Jr. There is also an extensive study collection.

NORTH CAROLINA

Raleigh

Hall of History, State Education Building

Open: Monday-Saturday 9:00-5:00; Sundays and holidays 2:00-5:00   *Admission:* Free

The Hall of History has a good collection of percussion rifles made in North Carolina plus some good Confederate arms. Work is now underway on a new museum building which will allow all of the major pieces to be placed on display rather than the sample now exhibited.

OHIO

Cleveland

Cleveland Museum of Art, Wade Park

Open: Sunday 1:00-6:00; Tuesday, Thursday 10:00-5:00; Wednesday, Friday 10:00-10:00; Saturday 9:00-5:00 *Admission:* Free

The John Long Severance Collection of arms and armor contains some specimens of finely decorated early European firearms.

Columbus

Ohio Historical Society, Ohio State Museum

Open: Monday through Saturday 9:00-5:00; Sundays and holidays 1:00-5:00   *Admission:* Free

There is a good general collection of firearms with some important historical association pieces. Because of limited space a good portion of the collection is usually in storage.

OKLAHOMA

Claremore

J. M. Davis Collection, Mason Hotel

Open: A portion of the exhibit is in the hotel lobby and may be seen at any hour.   *Admission:* Free

The J. M. Davis Collection numbers some 25,000 pieces, covering almost every field of American firearms.

Lawton

Fort Sill Artillery Museum

Open: Daily except Saturday afternoon and Monday *Admission:* Free

Both artillery and small arms are exhibited in the museum,

and the collections of the Cherokee County Historical Society, which are also displayed on the post, contain a number of percussion long arms with Western history association.

PENNSYLVANIA
Doylestown
Bucks County Historical Society, Pine and Ashland Streets
Open: Monday through Saturday 9:00-5:00; Sunday (April-October) 1:30-5:30   *Admission:* Free
The collection of Pennsylvania-made rifles is especially noteworthy, but the rambling Mercer Building also houses a large number of firearms of all types.

Harrisburg
William Penn Memorial Museum, Third and Forster Streets
Open: Monday through Friday 8:30-5:00; Saturday 9:00-4:00, Sunday 1:00-4:00   *Admission:* Free
The collection contains a general assortment of guns with some Pennsylvania-made rifles.

Lancaster
Pennsylvania Farm Museum, Landis Valley
Open: Monday through Friday 8:30-4:30; Saturday 10:00-4:30; Sunday noon-4:30. During the summer months the closing hours are extended half an hour on weekdays, one hour on Sundays   *Admission:* Adults 50¢, children free
The specialty of the museum is Pennsylvania-made rifles, and the original collection formed by the Landis brothers contains a great many, plus rifle-making tools and accouterments. There is also a general firearms collection.

Pittsburgh
Historical Society of Western Pennsylvania, 4338 Bigelow Boulevard
Open: Tuesday through Friday 10:00-4:30; Saturday 10:00-noon   *Admission:* Free
There is a medium-sized general collection of firearms with a number of locally-made rifles.

Valley Forge
Valley Forge State Park
Open: Daily, 9:00-5:00   *Admission:* Free
The Museum of American History contains a small but good collection of weapons and equipment of the Revolutionary War period, including some rare American-made muskets.

SOUTH CAROLINA
Charleston
Confederate Museum, Market and Meeting Streets
Open: Monday through Friday 10:00-2:00 November through June   *Admission:* 25¢
The collection of firearms in the museum is small, but there are some excellent Confederate pieces.

TEXAS
Austin
Texas Memorial Museum, San Jacinto Boulevard at 24th Street
Open: Monday through Friday 9:00-5:00; Saturday 10:00-noon, 2:00-5:00; Sunday 2:00-5:00   *Admission:* Free
The gun collection is general with some excellent Colts.

Canyon
Panhandle-Plains Historical Museum
Open: Monday through Saturday 9:00-500; Sunday 2:00-6:00   *Admission:* Free
The museum has a good general collection, strong in Colts.

College Station
The Carl Metzger Gun Collection Room, Memorial Student Center
Open: Daily 8:00 a.m.-11:00 p.m. Closed during college vacations.   *Admission:* Free
The Metzger Collection is one of the finest assemblages of Colt firearms on public display in the United States.

Houston
San Jacinto Battlefield Museum, State Route 134, 22 miles southeast of Houston
Open: Tuesday through Saturday 9:30-5:30; Sunday 10:00-6:00   *Admission:* Free
The firearms collection is general and of average quality. There are also exhibits relating to the history of Texas and the Southwest.

San Antonio
The Alamo, Alamo Plaza
Open: Monday through Saturday 9:00-5:00; Sunday 10:00-5:00   *Admission:* Free
Most of the firearms relate to the history of the Alamo, but there is also a small general collection.

Witte Museum, 3801 Broadway
Open: Daily 9:30-5:00   *Admission:* Adults 10¢, children under 12 free
There is a good collection of Indian weapons plus a general gun collection with emphasis on military pieces.

VIRGINIA
Fredericksburg
Fredericksburg National Military Park
Open: Daily 9:00-5:00   *Admission:* Adults 25¢, children free
The headquarters building contains a collection of Civil War guns, including a few rare Confederate pieces.

Newport News
The War Memorial Museum of Virginia, 9285 Warwick Road, Huntington Park
Open: Weekdays 9:00-5:00; Sundays 2:00-5:00   *Admission:* Free
There is an excellent collection of the weapons of World Wars I and II plus some specimens from earlier wars.

Quantico
U.S. Marine Corps Museum
Open: Monday-Friday 9:00-6:00; Saturday 9:00-5:00; Sunday noon-4:00   *Admission:* Free
The collection is devoted to arms used by the Marine Corps with an especially strong representation of automatic weapons, including developmental and experimental pieces.

Richmond
Confederate Museum, 12th and Clay Streets
Open: Monday through Friday 9:00-5:00   *Admission:* 30¢
Scattered throughout the former White House of the Confederacy are a large number of Confederate firearms. The collection is especially rich in weapons used by prominent persons, including Robert E. Lee, Jefferson Davis, and Jeb

26-4. A few of the many interesting weapons in the U. S. Marine Corps Museum at Quantico, Virginia. An outstanding group of automatic weapons may be viewed here, along with other types.

Stuart.

Virginia Historical Society, 428 North Boulevard
Open: Tuesday through Friday 9:00-5:00; Saturday and Sunday 2:00-5:00   *Admission:* 30¢
The Richard D. Steuart Collection of Confederate firearms housed in "Battle Abbey" is one of the most varied and complete in the United States.

Williamsburg

Powder Magazine, Colonial Williamsburg
Open: Daily 10:00-5:00   *Admission:* 75¢
The magazine contains an excellent selection of British service arms of the 18th century plus related equipment. There are also some guns on exhibit in other exhibition buildings especially the Governor's Palace.

WEST VIRGINIA

Huntington

Huntington Galleries
Open: Tuesday through Friday 1:00-5:00; Saturday 10:00-5:00; Sunday 2:00-6:00   *Admission:* Free
The Galleries were recently given a large portion of the famous Herman P. Dean Collection of firearms. Notable are the displays of Kentucky rifles and pistols and of the evolution of ignition systems.

WISCONSIN

Janesville

Lincoln-Tallman Museum, 440 N. Jackson Street
Open: Monday through Saturday 9:00-5:00; Sunday 11:00-5:00   *Admission:* Adults 50¢, students 25¢, children 10¢
The George K. Tallman Collection of firearms is a general collection of 166 pieces.

Madison

Wisconsin State Historical Society, 816 State Street
Open: Monday through Saturday 8:00-5:00; during the summer the Saturday hours are 8:00-noon.   *Admission:* Free

The good general collection of firearms was recently augmented by the addition of the Waldo E. and Franz H. Rosebush Collection of fine handguns and rifles.

Milwaukee

Milwaukee Public Museum, Wisconsin Avenue between 8th and 9th Streets
Open: Weekdays 9:00-5:15; Sundays 1:30-4:45   *Admission:* Free
The famous and extensive Rudolph J. Nunnemacher Collection of firearms is general but far better than average in both the quality and rarity of its specimens. There is, for instance, an excellent marked Cookson repeater.

WASHINGTON, D. C.

National Rifle Association of America, 1230 16th St., N.W.
Open: Monday through Friday 9:00-4:30   *Admission:* Free
The museum collection is extensive with more than 600 firearms on exhibit. There is an exhibit on the history of ignition systems plus a general collection of arms from all over the world. Basic models of all firearms currently being manufactured in the United States are also shown.

United States National Museum, Smithsonian Institution
Open: Weekdays 9:00-4:30; Sundays 2:00-6:00   *Admission:* Free
The new Museum of History and Technology opened in 1964 on Constitution Avenue. In it is an ordnance hall with a fine general firearms exhibit. Other firearms, especially association pieces, are scattered throughout the historical exhibits. The collection is especially rich in these association weapons and also in patent models and pattern specimens.

CANADA

ONTARIO

Kingston

Fort Henry
Open: Daily May 24-September 15, 9:00-9:00
The fort contains a representative collection of weapons associated with the history of the fort from the War of 1812 through the middle years of the 19th century. A trained guard performs period drill with both small arms and heavy ordnance.

Murney Redoubt, Macdonald Park
Open: July and August daily, except Mondays, 2:00-8:30
The redoubt, a martello tower built between 1846 and 1851, contains a miscellaneous collection of firearms, most of them formerly owned by Porfirio Diaz, President of Mexico.

Toronto

Royal Ontario Museum
Open: Monday-Saturday 10:00-5:00; Sunday 1:00-5:00
The Modern European Department of the museum contains a small but fine collection of firearms, including some rare early breechloaders and repeaters. Outstanding is the Herbert J. Jackson collection of gunlocks.

QUEBEC

Quebec

The Citadel

Open: June 1-September 30 daily 8:00-8:00

The museum contains a small collection of portable firearms and quite a good collection of artillery.

SASKATCHEWAN

Regina

The Royal Canadian Mounted Police Museum

The museum, located in the RCMP training school, contains a small collection of firearms related to the history of the Force from its founding in 1873.

WESTERN EUROPE

AUSTRIA

Graz

Steiermarkisches Landeszeughaus (Styrian District Arsenal)

Open: April-October, daily 9:00-12:00; also 3:00-5:00 Monday, Tuesday, and Friday

The Landeszeughaus is a surviving armory built between 1642 and 1644. It contains some 30,000 specimens of arms and armor, including many firearms, from the 16th and 17th centuries. These were not collected but actually formed part of the original contents of the building when it was used as an armory. Here one can see many of the smaller items that are so rare today, such as tools, bullet molds, etc.

Vienna

Heeresgeschichtliches Museum (Army Historical Museum)

Open: May-September, daily except Monday and Friday, 10:00-5:00; Monday 10:00-1:00; closed Friday

A large collection of some 80,000 objects includes cannon, small arms, uniforms, decorations, models, paintings, etc., all related to the military history of Austria.

Kunsthistorisches Museum (Museum of Art History)

Open: Monday, Wednesday, Thursday, Saturday, 10:00-1:00; Friday 2:00-7:00; Sundays and holidays 9:00-1:00

As an art museum the Kunsthistorisches Museum is primarily concerned with arms and armor of exquisite workmanship and design. The collection of fine guns is unsurpassed.

BELGIUM

Brussels

Le Musée Royal de l'Armée et d'Histoire Militaire (The Royal Museum of Army and Military History)

Open: Daily except Friday 10:00-12:30, 1:30-5:00

The collection is devoted to the history of the Belgian Army. There is some 18th century material, but the strongest parts of the collection relate to World Wars I and II.

Musée Royal d'Armes et d'Armures (Royal Museum of Arms and Armor)

Open: Daily except Friday 9:30-5:00

The historic Porte de Hal, one of the ancient city gates, has been filled with a synoptic collection covering the development of arms and armor from antiquity to the present. Cannon are included as well as small arms.

Liège

Musée d'Armes de Liège (Arms Museum of Liège)

Open: June through September, daily except Fridays, 10:00-noon, 2:00-4:30; Sundays the closing hour is 2:00

Founded in 1885, the museum has systematically sought to collect all types of firearms from the 14th century to the present. Of especial interest to Americans is the only surviving specimen of a Chambers repeating swivel gun used by the American Navy during the War of 1812.

DENMARK

Copenhagen

De Danske Kongers Kronologiske Samling Po Rosenborg (The Chronological Collection of the Danish Kings at Rosenborg Castle)

Open: June-October, daily 11:00-3:00

The firearms exhibited all belonged to the Danish royal family. There are some 200 items in the arms collection, including edged weapons and crossbows as well as guns.

Tøjhusmuseet (The Royal Arsenal Museum)

Open: May through September, weekdays 1:00-4:00; Sundays and holidays 10:00-4:00

The firearms collection of the Tøjhusmuseet includes cannon as well as small arms. It is one of the finest if not actually the finest public gun collection in Europe. It is especially rich in rare early breech-loading and repeating weapons.

FRANCE

Paris

Musée de l'Armée (Army Museum)

Open: Weekdays except Tuesday 10:00-12:15; 1:30-5:00; Sundays 1:30-5:00

Housed in the famous Hotel des Invalides, the museum has an exceptionally fine collection of firearms, including both artillery and small arms. There are also excellent edged weapons, armor, uniforms, trophies, and models related primarily to the history of France but not limited to it. The Musée de l'Armée is one of the largest and most important military museums in the world.

GERMANY

Emden

Rüstkammer der Stadt Emden (Armory of the City of Emden)

Open: Weekdays 11:00-1:00; 2:30-6:00; Saturdays and Sundays 11:00-1:00

The historic armory of the City of Emden was destroyed during World War II, but the arms themselves had fortunately been removed. They are currently exhibited in a modern building and comprise a fine selection of the arms and armor which were maintained for the defense of the city from the 15th century through the middle of the 17th century. There are more than a thousand firearms as well as edged weapons, armor, flags, and equipment.

Nuremberg

Germanisches National-Museum (Germanic National Museum)

Open: April-September, Saturday-Monday 10:00-4:00

The museum is devoted to all phases of German art and culture, arms and armor included, from prehistoric times until the 19th century. Prior to the War a number of rare firearms were on exhibition, including some fine early cannon. There was some damage during the war, but its effect on the arms collection is not known.

GREAT BRITAIN

Edinburgh

The National Museum of Antiquities of Scotland
Open: Weekdays 10:00-5:00; Sundays 2:00-5:00
The museum collections are devoted to Scottish prehistory and history to the mid-nineteenth century. Firearms are represented by a large and important group of Scottish guns, powder horns, and other equipment. There are also excellent swords, dirks, and targets. This is the finest single collection of Scottish weapons. Special students should make an attempt to see the weapons in storage as well as those on display.

The Scottish United Services Museum
Housed inside historic Edinburgh Castle, the museum is a repository for material related to all Scottish armed forces. Included are arms, uniforms, equipment, flags, and pictorial material from the 17th century to the present.

Glasgow

Glasgow Art Gallery and Museum
Open: Weekdays 10:00-5:00; Sundays 2:00-5:00
The extensive R. L. Scott collection contains firearms as well as armor and edged weapons. The C. E. Whitelaw collection is an exceptionally good assemblage of Scottish weapons. These two groups plus the A. Martin collection of firearms comprise the weapons holdings of the museum.

London

The Armouries, H. M. Tower of London
Open: May-October weekdays 10:00-5:30; Sundays 2:00-5:00
Housed in the historic White Tower is an exceptionally important collection of arms and armor open to the public. Included are many important firearms including the earliest dated breechloader (1537), the Puckle gun, and several pieces with American associations. In the student rooms there is a truly extensive collection of military firearms of all types. Application to visit the student rooms must be made in advance.

Victoria & Albert Museum
Open: Weekdays 10:00-6:00; Sundays 2:30-6:00
The Victoria & Albert Museum is devoted to the fine and applied art of all countries. The firearms collection is small and selected on the basis of decoration and workmanship.

The Wallace Collection
Open: Weekdays 10:00-5:00; Sundays 2:00-5:00
The collection of firearms is especially strong in finely decorated guns of the pre-percussion period.

Woolwich

The Rotunda
Open: Summers, daily 10:45-12:45; 2:00-5:00
The collection of the Royal Artillery Institution offers a large number of cannon and small arms from all over the world. Of special interest to American students is the only known example of a repeating musket invented by Joseph Chambers of Pennsylvania and used during the War of 1812.

ITALY

Naples

Museo e Gallerie Nazionale di Capodimonte (National Museum and Gallery of Capodimonte)
Open: Daily 9:30-4:00
The collection contains many fine examples of arms and armor. Among the firearms are specimens signed by many of the most famous Italian makers and by foreigners. There is a good collection of airguns and of unusual percussion systems.

Rome

Museo Nazionale di Castle S. Angelo (National Museum of Castle St. Angelo)
Open: April-September daily 9:30-6:00
There is an extensive collection of arms used in Italy, including both artillery and small arms.

Turin

Museo Nazionale Storico d'Artiglieria (National Museum of the History of Artillery)
Open: Weekdays except Mondays and Fridays 10:00-noon, 3:00-5:30; Sundays 9:30-noon
The museum contains an extensive collection of firearms designed to trace the history of both artillery and small arms from the 14th century to the present.

Armeria Reale (Royal Armory)
Open: Summer weekdays 9:00-12:30, 3:00-5:30; holidays 9:00-12:30
An exceptionally rich collection of all forms of arms and armor, including firearms.

NETHERLANDS

Leiden

Het Nederlands Leger-en Wapenmuseum Generaal Hoefer (The Dutch Army and Arms Museum General Hoefer)
Open: Weekdays 10:00-5:00; Sundays and Holidays 1:00-5:00
The collections comprise all forms of arms and armor from prehistoric times to the present day as well as uniforms, orders and decorations, pictorial material, etc.

NORWAY

Oslo

Haermuseet (Army Museum)
Open: The museum is still being reorganized following the

26-5. In the historic White Tower of the Armouries, H. M. Tower of London, the visitor will find many interesting public exhibits. Special student room exhibits are available upon advance application.

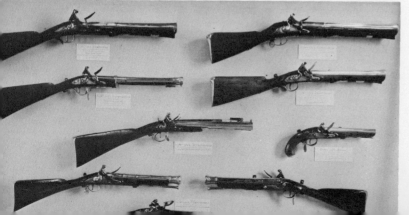

evacuation of the collections during the War. It is expected to open in 1965.

The firearms collection is largely restricted to guns used by the Norwegian armed forces from 1600 to the present. There are also accouterments, flags, and uniforms.

PORTUGAL

Lisbon

Museu Militar (Military Museum)
Open: Daily except Monday, 10:00-5:00
The museum, housed in part of the old arsenal, contains a collection of cannon and small arms ranging from the 14th century through World War I.

SPAIN

Madrid

Museo del Ejército Español (Museum of the Spanish Army)
Open: Sunday-Friday 10:00-2:00
The museum houses an extensive collection both of artillery and small arms as well as projectiles and other military materiel related to the history of the Spanish Army.

Museo de la Real Armería (Museum of the Royal Armory)
Open: June through September, weekdays 10:00-1:30, 4:00-7:00; Sundays and holidays 10:00-2:00
This is one of the great arms and armor collections of Europe. There are many fine firearms, including association pieces.

SWEDEN

Skokloster

Skokloster Castle
Open: May-October daily 11:00-5:00
The castle contains two armories which have remained unchanged since the 17th century. Surprisingly enough they include such widely differing weapons as Scottish pistols and Malay krises.

Stockholm

Hallwylska Museet (Hallwyl Museum)
Open: Tuesday-Friday 10:00-1:00
The collection is a general one. There are about 300 specimens of arms and armor, including firearms, most of them European and dating from the 16th and 17th centuries. There are also some Oriental arms.

Kungliga Armémuseum (Royal Army Museum)
Open: Daily 1:00-4:00
The Royal Army Museum has one of the finest modern exhibits of arms and armor in Europe. Both heavy artillery and small arms are included among the firearms. Some are Swedish, some trophies captured during the many wars of the 17th and 18th centuries.

Kungliga Livrustkammaren (Royal Armory)
Open: Weekdays 11:00-5:00; Sundays and holidays noon-5:00
The Royal Armory contains the weapons of Sweden's ruling family. There are many fine firearms, including presentation Colt revolvers.

SWITZERLAND

Basel

Historisches Museum Basel (Basel Historical Museum)

26-6. A section of the Royal Army Museum at Stockholm, Sweden. Here is housed one of the finest modern exhibits of arms and armor in Europe.

Open: Summer weekdays 9:00-12:15; 2:00-5:00, Sundays 10:15-12:15, 2:00-4:00
The gun collection contains both artillery and small arms dating from the late 15th century through the 19th century. Many are from the old town arsenal. There are also edged weapons, armor, flags, and uniforms.

Bern

Bernisches Historisches Museum (Bern Historical Museum)
Open: Weekdays 9:00-noon, 2:00-5:00; Sundays 10:00-noon, 2:00-5:00; closed Monday mornings.
The Bern museum has probably the best general collection of arms and armor in Switzerland.

Geneva

Musée d'Art et d'Histoire (Museum of Art and History)
Open: Daily 10:00-noon, 2:00-5:00; closed Monday mornings.
The museum has an excellent collection of arms and armor, including many fine firearms of the pre-percussion era.

Solothurn

Altes Zeughaus Solothurn (Old Solothurn Armory)
Open: Weekdays April through September 8:00-noon, 1:00-6:00; Sundays and holidays 10:00-noon, 1:00-5:00
The collection was begun in 1833 and contains both artillery and small arms from the 15th century to the present.

Zurich

Schweizerisches Landesmuseum (Swiss National Museum)
Open: May through September, daily except Mondays 10:00-noon, 2:00-5:00
The arms collection numbers some 30,000 items, all related to the history of Switzerland. Both artillery and small arms are included.

27-1. One of the pioneer gun collectors associations was formed in New York in 1932. This pictures the entire attendance at the first formal meeting near Ithaca, New York. The editor of this book (third from right, front row) was one of the organizers and officers.

27.

the Collector's Organizations and Gun Shows

Since Collector associations and their accompanying firearms displays provide much of the vitality for the arms collecting hobby, any treatment of this subject requires that we give thought to its past, present, and future.

The hobby of arms collecting is probably almost as old as the use of firearms. Many persons, past and present, have been fascinated by the historical importance of firearms or by family association with certain arms. Because of this, many old guns and other arms have been retained as decorative pieces or as cherished mementoes of the past.

There were some arms collectors who were more inquisitive than others, and some who wanted larger or finer collections than they could acquire from prevailing local sources. These folk sought a better means of satisfying their desires than that of "beating the bushes" for specimens in their own localities. The logical result of these efforts toward greater accomplishment has been the formation of Arms Collector associations. Pioneering these collector groups were organizations like the Arms and Armor Club of Columbus, Ohio, organized in March 1932, the Eastern Arms Collectors Association (now the New York State Arms Collectors Association) which held its first meeting at Ithaca, New York in 1932, and the Southern California Arms Collectors Association, formed the same year.

At first, the objectives of collector organizations were: *1. To exchange knowledge of arms, because the few books which were available on the subject were incomplete in their coverage, contained inconsistencies and misinformation, and often employed crude illustrations.*

2. To provide a means and place for the exchange of arms—a place or occasion in which club members could buy, sell, or trade with other members.

3. To develop organized efforts in combatting unjust anti-firearms legislation of the type which would discriminate against the lawful use, possession, or collection of arms by responsible citizens, a right defined in the Constitution of the United States, and reasserted in practically every State Constitution.

To accomplish these objectives, organizational constitutions were adopted, setting forth the purposes, qualifications for membership, rules for the election of officers, collection of dues, and the conduct of meetings.

Although there were always a few who were more willing than others to assume the responsibilities of planning for and arranging meetings, most members of a new group were willing to assist at the meetings. The quality and consistency of these meetings and their accompanying arms displays were to establish the stature of the organization.

As these early associations grew in membership, they suffered the same kind of "growing pains" experienced by any democratic form of government. They learned that just having a constitution did not automatically make every member become an ideal member, or insure "peace and tranquility" within the organization. They learned that any democratic form of government is only as strong and effective as the support given by the membership, and that the stature of the association was the reflection of the stature of the majority of its individual members.

Those associations which grew strong did so by continuous effort—not by accident. New problems arise in every meeting which require positive and unbiased action on the part of the associations' officers and directors. Because the conduct of meetings and displays are so important in the life of Arms Collector groups, the officers and members of many associations have been questioned as to what problems they have faced and how they were able to overcome them. For the benefit of organizations which still have these problems, or for new groups which are planning to organize, the next section of this chapter will be devoted to a statement of some of the problems faced by gun collector organizations, followed by the solutions suggested by a consensus of reports.

Membership in Collectors' Associations

Whether through enthusiasm for the hobby, a desire to make the club appear strong and important because of the number of its members, or just through carelessness, some organizations have made memberships easy to obtain, and the qualifications for membership either have not been strict enough, or have not been enforced. This situation can only result in the inadvertent acceptance of some members who will place selfish interests ahead of the good of the club, those who are after the "fast buck," and even those whose dealings are sometimes ethically unsound. Once in control of an organization, such a group can turn the club's displays and buying and selling activity into little more than rummage sales. Articles unrelated to arms collecting take the space of the fine arms which no longer appear, and the discriminating collectors who are interested in good items will drop out.

Membership in an Arms Collector association should be a matter of pride and a serious responsibility for each applicant and for his sponsors. (The size of an organization is not necessarily an indication of a respected position or integrity.) Qualifications for membership need not be "high-hat," but they should be strict enough to require very good citizenship on the part of the applicant and full knowledge of his qualifications by his sponsors. Since no human judgment is perfect, it follows that some undesirable individuals may become members, or some members may become undesirable after attaining membership. Any disregard of the organization rules, safety rules, or evidence of unethical conduct should be dealt with immediately and firmly by the directors.

Officers, Their Selection and Qualifications

In some instances, the selection of candidates and the election of officers may take on the character of a popularity contest. When this occurs, candidates may not have the executive ability and sound judgment necessary to retain the respect and confidence of the membership.

Since theirs are not easy jobs, they may not be willing to make what would be unpopular decisions concerning some members, even though they know that such decisions would be in the interest of the membership as a whole.

Because candidates are to be representatives of the membership as a whole, their selection should not be the result of a hurried business meeting. In the case of the larger organizations, a nominating committee should be selected to sound out the desires of the membership, and to interview candidates several months in advance of the election. Candidates should be experienced, capable, and willing to serve. Because jobs of this sort are becoming more complex year after year, some of the associations require that a candidate serve on the Board of Directors for at least one term so that he may become familiar with the details of club management, and the membership may thus have an opportunity to judge his

ability as a worker and potential administrator.

Control of Meetings

If meetings are not firmly controlled, the association is likely to suffer. When safety rules are not vigorously enforced, incidents may occur which will affect the reputation and public image of the club. If rules specifying what items may or may not be displayed are not enforced, some members may load tables with all sorts of items having no connection with arms collecting, and the meeting resembles a rummage sale. A serious result is that less space remains for legitimate arms displays. Dedicated arms collectors become so discouraged that they no longer attempt to bring their good material and may withdraw from the association.

Since display rules and safety rules are usually voted into force by the entire membership, the enforcement of these rules should be the responsibility of each member. Unfortunately, it is human nature to shun responsibility whenever possible, and there is a tendency to "wink at" rules infractions even though a member may not actually break the rules himself. Such being the case, the enforcement of rules usually falls upon the officers, directors, or certain individuals who accept appointments as rules advisors. Enforcement is not an easy or a pleasant job, but in many instances, the infraction is caused by thoughtlessness, and the member willingly complies with the rules when reminded. It is a wise precaution to be sure that the rules are posted prominently so that those in attendance have no excuse for noncompliance. Then *enforce* them!

Nonmember Attendance at Meetings

Meetings and displays which are open to the general public are especially difficult to manage. Unless locked cases are used for exhibits, sometimes damage or loss occurs due to unauthorized handling and other causes. Also, unless sales are scrupulously checked, transactions may be made with unauthorized buyers. Some nonmembers may innocently or ignorantly bring an unauthorized weapon to such an open meeting.

Certainly, all associations should be mindful of sound practices and anxious to give the association a good public image. Nor is the fact that many meetings are not open to the public any guarantee against a poor image.

Many associations have adopted the "guest" method of permitting nonmembers to attend. A member is usually limited to the admission of from three to four guests (exclusive of his immediate family) and he is to be personally responsible for the entertainment and deportment of his guests while they are in the meeting hall. Usually each member must wear a badge of identification, and his guests are provided with appropriate badges displaying their names and the name of the sponsoring member. This method is doubly effective. It causes the member to be more selective of those whom he invites as his guests, and it confers a special privilege on those who are admitted as guests. Guests are frequently potential members. Purchases or sales for guests should, of course, be made only through the sponsoring member.

Obviously, the foregoing paragraphs have not covered all of the problems which confront Arms Collector associations, nor have they provided all of the answers, but they have covered major issues. If an association has been able to cope with the problems covered, its management and membership will be progressive enough to find the answers to other problems as they arise.

Association Exhibits and Commercial "Gun Shows"

Exhibits are a very vital activity of Arms Collector organizations, and each club, large or small, has a definite purpose and program in the presentation of its exhibits. Actually there are two separate types of gatherings—those which are primarily of the "meet-ing" type, and those which have become classed as the "commercial" type. Each type, if it is to be successful, must follow the same safety rules and similar rules of meeting management. Each type of gathering fills specific collector needs and each type can be made to complement the other.

The basic Arms Collector gathering is of the "meeting" type. It usually is conducted by a group of collectors and shooters with kindred interests, and living near enough to each other to develop their meetings into a social as well as an educational and trading unit. Originally, displays in these meets were devised to encourage comments and exchanges of opinion concerning the items exhibited because there were few authoritative books available to explain finer differences and varied types.

Now, with many excellent books available, displays at these meetings serve the worth-while complementary purpose of demonstrating points described in these books in a more dramatic manner than text and photography could.

To be most effective, exhibits should be carefully planned, and the items described by identifying cards. If awards are given for displays, much more interest will be stimulated if displays are graded upon completeness, ingenuity shown in the layout, and effective description of the items, rather than upon the monetary value of the items exhibited.

These meeting-type gatherings lend themselves well to an occasional "display only" program at which nothing exhibited is for sale, and an interchange of knowledge and appreciation can be enjoyed at a leisurely pace. A banquet and a competent guest speaker, presenting a vital subject related to arms collecting, can add much to such a club's program.

Space is usually not a serious problem for the average meeting-type gatherings, but even here, table allocation by reservation, rather than by the old "first come, first served" basis invariably will result in more displays of the better material. These meetings present excellent opportunities for the encouragement of new studies of arms along specific lines. Cooperation with other organizations and with other individual collectors interested in the same lines can provide a wealth of background material.

The so-called "commercial" type of gun show falls into two distinct categories:

1. The show promoted by professional promoters; some of these are conducted on a very commendable plane—others are of questionable value to the collecting fraternity.

2. The show sponsored by a collector organization, or by several such organizations, in concert, in order to avoid conflicting dates and to increase the overall attendance.

For the purposes of this discussion, the second category is the one which is believed to be of the most interest to collectors.

This "commercial" type of gathering is a direct outgrowth of many factors, some of which were good and others which were less desirable. However, the associations which have sponsored successful "commercial" type meetings are those which have been able to employ the good practices and to subordinate or eliminate those which were found to be less desirable.

Inherent in the arms collecting hobby is the desire of the member to do the following:

1. Increase (or decrease) the size and/or scope of his collection on a basis of sound values.

2. Upgrade the specimens he has in his collection by sale or trade.

3. Dispose of the arms in one category in order to begin on another line.

The fulfillment of these desires is often a frustrating project for a collector acting as an individual, and is not much easier for members within a localized collector group. The amount and expense of "legwork" hunting new or better specimens, or disposing of a collection frequently makes the cost of such operations prohibitive for many collectors. Of course, collectors can satisfy many of these desires through transactions with dealers. But the problems of having to buy "sight unseen," often from a limited selection of material, plus insurance and shipping costs (both ways in case of dissatisfaction with the item) introduce expenses which may present serious handicaps to the joys of collecting.

Small local meetings cannot satisfy these desires to any great extent because of their relatively limited market, and the lack of enough new and different material to be displayed, show after show.

27-3. An attractive display of antique pistols at the largest of all collectors meetings—held annually at Columbus, Ohio. The author of this chapter has served several terms as president of the Ohio association, and has played a leading role in the growth and popularity of its meetings.

In the "growing pains" process over the years, some associations have enjoyed tremendous increases in membership. As the membership expanded, the market potential expanded with it, and the amount and selection of material changed quite frequently. The geographic location of these clubs was such that their meetings could attract a maximum attendance from all sections of the country with a minimum of travel in relation to the probable results to be derived from the journey. They have been fortunate enough to have space facilities of sufficient size to accommodate large crowds; lighting specifically designed for exhibit purposes; airconditioning and heating which permits holding meetings in the hottest or the coldest weather; adequate parking, unloading, and loading equipment; and good food available in the hall.

The large associations are those whose meetings and displays have developed into the commercial-type "gun shows" of real quality. They are not to be confused with the "flea-market" type of meeting at which anything and everything is available (at the buyers' risk). At such a hodgepodge show there may even be some good weapons offered for sale or trade; but you have a better chance of finding old tools, cameras, glass, china, coins, stamps, farm equipment, pictures, knives, buttons, motors, books, imitation jewelry, imitation antiques of all sorts, and other material unrelated to arms collecting.

In the high-quality commercial-type meetings, no effort is spared to maintain the identity of the show as an Arms Collectors' venture. The purpose of the commercial-type gathering is to bring together collectors, shooters, traders, and dealers from all parts of the country. It is common knowledge that what is a hard seller in one part of the country, is often a sought-after prize in another part. By bringing buyers and sellers and many kinds of collectible arms together at one time and in one place, the best interests of all facets of arms collecting are served. Dealers and clients can meet face to face. Choices can be made from a wide selection of material, and comparisons can be made in grades of material and prices. Specialist collectors can meet similar specialists from other parts of the country. In other words, a quality commercial meeting performs the same functions in

27-4. Collectors and dealers discuss the merits of antique weapons and accessories, and enjoy buying, selling and trading at the various meetings and gun shows.

relation to the meeting-type exhibits that a large department store does in relation to the neighborhood store. The basic needs are supplied by the neighborhood store, and the special or unusual needs are provided by the large department store. One is as necessary as the other in serving its clients in the fullest manner.

In operating a successful commercial meeting sponsored by a collectors' organization or other responsible party, the problems of show management become vastly greater than the mere increase in the number of tables provided. Because of the large crowds, security becomes a tremendously important factor if collectors of fine material are to be encouraged to bring their valuable arms for display, sale, or trade. The general public is invited to some commercial gatherings, but excluded from others because most exhibits and sales or trade material are displayed on open tables. Some special exhibits are shown in locked glass cases.

The "guest" method of handling nonmember attendance at closed shows is used. Paid-up members of recognized Arms Collector groups are admitted, but must wear identification badges.

Preferably one entrance is used for admission or exit, and members of the local police usually act as guards. No one is permitted in the exhibit hall before or after certain hours except the guards. Rules governing safety and those concerning the non-display of prohibited items must be strictly enforced.

The future of Arms Collector organizations can be greatly brightened by close cooperation. Without such cooperation, collectors may face curtailment of their hobby by restrictive anti-firearms legislation, often fostered by well-intentioned but uninformed public groups.

Within recent years, the National Rifle Association of America (a 92-year old organization) has become the most effective medium through which the arms collecting groups can cooperate and become centrally organized. Although the National Rifle Association concerns itself with all aspects of arms possession and lawful use (collectors and shooters, alike), affiliation with the N.R.A. by arms collector organizations has these advantages to recommend it:

1. The N.R.A. legislative staff is composed of a group of men who are experienced in ferreting out and analyzing proposed anti-firearms legislation in all levels of government. They issue timely bulletins to N.R.A. members, explaining the probable effects of such legislation, and offering suggestions as to what positive action can be taken by members in the specific areas affected.

2. At present, there are over 75 Arms Collector associations affiliated with the N.R.A., and the address of each organization and its current secretary is available to any member. Each year more arms groups recognize and avail themselves of the advantages of N.R.A. affiliation.

3. One of the six N.R.A. standing committees is the Gun Collectors Committee which is composed of collectors with experience in the problems of arms collectors and their associations, both large and small. Members affiliated with the N.R.A. can submit problems for consideration, advice, and action.

4. N.R.A. affiliated member organizations have a prominent part in the displays and program at the N.R.A. annual meetings which are open to the public, and at which arms collector associations have an opportunity to compare notes with other similar as-

27-5. Collectors' meetings are occasions for fun and good fellowship. Here Frank SoRelle, prominent as a rancher and chairman of the N.R.A. Gun Collectors Committee, demonstrates to Admiral M. C. Mumma, past president of N.R.A., that they grow even the pistols big in the West.

sociations, discuss problems, and to demonstrate to a usually astounded and appreciative public the beauty and great variety of our historic weapons.

These are but a few of the advantages which accrue to arms collector organizations through affiliation with the National Rifle Association; there are many more features of a very real and practical nature.

It is hoped that this chapter may be helpful in reminding collectors that they need good active associations, and that for an association to be both good and active, its members must be ready and willing participators in supporting the best interests of the association.

The pleasures and rewards of arms collecting will increase as our knowledge increases through education in the many fascinating fields of the hobby. To this end, arms collector organizations can render significant services to themselves and to the entire fraternity by encouraging willing members to undertake research studies in the lesser-known lines of arms, or to deepen studies in fields where some exploration has been done.

In the pursuit of greater knowledge, all groups interested in similar lines will find great value in cooperative efforts to compile known facts, make comparative studies, and record their findings in permanent form.

In such a union of ideals and efforts, collector organizations will not only gather greater strength, but each individual member will discover greater opportunities for pleasure and profit by contributing to the strength of his organization.

the Care
& Repair
of Old Guns

This chapter can not presume to provide answers to all the questions in the broad field of gun care and repair, but important basic problems which a collector will face are here presented in question-and-answer form with accompanying drawings; it is hoped that this format will make the details easy to understand and the information very usable.

A well-cared-for gun collection can illustrate in a fascinating manner man's great ingenuity and progress in the field of weapons. Many of these weapons will have a substantial value, and their condition is a vital factor. Reconditioning and care become very important in establishing value and desirability. If a fine old gun is injudiciously scrubbed on a wire wheel or otherwise poorly handled, it may lose much of its potential worth.

Gun collectors, skilled or unskilled, may find guidance here that will enable them to take a rusty old gun, possibly one with a broken stock, and turn it into a specimen that is a valuable asset to their collection. As values increase and demand for old guns grows, the ability to reclaim specimens will pay good dividends.

Starting with an old, neglected gun, the first objective is to remove all excess rust and grime from the metal parts and to clean the wooden parts without disturbing whatever original finish may be present. To accomplish this with maximum efficiency, the gun must be carefully taken apart and the several parts treated in a manner best suited to their individual need.

28.

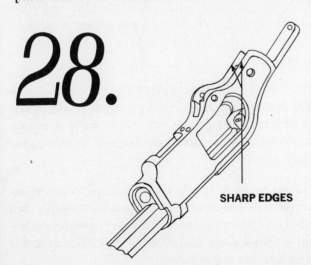

SHARP EDGES

A FEW PRECAUTIONS

When work is started on an old gun, be sure that there are no live charges in cylinder, magazine, or barrel. Many antique guns are found to contain old loads, and that old charge can be set off with unhappy results.

If one should receive a cut, or pick up a wood splinter, attend to the wound without delay. One cannot know where that old gun may have been or what sort of infection could develop.

Clean up around the sharp edges first, and then cover those edges with masking tape before proceeding to other areas for cleaning. The accompanying drawing of a stripped Model '73 Winchester receiver illustrates dangerously sharp edges which are exposed when the stock and lower tang are removed.

FIG. 1

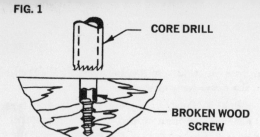

CORE DRILL

BROKEN WOOD
SCREW

236   While working with flint gunlocks out of the stock, keep fingers away from the pan area when the hammer is cocked. Some of these locks have powerful mainsprings and the front edges of the jaws are very sharp. The sear may be accidentally tripped and the force of the falling hammer is capable of inflicting serious injury.

Before starting any major restoration on a gun, one must become thoroughly familiar with the old original finish on the wood and metal parts of that particular model; if a part is missing, its proper dimensions and shape must be ascertained. A study of similar specimens in museums or other private collections can provide this needed basic information.

When one becomes a gun collector, it is a great advantage if he is able to master effective cleaning methods and do simple repair work; this chapter is designed to help him along that road.

STOCK WORK

Q. What is a good way to clean the checkering on a gunstock that is plugged full of dirt?

A. Apply masking tape around the area that is checkered to protect the surrounding stock finish. Then apply varnish remover to the checkered area, and allow the varnish remover to stand for several minutes to soften the dirt in the checkering. Then with a stiff toothbrush, brush out the checkered area. Repeat this process until the checkered area is clean. After this, if necessary, use a checkering tool to sharpen the checkering, but only after the wood has become thoroughly dry. The reason for using varnish remover is that in the past the stock may have been refinished, and linseed oil has been brushed into the checkering.

Q. How is a replacement stock made to look as though it has seen some service?

A. After the stock surface has been prepared for the stock finish, rub some dirt into the wood, or apply some dark stain in the places that are likely to get dirty from handling, standing in a corner, or hanging up over a fireplace. If you wish, strike the stock in several places to create some nicks and jams, using a blunt instrument. The nicks and jams, for best results are made after the stock has been finished. When the necessary dirt and stain have been applied to the wood to make the stock look "aged," apply several coats of stock finish before attempting to finish the stock. If this is not done, the undercoat of dirt and stain will be rubbed off while rubbing down the stock finish.

Q. What sort of stock finish is used to polish guns that are set out for display at gun shows?

A. Gun owners sometimes apply neutral shoe polish to the stock and polish it with a soft rag. Try it sometime and see how it works.

Q. What sort of permanent stock finish should be applied to an old gun stock?

A. In the old days linseed oil was used. It took many coats of the linseed oil to get a high luster on the surface of the stock. It is best to continue the use of linseed oil, or oil-based wood finishes.

Q. How it is possible to clean dirt off a gunstock without disturbing the original finish?

A. The finished gunstock is more or less waterproof. Remove the stock from the action and barrel, and with a rag or sponge and some soap, wash the stock with soap and water. It might be wise to leave the butt plate on the stock. Unprotected end grain in that area chips out very easily and the wash job could lead into a repair job.

Q. How is a broken wood screw removed from an old stock?

A. A special type of drill will have to be used for this operation. The drill is called a core drill. The drill is hollow for about two inches, and on the cutting end are saw teeth. This drill is placed over the broken screw and run down into the stock to a depth that may equal the length of the broken screw. The drill is then extracted from the stock. At times the stock wood will break off at the bottom of the hole, and the core of wood inside the drill will contain the broken screw. If this is not the case, the core of wood containing the screw will

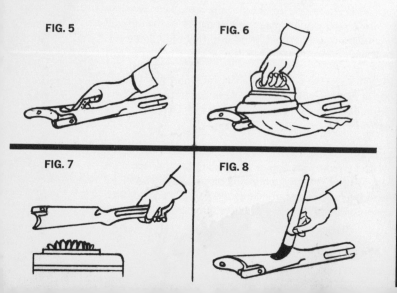

FIG. 5

FIG. 6

FIG. 7

FIG. 8

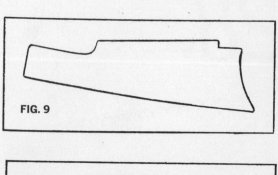

FIG. 9

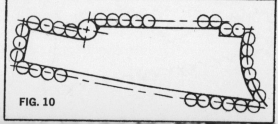

FIG. 10

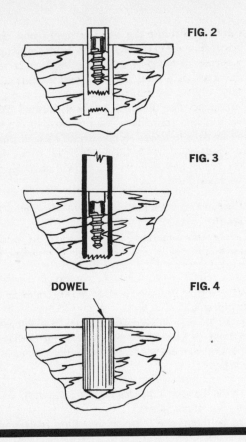

FIG. 2

FIG. 3

DOWEL   **FIG. 4**

been removed from the surface of the gunstock. First detach the stock from the metal parts of the gun.

Fig. 5 Remove all stock finish from around the dent. If the stock finish is not removed from around the dent, the steam will not be able to enter the pores of the wood to raise the grain of the wood in the damaged area.

Fig. 6 Place a damp cloth over the dent and apply the hot iron to the damp cloth. Repeat this operation until dent has been raised.

Fig. 7 Hold the stock over the open flame of a gas stove burner to dry the exposed stock wood. This will also raise the grain of the stock wood which will have to be sanded smooth when dry. Use caution during this operation, because it is easy to char the wood and existing stock finish.

Fig. 8 Apply stock finish to area around dent. Possibly several coats may be necessary.

Q. What is the best lubricant to use on a wood screw?

A. Soap. Fill the threads of the wood screws with soap. If grease is used, there may be a chance of the grease getting on some unfinished wood, and stock finish will not dry over greasy wood.

Q. How can one replace wood screws so that it is possible to have all the screw driver slots in the screws parallel with the stock and barrel center lines?

A. The correct size of commercial wood screws will have to be used. Obtain a dozen or so screws and keep trying them in position until the screw driver slots line up with the stock and barrel center lines.

Q. What sort of compound, other than plastic wood, or wood filler, could be used to fill holes and chipped out areas in a gunstock?

A. Beeswax (easily colored) has been put to use quite often for filling holes and chipped out areas in gunstocks. Beeswax is about as old as time. So the question could arise: "By whom and when was that repair made?"

Q. Is it possible to make a gunstock by using a drill press, handsaw, wood rasp, and various wood carving tools?

A. Yes, it is possible, and it is not too hard to do because wood cuts easily with sharp tools. The first step is to obtain a piece of stock wood of proper proportions and follow the sug-

have to be broken out of the gunstock. There will be a round hole left in the gunstock that will have to be plugged with a piece of doweling. Glue the dowel in place, and after the glue has set, trim off the excess dowel. Once more there is a solid base for a new screw.

Fig. 1 shows the starting of the drill. *Fig. 2* shows the drill below the depth of the screw. *Fig. 3* shows the core of wood containing the broken wood screw being extracted from the stock. *Fig. 4* shows the dowel in place after the core has been removed from the stock.

Q. How is it possible to remove dents and nicks from the surface of a gunstock?

A. This is done by steaming out the dent or nick by using a hot flat iron. This process will not work if a piece of wood has

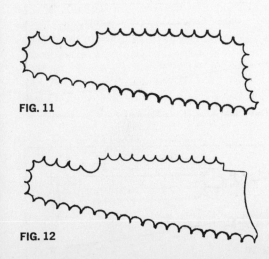

FIG. 11

FIG. 12

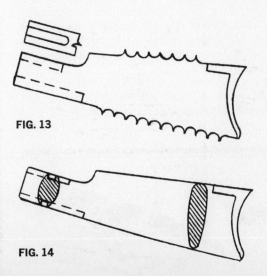

FIG. 13

FIG. 14

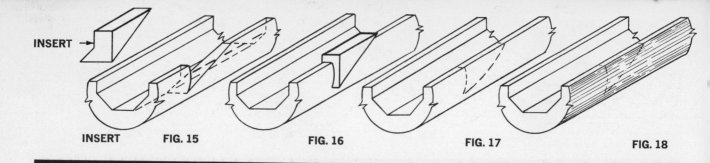

INSERT →

INSERT   FIG. 15   FIG. 16   FIG. 17   FIG. 18

gested methods as listed below.

Fig. 9 shows the outline of the stock on the selected piece of stock wood. This outline should represent the finished shape of the stock.

Fig. 10 shows a line scribed one-eighth of an inch from the outline of the stock. This second line will become a center line for a series of drilled holes. On this second line, lay out and mark every quarter of an inch all around the stock. Then use a quarter-inch diameter twist drill and drill a hole at every quarter-inch mark on this second line. When this is done, remove the drilled outline of the stock from the blank of wood. The rough stock will look like *Fig. 11*.

Fig. 12 shows the rough stock shaped to accept the butt plate. Once the butt plate has been fitted and installed, leave it in position during shaping operations. The butt plate will serve as a guide for the contour of the stock and also protect the end grain of the wood from chipping.

Fig. 13 shows the rough stock inletted for the upper and lower tangs of the receiver.

Fig. 14 shows the finished stock. To finish the stock, the problem is to hold the stock in some fashion and at the same time have access to all surfaces to be worked. In some cases the stock to be shaped can be installed on the receiver of the gun which will serve very well for making the stock accessible. If this system is used, apply masking tape to the portions of the receiver that are likely to become scratched while shaping the stock.

Q. How can broken out wood be replaced in gunstocks?
A. If wood has to be replaced, replace the wood before any cleaning or refinishing is done. The reason for doing things in this order is that the excess glue that spills out from glued joints will not stick to old stock finish and dirt on the surface of the stock. If the stock wood is finished around a joint to be glued, the glue will be absorbed by the exposed wood. Therefore, when it comes to blending the old wood with the new wood, the various stains and dyes will not penetrate the wood that has absorbed the glue.

When the stock is split, if possible, spread this break so that both surfaces can be cleaned. In order to make a good glued joint, the surfaces of the wood have to be clean.

Cleaning the wood surface in the broken section of a stock may not be a simple task. Sometimes a good scrubbing with soap and water will do the job. But if the wood is oil soaked, the soap and water treatment will not be of much help. The broken sections of the stock that are oil soaked will have to be washed and soaked in a cleaning fluid similar to what dry cleaning establishments use. The concentration of oil in the wood governs the amount of time to soak the sections of stock; the longer the better. This method is not exactly foolproof but it is a step in the right direction. In a bad break the use of dowels is desirable. The dowels of course are made of the same type of wood as the stock. The dowel pin holes are drilled through the heaviest sections of the wood. The dowel pins are then sized to the holes drilled in the stock, but do not make the dowel pins fit the holes too tight. Otherwise the moisture in the glue will expand the dowel pins and, therefore, the dowel pins will not go into the holes.

Stock breaks along the barrel channel are usually difficult to repair because the broken area is so small. Therefore, the small exposed area does not offer a good surface for gluing. The best thing to do in a case like this is to cut out the whole area where the break is located, down to the bottom of the barrel channel. Make the cut-out section good and square so the insert can be fitted easily. After the insert has been made and fitted, apply glue to the insert and stock, and clamp the insert in place. After the glue has set, trim the insert to match the inside and outside of the stock contour.

After the insert has been made to match the stock contours, the insert will have to be blended to match the color of the stock wood. This is done by first using a saturated solution of Potassium Permanganate and water, which is a very strong oxidizing agent. This solution will turn the stock wood a dark brown color. Try to control the spreading of the oxidizing agent so it will not run or spread too far beyond the border of the insert. If anything, try to blend the oxidizing agent with the new and the old wood. The oxidizing agent will raise the grain of the wood, and after the wood has become dry, use fine sandpaper to reduce the raised wood grain. This operation may have to be repeated several times to attain the desired effect. When the area is thoroughly dry, apply some linseed oil. This will usually show if the old and new wood have been properly blended in color. If the conditions are still not quite right, try blending the wood again by using a mixture of burnt umber and linseed oil. This is done by smearing the mixture

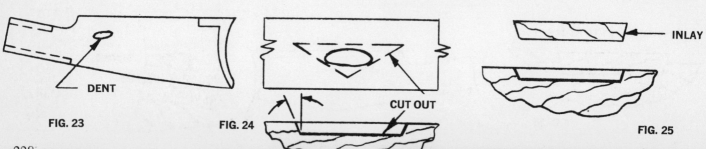

DENT

FIG. 23   FIG. 24   CUT OUT   INLAY   FIG. 25

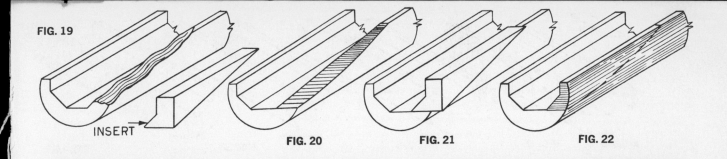

FIG. 19

INSERT→

FIG. 20   FIG. 21   FIG. 22

of burnt umber and linseed oil around on the stock in the re-paired area until the desired effect is attained. Allow the repaired area to dry before any stock finish is applied. When the area is thoroughly dry, apply several coats of stock finish before finishing the area with fine sandpaper or steel wool. As an extra precaution, it would be best to favor the repaired area while working on the rest of the stock surface. Otherwise the blending finish may be rubbed off.

See *Figs. 15, 16, 17, 18, 19, 20, 21 and 22* for barrel channel repair.

Some stocks have nicks and dents so deep that it is impossible to steam them out. This being the case, it is necessary to actually cut out the nick or dent and insert what is called an inlay. To do this type of repair, make the cut for the inlay as simple as possible, and not too deep. The edges of the hole cut for the inlay should be tapered inwards, and the edges of the inlay shaped accordingly. The reason for tapering the edges of the inlay is to insure a wedging effect. This method produces a very tight fit around the border of the inlay, thus making the repair almost invisible after blending. On dark stocks a little shellac and umber can be applied in such a way as to conceal cracks, mends, or inlays.

See *Figs. 23, 24, 25 and 26* for inlay repair.

Decorative inlays are usually made of some sort of metal, bone, or horn. This type of inlay has the habit of falling out or becoming loose. If one encounters this condition, use a type of cement that is called "Contact Cement." Follow the instructions that come with the "Contact Cement," and that loose inlay will be firmly attached to the stock.

The toe of the gunstock breaks out easily, due to the thin portion of the butt plate flexing under sudden impact loads.

If a large section of the toe of the gunstock is broken out, use a mortise and tenon-type joint. This type of a glued joint is stronger than a butt-type glued joint. For the tenon, use a piece of plywood which is next to impossible to split.

METAL WORK

Rust seems to be the worst enemy of guns. The museum curators watch like hawks for its appearance on the weapons they have on display.

Let's take a closer look at this substance called rust. What is rust? Rust is Iron Oxide, and it is rather abrasive as it appears on the outside surfaces of iron and steel. When rust is starting to appear on the metal parts of a gun, it is old Mother Nature doing her best to get that gun back into its original state of Iron Oxide. First a bit of light surface rust appears, which is usually quite easy to remove. After this light surface rust has been removed, there may be small telltale pit marks left on the surface of the part to let you know that rust has been there. If surface rust is left on a gun part for any great length of time, the rust becomes attached to the steel or iron. This type of rust takes the form of pits that run deep below the surface. Another type of rust that is caused by fire is very difficult to remove, because it is created at such a rapid rate. The result is a hard scale formed over the metal parts, and it is usually a black color.

Rust and old guns go hand in hand. But by the same token, the old-timers who made guns created that brown finish on the barrel and other metal parts by controlled rusting. This process is called "browning," and the same process is used to this day.

If an old gun has all the parts rusted to a deep brown color, but not pitted, try to utilize what is there by removing the excess rust from the metal parts down to near the original finish. Success depends on how severe the rusting is. If the rust is of a light nature, it will not be too difficult to handle. If the rusting is of a heavy nature, it will be a difficult task. Fine steel wool is all right to use for light surface rust but it will not be of much help for the medium and heavy deposits of rust. The rust being abrasive and firmly attached to the steel or iron, it will have to be attacked by some other means.

To make matters easier for the removal of any type of rust, soak all parts in kerosene for a period of two to three weeks. This treatment will have a softening effect upon the rust. For the removal of the medium type of rust, a sharp instrument like a single-edged razor blade makes an excellent scraper. If a reasonable amount of care is exercised, the rust can be scraped down to near the original finish. But, before scraping the metal parts, examine them carefully for nicks and dents. If the nicks and dents are not reduced, or removed, they will cause the razor blade to become nicked. The nicked razor blade will cause deep scratches on the metal surface during

the Care and Repair of Old Guns

239

TRIM INLAY TO STOCK LEVEL

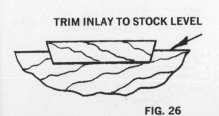

FIG. 26

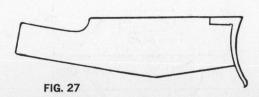

FIG. 27

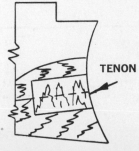

TENON

the scraping operation. If the razor blade becomes nicked or dull, sharpen the razor blade on a smooth oil stone. After the metal parts have been scraped free of excess rust, burnish the parts with fine steel wool. This act will show up any places that were missed in the scraping operation. If the parts were originally blued and look all right, but there are a few bright spots showing through, apply some touch-up blue, covering the whole part. The touch-up blue will make the rusted part look a bit darker and the bright spots seem to blend in with the rest of the finish.

A heavily rusted surface that is made up out of a lot of rust deposits that extend above the surface of the metal is much harder to remove. A scraper will not be of much use in this case. The rusted surfaces will have to be attacked by other means. This type of rust, if one is careful, can be used as a base for a brown finish such as may have been originally on the barrel or other parts. To remove this type of rust, emery cloth backed with a flat piece of steel will do very well. Work on the highest deposits of rust first to get them down to the level of the remaining rust. After this is done, pass the emery cloth lengthways along the surface of the parts until they become smooth. This action will bring out some bright spots, but that can be expected from such a treatment. To cure this condition, the barrel and parts will have to be re-rusted to cover the bright spots. Apply the rusting solution to the barrel and parts, set them up in a damp place for a few days, and note the results. The bright spots will rust again. This new deposit of rust will have to be scuffed off with steel wool, and once more the rusting solution will have to be applied to the parts. When handling the parts, use a clean pair of work gloves to prevent oil from getting on the newly rusted surfaces. Repeat the rusting process until the desired effect is attained and, afterwards, wash all parts with hot water using a strong soap. When the parts are air dried, apply a light coat of linseed oil. This will make the parts turn a dark brown color. Also the linseed oil when dried will give the metal parts a light shine, and it will protect the parts from future rusting.

Rust that has been caused by fire, thus causing a hard scale to form on the metal parts, is extremely difficult to remove. The scale is so hard that it will have to be chipped off the metal parts. To start the process, tap the part that is covered with this hard scale with a small hammer. This action will break a small section of the hard scale loose from the steel or iron part. Hereafter use a chisel with a slightly rounded edge, held in a vertical position, and tap lightly with a small hammer. The scale will chip off in small sections. It is wise to wear some sort of eye protection during this operation because the scale leaves the surface of the metal with considerable velocity. After the scale has been removed from the metal parts, the parts will have to be re-rusted again to attain that deep brown color.

Scrapers can be utilized to remove rust. A razor blade is one form of scraper that is often used. The idea is to get a sharp edge of some kind that will dislodge rust from a metal surface. There are some places on a gun where it would be impossible to use a razor blade for removing rust. In these cases, one will have to devise other types of scrapers. A six-inch flexible scale is good to use. A piece of clock spring that can be cut to size and shape and inserted into a wooden handle so the scraper blade can be controlled, is quite good. Very irregular surfaces, like the rear end of a percussion revolver cylinder, can be cleaned by using a wire brush. The bristles of a wire brush act like a thousand scrapers. This cleaning is done by hand. If the operation was done by using a wire wheel on a polishing head, the rust pits would become enlarged.

Flat surfaces are easier to scrape than round surfaces. A round surface offers so little contact with the scraper blade that there is a great danger of digging into the metal, therefore great care must be exercised. Whatever the shape of the surface, keep a film of kerosene on the metal part at all times while scraping. This serves as a lubricant and helps to keep the edge of the scraper from digging into the metal.

Case-hardened parts are relatively easy to scrape. They are hardened and there is not too much danger of damaging the part while scraping, but just the same care must be exercised to insure a good job.

Figs. 1 and 2 show the use of a single-edged razor blade being used for removal of rust.

Figs. 3 and 4 show the use of a flexible flat scraper and wire brush for the removal of rust.

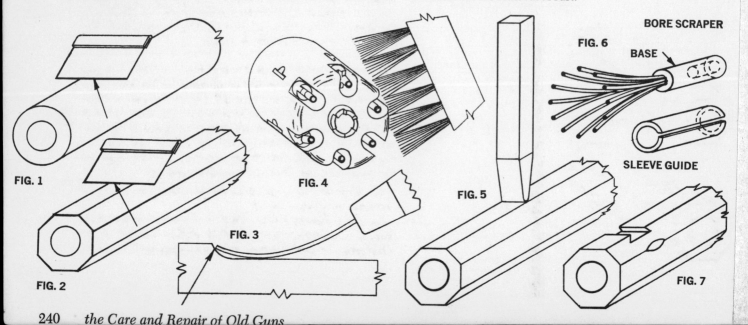

FIG. 1

FIG. 2

FIG. 3

FIG. 4

FIG. 5

BORE SCRAPER

FIG. 6

BASE

SLEEVE GUIDE

FIG. 7

Fig. 5 shows the use of a round-ended chisel for removing rust in scale form.

Q. What is a good way to clean checkering on metal parts?
A. Use a file card. In a sense a file is being cleaned.

Q. Is there any way to get old dried oil and grease off of gun parts without doing a lot of picking, poking, and scraping?
A. Yes, there is. Just soak the parts in carburetor cleaning fluid that can be obtained in any automobile service store. Leave the parts in the solution over night and then brush the residue away with a good stiff brush.

Q. Is there any way to clean engraving that is packed full of dirt and dried oil?
A. Apply carburetor cleaning fluid to the area and brush out the engraving with a stiff brush. Be careful not to get the carburetor cleaning fluid on the stock; it is very injurious to stock finish.

Q. When a gun is taken apart, what sort of a system can be used to keep track of the location of screws?
A. Put the screws back into the screw holes, and leave them there until the gun is ready to be assembled. This also applies to stock screws. The thread pitch on wood screws varies in relation to the slot in the head.

Q. Should any particular care be taken as to which way sights are to be driven out of their slots in the barrel?
A. The sight is tapered, and the general rule is to drive the sight out from left to right while facing the butt plate.

Q. What sort of preparation is necessary before one attempts to remove screws from a gun that has lain around for awhile collecting dirt and dust?
A. Clean out the screw slot so the screwdriver blade can be inserted to the full depth of the slot. Dirt in the screw slot in the heads of screws gives the illusion of a shallow slot.

Q. How is a rusted-in breech plug removed from the end of the barrel?
A. Sometimes the breech plug in a barrel is rusted tight and it is best to leave well enough alone before the tang is sheared off while attempting to unscrew it. To help matters, plug the nipple, then pour some penetrating oil down the barrel, and let the barrel stand breech down for several days. Pour out the penetrating oil, and then place the breech end of

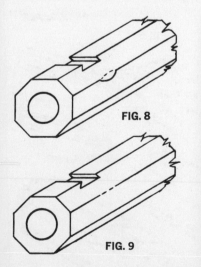

FIG. 8

FIG. 9

the barrel on a smooth flat piece of steel and strike all around the barrel in the area of the breech plug with a smooth-faced hammer. This type of treatment jars the rust loose from around the threads. Then apply heat to the same area, and while the barrel is still hot, try to unscrew the breech plug. If this does not work after several applications, the breech plug is securely frozen and very drastic measures would be required to replace it.

Q. How are rusted-in nipples removed?
A. There is not much to get hold of on a rusty and broken nipple, so the only thing that can be done is to drill out the old nipple. This is done by shoving drills through the old nipple until there is just a thin shell left which contains the threads. This thin shell can usually be dislodged by a small pick.

Q. Is it possible to replace the "safety pins" in Colt revolver cylinders?
A. Yes, but it is a tricky job to do correctly. First the old "safety pin" locations have to be found, and the old battered down "safety pins" will have to be drilled out. Then new "safety pins" of proper length will have to be made and pushed into the rear of the cylinder.

Q. How are broken and rusted-in screws removed from parts?
A. Same method as removing nipples, described above.

Q. How are newly-made exposed parts treated?
A. The parts should be rusted or blued to match the rest of the gun parts.

Q. Is it possible to re-rust repaired parts?
A. Yes, by using rusting solutions that can be purchased from antique gun supply houses, or making up your own from a formula provided near the end of this chapter.

Q. Is it possible to put an antique finish on brass?
A. Yes. Use a diluted solution of touch up gun blue. Swab the solution on the part, and the part will turn a dark color.

Q. What sort of a tool could be devised to clean out rusty gun bores?
A. A tool which can be used successfully is illustrated herewith (*Fig.* 6). The tool is made of a dozen pieces of curved music wire .062 inches in diameter by 4.000 inches long soldered into a brass base .350 inches in diameter by 2.000 inches long. The opposite end of the brass base is tapped to accept a heavy cleaning rod. Depending upon the size of the bore to be cleaned, various sizes of sleeve guides are required. The sleeve guide is pushed over the base.

When this type of tool is inserted into the bore of a gun barrel, the music-wire section is collapsed by the bore diameter, thus making an almost solid ring of scraping surface. The sleeve guide riding the bore surface will keep the end-scraping surfaces of the music wire 90 degrees to the bore surface. If a stiff wire brush were used for this operation, the rusty surface of the bore being abrasive, it would wear out the brush and very little rust would be removed.

Q. How can nicks and dents be removed from along the corners of an octagon barrel?
A. First, examine a dent or nick on the corner or end of the barrel. How does it appear? Could it be that the metal is just displaced, and could be pushed back into position? It may be

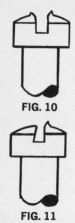

FIG. 10

FIG. 11

FIG. 12

FIG. 13

metal that has been displaced by a good hard bump. So the idea is to "bump" it back into place and touch up around the edges afterwards. By using a small, hard, smooth-faced hammer this can be done, and the result is that just a small mark shows where the metal has been displaced. This process can be applied to any dent or nick where the metal has been displaced but it will not work on a spot where the metal has been removed.

Fig. 7 shows a dent on a gun barrel. *Fig. 8* shows one-half of the dent "bumped" back in place with a smooth-faced hammer. *Fig. 9* shows the dent removed.

Q. How can battered screw heads, usually caused from ill-fitting screwdrivers, be repaired?

A. In much the same manner as described in the answer to the preceding question.
See *Figs. 10, 11, 12 and 13.*

Q. Is it possible to repair a broken tang that is part of the breech plug without welding, drilling, and countersinking a new hole in the tang?

A. Yes, but it takes a bit of skill and a sweat-soldering job. See *Figs. 14, 15, 16, 17 and 18.* Barrel tangs usually break across the screw hole as shown in *Fig. 14.*

Fig. 15 Remove all rust and dirt from the under side of the tang. To do a good soldering job the parts have to be clean. A coarse file does a good job of cleaning for this type of work.

Fig. 16 Make a piece of steel to fit the under side of the tang. The thickness of the steel would be about ⅛ inch. Tin the under side of the broken barrel tang and one side of the ⅛ inch piece of steel. Clamp together as shown in *Fig. 17* using a brass shim as indicated by the arrow between the tang and the clamp. The brass shim prevents the clamp from scratching the upper surface of the barrel tang. Apply heat to the parts to melt the solder and add more solder if necessary.

Fig. 18 When the parts have cooled, remove the clamp and drill a hole as indicated by the arrow in the ⅛ inch piece of steel for the stock screw.

Inlet the stock to allow for the extra thickness of the tang before assembly of the gun.

Q. Is it possible to make rather complicated parts, like a hammer, by using a drill press, hack saw, and a file?

A. Follow the same idea as shown in *Fig's. 9-14* under Stock Work.

Q. How is it possible to gage the correct length of metal stock for an irregular-shaped part that has to be replaced?

A. If the part to be replaced is something like a trigger guard, use a thin strip of copper about a quarter of an inch wide. Bend the strip of copper to the desired shape. The result will be the length of stock that is required to make the trigger guard. Trace an outline of the bent shape before straightening out the piece of copper.

Q. What is the best way to solder ramrod guides to a barrel?

A. The ramrod guide being made of thinner metal than the barrel, it would be impossible to use a soldering iron for this type of work. The soldering iron could not get the barrel hot enough to melt the solder.

In this case, the barrel will have to become the soldering iron. Clean out the recess where the ramrod guide is located and tin the portion of the ramrod guide that rests against the barrel. Wire the ramrod guide to the barrel, and apply heat to the barrel opposite the ramrod guide. Use a rosin core solder and when the barrel is hot enough to melt solder, flow the necessary amount of solder between the barrel and ramrod guide. The excess solder can be scraped off after the parts have cooled.

Some barrels have a decorative rib to which the ramrod guide is soldered. It would be advisable to apply a clamp, or wire tie this decorative rib to the barrel, before applying any heat. This decorative rib is sometimes soldered to the barrel, and it may come off while one is attempting to solder on the ramrod guide.
See *Figs. 19 and 20.*

Q. What is the best way to remove tight pistol grips and side-plates without marring or scratching the surrounding wood and metal?

A. *Figures 21 and 22* show pistol grips. Loosen the grip screw, indicated by the arrow, until the head of the grip screw appears above the surface of the grip. Using the screwdriver handle, tap the head of the screw lightly. This action as a rule will dislodge the opposite grip from the frame. Once one grip is loose, it can be removed from the frame and it is a simple matter to remove the other grip, tapping it loose through the frame.

242

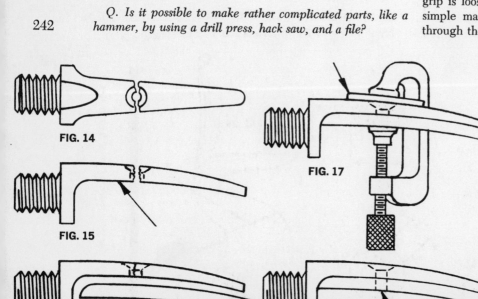

FIG. 14

FIG. 15

FIG. 16

FIG. 17

FIG. 18

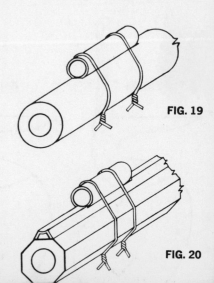

FIG. 19

FIG. 20

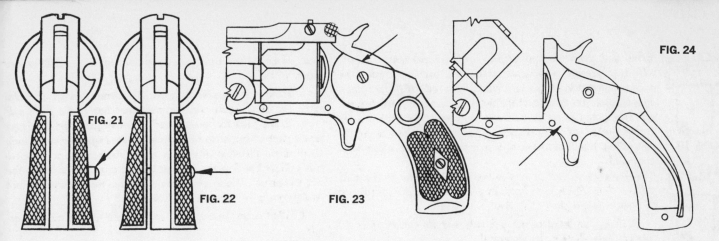

FIG. 21

FIG. 22

FIG. 23

FIG. 24

Figs. 23 and 24 show a side plate on a pistol. To remove a sideplate of this type, remove the screw in the center of the sideplate, and also remove the grips. Swing the cylinder out of the way and with a soft-faced hammer strike the frame a sharp blow at the spot indicated by the arrow in *Fig. 24.* The sideplate should come out of position after one or two sharp blows with the soft-faced hammer.

Q. How can model parts be made that can be used at a later date for actual part manufacture?

A. To copy a part from a rare gun will consume a lot of time. To avoid this bit of labor, if someone is good enough to loan a gun to copy a part, make a plaster of Paris mold of the part, and after the mold has dried out, fill the cavity with type metal. The casting will make a good model to work from and if the casting is kept on file, it may be used many times.

Q. How is it possible to install a misfit hammer to a lock?

A. The initial efforts are often not very good because the misfit hammer will not assume the correct full-cock position.

Fig. 25 shows a hammer. The first step will be to anneal the hammer around the square hole. Most hammers are heat treated to make them more durable. After this has been done the square hole that has been timed for another lock can be eliminated. Before any drilling is done, refer to a standard tap chart and choose a tap that will be large enough to contain the dimensions of the square portion of the tumbler within the root diameter of the tap. Use the proper size tap drill, and drill out the square hole in the hammer as shown in *Fig. 26* and tap the hole square with the rear surface of the hammer. Next make a threaded plug as shown in *Fig's. 27 and 28. Fig. 27* the "T" represents the thickness of the hammer, and "A" represents the diameter of the threaded

hole in the hammer. *Fig. 28* "B" represents a square hole that will have to be filed out to fit the square portion of the tumbler.

Insert the threaded plug into the hammer as shown in *Fig. 29* until both surfaces are flush with the hammer. Set the lock in the fired position and then place the hammer in position so that the inner shoulder, indicated by the arrow in *Fig. 29,* rests on the top of the lock plate when the hammer is in the fired position. Remove the hammer carefully from this position on the lock and sweat solder the plug in position.

HELPFUL HINTS

Packing Guns for Shipment. It pays dividends to do a thorough job, although sometimes if long guns are involved it may take several hours to make a packing case. The objective is to keep the gun from moving about inside the box during transportation, and to keep it from being crushed if heavy objects are piled upon it.

Colt Revolvers (Percussion). Most parts from the Colt Single Action Army revolver will function with a minimum amount of fitting in the Colt large framed percussion revolvers.

Hose Clamps. This type of clamp works well for gluing stocks that are broken through the grip section.

Small Nails and Pins. Common straight pins made of brass or steel, when cut to the proper length, can be used for holding down patch boxes and decorations.

Old Bone and Horn. A source for old bone and horn can be found in your friendly farmer's animal graveyard.

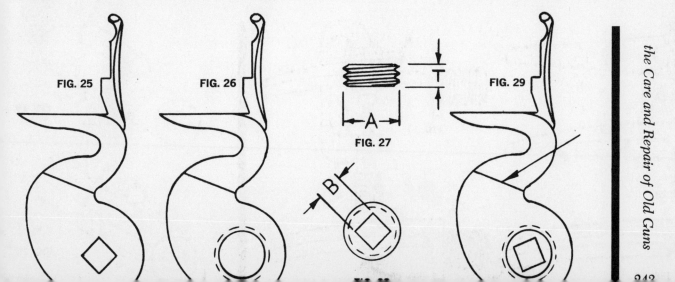

FIG. 25

FIG. 26

FIG. 27

FIG. 29

the Care and Repair of Old Guns

Browning Barrels and Parts. To obtain a brown finish on a gun barrel or part they will have to be rusted by use of chemicals. The chemicals that are used to produce such a finish are poisonous. Whatever is mixed for this process of browning barrels and parts, *label the bottle as being poison, and keep the bottle in a safe place.*

Browning Formula:	Nitric acid C.P.	1 ounce
	Spirits of Nitre	2 ounces
	Powdered Copper Sulphate	1 ounce
	Tincture of Iron	2 ounces
	Distilled water	3 quarts
	Corrosive Sublimate	3 ounces

To mix the browning formula given above, proceed as follows:

1. Dissolve the Corrosive Sublimate in the 3 quarts of water.
2. Add the powdered Copper Sulphate. Stir until dissolved.
3. Add the Tincture of Iron.
4. Add the sweet Spirits of Nitre.
5. Add the Nitric acid.

Preparation of parts to be browned—look the parts over carefully, looking for heavy rust deposits. These heavy rust deposits will have to be smoothed down with a file or emery paper to the surface of the part to be browned. After this is done remove as much of the old finish as possible. The parts do not have to be bright metal color in order for the parts to rust. What was browned before will turn brown again when the rusting solution is applied.

To brown a barrel or part, pour a small quantity of the solution out into a small dish after the solution has been bottled for a week. Apply the solution to the barrel or part with a cotton swab wrapped around the end of a small stick. Wet the barrel or part with the solution, but not to such a degree that the solution will run on the surface of barrel or parts.

To make the barrel or parts rust, they will have to be placed in an area where there is heat and moisture. A great deal depends upon this condition. The chemicals work best during hot and humid weather.

The first coat of solution applied to the barrel and parts will produce a strange color or corrosion, ranging from red, blue, and green. This usually appears in eight to twelve hours, if the temperature and moisture conditions are good. At any rate, let the parts stand until a dry rust has formed.

After this dry rust has formed, it will have to be removed from the surface of the parts by scratching it off with "O" grade steel wool. During this operation of removing the rust, it is very important that the hands do not come in contact with the rusted surface. To prevent this, wear a clean pair of cotton work gloves. There may be rather heavy and light deposits of rust on the parts and the idea is to remove these heavy deposits down to a smooth and even coat of rust. What will be left of the first application is a very light coat of brown rust on the parts. This first coat of rust will form a base for the final finish. To arrive at the final finish, apply as many coats of the solution as needed until the desired color of brown is reached, scratching off the rust between each coat. The process may take several days before the job is complete.

When the parts are dark enough, boil them in water; after they come out of the water, let them air dry and while the parts are still hot, apply a light coat of boiled linseed oil. This will bring out the full color of the browned parts.

To assure a successful job, be sure the metal parts are free of all grease and oil before applying the browning solution. This also applies to spots where only a touch up job is needed.

It may be wise to practice this art of browning on some pieces of steel or on an old barrel before doing an actual job.

EDITOR'S NOTE: There are competent gunsmiths, with modern power tools, to do major restoration or intricate jobs, and very valuable pieces which need attention should be entrusted to the highly skilled specialists who restore antique guns. But for the simple jobs, there is great convenience and personal satisfaction in "do it yourself" care and repair. It is hoped that the information given here, along with the sketches prepared by the author (an excellent draftsman as well as a working gunsmith), will provide practical guidance of considerable value.

29. *the Protection*

Every gun owner in the Free World has an interest in this subject, no matter whether he owns one single-barrel shotgun for rabbit hunting or shows with pride one of the world's great collections of antique weapons. His failure to appreciate his own stake may easily result in an irreplacable loss by default. Careful consideration here and now of the many facets of the problem may well be a continually rewarding experience.

When one mentions safeguards for your guns, the natural and immediate first thoughts are of prevention of loss by burglary or fire, and if those losses should be sustained, then insurance against financial loss. Certainly these areas are important and deserve serious study. They are the types of losses which draw the attention of news media and are spectacular to the average citizen. Yet less spectacular but more insidious factors, such as faking, neglect of condition, and even more important, legislative restrictions on ownership, pose threats of more far-reaching importance.

Writing in *The American Rifleman* a few years ago, Paul C. Mitchell of Decatur, Illinois, set up some good guide lines on physical safeguards. Mitchell lost a large proportion of a fine Colt collection to burglars. His advice covered five salient points:
1. Insure adequately
2. Safeguard your home and collection
3. Screen visitors carefully
4. Keep neighbors informed on your movements
5. Catalog and describe individual pieces in detail

INSURANCE:

Perhaps nothing is so thoroughly misunderstood, even by the people who sell it, as insurance on firearms. A sound knowledge is imperative where any appreciable investment is involved. Many types of gun insurance are available. Study the one or ones that suit your needs. Such study can save you money now and maybe prevent considerable grief in case of loss. Try this experiment. Walk up to or call the average insurance agent and tell him you want to insure a gun collection. In 75 percent of the cases he will look frantically through his rate book and finally read you a paragraph on a "Gun Floater." It is almost standard in the insurance industry and carries a flat rate of 1 percent of the insured valuation per year or 2½ percent for a three-year contract. In other words your premium is $10 per $1,000 worth of guns insured. This type of policy has a definite place and you may well need it, but it should be confined to guns used for hunting or shooting, whether for competition or for fun. For the serious collector, it is entirely unnecessary and far too expensive.

A fallacy in many people's minds is the belief that a "Home Owner's" blanket policy provides adequate protection. A generalization here is dangerous and one can only suggest a thorough study and understanding of the fine print and limitations of the policy under consideration. Most of those studied would cover losses of one or two items. However, there is a major pitfall. In the event of catastrophe, such as a total collection burglary, a total loss by fire, or a total loss by flood, of the type which hit Los Angeles in 1963, the indemnity recoverable on an arms collection may be but a small percentage of the face value of the policy. A qualification of this type generally is set out in the policy and almost always is included in so-called blanket coverage.

All major casualty insurance companies write Marine Insurance which includes a type peculiarly applicable to most antique gun collections—the Fine Arts Floater. The term "Marine" apparently indicates that the underwriter swims out in the current to an unknown point and swims back with a rate for the coverage desired! No fixed rules cover it, and few insurance men understand it.

Seriously, the rates are based on the fire rate for the particular location of the insured property with cer-

# of Your Guns

tain "loads" for other risks. In this type policy, the guns (and other antiques, paintings, art objects, and jewelry that may be combined in the same policy) are "scheduled." In other words, they are listed with an adequate identifying description and given a fair market value. The rate on this type insurance ranges from one-fourth to one-third of that on the Gun Floater; in other words, $2.50 to $3.50 per $1,000 valuation.

Since the fire rate is the basis of a Fine Arts premium, collectors living in rural areas or localities with high fire loss may find rates nearly as high as the Gun Floater. For these people the National Rifle Association has performed a very real service for its members. Some years ago, as a project of its Gun Collectors Committee, the N.R.A. negotiated a flat-rate Fine Arts policy with a major insurance company of $3.50 per $1,000 valuation and 2½ times that rate for three years, regardless of location. This policy is written by the company, not the N.R.A., but one must be an N.R.A. member to enjoy the benefit.

All such policies, regardless of the company writing them, have certain reservations, and the owner should know them. Three that come to mind are: *(1) You are not covered if you entrust a gun to a friend or a gunsmith and he absconds with it. (2) You are not covered if possession at a particular place is a violation of local law and it is confiscated. (3) You are not covered for exhibition on a public fairground.* This latter is an archaic provision in most policies but important if you plan to compete for the blue ribbon in the Podunk County Fair or have a display in a gun show held on a fairgrounds. Generally on request, your company will issue a special waiver to cover you, but get it in writing.

In scheduling such policies it is impossible to list every feature of individual arms. However, in the event of loss you will be called upon to substantiate the values of the loss claimed. It is highly important that you have an accurate catalog description. This should include not only make, model, and serial number, but also any unique feature such as a presentation inscription, nicks, dents, replaced parts, overstamping, or anything which would make identification more positive. Clear individual photographs would be invaluable in such a case.

Finally, values should be periodically reviewed and brought up-to-date with current market trends. Dozens of cases can be cited of arms that sold in the 1920s and 1930s for a few dollars but that now bring hundreds or even thousands of dollars. If in doubt and large valuations are involved, it might be worthwhile for you to have a professional appraisal by an authority acceptable to the insurer.

Nearly every large dealer and many individuals locally recognized as experts in the field are almost daily harassed on values. Insurance adjustors call to ask the value of a gun burned or stolen and rarely can they give any information on condition, serial number, while usually the basic model designation is too sketchy for even an educated guess. Invariably the owner is the loser from inadequate description and proof of loss.

It is not our purpose here to sell insurance. Still, many collections represent a sizable proportion of the owner's estate. Such collections should be accorded the same protection as that given any other valuable asset. Few persons can afford self-insurance.

PHYSICAL SAFEGUARDS:

In the area of physical safeguards we encounter some real problems. Whose idea or ideas are best? Mitchell's article in *The American Rifleman* suggests a simple form of burglar alarm. Some collectors have built virtual vaults and a few have built very real ones with bank-vault-type doors. Other collectors have installed intricate burglar alarm systems. Most of us are familiar with ADT and similar setups where an alarm rings in a constantly supervised office connected directly with police when any entrance to room or case is made. This type of service is generally available in metropolitan areas only. A similar system with bell or gong alarm is available almost anywhere. In this connection, we can never forget the words of the president of a burglar alarm company who remarked, "With a central station alarm we are frequently able to catch the burglar, but not always without loss. With an audible alarm (ringing bell) we have never caught a burglar but we have never sustained a loss."

Actually one does not always need professional help in this type situation. Frequently a refrigerator-door-type switch on a gunroom door providing an alarm in another part of the house will suffice.

On the other hand, a type of camouflage may be the best answer. Illustrated here is a wonderful idea in concealment. This collector brought in a professional cabinet maker and produced a gun cabinet that is

29-1. Behind the doors of this normal-appearing cabinet one will find a beautiful display of collector's firearms.

29-2. When the outer doors are opened, drawers and panels are shown to contain a large and attractively arranged group of weapons.

almost a piece of fine furniture. When closed, as it would be to the casual visitor, the appearance is that of a storage cabinet. Opened, it reveals that it will hold and display four to five hundred handguns. This type setup could be readily modified to accommodate rifles and other long guns.

In overall consideration two views are constantly at hand. On one side is the collector, hoarder, or miser who consistently buries or hides everything he owns. On the other is the man who feels that whatever he has accumulated he wants to enjoy, and to do so he hangs it in the open where it can be seen and handled.

Advice cannot resolve these differences; only an individual determination with, we hope, adequate insurance coverage, can establish the policy.

ATMOSPHERIC PROBLEMS:

Collectors with a considerable investment in fine guns face another threat of damage or loss which varies considerably from place to place throughout the country. That is damage from changing atmospheric conditions.

Collectors along coastal areas with a high humidity combined with salt air face probably the most serious problem of all. Here only constant vigilance in cleaning and protecting with proper oils or silicones can avoid rust, loss of finish, and other damage.

In extremely arid climates one may find an entirely different problem in damage to wood stocks, particularly the highly ornate ones with inlays, and to cases of dueling sets and similar pieces. Some collectors in these arid locations have worked out methods of humidity control either by humidifiers or dehumidifiers as the need arises. After a stock or a case lid has seriously warped or cracked, it is too late. Study the problem in your own community. If necessary, seek professional advice and experiment under the peculiar conditions of your own storage area.

TRAVELING AND LEGAL PROBLEMS:

A generation ago the "Gun Show" was unknown. In the past fifteen years a wholly new picture has evolved. Collectors, dealers, and "horse traders" travel the length and breadth of the land to attend shows sponsored by state organizations, local civic groups, or by individual promoters. There is also much traveling when calling on prospective buyers or sellers. By a long percentage margin, this travel is by private automobile. In the same connection it should not be overlooked that serious competitive shooters follow the same pattern of travel to matches, tournaments, and even to the National Matches. In most cases, travel is by private conveyance and the firearms used are carried in the car.

In either case, whether collector or shooter, the persons transporting these arms have probably violated the law before they reach their destination. The tremendous number of state laws and local ordinances on firearms are so complex and in many cases so conflicting that almost any traveler with firearms becomes a witting or unwitting violator.

Listing all such situations is not possible here, but to illustrate, here are a few examples:

In Hawaii a permit is required to purchase a handgun. All firearms must be registered. No exception is made for antiques or other collector items.

In South Carolina not much is said about long guns, but the law on handguns is indeed weird. It is absolutely illegal to manufacture a handgun in the state, with a further ordinance of the same type in the city of Columbia. It is illegal to sell, give, or in any way transfer a handgun "weighing less than three pounds and measuring less than twenty inches in length." There are no exceptions. However, there is this strange exception on machine guns: "The provisions hereof (making illegal the sale or possession of a machine gun) shall not apply to machine guns kept for display as relics and which are rendered harmless and not usable."

It is difficult to fathom the legislative reasoning that the famed single shot cap-and-ball pistol manufactured at the Palmetto Armory in South Carolina in 1852 is a threat to the peace and security of the state, while a gangster era, World War II full automatic weapon is not!

The California law, briefly summarized, is fairly reasonable and clear. A license (dealer's) is required for the business of selling handguns. A waiting period is required between purchase and delivery of a handgun to permit police to check for criminal records. A license is required to carry a handgun on or about the person. On the latter point we again face the proposition of capriciousness of responsible officials. In this case local police officials have the authority to issue the license to carry. In at least one metropolitan area the police chief simply refuses to issue a license regardless of the person or the circumstances. There is no appeal authorized in the law. The same license is required for carrying a concealed handgun in an automobile. Carrying a loaded rifle or shotgun in a vehicle is prohibited. An alien may not possess a handgun.

While the survey used covered only cities of 100,000 or more, many smaller towns and cities probably should be included in this list. Such cities as Anaheim, Berkeley, Fresno, Long Beach, Los Angeles, Oakland, Pasadena, Sacramento, San Diego, San Francisco, San Jose, and Torrance all have special ordinances in addition to state law. Berkeley even

requires the registration of handguns. It is readily apparent that one may comply with state law and yet run afoul of a municipal ordinance.

Massachusetts re-codified its firearms laws five years ago, greatly improving them. A permit is required to purchase a handgun; a license is required to carry one. However, a license to carry eliminates the necessity of a permit to purchase. Highly important, however, is the right to appeal for judicial relief if the police refuse a permit or license. A loaded gun may not be carried in a vehicle. Sane restrictions are placed on the sale to and use of firearms by minors and aliens. No license is required to purchase or carry arms made before 1870.

In New York the infamous Sullivan Act is without doubt the prime example of the utter failure of firearms restrictions to prevent or reduce crime. It has been amended "to put teeth in it" until it is a dental marvel. Once the legislature voted its repeal only to have the then Governor, Franklin D. Roosevelt, veto it. I believe it to be an unconstitutional encroachment on the rights of New York's citizens, but up until now, not enough of its citizens have become sufficiently angry to impress their solons.

The law requires a permit to purchase; a license to carry, and complete registration of ownership. The Penal Law makes no distinction between modern and antique concealable firearms. While some distinction might be achieved by going to court, in the absence of such a judicial determination it is the height of folly to transport arms of any kind through the State of New York.

Some four or five years ago the *New York Journal-American* ran a survey on the "licenses to carry" issued by the New York City Police. It seems more than a coincidence that over 50 percent of the licensees had criminal records.

Obviously it is impossible here to list all the state and local laws which might affect ownership and transportation of firearms, but those noted should point up to any individual collector, dealer, or shooter that for his own protection he should familiarize himself with the laws in the area he expects to travel and arrange to comply with them.

As a passing thought on this subject, it is most interesting to note that the two states, Vermont and New Mexico, which have the least restrictions on ownership and use of firearms also have the lowest crime rates in the nation.

FAKES AND REPLICAS:

Another chapter of this book deals primarily with this subject. The comment here is intended only to emphasize a point frequently overlooked. A collector with a reputation of playing around with fakes and replicas or misrepresenting them is doing himself and his collection irreparable harm. There are few collectors or dealers who are not occasionally stung on a bad gun. Economically they would be far better off to destroy the gun or in some other manner get it off the market, so that it may not be passed on to some unsuspecting beginning collector down the line. The dealer who builds himself a reputation of selling "doctored" or fake guns, soon finds himself without clients. The collector who incorporates them in his collection, brings suspicion upon all his guns, good or bad. There are cases known where men have had magnificent, rare guns, such as cased Patersons, who have sold them and replaced them with a replica bearing the same serial number. When it comes time for either that man or his heirs to liquidate the collection, the probability of disinterest on the part of the buying collectors or dealers is extremely strong. Guard yourself and your collection against this kind of reputation. Clean dealing in selling and trading will bring many hours of happiness. The sad old dodge of offering a gun that one knows is not right with the explanation that "I don't know what it is" or the approach of "Caveat Emptor" can have a strong hand in destroying the sound things you have built up.

There is a definite place in the American market in the shooting field for a good, modern-made percussion revolver, but the proper and ethical thing for the manufacturers and importers of such guns to do is to so design it that it can not be mistaken for, nor readily converted to, a fake of a known and desirable collector's item. In buying a gun, if in doubt or if you don't know, ask advice and demand a legal bill of sale. See photo 2-4.

THE ESTATE PROBLEM:

In the light of today's increasing interest in gun collecting and shooting, too, together with the increasing prices brought on by monetary inflation, the investment in the average collection gets into sizable figures. Many collectors hurt themselves and their potential heirs by a foolish approach to the economic questions involved.

Some collectors tell their wives that they paid only a few dollars for an item to keep them from knowing what was actually spent. If that wife then must liquidate the collection, she has a totally unrealistic idea of its value. On the other hand, there is a type of person who puts a highly inflationary value on everything he owns and his heirs then receive a rude shock when they find what he actually has.

It is wise in this connection to keep an accurate catalog, periodically re-appraising values in line with the changing market. This is not only the basis for insurance scheduling but just plainly makes practical business sense, as does a proper accounting of all other elements of an estate. If one is afraid to tell his wife what he has invested, keep the list in a safe deposit box or in the hands of a trust officer or an attorney. If there are special bequests of specific items to someone else, they should be clearly outlined. If a commitment has been made to allow a friend first chance at a gun, instructions should be given for that purpose. All too often some joker comes to the executor or the grieving wife and says, "Dear old John promised me that the day before he died." (Usually at about half of what it is worth.)

Most collectors have a better idea than anyone else of the best method to dispose of their guns in the event something happens to them. If they have specific ideas on these subjects, information should be left in writing with those responsible for carrying out that individual's wishes.

LEGISLATION:

The greatest threat existing today to the enjoyment of collecting, of field shooting, of competitive target shooting, and all the other facets of interest in firearms, is the whole interlocked field of restrictive legislation. For some strange reason the legislator, councilman, or commissioner frequently jumps on the wagon of anti-gun legislation thinking that he can make a quick name for himself by enacting a law. Almost daily there is introduced at some level of government—local, state or federal—some ill-advised law that can further restrict your right to own and lawfully use the firearms of your choice.

In the event more restrictive legislation actually becomes effective in this country, it can very well almost completely destroy these hobbies and sports as we know them. On the one hand, if it becomes so difficult and obnoxious to contend with the various laws and regulations, thousands of people will simply give up rather than be harassed to that extent. Secondly, if that does happen, the market for guns is simply dried up or destroyed. If there is no market, the commodity offered has no value, and one may well find himself with a serious economic loss from such legislation.

First and foremost the collector and shooter should know thoroughly the laws of his own community and his own state, as well as those in which he might travel. Secondly, he should through some means maintain a constant and vigilant watch on legislation that may be introduced that affects his interests. For many years the National Rifle Association has maintained a legislative service informing affected members of proposed laws that might be introduced in the member's place of residence. However, it is almost impossible for them to maintain sufficient channels to learn of local legislation at the city or county level. There, more than ever, the eternal vigilance to protect one's rights must be maintained.

What can you as an individual do to prevent this sort of thing? First, know the lawmakers who might be in a position to act on such legislation. Know who they are and if possible, know them personally. Second, never forget that the one person to whom a lawmaker will always listen is the constituent in his home community who can vote for or against him. Nothing has so much effect as a personal contact by telephone or face to face, explaining your views logically and reasonably.

The next best thing to personal contact is a letter, personally written and clearly and fundamentally expressing your opinion on the legislation under consideration. Here all too often those who are most vitally interested do not use good judgment. How often have you heard someone say, "I wrote him a real nasty letter and gave him a piece of my mind." That type of letter is more harmful than helpful.

Avoid profanity, insulting remarks, threats, or any remark that would question the patriotism or loyalty of the person to whom the letter is addressed. Letters that contain such an attack receive short shrift and usually breed animosity toward your viewpoint rather than favorable consideration.

A brief and concise communication offering reason and logic, expressed in courteous phraseology, will do more to influence a legislator than any wild accusations or abuse could ever accomplish. Finally, a petition has little if any value. Form letters or mimeographed communications find their way usually to the wastebasket.

When you are alerted to the danger of this type legislation, act yourself immediately. Try to influence your friends and others with parallel interests to express their opinions also. Some collectors feel that an organization in Washington or in the State Capital can best handle these things. While such organizations are extremely helpful in presenting face to face information and fact, nothing counts like a letter from home.

Finally, know the laws in your own community, your state and your nation. Know the people who have the capability of changing or amending those laws. When the occasion demands, express yourself promptly, briefly, politely, and forcefully. You may be going a long way to protect one of your principal investments.

29-3. Loss by legislation is one of the dangers facing gun owners. In the various legislative chambers of the nation, efforts to enact harassing anti-firearms laws are sometimes attempted. We must be ever vigilant and quick to oppose misguided encroachments on a basic American constitutional principle. The record of gun laws shows that the *criminal use,* not the inanimate tool, should command the strong legislative concern.

30-1. Simple 3 inches x 5 inches record card printed on one side.

NO.	MAKE	
TYPE		CAL.
SERIAL NO.	FINISH	GRIPS
CONDITION	BARREL LENGTH	OVERALL LENGTH
PROCURED FROM		195
COST	VALUE	
GENERAL DESC. AND MARKINGS		
HISTORY		

the Cataloging
of Your Guns
by Pen
& Camera

Too much cannot be said in favor of maintaining up-to-date records of your gun collection and of your buying and selling transactions. Besides being good business, it is quite interesting to look back over the years and review the trend in gun prices as well as the changes in your collecting taste.

The keeping of sensible records in the degree of detail needed may stand you in good stead some day should you require substantiation of a claim due to fire, theft, or loss in transportation. Sometimes it is hard to convince an insurance company or any carrier that an 1851 Colt Navy which has a trigger guard straight at the back instead of round and has a little screw under the wedge is worth much more than the common model. Also there may be the legal matter of settling an estate, or records for tax purposes. Then again the fellow who sold you a gun may get into trouble with the Internal Revenue boys and you may be requested to show when and where you bought the gun, how much you paid for it, and even asked to produce your canceled check covering the transaction. So keep your canceled checks and receipts, too.

In cataloging your collection, do not *overstate* or *understate* the purchase price or the prevailing market price. Don't give that old routine to your beloved spouse that you got it for a song but it really is a valuable arm—that story can backfire in many ways. Any dealer can tell you of cases where he has been called in to buy or appraise a collection left to a widow, only to find a lot of iron that she had been led to believe was gold. By the same token, it is just as bad to underestimate or undervalue guns and later have them sold for too little. Keep the Little Lady correctly informed. She may not be interested in guns as such but almost any collection of arms today represents a sizable investment, and I do mean they are a valuable investment, the same as other good antiques. Getting back to the legal aspect, in states where "Community Property Laws" prevail, in the unhappy event of a divorce, at times splitting of the collection is necessary and you had better have good, honest records or you may end up with the short end of the deal.

Should you own some fairly valuable arms and intend to insure or sell them, don't hesitate to pay for professional appraisal service. Almost any nationally known dealer offers such service at a nominal fee, and it is money well spent. Their word carries a lot of weight should any controversy arise later.

As to the type or amount of data you wish to record, that is purely a personal matter dependent upon the use to which the records may be put later. Whether you simply want to make a record of the arm, its cost, approximate value, from whom purchased, and enough of a description to tie it down in case of a loss; or if you want a complete record of variations, barrel lengths, odd features, etc., for use in research later on, these factors will determine the type and size of the record card or loose-leaf sheet that will be required.

Printed record cards, such as the sample shown, are frequently available. These 3x5-inch cards carry about as much information as is generally needed. Some collectors have had their own loose-leaf sheets printed, such as the two examples shown. These both are printed on two sides and carry considerable information. I would suggest keeping them in duplicate, one copy for your insurance company or to keep with the collection and the other copy to be kept in your safe deposit box. And by all means keep the records current! When you dispose of a gun, remove the card or sheet from your active records. Where there is a more or less permanent collection, owners often tag the arms in some manner and record the tag number on the record card. I have for years used small round aluminum tags about ¼-inch in diameter. I stamped out the tags, drilled a small hole at the edge and hand-numbered them with a set of small numbering dies. This entails quite a bit of work at the start, but the tags last forever and are small and neat. If you dispose of a gun, save the record card; it may come in handy.

I have always been a strong believer in photographic records to supplement the card or record system. I think it was Confucius who said, "A picture is worth ten thousand words." That may be a little strong but to illustrate the value of photography, I will cite a specific case.

Recently a very rare pistol was brought to me by a prospective buyer, as he had been told that I knew something about the piece. The pistol was in very fine condition considering the age, one of the best that I had seen. In taking it apart, I noted the serial number, which at once rang a bell in my mind. This piece was cataloged as serial number 174, whereas the one I recalled had been 114. At the time that pistol was numbered, they used rather crude dies and it was easy to mistake a 1 for a 7. Fortunately, when the pistol was offered for sale to me several years before, the seller had sent me a picture of the pistol as it had been found. The stock was badly in need of repair, lock parts were missing, and the rammer was missing; all in all, it was quite rough. Comparing the serial numbers left doubt, but when we compared the gun with the picture there was no question; you could tell by the dents in the frame and other scars that the pistol pictured and this pistol were one and the same. The pistol had been completely worked over. This of course affected the value of the arm considerably. Detail can be obtained and retained in a picture that is mighty hard to put into words.

Photographing guns need not be complicated, and good pictures can be had with a minimum of moderately priced equipment. Adopt the method that suits you best. Use the same lighting, the same film, the same exposure, and you should get uniform results. You will be striving for flat lighting, eliminating shadows. You will be after black and white pictures for record purposes. Later you can get fancy and shoot magazine covers.

Now for a few words on equipment. There are two types of cameras which I prefer for this type of photography. The small "Single Lens Reflex Camera" in the 35mm or the 2¼x2¼-inch size is quite portable and can be taken to a gun meeting if you wish. With this type of camera, instead of a view finder, you look directly through the lens and see just what the picture is going to look like as to arrangement up to the instant you take the picture. Furthermore, if

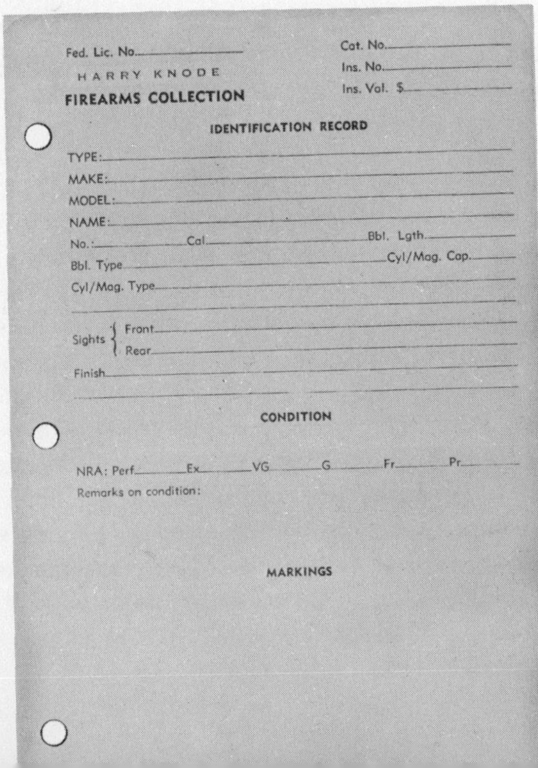

30-2. Loose-leaf 3¾ inches x 6¾ inches record card printed on two sides.

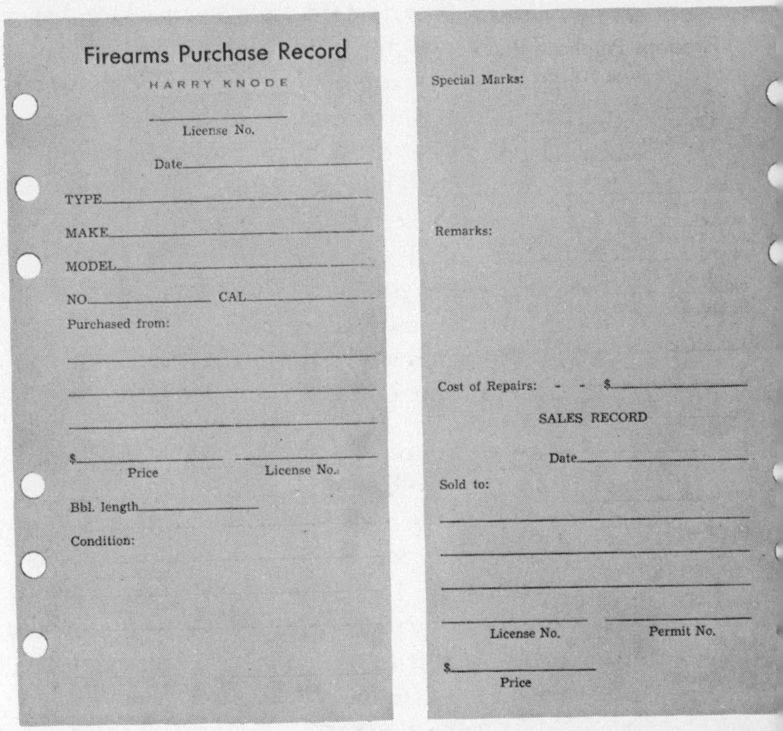

Firearms Purchase Record
HARRY KNODE
License No.
Date
TYPE
MAKE
MODEL
NO. CAL
Purchased from:

$ Price License No.
Bbl. length
Condition:

Special Marks:

Remarks:

Cost of Repairs: - - $
SALES RECORD
Date
Sold to:

License No. Permit No.
$ Price

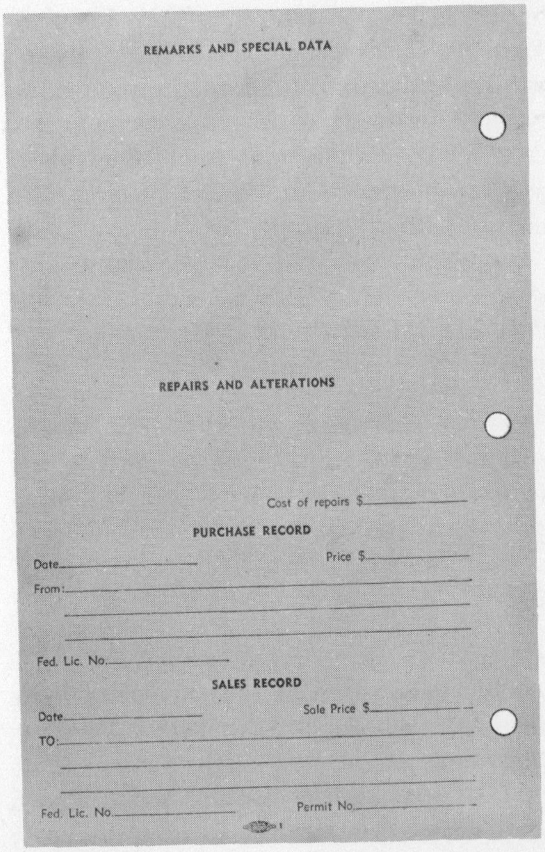

Fed. Lic. No. Cat. No.
HARRY KNODE Ins. No.
FIREARMS COLLECTION Ins. Vol. $
IDENTIFICATION RECORD
TYPE:
MAKE:
MODEL:
NAME:
No.: Cal. Bbl. Lgth.
Bbl. Type Cyl/Mag. Cap.
Cyl/Mag. Type
Sights { Front Rear
Finish

CONDITION
NRA: Perf. Ex. VG. G. Fr. Pr.
Remarks on condition:

MARKINGS

REMARKS AND SPECIAL DATA

REPAIRS AND ALTERATIONS

Cost of repairs $
PURCHASE RECORD
Date Price $
From:

Fed. Lic. No.
SALES RECORD
Date Sale Price $
TO:

Fed. Lic. No. Permit No.

30-3. Loose-leaf 5 inches x 7¾ inches record card printed on two sides.

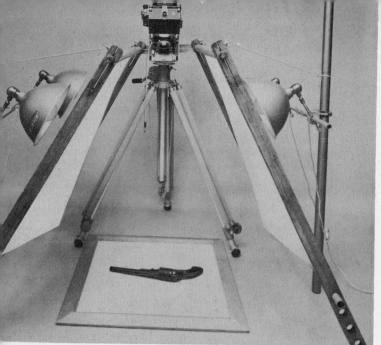

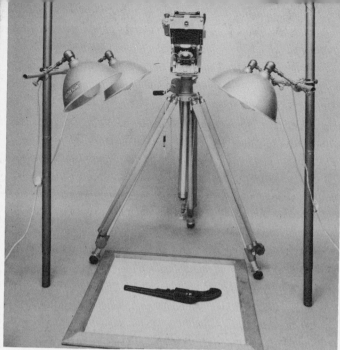

30-4. **Direct lighting through "tent" to diffuse light. Acetate is** stretched on adjustable frames between lights and subject.

30-5. **"Direct lighting" setup. Center the lights both ways over** subject.

you want to move in close and take proof marks, barrel markings, etc., you merely place an extension tube between the lens and the camera body and still look through the lens to see what you are getting. The other type, that is equally as good and usually gives a larger negative, is the "View" or "Press" camera. This type of camera has a ground glass focusing back that permits the arranging and viewing of the proposed picture on the ground glass. It also has a long bellows that permits taking of close-ups without attachments. This type of camera will run from a negative size of 2¼x3¼-inch to 8x10-inch. The 4x5-inch negative is very satisfactory.

Don't use film of extremely high speed; it isn't necessary. The guns aren't going any place, so stop down the lens, give longer exposure, and as a result get better detail. A film speed rating of 100 ASA is plenty for black and white.

To me, an exposure meter is a must in all methods except "Painting," as will be explained later. There are two general types of meters, "Incident" and "Reflected" light. With the Incident meter you read the amount of light that falls on the subject, and with the Reflected meter you read the amount of light reflected from the subject, and this can vary considerably depending on the part of the subject from which you take your reading. Some meters will take readings both ways. I prefer the Incident method. Your camera store man will go into more detail for

you. In either case, take readings at all four corners and the center of the proposed picture to see that you are getting even lighting at all points; if not, move your lights until you do. Remember, if it doesn't look good before you take the picture, the chances are it will not look good afterward.

For background use a piece of non-glossy white paper. A roll of plain shelf paper does a good job and is easy to get. A good steady tripod is a must. Move in close and fill up the negative. Photoflood bulbs #1 or #2 size in large reflectors give even lighting; keep them in multiples of two, that is 2, 4, or 6 so that you have the same number on each side. I do not care for reflector floods—that is a lamp made like a headlight for a car. They are more expensive and give hot spots.

There are many methods of taking gun pictures, but probably the simplest way is to go outdoors in the middle or late afternoon and set up your camera in the shade of the eaves of your house. There will be plenty of light, and since you are using no direct sunlight, you get soft, even lighting without shadows. Put your gun on the background, take meter readings at all four corners and the middle, and then shoot. Expose at about f:16 or f:22 at whatever speed the meter indicates. If you want to play safe until you are sure of yourself and your camera, do what we call "boxing." Take one exposure as the meter indicates, then one exposure at the same shutter

30-6. "Bounce lighting" setup. Note lights are pointed at the ceiling.

30-7. Professional lighting setup for photographing firearms, as prepared by E. Irving Blomstrann. This gives museum-quality photographs.

speed but open the lens one stop, and for the third negative use the same shutter speed and close down the lens one stop. One of the three should do it. Generally you have enough latitude in the film speed so that if you are off a little you will still get a good negative.

Another simple way to get good, shadowless pictures is to make your setup indoors in the normal way, and for lighting use a #1 photoflood lamp in a hand-held reflector on an extension cord (this can also be done with a 75- or 100-watt light bulb, but it takes a longer exposure). Set the shutter on "time," turn on the light, open the shutter, then pass the light back and forth around the background in a circle between the camera and the floor with the reflector pointed down. The lens should be set at about f:16 or f:22; it isn't critical, and you will soon learn how many passes you have to make to get a good negative. Here no meter reading is necessary; the process is called "Painting."

Bounce lighting has proven very satisfactory for soft shadowless lighting. Here again you make your setup in the normal way. Point two or four photoflood lamps in reflectors at a light-colored ceiling. Take your reading on the subject to be taken and make your exposure accordingly. Don't try this with color film if you have a colored ceiling.

The method that I prefer is what is called "using a

tent." Here the lights are pointed at the subject, but to break up the light and diffuse it, a screen made of translucent sheet plastic called 10 mil Acetate is placed between the lights and the subject on both sides. The light goes through the screen and bounces back and forth giving even, soft lighting which brings out the engraving and other details. You take the meter reading under the tent, of course, and proceed in the normal way.

In the use of direct light, which is the same setup as above without using the tent, you have to be very careful that your lighting is even or you will get multiple shadows and plenty of hot spots. I seldom use it unless shooting color with a colored matte finish background that kills shadows. As a final tip, if you have a gun that is nickel- or silver-plated or very high blue and you are getting hot spots, get a piece of putty, roll it around in your hand until the oil is worked in, then pat the bright spot and you can see it disappear.

Final suggestions: When you have taken your pictures, they have turned out well, and you perhaps wish to mail copies for publication, do not clip them together with paper clips. These often cut into glossy prints and can ruin your prints. Place your pictures between two pieces of stiff cardboard, larger than the prints, and held together by scotch tape. Send your pictures first-class mail.

Good shooting!

Restoration of antiques has been a general practice for years and is not frowned on by the trade or by buyers. It would just about be a sacrilege to let some fine, rare antique deteriorate for lack of authentic and proper repair. It is an entirely different matter when a person or a dealer with an antique chair, for an example, takes it apart and makes four similar chairs, one original leg and a part of the seat in each of the new chairs. This principle also holds true with antique firearms. There is a quaint old saying we use to the effect that, "You can see traces of original metal in the arm." The separation point between restoration and faking seems to be the intent for which the work was done. If it is to restore a fine or rare arm, that is one thing and is unobjectionable. But if the work done is to mislead, commit fraud, and enhance the value of the arm far above normal value, then it is wrong.

Faking is not new and is not confined to firearms alone. Like death and taxes, faking has been with us for centuries and probably will remain. Our greatest fear is not for the experienced collector but for the beginner. I have seen several cases where new collectors have sold their collections and quit collecting entirely because of being mislead by an unscrupulous seller who was only interested in making a "fast buck." I feel that it is the duty of every advanced collector and dealer to help, advise, and guide these new collectors. They tell me that in the early days of arms collecting in the eastern part of the United States, faking was quite the thing, not for the sake of making a few extra dollars but to have some "rare specimen" that the other fellow didn't have. Some of the collectors would have pistols such as "Trap-door Springfields" made up at considerable expense just to fool their friends.

Any discussion of replicas can become quite involved and controversial. I cannot be convinced that exact replicas or replicas with but minor changes in shape, rifling, hammer contour, screw locations, etc., need be made for those who like to shoot the black powder caplock pistols. Excellent pistols for shooters can be made without employing the precise configuration of established antique firearms. Then there will be no temp-

Restoration, Replicas, and Fakes

31.1. Comparison of faked "North & Cheney" (right) with original specimen at left. Close examination would disclose many differences.

tation to doctor up a replica to make it appear to be an antique. The advanced collector will probably recognize a replica, but a beginner may not. This matter of replicas has not been limited to arms alone; a picture is shown herewith of a fine pair of cased Colt 1851 Navy Pistols, and today just about every accessory shown can be purchased, modern made, even to Colt's design and name on the flask.

It is unfortunate that we must be suspicious of many fine and rare arms that we see, but remember, anything that has been made before by man can probably be made again. Fakers or the men they hire to do their jobs are usually excellent mechanics equipped with fine machine tools and have the ability to do work as perfect as Colt, Remington, or any other maker if they have a good example to copy. It may be some consolation to know that if you compare an original pistol with a replica, piece by piece, you will usually find some place where the maker has slipped.

At a gun show recently there were almost enough fake "Walkers" there to equip Captain Sam Walker's entire company! One "under-the-table" dealer asked me if I would like to see a good Walker, and I replied that I sure would. He pulled from a zipper bag under his table about as pretty a Walker as I have ever seen and informed me that it was for sale. With it he showed me a letter from a nationally known dealer stating that the gun was worth about $6,000.00. I immediately thought of a friend who was looking for a fine Walker and asked the dealer if I could take the gun down and examine it. He hesitated but finally said, "Yes." The gun looked fine; the workmanship was superb, the color fine, even the engraving on the cylinder was perfect. My eye caught one thing; there wasn't the slightest sign of a *safety pin* on the back of the cylinder. It was a beautiful fake, six thousand dollars worth.

Obvious fakes like some pictured here do not bother us too much; they speak for themselves. You have to be rather naive to be taken in by a dragoon barrel, square-back trigger guard, engraved Colt Pocket Model. Faking takes place where there is either rarity or great value, or both.

31.

The main fields for fakers presently are Colts, Confederates, U. S. Single Shot Martials, and Kentucky Pistols although unscrupulous practices are not limited to these fields. In Colts, watch for the Walkers, Patersons, Baby Dragoons, Wells Fargos (Pocket Model and Navy), any square-back trigger guard model. Colts with fake Tiffany all-metal grips have been hitting the market in both the Civil War Commemorative and the Mexican Eagle designs; they are good jobs and so far have mostly been on the Colt 1862 Model. In another field, a mediocre pair of English dueling pistols was made into a pair of Simeon North American dueling pistols—sunken gold name and all. The rare North & Cheney martial pistols have also been the subject of faking, the fakers employing Model 1777 French pistols, which have a close resemblance.

Naturally the question arises, "How to detect fakes?" In difficult cases that is the job for someone who can qualify as an expert. There are a lot of fine dealers and collectors that know a lot about many arms, but no one can know everything about all arms. If in doubt, take it to more than one. Several magazines have asked me for pictures of an original gun and a fake, with captions to point out the differences. It is axiomatic that if it is a good fake, there will be no differences to show. It is generally agreed that the surest way to check a fake is to compare it with a gun that is known to be original. There are some points to look for such as: Size differences in frame, barrel, and other parts; on square-back trigger guards, watch for welding or brazing potholes or the general shape, thickness, and width; for barrel "stretching," look for a ring inside the barrel, whether the rifling lines up, or if welding pits show on the outside. It is mighty hard to put an "aged" patina on a gun once the original finish is gone; re-bluing generally shows up, cold-blue is worse; and be careful of new silver or nickel plating. Watch for replating over scratches or dents; it takes a good mechanic to refinish a gun by either bluing or plating and not round the flats and corners or cup out the screw holes and destroy the sharpness of stamped markings. Watch to see that the stamped markings on the gun haven't been re-stamped or engraved; look for differences in size and type in stampings of serial numbers (also for overstampings), but remember, the same die struck in brass and in iron can make quite a different mark. Watch for reconversions of flintlocks; usually welding will show if a new pan has been added, and x-ray will show whether the touchhole has been bushed. U. S. martial pistols most often carry inspector's marks on many of the parts including the screws. Switching of locks on flintlocks and percussion arms, although not often done, can occur to make a rarity. Take the lock off and see if the wood has been worked on. This list of warnings could go on and on, but comparison and experience will always be the best teacher.

Every now and then a "rare" specimen shows up that to the best of our knowledge and belief was never made. A few of them are as follows: square-back trigger guard Colt 1860 Army, square-back trigger guard Colt London signed Pocket Model, square-back trigger guard Colt 1862 Model, semi-fluted Cylinder Colt 1860 Army, Wells Fargo Type Colt 1851, and the Maynard Single Shot Pistol.

31-2. Above: The cylinder of an original Colt 1860 Army "full fluted cylinder." Note word "Patented" is spelled out. Some carry serial number in the flute, others on back of cylinder. Right: Cylinder of the fake Colt 1860 Model Army "semi-fluted cylinder." Believe the maker turned out about 10 or 12 of them and even had a die made to stamp patent date in the flute.

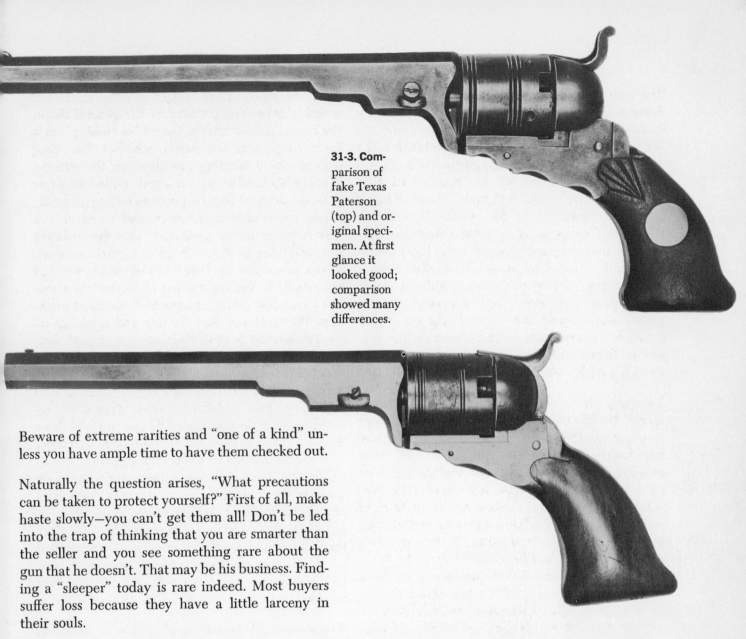

31-3. Comparison of fake Texas Paterson (top) and original specimen. At first glance it looked good; comparison showed many differences.

Beware of extreme rarities and "one of a kind" unless you have ample time to have them checked out.

Naturally the question arises, "What precautions can be taken to protect yourself?" First of all, make haste slowly—you can't get them all! Don't be led into the trap of thinking that you are smarter than the seller and you see something rare about the gun that he doesn't. That may be his business. Finding a "sleeper" today is rare indeed. Most buyers suffer loss because they have a little larceny in their souls.

Above all, get a detailed "Bill of Sale" (see page 40) or a sales slip giving a full description of the arm and what it is represented to be. The National Rifle Association, through their Gun Collectors Committee, have drawn up an excellent *Uniform Bill of Sale,* and they will furnish copies at a nominal fee or permit you or your association to copy it. A sample appears herein. A lot of faking could be stopped by the use of the bill of sale, because giving a false statement in writing is a fraud and the seller can be prosecuted. Without evidence of a false bill of sale in court, it is your word against his. A few prosecutions would deter many fakers. No reliable dealer or seller would hesitate to give you the above papers if requested.

The Texas Gun Collectors Association has these bills of sale for their members as well as an Authentication Committee composed of three nation-

ally known dealers and three advanced collectors. For a nominal fee paid to the association at a regular meeting, the committee will examine an arm and issue a certificate stating whether the arm is original in all respects and if not original will list the alterations, replacements, and/or defects. This is very cheap insurance for the buyer and the seller. I wouldn't say that the committee is infallible, but if a bad gun gets by all six of these men it has to be a near-perfect job.

There are other ways to authenticate an arm. Several national dealers offer appraisal and authenticating service. They rely on years of experience, sometimes the help of other dealers or collectors, the use of x-ray, and by comparison. Their fee is commensurate with the work done and the value of the arm. This, too, is very good insurance. Be willing to pay for this service.

31-4. Fake Edward Maynard .50 caliber single shot pistol made from a Maynard rifle. Purportedly made for U. S. Government tests but never adopted. Barrel marked U. S. with small "s" on side of barrel.

31-5. Note on original 1851 Navy "cut for stock" (top) metal was left protruding above frame when cut-out was made. On fake, it was not and cut-out is of improper shape.

31-6. Fake cast "Tiffany" grips on Colt 1862 Model; apparently gun has been recently engraved. This type of fake comes high.

Buy from legitimate dealers or from collectors whom you know will be around should you want to see them; it is much safer. Don't be rushed into a sale believing that someone else is about to grab the piece. Go slow, and if the seller won't give you time to have the gun checked . . . pass it up. To borrow the slogan of the Better Business Bureau,

"Investigate Before You Invest."

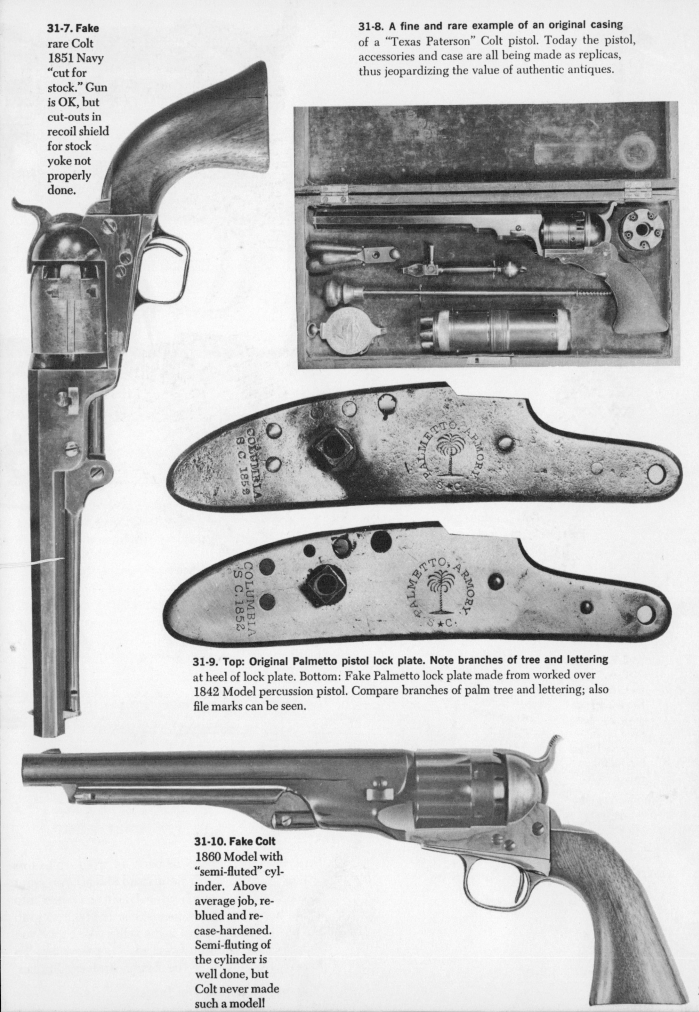

31-7. Fake rare Colt 1851 Navy "cut for stock." Gun is OK, but cut-outs in recoil shield for stock yoke not properly done.

31-8. A fine and rare example of an original casing of a "Texas Paterson" Colt pistol. Today the pistol, accessories and case are all being made as replicas, thus jeopardizing the value of authentic antiques.

31-9. Top: Original Palmetto pistol lock plate. Note branches of tree and lettering at heel of lock plate. Bottom: Fake Palmetto lock plate made from worked over 1842 Model percussion pistol. Compare branches of palm tree and lettering; also file marks can be seen.

31-10. Fake Colt 1860 Model with "semi-fluted" cylinder. Above average job, reblued and re-case-hardened. Semi-fluting of the cylinder is well done, but Colt never made such a model!

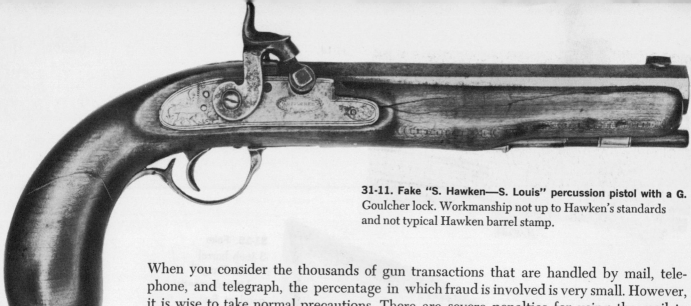

31-11. Fake "S. Hawken—S. Louis" percussion pistol with a G. Goulcher lock. Workmanship not up to Hawken's standards and not typical Hawken barrel stamp.

When you consider the thousands of gun transactions that are handled by mail, telephone, and telegraph, the percentage in which fraud is involved is very small. However, it is wise to take normal precautions. There are severe penalties for using the mail to defraud. Confirm by mail all arrangements and agreements made by phone, and keep copies. A safe transaction consists of having the gun shipped to you by express subject to an inspection period of a day or so. You pay the express company when the gun arrives, take it, and examine it. If you decide not to buy the gun you return it and get your money back.

I would venture to say that there are very few dealers or collectors who have been at it very long who haven't been "taken" a few times. Some fakes take much checking before you can be sure, and in buying entire collections bad pieces are sometimes overlooked. I know of one dealer who has quite a collection of fakes set aside. This collection will be given to a museum for the education and protection of others. When I was editor of the *Texas Gun Collector* magazine, another dealer sent me two fake Colt pistols to photograph and destroy; they are now in the bottom of the Trinity River. These measures cost dealers and collectors many a dollar, but are very commendable.

I feel that the greatest protection and satisfaction a collector can get is through self-education. Buy good reference books. Keep records as to variations and other important details of the arms that you collect or that interest you. Best of all study firsthand the actual arms—nothing takes the place of that. Visit your collector friends; study their collections. Visit museums and don't be afraid to ask questions. You will find that gun collecting is a wonderful hobby even though you may meet a "sharpie" now and then. Remember, *"Investigate Before You Invest."*

31-12. Fake "London" signed Colt pocket model with iron square-back trigger guard. As far as we know, no square-back pocket models were made in London. Now and then a fake brass square-back trigger guard shows up.

31-13. Trigger guard of the fake "London" signed Colt pocket model. The welding potholes show up plainly at the back end of the square-back guard.

31-14.
Barrel signing
on fake
"S. Hawken"
pistol.

31-15. Fake
3 inch barrel
"Wells Fargo"
and it looks pretty
good at first
glance except the
barrel lug doesn't
appear to be
the right shape.

31-16. Com-
parison of
fake 3 inch
barrel of
"Wells Fargo"
model with
original barrel
at bottom.
Note contours
of the barrel
lug are far
from correct.

31-17. Comparison of fake 3 inch
barrel of "Wells Fargo" model
with original barrel at bottom.
Again the contours on the fake
are entirely wrong; they should
taper to width of barrel flat.

the Sources of Firearms Facts

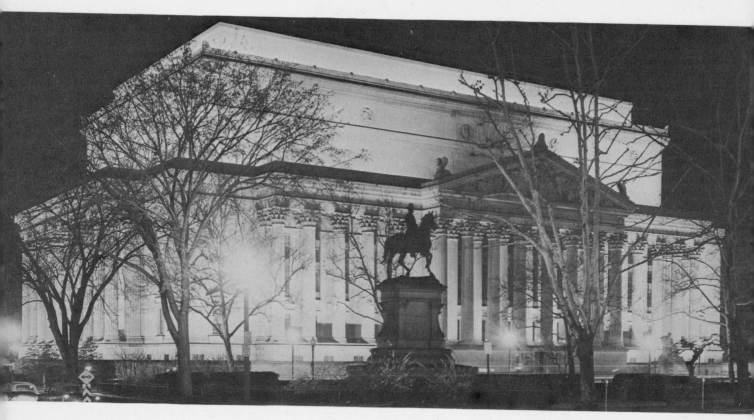

32-1. A great wealth of information, supervised by the National Archives and Record Service, is available to the serious researcher within this beautiful building in Washington, D. C.

Collecting is more than accumulating. The true gun collector wants to know exactly what he has and how each specimen fits into the general history of arms. More than that, he is interested in what uses were made of each type of gun he acquires, what sort of person might have carried it, and how well it actually performed as a weapon. Such information makes a gun more interesting and meaningful.

A generation ago collectors were largely on their own. They could recognize differences in mechanisms, sizes, shapes, and makes; but they had to depend for the most part on their own experience. There were few books about guns, and there were almost no clubs or other organizations where they could gather with fellow enthusiasts to pool their information and to compare notes. A few pioneer students expended great energy in research to build meaningful collections. These were the only ones who truly understood and enjoyed their guns. For the others, a gun collection was little more than a cabinet of mechanical curiosities.

Today the situation is vastly different. More than three thousand books on firearms are known to have been published. Most of the good ones have appeared in the last twenty years and so are readily available to anyone who is willing to seek them out. The results of hundreds of thousands of hours of exhaustive study stand ready in print for those who wish to take advantage of them. In addition there are hundreds of museums, libraries, and research repositories throughout the world to which the collector can turn for help.

Learning how to use all of the available sources takes time. Many a collector searches for information for years before learning that he could have found the answer he sought quickly if he had known where and how to look for it.

Historians generally recognize two types of sources, which they call "primary" and "secondary." Primary sources consist of writings which tell of things the author has seen personally and knows from his own experience. These might be personal narratives, reports of investigating boards, transcripts of tests and experiments, minutes of meetings, inventories, and the like. They must deal with events or facts which the writer has personally seen or done. As soon as the document deals with something which happened when the writer was not present and which he knows only through the word of someone else, it becomes a secondary source. This is true whether the document was written the same day as the event described or several hundred years later. An analogy in another field would be the distinction between admissible evidence and hearsay in a court of law.

Naturally nearly all firearms books do in fact fall into the category of secondary sources. Here the reader must be especially careful in sifting fact from fancy. The best books are those based on primary sources or on the work of others who have used primary sources. A careful writer of a serious book usually indicates the source for any important statement he makes. As a start, a bibliography is appended to this book giving some of the most useful and reliable books published recently in English for a number of fields of firearms history. In the space available it is impossible to list even all of the best works, but most of these books have bibliographies of their own which will lead the reader on, down an ever-lengthening path.

Every collector should join at least one and probably several clubs or associations of weapons collectors. Contacts with people of like interests are among the most enjoyable aspects of collecting. At the same time they increase the opportunity to see guns and to learn more about them. Many state and local associations schedule educational programs as part of their regular meetings. Some publish magazines or special booklets. The biggest organization devoted to firearms, and this includes collecting as well as hunting and target shooting, is the National Rifle Association of America, 1600 Rhode Island Avenue, N. W., Washington 6, D. C. Joining it should be one of the first acts of any serious collector. Few other organizations of any sort can match the services it offers. From the standpoint of knowledge, these include a monthly magazine and the services of a panel of specialists on all phases of firearms lore. The magazine, *The American Rifleman,* contains at least one article each month devoted to collector firearms. It also offers critical reviews of all the latest books on guns, the best guide a collector can obtain to what he should and should not read. The panel of specialists stands ready at all times to answer questions sent to them by members. This includes the identification of firearms, and there is no charge for the service. The National Rifle Association can also provide the collector with the names and addresses of affiliated local collectors' organizations in any part of the country.

Another suggestion for building a general background of firearms knowledge is to visit as many museum collections as possible. Another chapter in this volume lists some of the more prominent museums that include firearms collections and indicates their specialties. If you have a special interest, it is frequently worthwhile to write to the director of the museum in advance of a visit to see if there are specimens tucked away that may be of importance to you. Sometimes it is possible to make special arrangements to see these arms. Most museums will do all that they can to help bona fide students, and a few have special facilities set up for just such study of their collections.

There comes a time for every collector when he needs to obtain special data about some particular gun, data that he cannot find in the standard references on the subject. Usually his quest relates to the original owner of the weapon or to its individual history. Such searches are often fruitless, but in some instances it is possible to find out a surprising amount about a gun and the man who carried it.

The first thing that a collector must have is the name of the original owner. If the former owner was an officer in the regular Army or Navy or Marine Corps prior to 1900, his name and synopsis of his career will appear in either: Francis Heitman, *Historical Register and Dictionary of the United States Army*, 2 volumes, Washington, 1903; or Edward W. Callahan, *List of Officers of the Navy of the United States and of the Marine Corps from 1775-1900*, New York, 1901. Heitman also lists general officers of the Confederacy, staff and field officers of volunteer forces, and a few other non-regular officers. Generally speaking, however, it is necessary to look elsewhere for the record of an enlisted man or of an officer of state troops or volunteers.

The National Archives in Washington is usually the best source for information on such men. If you know the state from which a man enlisted, it is usually possible to find a file on him in the Old Army Section of the Archives. These files are maintained by states, and so that bit of data is absolutely essential in order to track down the soldier. The exception to this would be if the subject was a Confederate. All files on Confederate soldiers are kept together without a state breakdown.

If the owner should turn out to have been a soldier in the Civil War, and if you have been able to learn the name of his regiment or battery, there is one step that might provide further information. This would be to check the regimental histories of the war to see if there is one for the soldier's unit. This will tell in detail about the regiment's service and might even contain some personal data about the individual soldier in whom you are interested. There are literally hundreds of these regimental histories; and fortunately The New York Public Library has just published a complete checklist of them, compiled by C. E. Dornbusch and entitled *Regimental Publications and Personal Narratives of the Civil War*.

One of the most vexing problems that faces private collector and museum curator alike is the authentication of a gun that is supposed to have belonged to a specific person. Arms that belonged to famous or notorious individuals have a special appeal for almost all collectors, and as a result they command premium prices when they appear on the market. There is thus a great temptation for both the wishful thinker and the unscrupulous dealer to fabricate such an association. Sometimes they go to great lengths, engraving inscriptions on the pieces themselves and even obtaining false "documentation."

If the collector is sufficiently interested in an association piece to pay a premium price for it, it is up to him first to try to analyze the evidence offered by the seller to back up his assertion of the historical significance of the gun. An affidavit signed by the individual identifying a gun as his property is valid evidence, since the owner would know from personal knowledge that this was indeed his weapon. An affidavit signed by a person stating that a gun had belonged to his father might very well represent something the deponent knew from personal experience, having seen his father with the piece. At the same time, it might represent conjecture, and so an element of doubt creeps in.

Other documents that can establish a gun's original ownership include such things as wills, letters, inventories, photographs, or paintings—if they describe the piece sufficiently to preclude the possibility that they refer to another gun.

In some instances among later firearms it is possible to obtain evidence about a piece by writing to the manufacturing company if it is still in existence. The Colt company is especially helpful in this field, for it maintains a record of serial numbers of its cartridge arms and can tell who purchased each piece from the company and when he purchased it. Often the purchaser will turn out to be a jobber or retailer, but if the gun happened to be a special order the individual's name will be on record.

Just as important as the documentation is the evidence offered by the gun itself. The knowledgeable collector will know immediately if a gun is of the proper type and age for its supposed association. This would normally be the first factor he would consider well before he went to the trouble of checking for supporting documentary evidence. Sometimes guns also bear engraved initials or names. If these are authentic, they are of the greatest assistance in establishing a gun's "identity." Again, the knowledgeable collector will examine such markings with care to see if the style is proper for the period and if there are proper evidences of age and wear.

33.

the Problem of Display

Throughout this book we have presented a number of subjects designed to help the collector and the historian in his search for knowledge regarding weapons of the past. We hope that the information on these pages will contribute to the building of important and valuable collections of historic arms.

As these arms are assembled the problem of display will become more pressing, and this is a matter for careful study and forethought. There can be no standard specifications for display, as each home is different, available space varies, and the nature of the collection itself is a major factor.

Pistols, of course, present the lesser problem. You

33-2. Collections of the past tended to contain any kind of old gun. Today the tendency is to cover less ground and limit collecting to periods, types, one manufacturer, or other special categories such as some of those described on the accompanying pages.

will find pictured in Chapter 29 the solution of one well-known collector. His plan combines drawers and wall panels, all concealed behind solid doors. On the other hand, some collectors prefer to exhibit their pistols where they can be continually visible, and therefore place them in shallow box wall-cases with hinged or sliding glass doors.

One disadvantage of the wall display is that as one's collection grows or changes, there is often the

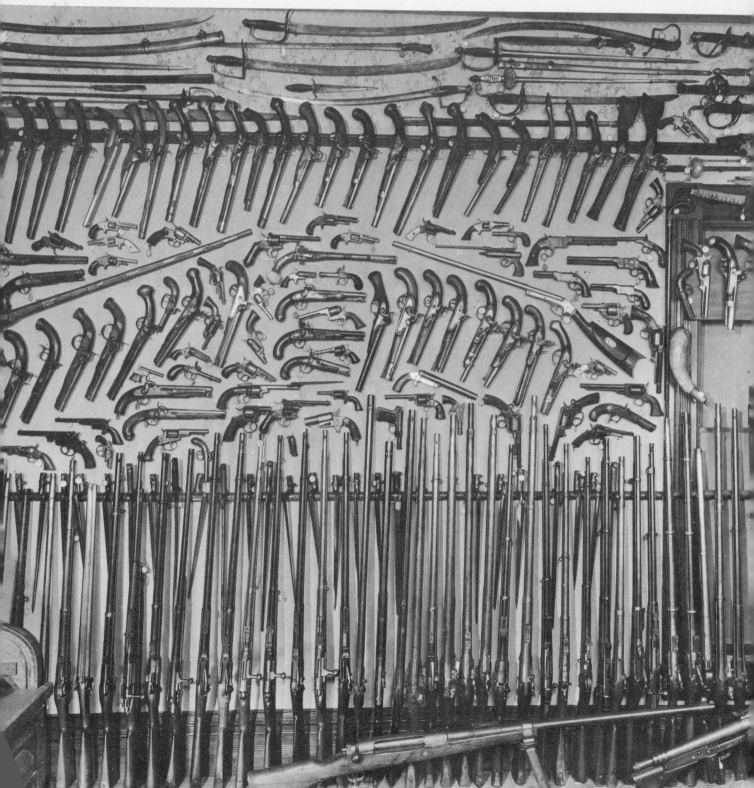

problem of rearranging the L hooks or the fine tie wires which hold the pistols to the backing. If the wall case is so constructed that it may be removed easily from the wall, the fine wire system of fastening the pistols from the back permits a neater appearance than L shaped screw hooks, but of course the pistols cannot be taken down and replaced quickly. In either case, it is desirable to glue a cloth facing to the plywood backing of the case. Loosely-woven material, such as monk's cloth, is best suited to this purpose, as the inevitable changes you will make will thus leave a minimum of evidence. If screw hooks of brass or iron are employed, they should be covered with plastic or rubber tubing.

Pegboard, of course, eliminates any problem of adjusting or readjusting the hooks, but many people object to its perforated appearance. It can, however, be used for backing and covered with loose-woven cloth.

Chests of drawers in proper dimensions, while making it impossible to view a fine group of arms at one glance, make it possible to store the greatest number of pistols in the smallest space. One complaint of the past has been that some damage occurs when unlined drawers are opened and closed, causing the pistols to rub together or slide back and forth. This problem can be easily solved by lining the drawers with the thin foam rubber now available or with the thin, waffle-design, tan rubber matting used widely under rugs to keep them from sliding.

Some collectors make a coffee table by building a shallow box, mounted on legs, and so arranged that pistols can be placed in the cloth lined interior, using inletted plate glass for the top. Those who have especially ornate pieces sometimes display them in showcases fitted with glass shelves.

Shoulder arms present a somewhat more difficult problem because of their size and weight. Where wall space is available, few arrangements can be more effective than the simple two wood strips and dowel system. Two pieces of clear lumber 3 inches wide and 1¼ inches thick are cut to the desired length. They are marked or scored down the middle and ½-inch holes drilled 5 inches apart. The holes for the dowels which support the gun at the trigger guard are bored so the holes on this strip start 1½ inches lower than the strip which supports

the barrel. The holes should be machine bored and made perfectly uniform; they should be bored at a slight downward angle, thus the ½-inch dowel to be inserted will be slightly higher at its tip than where it enters the 1¼x3-inch strip, holding the gun securely. The dowels may be any length found suitable; dowels extending 2¾ inches from the face of the strip will usually support the bulkiest of guns. These two wooden strips can be firmly anchored to either masonry or wood walls, and are normally spaced about 18 inches between the dowels. The best effect is obtained when gun racks are painted or stained to match the wall.

Where space in the center of a room is available, a very simple but effective gunrack can be constructed in a form resembling an elongated high sawhorse. Clear lumber must be used for the long 2x4-inch piece which connects the end legs. This 2x4-inch member should be machine drilled so that properly spaced ½-inch dowels can be driven completely through, extending evenly on both sides. To maintain secure rigidity, the rack should be anchored at both ends. Screw eyes, wire, and a turnbuckle will serve very well. If you do not wish to bother with elevating the base to raise gun butts off the floor, merely go to any store where rubber matting may be obtained and place this along the base of the rack; it is usually sold in 2-foot or 3-foot widths and will serve to keep dampness away from your metal butts and prevent them from slipping. Shoulder arms can be lined up on both sides of the rack.

Another popular method to display shoulder arms is that often employed in sporting goods stores. In homes with the average 8-foot ceiling, a base or counter is built, usually 16 to 30 inches deep and 24 to 30 inches high. Under this counter can be drawers or shelves, enclosed by hinged or sliding doors. Extending directly out from the wall, at proper barrel height and angled to right or left, notched brackets are firmly secured. The extended brackets are cut out to receive the barrels of four to six guns. Plywood is most often used, but plastic-covered metal brackets can be purchased from store-fixture supply houses—some are so designed that each bracket has a lock to secure all the guns in that bracket. The butts can be held secure by covering the counter on which they rest with carpet or rubber matting.

Bibliography

GENERAL

Blair, Claude A., *European and American Arms*, London: Crown, 1962.

Chapel, Charles E., *Gun Collector's Handbook of Values*, New York: Coward-McCann, Inc. Revised editions published every few years.

Hayward, John F., *The Art of the Gunmaker*, 2 volumes, London: St. Martins, 1962, 1963.

National Rifle Association, *Gun Collectors Handbook*, Washington, D. C., 1959.

Peterson, Harold L., *The Treasury of the Gun*, New York: Golden Press, 1962.

Peterson, Harold L., Editor, *Encyclopedia of Firearms*, London and New York: Dutton, 1964.

Riling, Ray, *Guns and Shooting, a Bibliography*, New York, 1951.

SPECIAL STUDIES

Abridgements of the Patent Specifications Relating to Firearms and Other Weapons, Ammunitions & Accoutrements, 1588-1858, reprint edition, London: Saifer, 1960.

Albaugh, William A., III, and Edward N. Simmons, *Confederate Arms*, Harrisburg: Stackpole, 1957.

Albaugh, William A., III, Hugh Benet, and Edward N. Simmons, *Confederate Handguns*, Philadelphia: Riling, 1963.

Blackmore, Howard L., *British Military Firearms, 1650-1850*, London and New York: Arco, 1961.

Campbell, Clark S., *The '03 Springfield*, Beverly Hills, Cal., 1957.

Cline, Walter M., *The Muzzle Loading Rifle Then and Now*, Huntington, W. Va., 1942.

Dillin, John G. W., *The Kentucky Rifle*, Wilmington, Del., Hyatt, 1950.

Dowell, William Chipchase, *The Webley Story*, Kirkgate, Leeds, 1962.

Edwards, William B., *Civil War Guns*, Harrisburg: Stackpole, 1962.

Edwards, William B., *Story of Colt's Revolver*, Harrisburg: Stackpole, 1954.

Fuller, Claud E., *The Breechloader in the Service*, Topeka, Kans., 1933.

Fuller, Claud E., *The Rifled Musket*, Harrisburg: Stackpole, 1958.

Fuller, Claud E., *The Whitney Firearms*, Huntington, W. Va., 1946.

George, John N., *English Guns and Rifles*, Harrisburg: Stackpole, 1947.

George, John N., *English Pistols and Revolvers*, Plantersville, N. C., 1938.

Glendenning, Ian, *British Pistols and Guns, 1640-1840*, London, 1951.

Gluckman, Colonel Arcadi, *United States Martial Pistols and Revolvers*, Harrisburg: Stackpole, 1939.

Gluckman, Colonel Arcadi, *United States Muskets, Rifles and Carbines*, Harrisburg: Stackpole, 1959.

Grant, James J., *Single Shot Rifles*, New York: Morrow, 1947.

Grant, James J., *More Single Shot Rifles*, New York: Morrow, 1959.

Hamilton, T. D. (compiler), "Indian Trade Guns," in *The Missouri Archeologist*, December 1960, Columbia, Mo.

Hanson, Jr., Charles E., *The Northwest Gun* (Nebraska State Historical Society Publications in Anthropology, No. 2), Lincoln, Neb., 1955.

Hanson, Jr., Charles E., *The Plains Rifle*, Harrisburg: Stackpole, 1960.

Hatch, Alden, *Remington Arms in American History*, New York and Toronto: Holt, Rinehart & Winston, 1956.

Hicks, James E., *French Military Weapons*, New Milford, Conn.: Flayderman, 1964.

Hicks, James E., *Notes on United States Ordnance*, 2 vols., Mount Vernon, N. Y., 1940, plus later reprints of volume one.

Hicks, James E., *U. S. Military Firearms, 1776-1956*, Borden.

Hicks, James E., *German Weapons, Uniforms, Insignia, 1841-1918*, La Canada, Calif.: Hicks, 1963.

Johnson, Peter H., *Parker—America's Finest Shotgun*, Harrisburg: Stackpole, 1961.

Karr, Jr., Charles Lee, and Karr, Caroll Robbins, *Remington Handguns*, Harrisburg: Stackpole, 1960 (4th edition).

Kauffman, Henry J., *The Pennsylvania-Kentucky*

Rifle, Harrisburg: Stackpole, 1960.

Kindig, Jr., Joe, *Thoughts on the Kentucky Rifle in its Golden Age*, Wilmington, Del., 1960.

Logan, Herschel C., *Underhammer Guns*, Harrisburg: Stackpole, 1960.

Madis, George, *The Winchester Book*, Dallas, Tex., 1961.

McHenry, Roy C., and Roper, Walter F., *Smith & Wesson Hand Guns*, Harrisburg: Stackpole, 1958.

National Rifle Association, *Illustrated Firearms Assembly Handbook*, Washington, D. C., n. d.

Neal, W. Keith, *Spanish Guns and Pistols*, London, 1955.

Nutter, Waldo E., *Manhattan Firearms*, Harrisburg: Stackpole, 1958.

Parsons, John E., *The First Winchester*, New York: Morrow, 1955.

Parsons, John E., *Henry Deringer's Pocket Pistol*, New York: Morrow, 1952.

Parsons, John E., *The Peacemaker and its Rivals*, New York: Morrow, 1950.

Parsons, John E., *Smith & Wesson Revolvers*, New York: Morrow 1957.

Peterson, Harold L., *Arms and Armor in Colonial America, 1526-1783*, Harrisburg: Stackpole, 1956.

Reynolds, E. G. B., *The Lee-Enfield Rifle*, London: Arco, 1960.

Roberts, Ned H., *The Muzzle-Loading Cap Lock Rifle*, Harrisburg: Stackpole, 1958. (3d edition, fifth printing.)

Russell, Carl P., *Guns on the Early Frontier*, London, and Berkeley and Los Angeles: U. of Calif., 1957.

Sell, DeWitt E., *Collector's Guide to American Cartridge Handguns*, Harrisburg: Stackpole, 1963.

Serven, James E., *Colt Firearms from 1836*, Santa Ana, Calif.: Serven, 1954. (New edition.)

Shumaker, P. L., *Colt's Variations of the Old Model Pocket Pistol, 1848-1872*, Beverly Hills, Calif.: 1957.

Smith, W. H. B., *Gas, Air and Spring Guns of the World*, Harrisburg: Stackpole, 1957.

Smith, Winston O., *The Sharps Rifle*, New York, 1943.

Stebbins, Henry M., *Pistols—A Modern Encyclopedia*, Harrisburg: Stackpole, 1961.

Stebbins, Henry M., *Rifles—A Modern Encyclopedia*, Harrisburg: Stackpole, 1958.

Stockbridge, V. D., *Digest of U. S. Patents Relating to Breech Loading and Magazine Small Arms (Except Revolvers), 1836-1873*, reprint edition, Greenwich, Conn., 1963.

Webster, Jr., Donald B., *Suicide Specials*, Harrisburg: Stackpole, 1958.

Wesley, L., *Air-Guns and Air-Pistols*, New York, 1955.

Whitelaw, Charles E., "Treatise on Scottish Hand-Firearms" in *European Hand Firearms of the Sixteenth, Seventeenth and Eighteenth Centuries*, edited by Herbert J. Jackson, London: Quadrangle, 1933.

Williamson, Harold F., *Winchester, The Gun that Won the West*, Washington, D. C.: Barnes, 1952.

Wilson, J. Larry, and du Mont, John S., *Samuel Colt Presents*, Hartford, Conn., 1961.

Winant, Lewis, *Early Percussion Firearms*, New York: Morrow, 1959, and London, 1961.

Winant, Lewis, *Firearms Curiosa*, New York: St. Martins, 1961 (2d ed.).

Winant, Lewis, *Pepperbox Firearms*, New York, 1952.

Wolff, Eldon G., *Air Guns*, (Milwaukee Public Museum Publications in History, No. 1), Milwaukee, 1958.

Wolff, Eldon G., *Ballard Rifles in the Henry J. Nunnemacher Collection* (Bulletin of the Public Museum of the City of Milwaukee, Vol. 18, No. 1), Milwaukee, 1961 (2d ed.).

AMMUNITION AND ACCOUTERMENTS

Grancsay, Stephen V., *American Engraved Powder Horns, a study based on the J. H. Grenville Gilbert Collection*, New York, 1945.

Lewis, Colonel Berkeley R., *Small Arms and Ammunition in the United States Service*, Washington, D. C., 1956.

Logan, Herschel C., *Cartridges*, Harrisburg: Stackpole, 1959.

Partington, J. R., *A History of Greek Fire and Gunpowder*, Cambridge, England, 1960.

Riling, Ray, *The Powder Flask Book*, New Hope, Pa.: Riling, 1951.

Suydam, Charles S., *The American Cartridge*, Santa Ana, Calif.: G. Robert Lawrence, 1960.

White, Henry P., and Munhall, Burton D., *Cartridge Identification*, 2 vols., Washington, D. C., 1948, 1950.

MAKERS

Gardner, Colonel Robert, *Small Arms Makers*, New

York, 1963.

Gluckman, Colonel Arcadi, and Satterlee, L. D. *American Gun Makers*, Harrisburg: Stackpole, 1953 (revised ed.).

Gooding, S. James, *The Canadian Gunsmiths*, Toronto, 1962.

Kauffman, Henry J., *Early American Gunsmiths, 1650-1850*, Harrisburg, Stackpole, 1952.

MODERN

Allen, Major W. G. B., *Pistols, Rifles and Machine Guns*, London: Borden, 1953.

Bady, Donald B., *Colt Automatic Pistols, 1896-1955*, Los Angeles: Borden, 1956.

Burrard, Major Gerald, *The Modern Shotgun*, 2 vols., New York: Barnes, 1962.

Datig, Fred, *The Luger Pistol*, Los Angeles: Borden, 1958 (rev. ed.).

Hatcher, Major General Julian S., *Hatcher's Book of the Garand*, Washington, D. C., 1948.

Hatcher, Major General Julian S., *Hatcher's Notebook*, Harrisburg: Stackpole, 1962 (3d ed.)

Jones, Harry E., *Luger Variations*, Los Angeles, 1959.

Olson, Ludwig E., *Mauser Bolt Rifles*, Beverly Hills, Calif., 1957.

Smith, W. H. B., *The Book of Pistols and Revolvers*, Harrisburg: Stackpole, 1962 (5th ed.).

Smith, W. H. B., and Joseph E. Smith, *Small Arms of the World*, Harrisburg: Stackpole, 1962 (7th ed.).

Smith, W. H. B., and Joseph E. Smith, *The Book of Rifles*, Harrisburg: Stackpole, 1963 (3d ed.).

Smith, W. H. B., *Mannlicher Rifles and Pistols*, Harrisburg: Stackpole, 1947.

Smith, W. H. B., *Walther Pistols and Rifles*, Harrisburg: Stackpole, 1962 (2d ed.).

CURRENT PUBLICATIONS

The inexorable process of change is certain to be important to those who collect, shoot, or just have a general interest in guns. New information is often of great value, and thus the firearms enthusiast must keep well informed. To do this, he turns to those publications which make the periodic dissemination of firearms news and information their business. Among the current publications devoted to firearms and associated subjects are:

AMERICAN RIFLEMAN, 1600 Rhode Island Ave., N.W., Washington 6, D. C.

GUN DIGEST 4540 W. Madison St., Chicago 24, Ill.

GUNS, 8150 N. Central Park Avenue, Skokie, Illinois

GUNS & AMMO, 5959 Hollywood Blvd., Los Angeles 28, Calif.

GUN REPORT, P. O. Box 111, Aledo, Illinois

GUN WORLD, 550-A S. Citrus Avenue, Covina, Calif.

GUNS and HUNTING, 156 East 52nd Street, New York 22, N. Y.

MILITARY COLLECTOR & HISTORIAN, 77 Barnes St., Providence 6, R. I.

MUZZLE BLASTS, P. O. Box 211, Shelbyville, Indiana

SHOOTING TIMES, Box 1500, War Memorial Drive, Peoria, Illinois

THE SHOOTING INDUSTRY, 8150 N. Central Park Ave., Skokie, Illinois

THE SHOTGUN NEWS, Columbus, Nebraska

CANADIAN JOURNAL OF ARMS COLLECTING, P. O. Box 7, Town of Mt. Royal, Quebec.

JOURNAL OF THE ARMS AND ARMOUR SOCIETY, 14 Cerne Close, Hayes, Middlesex, England.

Publications which frequently contain material devoted to collector's guns and collecting are:

ARGOSY, 205 E. 42nd Street, New York 17, N. Y.

FIELD & STREAM, 383 Madison Avenue, New York 17, N. Y.

HOBBIES, 1006 S. Michigan Avenue, New York 22, N. Y.

HUNTING and FISHING in CANADA, 1231 St. Catherine St. W., Montreal 25, Canada

OUTDOOR LIFE, 353 Fourth Avenue, New York 10, N. Y.

SPORTS AFIELD, 959 Eighth Avenue, New York 19, N. Y.

TRAP & FIELD, 3516 N. College, Indianapolis 5, Indiana

TRUE, 67 W. 44 St., New York 36, N. Y.

WESTERN OUTDOORS, 325 N. Newport Beach Blvd., Newport Beach, Calif.

2812-21

OK
BM   65 y